Creon's Ghost

Creon's Ghost

Law, Justice, and the Humanities

JOSEPH P. TOMAIN

OXFORD
UNIVERSITY PRESS

OXFORD
UNIVERSITY PRESS

Oxford University Press, Inc., publishes works that further Oxford University's objective of excellence in research, scholarship, and education.

Oxford New York
Auckland Cape Town Dar es Salaam Hong Kong Karachi Kuala Lumpur Madrid
Melbourne Mexico City Nairobi New Delhi Shanghai Taipei Toronto

With offices in
Argentina Austria Brazil Chile Czech Republic France Greece Guatemala Hungary
Italy Japan Poland Portugal Singapore South Korea Switzerland Thailand Turkey
Ukraine Vietnam

Published by Oxford University Press, Inc.
198 Madison Avenue, New York, New York 10016

Library of Congress Cataloging-in-Publication Data

Tomain, Joseph P., 1948–
Creon's ghost : law, justice, and the humanities / Joseph P. Tomain.
p. cm.
Includes bibliographical references and index.
ISBN 978-0-19-533341-1 ((hardback) : alk. paper)
1. Law—Philosophy. 2. Law and literature. 3. Law in literature.
I. Title.
K230.T66A33 2009
340'.11—dc22 2008037793

1 2 3 4 5 6 7 8 9

Printed in the United States of America on acid-free paper

Note to Readers
This publication is designed to provide accurate and authoritative information in regard to the subject matter covered. It is based upon sources believed to be accurate and reliable and is intended to be current as of the time it was written. It is sold with the understanding that the publisher is not engaged in rendering legal, accounting, or other professional services. If legal advice or other expert assistance is required, the services of a competent professional person should be sought. Also, to confirm that the information has not been affected or changed by recent developments, traditional legal research techniques should be used, including checking primary sources where appropriate.

(Based on the Declaration of Principles jointly adopted by a Committee of the American Bar Association and a Committee of Publishers and Associations.)

To Michael and Rachel

To Michael for his luxurious hospitality, unparalleled generosity, and for his abundant *sprezzatura*, and to Rachel, *la serenissima*, who complements him, adding her own elegant beauty and quiet strength

Contents

Preface

BOOKS HAVE MANY MEMORIES and debts, and *Creon's Ghost* is no exception. The idea for this book was planted in 1970 in an undergraduate seminar called *Common Law* and taught by Law Professor Thomas Shaffer at the University of Notre Dame. Tom introduced me to the conflict between natural law and positive law through the Hart-Fuller debate. That debate captured my attention then as it does now, although I must confess to having changed allegiances.

From 1970, fast forward to1995. Michael Cioffi and I began offering a seminar entitled *Law in Literature & Philosophy* at the University of Cincinnati, both in its law school and occasionally to undergraduates. Also at that time, I approached Thomas Moyer, the chief justice of the Ohio State Supreme Court, with the idea of offering an Aspen Institute-style Great Books seminar to experienced lawyers and judges. With the support of the chief justice, the Ohio State Bar Association, and the Ohio State Bar Foundation, the first seminar was offered under the auspices of the Justice Institute for the Legal Profession.

Since the initial seminar, the Justice Institute was established as a nonprofit educational organization by Michael Cioffi, Judge Theresa Liston, and me. The institute continues to offer annual Great Books programs in Ohio as well as throughout the United States. Over the last few years, under the watchful and gentle guidance of our director Julie Palermo, the institute has offered a summer program at the Villa Buonriposo in Tuscany where, through his great generosity, Michael opened up his villa as well as his pantry and, and not least important, his wine cellar for our seminars.

Buonriposo is located on the grounds of the fifteenth-century estate of La Foce, about 10 kilometers due south of Montepulciano. La Foce is owned by the family of Iris and Antonio Arrigo who, until recently, owned the Villa Medici in Fiesole, once home to Lorenzo de' Medici who conducted his own Platonic Academy. The Villa Buonriposo sits amidst medieval towers and orchards of grape and poppy and olive. Buonriposo was also the setting for numerous early morning and late night conversations about the topic of this book—an echo, perhaps faint, of Il Magnifico's conversations at his academy.

Midnight in Tuscany is not the experience of Hamlet on the battlements. No fatherly apparition here. Instead, those midnight Buonriposo conversations were preceded by good food, better wine, and even better company. Our evening Tuscan disputes would start after bruschetta, then prosciutto e melone, then zuppa, and finally, pasta. Conversation would start before carne e contorni, salada, and dolci. Discussions might begin with a question such as: is Michelangelo's *David* an expression of universal beauty? The answers which followed would encompass contemporary culture and politics and would eventually lead to conversations about beauty, truth, and justice. The conversations carried on into the night, often concluding under the Tuscan stars with varietal grappa and Cuban cigars.

How is it that those sumptuous Toscana dinners birthed a ghost? Surely it was neither the Brunello nor even the Riserva. No, although vino is a likely suspect to make us see the unseen, and while it may have verily loosened the tongue, it decidedly was not the cause of seeing the ghost in the Italian night. *Creon's Ghost* is the product of a conversation that took place in those hills and in other venues, and it continues today because of the timelessness of the questions themselves and of the elusiveness of the answers. Most particularly: What is the higher law? What is Justice?

From those conversations, the writing of the book has taken place in different locales. I am grateful to Dr. Ralph Waller and his board of trustees for appointing me a visiting fellow at Harris-Manchester College, Oxford University. I began writing the book at the college where I was greeted each day that cold, Hilary term by librarian Sue Killoran, with a smiling face and a toasty place for me in the well-appointed and well-stocked Tate Library. The library collection suited my work particularly well, and what I could not find on the shelves there, I could find by only a short walk to either the law library or the Bodelian.

The second phase of writing occurred during an even colder winter term at the University of Notre Dame where Dean Harvey Shapiro graciously appointed me as a visiting scholar in the Program of Liberal Studies. The book was completed in my home university with the gracious help of Virginia Thomas and her staff.

Over the years, there have been hundreds of students and hundreds of seminar participants who have enriched my understanding and love for this subject. I thank them even though they go unnamed.

Finally, I thank my editor at Oxford University Press, Chris Collins, who promoted a book proposal through the review process and took a chance on a book that might accurately be called a "betweener." Neither strictly law nor strictly the humanities, this book falls between the stacks of both, and I am grateful for having the opportunity to publish it.

Introduction

At the dawn of reason, at the birth of man's law, was also born a ghost haunting us still. The ghost is the conflict between our desire for just laws and our experience of unjust ones. Sophocles told the story through Creon and Creon's tale has been the curse of the human condition. How arrogant is man to tempt the gods? To desire to rule beyond man's authority? To impose law under the guise of right regardless of the virtue of Justice? Yet, how foolish is man not to seek the Good? Not to struggle for Justice in the face of human imperfection?

On the first of day of spring in the year of our Lord 2005, in a rushed midnight ritual, the Congress of the United States of America passed a bill—an arcane law of federal civil procedure—to keep alive a brain dead, comatose patient.[1] *The bill was enacted into law with the signature of a president flown from his Crawford, Texas ranch to our nation's dreary March capitol. "In cases like this one, where there are serious questions and substantial doubts, our society, our laws, and our courts should have a presumption in favor of life. This presumption is especially critical for those like Terri Schiavo, who live at the mercy of others."*[2]

IN SOPHOCLES' *ANTIGONE*, King Creon, through man's law, attempts to punish Polyneices' soul which floats in a realm beyond his jurisdiction. Antigone resists his order prohibiting the burial of her brother by claiming obedience to a higher law. Twenty-five hundred years later a drama repeating Creon's tragic mistake was played on a national stage. Terri Schiavo had been in a coma since 1990, and she was declared to have been in a persistent vegetative state since 1991. In 1998, her husband sought a court order to have her removed from life support, a request that triggered seven years of federal and state litigation ending with the passage of federal legislation before she was allowed to die. In both cases, man's law attempted to thwart a higher law and failed. But it is not always so that the higher law triumphs.

Nor is it the case that conflicts between man's law and the higher law are easily resolved. Man should never tread on the soil of the gods. Nor can man ignore the gods' dreams of Justice. As humans, we live with the dissonance created by our desire for higher just laws and our experience of man's unjust ones. *Creon's Ghost,* then, is the story of the frustration born of that dissonance, and it is also the story of our attempt to ameliorate the conflict between desire and experience by attempting to reconcile the imperfection of man's law with the virtue of Justice.

The Message

Creon's Ghost, somewhat audaciously, addresses the enduring problem of the relationship between man's law and a "higher" law. The audacity is that somehow this book will resolve age-old controversies about two concepts—man's law and the higher law—for which there are no agreed definitions. Still, to apprehend *Creon's Ghost,* we must first understand what we mean by the word law:

> *Law, say the gardeners, is the sun*
>
> * * *
>
> *Law is the wisdom of the old*
>
> * * *
>
> *Law, says the priest with a priestly look*
>
> * * *
>
> *Law, says the judge as he looks down his nose*

These first lines of the first four stanzas of W. H. Auden's poem[3] facilely demonstrate that the word "law" is susceptible to many meanings.[4] When we use the word "law," do we mean a law of nature, the law of the sun? Or do we mean the law that comes with experience, the wisdom of the old? Or do we mean religious priestly laws such as the proper rites for a valid baptism or a consecrated burial? Or do we mean the pronouncements of authority, the law of the judge? Jurisprudents and philosophers of law have attempted to ascertain the meaning or meanings of the word law, and there is no shortage of commentary over this term.[5] For our purposes, we need only to concentrate on workable definitions.

The reference to "man's law" is a reference to Sophocles' great play, *Antigone.* Ismene rejects Antigone's entreaties to help her bury their brother: "I cannot ignore the laws of the city and of men." We will learn that man's law is inferior, imperfect, and too often, unjust. Paraphrasing Justice Potter Stewart, we know man's law when we see it. It is a decision handed down by a court, a statute passed by a legislature, or an order given by an executive; it is an order from some recognized human authority. In the *Minos*, Socrates asks, "What is law?" and the Comrade responds, "What else would law be, Socrates except the things that are lawfully accepted?"[6] From this response, law most simply is some piece of paper to which we can point.

The "higher" law is more difficult to define as this book demonstrates and as it offers several definitions for inspection. We might console ourselves about the ineffability of the higher law by saying that we know when a law is unjust. A law legitimizing racial segregation is unjust. Laws which deny women full rights to civic participation or employment are unjust. Laws which allow negligent or intentional injuries to persons or damages to property to go unredressed are unjust. Although we will not arrive at fixed definitions of either man's law or the higher law, we are able to converse about law and Justice. Man's law is positive, human law which is sometimes just and sometimes unjust. The higher law is natural or moral, but is always just. This asymmetry creates a problem when man's law and the higher law do not mesh. What should be done in the face of unjust law?

There are two general responses. The positivist John Austin offers the first. "Suppose an act innocuous, or positively beneficial, be prohibited by the sovereign under penalty of death; if I commit this act, I shall be tried and condemned, and if I object to the sentence, that it is contrary to the law of God . . . the Court of Justice will demonstrate the inconclusiveness of my reasoning by hanging me up, in pursuance of the law of which I have impugned the validity."[7]

The opposite response, called "stark nonsense" by Austin,[8] is offered by Saint Augustine: "*Lex injusta non est lex*"—an unjust law is no law at all. Both of these responses are extreme. If Austin is correct, then power prevails over the Good, and man's law always prevails over Justice. If Augustine is correct, then chaos prevails over order when man's law is unjust. Neither extreme is a sound basis for law, yet both responses recur in various guises throughout the book.

As a final preliminary matter, we must also distinguish between a *concept* and a *conception* of law. I treat the notion of the *concept* of law as Plato treats the Form of Justice. A *concept* of law is an ideal form; we can no more fully know the ideal form of law than we can fully know ideal beauty. A *conception* of law speaks more specifically about how we perceive law working in the world. When someone argues that law emanates from some official body and another argues that law is embedded in the political history and morality of a nation, they are offering different *conceptions* of law. When people argue about whether law does or does not exist, they are arguing about law as *concept.* The *concept* of law, like the *concept* of Justice, drives us even as we disagree about its content and as we offer competing *conceptions* to help us understand how it functions in the world.[9] In this book and for the most part, we will be discussing different *conceptions* of law.

The Method

Antigone's story ends in literature; Terri Schiavo's story ends in law. There is a strangeness[10] linking Antigone's dramatic dilemma with Terri Schiavo's litigation—a link between law and the humanities. We can bridge 2500 years of the Western tradition through the Great Conversation. Law and law's stories are embedded and interwoven into the great texts and fabrics of the humanities. We will find that the humanities provide "a faithful mirror of justice," aid our understanding of man's law, and continually challenge us in our search for the higher law.[11]

The more than occasional conflicts between man's law and the higher law and the frustration of experience failing desire are central to the study of the human. Because we are human, we find that our wants, needs, and desires are often in conflict. This conflict is true for us as individuals, and it is true for us living in society as we attempt to mediate that conflict through law tethered to the virtue of Justice.[12] We believe that law should be in the service of Justice and that law and Justice should be at peace with each other. They are not. We know this to be true. We may even know this to be forever true and yet. . . . And yet we continue, as we must, to seek reconciliation between them.

Here, then, the challenge: we have not one but three paths to reconciling the imperfect laws of man with man's desire for perfect Justice. No one path is complete. No one path is true. No one path is historically contained. Nor do the paths together serve as compass to a true and reliable reconciliation between law and Justice. Instead we try each path and wonder about its strangeness, its compulsion, and its attraction. And funny thing—we are occasionally satisfied with where each and any of these divergent, but not completely unconnected, paths lead us. So much for the ethereal; let's get down to cases.

The three paths along which we can travel in our search for a reasonable, if only tentative and provisional, reconciliation between man's law and the higher law are (1) law and Justice[13] are and ought to be connected—the connection thesis, (2) law and Justice are not and should not be connected—the separation thesis, and, (3) who knows? Let me be a little less cynical-sounding. The third choice is the admission, particularly in modern pluralistic societies, that no single moral world view is possible. There is no single acceptable definition of Justice or of the higher law. Because of the plurality of reasonable world views, we can only approximate Justice through fair and accepted procedures for conflict resolution. The third path is a second-best solution to the problem of defining Justice by designing a process or processes for managing the political and moral conflicts that plague modern society, including problems of evil.

No single volume can condense the libraries of moral and political philosophy, social and ethical theory, and jurisprudence and legal philosophy that have addressed and dissected this relationship through the ages. The madness of *Creon's Ghost* may lie in its ambition. Hopefully, its method can tell the tale. The conflict between man's law and higher law will be told through stories taken from the humanities—mostly literature and philosophy—and read alongside basic texts in jurisprudence. I consign the technical jurisprudence arguments to the endnotes and let the humanities tell their stories.

Each chapter of the book takes a similar approach. A principal text from the humanities is discussed, and then each text is paired with a text of legal philosophy. After pairing legal philosophy with a humanities classic, modern Supreme Court cases illustrate the point under discussion. This method of marrying classic text with jurisprudence and then with case law may appear cumbersome, but it is not. This is the approach I use in university classes as well as with lawyers and judges in advanced seminars. Classic text meets the modern bench and bar in peaceful and enlightening coexistence.

The sinister plot of *Creon's Ghost* should now be uncovered. The humanities have much to teach lawyers about the deepest problems they face, and law's cases have much to reveal about human nature and behavior to humanists. This method helps us better understand the enduring nature of legal problems. Perhaps we can learn from the past and correct our mistakes; perhaps we can simply better understand the problems themselves. Ludwig Wittgenstein wrote that philosophy may not answer or resolve our moral dilemmas, yet philosophy can help us untie the knots of the problems that we face. The humanities help us untie the knotty problem of the conflict between man's law and the higher law.

The Architecture

This book is arranged in four pairs of chapters. Chapters 1 and 2 identify and describe the nature of the problem. *Antigone* is used to establish the fundamental conflict between man's law and the higher law. Creon justifies his edict because the ship of state needs guidance, and as king it fell on him to provide it. The ghost that is the title of the book is Creon's human predicament. As ruler he must rule; as human he is fallible. Consequently, his law will not always be just, yet it remains law. His claim to rule, his claim of legitimate authority, is not without foundation. His rule was rebuffed as Antigone was compelled to follow another, a higher law. But what exactly is that higher law? We will see that Antigone's law may well be unsayable and, therefore, is not much help as a way to more brightly illuminate the higher law.

If Sophocles cannot help us too terribly much, then what does his near-contemporary have to teach us? Can Plato or Socrates help us "see" the higher law? For our answer we must descend in Chapter 2 into Plato's Cave.

The *Allegory of the Cave* is both more familiar and complex than it might first appear. The familiar part of this allegory is that a prisoner is unshackled and works his way into the warmth and light of sun where, *voilà*, he "sees" the Good, the True, the Beautiful, and the Just. But now comes the complex part. Neither the prisoner nor we can literally or figuratively see the sun. Nor can we know Justice beyond having a sense of it. Plato gives us less of a definition of the higher law than he provides a method, the dialectic, for trying to find it. The *Allegory of the Cave* confirms the notion that we all have a sense of Justice, that we must be educated to it, but that we can never completely obtain it.

The second part of the book investigates the stark conflict between natural law and positive law. In Chapter 3, Thomas Aquinas's natural law is offered as a useful way to define the higher law. Aquinas argues that there is and ought to be a necessary connection between law and Justice—the connection thesis. Natural law, Aquinas argues, is the way that humans participate in the eternal law through their use of reason. Just as Plato argued that we all possess a sense of Justice, Aquinas argues that we manifest that sense of Justice through the natural law.

Aquinas was enough of a realist to recognize that human imperfection is ubiquitous and that human law sometimes gets it right and sometimes not. While there might be a necessary, or at least desirable, connection between law and Justice, missteps will be made. There is a polestar, however, to guide us—the natural law. Thomist first principles can help us identify which laws are just and which are not. Natural law, then, appears to be a sturdy candidate for the higher law.

Niccolò Machiavelli demurs in Chapter 4 and takes the opposite approach from Aquinas. He is a separatist and rejects any necessary connection between law and the virtue of Justice. Law for Machiavelli operates in the service of power politics, and his realpolitik is based precisely upon divorcing morality from politics. Yet Machiavelli is not a nihilist. He does not say that law is irrelevant. Rather, law is not an intrinsic good—it is instrumental to acquiring and maintaining power. A prince uses law but is not constrained by it, and he must break it when necessary. Both law and Justice should be used to advance the civic greatness of princes. There is, then, no higher law; there is only law that works to perpetuate the power of the prince and perpetuate the principality.

Aquinas and Machiavelli present us with a true opposition. Is law a Thomistic intrinsic good which enables persons to live in harmony, seeking Justice, and perhaps even leading to individual human fulfillment? Or, as per Machiavelli, is law an instrument to be used by the ruler against the ruled?

From Machiavelli's Cinquecento, we move to the nineteenth century and revisit the contest between man's law and the higher law. The next two chapters recapitulate the contest between Aquinas and Machiavelli in more modern terms by posing Harriet Beecher Stowe against Oliver Wendell Holmes Jr.

Uncle Tom's Cabin is a direct descendent of the religiously inspired Abolitionist movement, and Stowe saw her book as a Christian higher law rebuke to man's law of slavery. Chapter 5 begins with Mrs. Bird challenging her husband, an Ohio state senator, about the newly passed fugitive slave law: "Now, John, I want to know if you think such a law as that is right and Christian?" His reply is, "You won't shoot me now, Mary, if I say I do!" The issue is joined. Senator Bird defends the fugitive slave law in the name of the state and its need to maintain order among men. John's defense is Creon's justification of his rule. Mary rebuffs such a justification with the Bible. Is religion constitutive of the higher law?

In contrast to *Uncle Tom's Cabin*, Chapter 6 examines Oliver Wendell Holmes Jr.'s *The Path of the Law.* Holmes intended to be provocative in his speech when, not unlike Machiavelli's view, he wrote, "I often doubt whether it would not be a gain if every word of moral significance could be banished from the law altogether."[14] Holmes was indeed troubled by the confusion of moral ideas with legal ones, and he argued strenuously for their separation. However, he was not unaware of the relationship between law and morality. His speech explains their relationship and his separationist argument. Holmes was telling us how to understand the seemingly contradictory impulses of the law. First, we must clearly understand what the law says with moral talk stripped away. Then we can critique man's law against a higher law or Justice standard.

The nineteenth century, then, pits the higher law of religion against the pragmatic necessities of man's law and, therefore, fails to resolve the conflict.

The last pair of chapters goes in a decidedly different direction. Instead of arguing about the connection or the separation between law and morality or between law and Justice, our search poses a more fundamental problem. If conflict is ubiquitous because of man's fallen nature, or if the religious reference is too much, then because of simple, ineluctable human fallibility, perhaps the search for Plato's Sun is unrealistic and should be abandoned in favor of something more useful like conflict resolution. If the conflict between man's law and higher law is a conflict between desire and experience, will we then be forever locked in an eternal struggle between the two, never realizing full Justice? Is there a second-best solution? The second-best solution to the conflict between man's law and higher law lies in legal or political processes.

Chapter 7 discusses Martin Luther King Jr.'s *Letter from the Birmingham Jail.* King was religiously educated, motivated, and inspired. Religion sustained King and the civil rights movement in a way not dissimilar from the Abolitionist movement a century before. But religion did not constitute King's path to the higher law—political morality did. For King, destroying racial segregation was the just thing to do, and its elimination had to come about through democratic participation open to all on equal bases.

Political equality is best manifest through democratic participation in the political process. The promise of representative democracy now confronts the segregationist policies, strategies, and tactics used to disenfranchise black Americans and keep them in bondage. Segregation is exposed for what it really is—injustice. Segregation laws are unjust, in part, because they are enacted without the full voice of the people. Political participation has appeal but may ultimately be too thin a theory of the higher law because the winds of politics change course so rapidly.

If democratic participation continues to result in unjust laws, then what are we to do?

The book closes with a discussion of *Justice is Conflict* by the late British philosopher Stuart Hampshire. Hampshire came to the conclusion that it is likely in a modern democracy that people with differing world views who hold them equally strongly and in good faith will continue to encounter conflicts. For Hampshire, the best that could be hoped for was to create a process for the resolution and management of contentious moral or political controversies. Hampshire describes a system of procedural justice as a substitute for a substantive conception of Justice.

The story of Justice is the story of struggle. Such is the human condition as struggle brings law in conformity with Justice when man's law otherwise goes lacking. Law is the tool we use to achieve Justice, and law's struggle for Justice is the story of this book. This story is told not as a matter of jurisprudence or philosophy of law; they are supporting actors here. The story is told as a central story of the humanities. If the thesis is correct that the relation between law and Justice is an eternal human conflict, then that conflict should appear in the great conversation that is the humanities. Indeed it does. Great works of drama, literature, philosophy, and poetry help us understand that law is not always just, but that the struggle for Justice is always with us. In short, the humanities teach us a method for navigating the sea of man's law that falls short of the ideal of Justice and help chart the course that leads us as close to Justice as human nature allows.

ONE

Creon's Ghost

The young woman, mourning a fallen soldier, stands in the dusty street outside the ruler's home, questioning his actions. The ruler justifies his laws as he must. As captain of the ship of state, his duty lies in protecting his citizens from the terror of foreign enemies. As commander of the country, his duty lies in resisting any treason from outside or within. In troubling times, strong leadership is necessary as dissent weakens his leadership, weakens the state, and it must be repelled. The ruler, forced by circumstance and by inclination, rejects the young woman's pleas in favor of the state and of his rule over it.

THIS SCENE COULD BE either Thebes in 441 BC or Crawford, Texas in 2005. It could also be 1958 Montgomery, Alabama. The young woman could be Antigone or Cindy Sheehan[1] or Rosa Parks. And the ruler could be King Creon, President George W. Bush, or a white bus driver. Sophocles' *Antigone*, whether performed in ancient Greece, sixteenth-century Italy, occupied Paris, or today in Dublin's Abbey Theater, retains its immediacy.[2] *Antigone's* genius lies not only in its theme of the one against the mighty, nor only in its poetic power as "a work of art nearer to perfection than any other produced by the human spirit"[3]; *Antigone*'s genius also lies in its timelessness and in its many faces. Neither history nor geography cabin its message.

Coming to *Antigone* for the first time, it is easy to accept Georg Wilhelm Friedrich Hegel's argument that the play is about the conflict between an individual and the state which, of course, is why it so easily lends itself to adaptation throughout history.[4] There are always those individuals who cannot march in step to the drumbeat of the state and who criticize its missteps. Hegel's point is attractive, and he develops it as a conflict between life and spirit, between our public and private selves.[5] *Antigone* can also be read as a struggle between woman and man. Antigone's sister, Ismene, warns of the dangers of women violating men's laws. And later in the play, Creon mocks his son, Haemon, for favoring a woman over his own father, the king, as he refuses to be bettered by a woman. The play bears these interpretations among others, including conscience against power or religious or familial duty against civic obligation.[6]

The standard reading of *Antigone* treats the action of the play as a conflict between two willful people situated in a moment of history. While *Antigone* is about the clash of wills, it is also about a clash between conflicting, and perhaps irreconcilable, conceptions of law. Creon's law conflicts with Antigone's law.[7] More deeply, this conflict of laws threatens the realization of justice. In the play, a tragic injustice has occurred leading to Antigone's death, among other ones, and to Creon's madness. Antigone, the heroine, faces down Creon, the powerful, to her doom and to his.

Antigone's heroism gives the play its timeless power, but let's not canonize her prematurely. Following Albert Camus, I take it that, "Antigone is right—but Creon is not wrong."[8] It is the person of Creon and his actions, as much as Antigone and hers, that capture my attention. One can be not wrong, or more accurately, not completely wrong, and suffer the horrid tragedy that is Creon's fate and, at times, our fate as well when laws conflict.

Law's claim on us derives, in part, from its authority.[9] When we refer to man's law, the authority for that law is man and the institutions that he creates. And when we refer to the higher law, the claim of authority is less clear. The authority of the higher law can be based on conscience, religion, duty, morality, or something other. The conflict between Creon and Antigone is a conflict about conceptions of law and about its authority. It is also a conflict which is as present today as when brash Antigone defied headstrong King Creon.

Creon's Law

Before the action of the play, let's situate Creon. Creon is a member of the house of Laius. Laius is Oedipus's father and originator of the fateful tale. Oedipus marries his mother, Jocasta. Creon is Jocasta's brother and, therefore, nephew and brother-in-law of Oedipus, Jocasta's husband/son. Antigone, Ismene, Polyneices, and Eteocles are the children of Oedipus and Jocasta, thus making Creon an uncle to each. The backstory of *Antigone* is rich with prophecy and tragedy. Oedipus, returning from exile, solves the riddle of the Sphinx, kills his father and marries his mother, and then blinds himself when he learns his fate. Jocasta, the wife/mother, bears her son's children, and upon learning the paternity of her children, hangs herself in fulfillment of the prophecy. As the concluding part of the prophecy, Oedipus and Joscasta's sons, Eteocles and Polyneices, suffer their dual death at each other's hands in the battle for Thebes. Once the brothers decide to share the throne in alternate years, Sophocles set the stage for Creon's rule and for his sad demise. Eteocles, enjoying his reign, was reluctant to leave the perquisites of office, and Polyneices attacked the city to claim his birthright. Creon's response to this attack begins the action of *Antigone*.

Creon enters the play through the opening dialogue between Antigone and Ismene in which the two sisters argue about King Creon's new "proclamation"[10] or "general order"[11] or "edict."[12] With a single and dramatic speech act, Sophocles not only sets the play in motion to its tragic conclusion, he gives life to Creon's ghost. "Edict," "general order," or "proclamation" all collapse into one word—law.[13] Creon and Antigone both acted on the authority of the law, but they disagreed about the basis of that authority and, consequently, their conceptions of law differed. Their disagreement proved to be deathly dangerous.

Creon's law is easily named. Creon's proclamation, general order, or edict was issued upon his authority as king, upon his authority as head of state. His exercise of authority makes Creon's law man's law. Creon's conception of law is equally straightforward. Law is the king's to proclaim because he has legitimacy. The orders of a king are law. Creon's specific law is that Eteocles, the patriot, would receive a hero's burial, and the traitor, Polyneices, would not. Instead, Polyneices would be dishonored and his body left as carrion for the birds that flew and the dogs that roamed those dry Theban streets. Moreover, anyone caught attempting to bury Polyneices would suffer death. Although his edict was clear, Creon never understood its implications nor anticipated its consequences.

Creon's desire to dishonor Polyneices through law might well have been quite enough for Antigone to act to honor her brother, family, and conscience. But there was so much more at stake for her. Quoting George Steiner, "Creon's edict is political punishment; to Antigone it is an ontological crime."[14] Antigone knew that the disgrace Creon imposed by law—man's law—on her brother Polyneices went beyond the incivility of having his dead body eaten and destroyed by animals, and her actions were more than simply giving Polyneices his due burial dress. For without proper burial, Polyneices' soul would never reach Hades and would be condemned forever to roam the space between this world and the next. Creon's law was intended to punish not only the soldier; it was intended to punish the soldier's soul. For Antigone, Creon's law went beyond insult and disgrace, and most importantly, beyond Creon's legitimacy.

Fully aware of Creon's law, the so-called "law of the land,"[15] Antigone sought to enlist the aide of her sister, Ismene, to help bury Polyneices in defiance of Creon. Rejected by Ismene, Antigone, in turn, rejects her sister and goes about executing her duty alone. Later, caught in the burial act, she is brought before her uncle, boldly admits her deed, and equally boldly, faces her sentence of death. Death is Antigone's end, and Antigone's death is Creon's end as well.

This description of the action makes the play look fairly simple. As characterized by classicist David Grene, *Antigone* is the story of a ruler who makes a mistake, finds himself opposed because of it, misunderstands the opposition, and persists in his mistake ending in his demise.[16] Were the story so simple, the play could have ended quite quickly. Once confronted with the perpetrator of the crime, punishment could have been swift and complete if Creon ordered Antigone to her death. Instead, Antigone is given the opportunity to respond to Creon, and in her search for justice, she challenges Creon's conception of law. By doing so, she challenges his authority as king as she offers us her own conception of the higher law.

Challenging Creon's Law

Creon faces three challenges by Antigone, Haemon, and Tiresisas. These challenges establish the architecture of the play, expose the weakness of Creon's conception of law, and therefore, contest his kingly authority all in the name of the higher law. Tone-deaf to these challenges, instead of reasoned responses, Creon is angered and insulted by his interlocutors. Although he eventually changes his death order, he does so too late in the action of the play to his everlasting regret.

The First Challenge: Antigone's Law

Antigone's challenge exposes Creon's wrong thinking and wrongdoing. Her direct claim is as poignant as it is simple—Creon's edict prohibiting Polyneices' burial was not Creon's law to give. Creon's law of the land had no authority over familial law, the law of the dead, or over the law of the gods. Creon's law had no authority over Antigone's law, a law which is yet to be named. Creon's pronouncement, as a kingly utterance, had the *de facto* force of law. Yet, to Antigone and to us, Creon's law was also clearly unjust and beyond the bounds of his legitimacy.

Creon indulges his niece's entreaties not as a matter of family loyalty but rather as a matter of his own weaknesses. Creon's tragedy is the result of his stubborn ignorance; his fatal and arrogant belief in the full, legitimate authority of his kingship; his failure to understand the nature and extent of that authority; his refusal to engage reason; and his adamant willingness to ignore the gods and the fates. He is moved only when the flesh of his flesh is threatened. Creon allows, indeed invites, Antigone to speak so that he can lord his will over hers and release his anger; he did not engage her challenge with measured replies. Theirs is a dialogue of power, not persuasion.

Unseen by the guards who stand watch over the corpse, Polyneices' body is covered in a way that could not have occurred other than by human hands. A guard enters the palace and tells King Creon, "Somebody has good as buried it . . . under this coat of dust."[17] Creon demands to know who committed the traitorous act.

The chorus responds that the gods may have buried Polyneices, and Creon rejects their suspect as "preposterous."[18] Creon then accuses the guard of taking bribes to allow the burial and to cover up the crime. The guard denies the accusation by saying: "What's happened here, Creon, is that the judge/Has misjudged everything."[19] And so Creon has misjudged. Creon should have understood these two warnings. He was wrong to accuse the guard of bribery and even more wrong to ignore the chorus who warned him that he should tread carefully and not interfere with the realm of the gods. Early in the play, the chorus and the guard recognize that Creon's law is a mistake and try to tell him so.

The guard reenters with Antigone, who was caught attending the corpse. The guard who brings Antigone before Creon is the same guard who first told him of the burial, at which time he swore that he would never return to face the king again. Yet, believing himself lucky to catch the criminal, the guard now says, "Circumstances change and your mind changes."[20] Another unheeded warning to Creon is that just as the guard changes his mind and returns to the palace, he should change his edict.

Creon asks the guard for the details of the crime before he turns to his niece and asks if she knew of his law. "I did know. How could I not?" she admits.[21] In disbelief, Creon asks Antigone directly if what the guard said was true, "And you still dared to disobey the law?"[22] Her response to her uncle is her challenge to Creon's legitimacy:

I disobeyed because the law was not
The law of Zeus nor the law ordained
By Justice, Justice dwelling deep
Among the gods of the dead. What they decree
Is in memorial and binding for us all.
The proclamation had your force behind it
But it was mortal force, and I, also a mortal,
I chose to disregard it. I abide
By statutes utter and immutable—
Unwritten, original, god-given laws.[23]

With these lines, the controversy is starkly presented. Antigone knows her crime; she willfully violated the law of man. Her conscience did not allow her to do otherwise; her moral obligation to disobey the law was clear. But how can this be? How can she supercede this law of state, her uncle's law?

The eternal tension between man's law and higher law is both an epistemological and metaphysical[24] problem: How can we come to know whether a law is just or unjust? How can we come to know the higher law? Against what should we measure man's law? Subsequent, but by no means subsidiary, problems follow. If a law is unjust, must it be obeyed nonetheless? Or, and we can put the point more strongly: If a law is unjust, then *must* it be *dis*obeyed? Somewhat more prosaically: What must we do in the face of unjust law? In the face of an unjust law, what actions are proper? Should someone who feels compelled to violate an unjust law rather than obey it be required to attempt to change the law before disobeying it? Should Antigone have attempted to persuade her uncle to rescind his edict? Or should Antigone have violated it outright? Antigone's response was swift and sure. Creon's law was unjust, and she had an obligation to violate that law and bury her brother—twice.

What can justify Antigone's violation of Creon's authority? Antigone does not contest Creon's claim to rule, though she might. Rather, Antigone contests the limits of Creon's power to issue law. She contests the law's reach, arguing that Creon's reach, and therefore his claim to full and legitimate authority, stops at the grave. Her claim is a powerful one. Repeating her words, she abides by laws that are "immutable—unwritten, original, god-given."[25] Antigone's law finds its authority in the gods, and it is both unwritten and infallible. What are we to make of unwritten and infallible law?

Antigone's transgression does not and cannot go unpunished if, as Creon believes, he is to hold onto his claims[26] of authority. Creon believes that he is punishing Antigone for violating a civil law; he does not understand that he is condemning her for her devotion and her piety, for revering what was right. He is oblivious of the line dividing man and the gods; he is also oblivious of having defied the gods. He does not understand that man's laws cannot overrule the laws of the gods. He is oblivious even though he stands forewarned.

Creon's law is the written law of man, the positive law. Antigone's law is something other. Naming that something other is no small matter. Is this something other a religious law? A moral law? A familial law? Natural law? Eternal law? Or something other still? Is it something higher than man's law? Is it something that can trump man's law?

The difficulty should be clear. Assuming that the authority of the gods is legitimate, questions still arise about the unwritten law. How do the laws of the gods manifest themselves? How is it that we can know the contents of unwritten, albeit, infallible laws? How are we to know and understand them? How are we to apply them in the world? What, exactly then, are the "unwritten, original, god-given laws" of which Antigone speaks?

In a sensitive reading of the play and in a scholarly study of the Greek, Philippe Nonet[27] offers a reading of Antigone's law that is challenging to apply in the world and even challenging to express. For not only is Antigone's law unwritten, it is literally unsayable.[28] The law that guides her also guides the gods; it is a law that even the gods must obey.[29] Nonet tentatively names Antigone's law *phusis* and says that it best stands untranslated from the Greek because the closest word in English is "nature," and it is better to leave *phusis* untranslated than confuse it with natural law.[30] Antigone's law is not natural law. Antigone "knows" this law not from any practical reasoning or human experience; instead it resides in the radiance of her being, says Nonet, following Martin Heidegger.[31]

Naming Antigone's law is a task which must fail of its ultimate purpose of discovering a completely satisfactory definition. For our purposes, Antigone's law is a "higher law." It is a law with a moral claim which prevails over man's law, and it is a law which comports with justice rather than with the mere exercise of power.

Imagine what Creon hears when Antigone tells him that his law is illegitimate. Imagine Creon's reaction. Imagine Creon's affront by this woman telling him he could not rule and him not understanding anything other than a woman's challenge to a man's authority. Not only is Creon unmoved by Antigone's challenge, he is angered by this mere woman and is made even more steadfast in his resolve to punish those who dare honor terrorists even if it means killing his son's bride-to-be. Creon's response to this effrontery is to have her taken and given her due by his decree as head of state:

When she defied the general order
Antigone had already gone too far,
But flaunting that defiance in my face
Puts her beyond the pale.[32]

Antigone's challenge to Creon is to appeal to a higher authority than Creon's kingship. Antigone appeals to the law that binds even the gods. Perhaps, though, we should not judge Creon too harshly. Antigone cannot persuade Creon that either the source of the higher law or what that higher law says should prevail over the interests of the state or his rule of it. Antigone may well follow her conscience and follow that higher law. Yet how can Creon let the violation of his edict pass without disrupting his rule? The higher law may well be the superior and the just law. But how does it work? How can Creon recognize the higher law and explain it to the citizens of Thebes even if he were so inclined? Antigone's challenge is insufficient to move Creon away from his already declared law and his death sentence.

The Second Challenge: Reason's Law

Enter son Haemon—loyal to father, loyal to Thebes, and betrothed to Antigone. How can he manage such sensitive, treacherous, conflicts? Not well as it turns out. The second challenge to Creon from Haemon takes another tack; he tries to reason with his father.

The chorus cautions that Haemon may be "wild" at his father's order to have Antigone executed. Creon attempts to preempt this reaction: "Haemon, son, the judgment I pronounced/ It's what the law requires."[33] Again, Creon relies on the authority of man's law. Haemon acknowledges the fact of the law and then addresses Creon as father and as king and professes love and loyalty befitting a royal son. He tells his father that his marriage promise cannot supplant his loyalty to him. Creon's judgment is sound and should be followed, Haemon tells his father. However, good kings can be strong kings as well as thoughtful kings. To these ends of strength, goodness, and statesmanship, kings should use all of the talents at their disposal, including the talent of reason given to men by the gods:

The use of reason, father . . . The gods
Have given us the use of reason.
But do we use it right? Do I? Do you?
It's hard to know . . . [34]

To support his appeal to reason, Haemon tells his father that the people of Thebes are sympathetic toward Antigone:

People are heartbroken for her. What
They're asking, did she do so wrong? What deserves?
A punishment like this? As far as they are concerned,
She should be honoured—a woman who rebelled.[35]

Creon, after feeling insulted by his niece Antigone is stung by Haemon's words. Haemon speaks words of filial loyalty, but to Creon his loyalty is suspect for love of a woman. Haemon's words are not the words of advice from an equal; they are heard as a lecture by a youth who never held the reins of state. As Creon says to the chorus, "So a man of my age, you are telling me,/Must take instruction from a man of his?"[36] Worse still, they are the words of a son betrothed to a traitor. Creon's anger toward Antigone as woman is transferred to his son for taking up the woman's cause. "Son you are pathetic. You give in to a woman."[37]

Haemon's call to reason and to public opinion falls on deaf ears. "Reconsider," Haemon pleads, it is the sign of wisdom; it is what wise kings do. Haemon simply and directly tells his father, like Antigone tried before him, that Creon's edict, his man's law, is beyond his kingly authority; it is unjust because it is not based on reason. Creon is deaf to this argument for he believes, as in part he must, in his authority to issue laws as king and have to them obeyed.

Creon: Wicked to try conclusions with your father.
Haemon: When you conclude unjustly, so I must.
Creon: Am I unjust when I respect my office?[38]

And,

Haemon: The rightness is what matters . . .
Creon: Rightness? What rightness? Aren't you against the law?
Haemon: I am not, and I don't want you to be."[39]

Creon and Haemon both acknowledge and accept the *de facto* authority of the law. Yet, they are talking past each other; they are pledging allegiances to different conceptions of law. Creon pledges allegiance to man's law and Haemon to reason's. Creon's crude conception of law suppresses law's flexibility; Haemon's appeal to reason allows law to adapt.

The confrontation between father and son is acrimonious and Creon vows to have Antigone killed before Haemon's very eyes. Creon also vows to have Haemon banished from his household, a vow that causes Haemon to flee Creon forever. Upon Haemon's leave, this threatened loss of a son causes Creon to reevaluate his edict. For rather than summary execution, Creon changes the death sentence and commands that Antigone should be placed in a cave with food, thus washing his hands of her blood. This softening of his punishment—entombment instead of execution—satisfies no one. Haemon has moved his father but not nearly enough. Reason has not prevailed over power.

The Third Challenge: Fate's Law

The final challenge to King Creon comes from Tiresias, the blind prophet, who lost his sight and gained the gift of prophecy at the hands of the gods.[40] Tiresias has watched over Thebes throughout the tragedy of the house of Laius and he has befriended Creon. With the help of his prophecy, Creon has saved the city by defending it against Polyneices' attack. When Tiresias enters the palace, he does so with Creon's welcoming blessing, and he is given Creon's full attention. That is until he speaks.

Tiresias wastes no time telling Creon of his dangerous position, "Where you are standing now/ Is a cliff edge, and there's cold wind blowing,"[41] he warns. Tiresias tells Creon that in all his days as a seer he has never heard the birds of prophecy screech and scream in such fury. Worse, when brought to the altar, Tiresias' offerings were refused by the gods:

But the fire had no effect. It wouldn't take
And none of the bits would burn.

Slime,
Slime was what I got instead of flame.
Matter oozing out from near the bone.
The fat stayed raw and wept into the ash.
Everywhere there was this spattered gall
From the gall-bladder.[42]

The gods are revolted, he tells Creon, yet "Mistakes don't have to be forever/ They can be admitted and atoned for."[43] Once again, Creon is asked to reflect and reconsider his edict.

Creon hears neither Tiresias' fears nor his plea for reconsideration. Instead, Creon reacts to Tiresias exactly as he did to Antigone and to his son Haemon. He lashes out at Tiresias as someone who sells his prophecies for gold, a mere hired gun. His bribery charge echoes the one leveled earlier at the guard and as Creon misunderstood the guard, he misunderstands Tiresias. All that is left for Tiresias is to tell Creon that his obstinacy will result in consequences for the "flesh of your flesh." Once again, Creon is told that his law was unjust for "No earthly power, no god in upper air/ Exerts authority over the dead."[44] Higher law takes precedence over man's law: otherwise fate will intervene with tragic consequences.

Creon has been told by Antigone that he has violated the higher law, told by Haemon that he has violated reason, and told by Tiresias that he has violated the fate of the gods. Only then, after repeated warnings and challenges, does Creon vow to release Antigone. But by then his fate has been cast, and he must bear the ensuing tragedy. Creon finally succumbs to these entreaties and goes to release his prisoner only to confront her hanging, his son's anguish and suicide by the sword, and then his wife's own suicide by a blade to her heart.

But why did Creon suffer? After all, he did change his ruling however reluctantly. Creon suffered, not because of his reluctance; he suffered because he was never conscious of his wrong to the gods. As the chorus tells him, "You have learned justice, though it comes too late."[45] Creon held on to the exercise of his authority as long as he could. He yields, finally, only because he knows he is up against a stronger force, the force of fate: "It goes against the grain. But I am beaten/Fate has the upper hand."[46]

Creon's consciousness of his plight is only a recognition that he has been "smashed to bits by a god."[47] Even as he yields to fate, Creon clings tragically to his claims of human, kingly authority and to his belief in the necessity of following man's law:

In my heart of hearts I know what must be done.
Until we breathe our last breath we should keep
The established law.[48]

Why does Creon cling so steadfastly to man's law? He never recognizes that his law exceeds his rule. He never recognizes that the higher law defeated his own command. He never recognizes that as king, he could issue a law to bind man as citizen but could not issue a law to bind the citizens of the underworld. His prohibition against Polyneices' burial interfered with the law of the gods, and that prohibition conflicted with justice by unsettling the order of the world. These failures of recognition had a devastating effect for Creon finally acknowledges that "I am nothing now"[49] and "I who am nothing more than nothing now."[50]

Justice in *Antigone*, as the citizens of Thebes knew, as Antigone knew, as Haemon and Tiresias knew, was a matter of letting Polyneices' soul come to rest in Hades. It could not roam forever the netherworld. Justice allows the laws of man and the laws of the gods to coexist for they have distinct ends. The laws of man bring order to our cities; the laws of the gods bring order to our souls. Creon's mistake was his failure to reason his way through the limits of his rule and to recognize and acknowledge the limits of man's law. Yet, despite its obvious weakness and, in our eyes, obvious injustice, Creon's law is not without support.

Understanding Creon

On the standard reading, Creon is so clearly wrong that it is difficult to recognize the dramatic and philosophical tension in Sophocles' play. Let's start not with what is wrong with Creon but with what is right about him, after which we can turn to Antigone's plight. Creon's conception of law, his claim to issue law, is not without merit. For Creon to purport to issue a law, he must have a claim to authority. And he does. "Authority in general can be divided into legitimate and into *de facto* authority."[51] Creon, by his position as king, had *de facto* authority to issue laws. Yet his authority to issue laws is not unconstrained; his authority is limited. He could not command the sun to revolve the earth nor the rising tides to stop simply because he was king of Thebes. For man's law to be fully effective and just, Creon must act with *de facto* and with legitimate authority.[52] Does his edict satisfy both demands?

On the one hand, Creon's authority is debatable. He has a questionable ascension to the throne,[53] this was the first law he issues, he needs to establish his full legitimacy and authority, and he needs to gain confidence as ruler. Thebes was attacked and Creon's kingship depends upon his response. On the other hand, Creon's claim of *de facto* authority can be justified. He does not claim his kingship by divine right; rather he asserts it as a matter of orderly succession, an assertion that goes unchallenged. More dramatically, his claim to issue laws is based upon a claim of state necessity. He does not say, *"L'Etat c'est moi."* He rules by more than whim; he rules not just because he is king. He rules because someone must guide the ship of state; someone must protect the city; and most important, someone must do so with the city at war. War, defensive in this case, is the strongest claim of necessity because unless state power is artfully exercised, death is probable and annihilation is possible.[54]

Creon's claim as war king and protector of Thebes does not fall on deaf ears. The chorus of elders recognizes that he saved their city from destruction and did so with the help of Zeus, the god of war. A city protected gives Creon great stature and confirms the *de facto* authority of his kingship: "He is a new king but he is right/For this city at this moment."[55] So sing the elders.

A state threatened is a state in need of protection. Creon's obligation is to protect the city, and he does so. To solidify his rule after battle he issues his law, one that has to be honored because to violate it would be to go against the good order. To violate his war law would be treasonous and punishable by death. Creon takes hold of the rudder of the ship of state and guides it through traitorous waters. He does so as much to prove himself and be his own man as he does to answer necessity's call:

You cannot learn of any man the soul,
the mind, and the intent until he shows
his practice of the government and law.
For I believe that who controls the state
and does not hold to the best of plans of all,
but locks his tongue up through some kind of fear,
that he is worst of all who are or were.[56]

Creon stakes his rule on his ability and authority to govern and issue laws. By relying on man's law to protect the state, Creon is moving boldly in the world. He justifies that move as leader of Thebes. The king must command the respect of the citizenry. Creon knows that he needs to prove himself as a ruler to gain the confidence of the people[57] because, "Failure of rule [is] the most destructive thing."[58] Creon rules, yet he fears and maybe even knows that unless he rules hard and swiftly, a "certain poisonous minority" will contest his edict and his rule.[59] Creon reacts to that fear by using man's law to maintain his order and authority. Those who would threaten the state can only be labeled traitor, and those who sympathize with traitors can only be labeled unpatriotic.[60] Polyneices, the man who "terrorized"[61] Thebes must pay, and it is precisely here that Creon's full authority to promulgate law falters because his second claim to legitimate authority is uncertain.

We can accept Creon's *de facto* authority to issue law. It is not hard to sympathize with Creon having been a war king, having fought the good fight, having repelled the terrorists, and having saved the state. Our country and our congress reacted to the 9/11 terrorist attack in exactly the same way, giving our president the *de facto* authority to command in response to the attack, even as we debate whether that authority was exercised legitimately. In victory, Creon can honor the heroes and condemn the traitors. Yet something is wrong here and it is this wrong that challenges Creon's legitimate authority; Polyneices is dead and King Creon's law of the land does not extend to the land of the dead.

Creon—The First Legal Positivist

Creon's *de facto* legitimacy rests on two breaks from the past. Creon needed to break away from reliance on the gods, and he needed to break away from the Theban legend; he did so through law, man's law. He acted on his human authority as king, not on any divine right. And by doing so, Creon plays an important role in the development of law. Creon's claim to promulgate man's law is a basic form of legal positivism.[62] This conception of law depends on the issuance of an order from a recognized authority, backed by the threat of sanctions, and obeyed by those persons subject to the recognized ruler. Creon's edict has, at least partially, all of these characteristics. Creon issues an order as a recognized king; disobedience is subject to death, and most citizens of Thebes obey the edict. The failure of all citizens to obey is Creon's undoing. Antigone's failure to obey undermines Creon's claim to legitimacy and shatters his edict and his conception of law. Creon can sustain neither his edict nor his rule because Creon's law confronts something other, something higher. Throughout the play, Creon tries to justify his law as he responds to the three challenges. His responses fail.

To better understand why Creon's responses fail, we should consider a stripped-down example of his positivist conception of law which comes from Herodotus who lived and wrote at the time Sophocles was writing his Theban plays. In the *Histories*, Herodotus tells the story of King Xerxes, who, upon his defeat by the Greeks at Salamis, commandeered a boat to retreat to Persia. The retreat was hazardous and Xerxes feared for his safety. The helmsman told the king that the boat was overloaded and would sink, drowning them all unless the load was lessened. When Xerxes heard the warning from the helmsman, he then said:

> '[Y]ou men of Persia, now let each of you prove your care for your king; for in you, it seems, lies my safety.' That is what he said, and the men did obeisance and jumped into the sea and the ship was lightened and came safe to Asia. As soon as Xerxes landed, he did the following: because the helmsman had saved the life of the King, he awarded him a golden crown; but for causing the death of many Persians, he had his head cut off.[63]

The story of Xerxes is a bare bones example of legal positivism. The king, claiming *de facto* authority, issued two orders backed by sanctions. Men jumped into the sea to their deaths for fear of sanction, and the helmsman lost his head as sanction for the death of the Persians. Do we consider Xerxes' orders to be law? H.L.A. Hart, the seminal legal philosopher in the last half of the twentieth century says, "No." Law, Hart argues, is more sophisticated. His canonical book, *The Concept of Law*, establishes our modern understanding of legal positivism and continues to command attention.[64] Hart's jurisprudence is significant both in its message and its method and supports Creon's conception of law.

As message, Hart argues that law can be identified independently of its moral content and that law is a recognizable rules system. As method, Hart draws his arguments from observation, from practice, and from "social facts." Instead of a naked theory of law, Hart's conception of law is based on how he perceives law operating in the world. Hart is describing what lawyers, judges, and citizens do from the inside of law.[65]

Hart rejects the idea that Xerxes' order constituted valid law. Hart was dissatisfied with and critical of John Austin's positivist idea that law was nothing more than orders backed by threats and obeyed by subjects out of fear.[66] He said that such a conception was analogous to a gunman demanding your money as he put a gun to your head. Surely you would obey, but does this threat, followed by obedience constitute law? Hart rejected the gunman conception of the law because he argued there is more to law. For Hart, the something more started with the obedience that subjects give to the orders of their rulers. In part that obedience is habitual. In other part, it is voluntary as people obey when no guns are pointed to their heads. Why then, do people obey the law? And is obedience enough to constitute a valid concept of law?

Introductory jurisprudence courses explore the question of obedience by posing a hypothetical: *If you are driving home at 2:00 AM and come to a stop sign at a deserted intersection, do you stop? If so, why?* People do stop at deserted stop signs. Some persons stop because they believe that they *ought* to obey the law. In other, and slightly more formal words, some persons stop because they believe that they have a moral obligation to obey the law. Others stop because even at deserted stop signs, there is a risk of getting caught. In other and slightly more formal words, they obey because they fear the sanction of the orders backed by threats. Finally, others obey simply out of unreflective habit. They obey without thinking about law's authority in any obvious way. Is obedience, even habitual obedience, enough to justify law? Hart says that law is more complicated still; obedience alone does not explain the continuity necessary to sustain a legal system. Hart, lawyer-turned-philosopher,[67] developed a conception of law as law is practiced in the world, not as it might operate in a theoretical vacuum.

As archetype, Xerxes occupies a position similar to Hart's Rex I.[68] Rex I is an absolute monarch who "controls his people by general orders backed by threats requiring them to do various things which they would otherwise not do and to abstain from doing things which they would otherwise do."[69] Hart makes the point that even though people chafe under Rex I's rule, they obey his orders, and that obedience makes Rex I the sovereign. This obedience is solely the result of power and is not based on the goodness or justness of the monarch's rules themselves. Hart doubts that such a primitive society ever existed yet says there is a certain unity that may constitute a state. Still, even habitual obedience to Rex I does not resemble what Hart considers law and therefore must be rejected as an inadequate conception.

Hart explains his rejection with a practical problem: How does law continue? If law is part of the machinery of the state, and we all experience that it is, then how does the state continue after Rex I's rule ends? What happens after Rex I's death? How is it possible for Rex II to succeed his father and enjoy the habitual obedience of his subjects? Why should Rex I's subjects obey Rex II at all, let alone habitually, when no habit has been able to form under Rex II? Hart argues that regular obedience depends on something other than blind habit, and that law's continuity is based on a set of observed rules, not habits. "What is required instead is the notion of a rule conferring powers . . . on persons qualified . . . to legislate by complying with a certain procedure."[70]

Note the moves that Hart makes. First, he expands the idea that law is an order backed by threats by noting that law also confers powers. Law confers power on some citizens, specifically legislators, to pass laws which bind themselves and others. Law also confers powers on other citizens to go about the civil life of getting married, making contracts, and creating businesses among myriad other legal activities of individual volition not based on compulsion.[71] Second, Hart stresses the importance of rules for law's existence, stability, and continuity.

Rules lie at the core of Hart's conception of law and he identifies two kinds of them. Hart's first kind, his primary rules, are familiar to us. Primary rules include orders backed by threats such as rules of criminal law which prohibit certain forms of conduct. Primary rules also include Hart's definition of rules as conferring powers such as the civil rules authorizing contracts, marriages, and various forms of business association. A society of only primary rules will be either primitive or defective because it will lack certainty, dynamism, and efficiency.[72] In short, a society of only primary rules cannot grow, adapt, or change.

The power of Hart's conception and the reason for law's continuity derives from his secondary rules which legitimate the primary rules and sustain a living society. As citizens, we elect legislators and presidents who appoint and confirm judges. We then recognize, through rules of recognition in Hart's vocabulary, the legitimacy of legislatures to issue laws, of presidents to execute them, and of judges to decide disputes arising under those laws. Through secondary rules, the orders of the sovereign have greater certainty, can be changed in orderly and necessary ways, and conflicts among or about the legitimacy of the primary rules can be adjudicated.[73] Through secondary rules, citizens acknowledge the continuity of primary rules and with them the continuity of government.

Is Creon's law more like Xerxes' orders backed by threats? Or is his law closer to Hart's legal positivism? Creon's law is a sophisticated advance from Xerxes' order. Xerxes' order exemplifies the gunman state. Creon's edict, while backed by threat of death, was justified in a way that Xerxes' order was not. Xerxes ordered men to their death for his own safety. Herodotus does not say that Xerxes claimed his safety was necessary to preserve Persia. Instead, Xerxes said that in his men "lies my safety." Creon's edict was justified as an act of state. Thebes was attacked by terrorists and no honor can be given to those who threaten the annihilation of the state. By justifying his edict on the basis of state necessity, Creon argued for the preservation of the state, not only his own preservation. In this way, Creon acknowledges the need for sovereign succession and for the continuity of Thebes. Is this enough to sustain his rule?

The Limits of Man and of Man's Law

Creon used man's law to protect the state and to set himself apart from the gods and apart from legend. Creon's heroic law confronted a society still in the thrall of both. Creon lived when Greek citizens and leaders still believed in and sometimes relied upon the gods and respected legend. Still, Creon's new world was not as ordered as Creon's law would have it because man's law does not exist alone and apart from or independent of something other, something higher.

The boldness and fragility of man, and of man's law, is revealed in *Antigone's* first ode, *The Ode to Man.* The chorus is much taken by this clever animal known as man who appears in control of the earth, the sea, and the beasts which inhabit them. This clever animal created language and thought and has "a temperament for the laws of towns."[74] The only force that man cannot resist is death. Still, man is clever but may be too clever by half as the chorus sings:

Full of skills and
Devising, even beyond
Hope, is the intelligent
Art that leads him
Both to evil and
To good. Honoring

Laws of the earth
And the justice of
The gods, to which
Men swear, he stands
High in his city
But outside any
City is he who dares,
To consort with
What is wrong:. . .[75]

Early in the play, the chorus adeptly situates Creon and Creon's law. As man, Creon exercises his intelligent art by passing a law, and the law that he passed was more sophisticated than Xerxes' order backed by threats. Creon's law was justified not on his gain alone; it was justified on the good of the city. Creon's law gave him stature in the city, but it alone could not give him the stature of justice. The chorus warns that man's cleverness cannot ignore the justice of the gods; it cannot ignore the higher law. Creon's edict against Polyneices' burial goes beyond his own cleverness. Creon could issue man's law to protect the state, but punishing Antigone for saving her brother's soul is beyond his reach.

Creon's conception of law is close to Hart's legal positivism as it embodies the separation of man's law from the higher law. There are strong theoretical and practical reasons for the separation, but with separation comes danger.

Theoretically, man's law and the higher law have distinct ends. Where man's law exists to keep peace among men, the higher law exists to bring men to the Good or to God. Also, particularly in a modern pluralistic democracy, we acknowledge and accept the existence and value of moral and political disagreement. We acknowledge that society is comprised of a variety of political, moral, and religious points of view. We are committed to toleration and endorse the idea that there can be no single moral viewpoint that can or should take precedence over others. Hans Kelsen's pure theory of law makes this point: "In view of the extraordinary heterogeneity, however, of what men in fact have considered as good and evil, just or unjust, at different times and in different places, no element common to the contents of the various moral orders is detectable."[76]

Practically, the separation of man's law and the higher law is also supportable. Much of man's law is either nonmoral or so far removed from moral considerations as to bring it beyond the conscious acceptance of law's moral content. Matters of life and death, abortion, racial discrimination, and marriage are obvious examples of laws with explicit moral content. Can the same be said about the allocation of the electromagnetic spectrum for broadcasting or setting a speed limit at 55 mph? Surely the distribution of information and entertainment as well as safe driving are moral goods, but where the law draws the lines is not obviously a matter of moral concern. Allocating the electromagnetic spectrum to broadcaster *X* or *Y* when each is similarly situated or setting the speed limit at 55 or 60 mph has no moral value or a moral value so ambiguous or attenuated as to be insignificant. Man's law, given its separability from the higher law, lets government function without continuous debate about the moral significance of every law that is issued.

Creon's law fits comfortably within this conception of legal positivism. His kingly edict was backed by a threat, it commanded the obedience of most of the citizens, it was intended to preserve and continue the state. Why, then, did it fail?

Sophocles' *Antigone* rejects Creon's brand of legal positivism. Neither the *de facto* authority of the law nor habitual obedience, nor even habitual obedience of rules of recognition are enough to sustain law. Rather, man's law cannot contrast too sharply with the higher law precisely because habitual obedience, even reflective obedience, is so fragile. Assume for the moment that Antigone did comply: how many such similar orders could Creon have given? How many times could the citizens of Thebes have accepted laws that conflicted with the higher law? How long could they have accepted unjust laws? As it was, Creon's single unjust order brought ruin to his rule. As the last chorus sings:

> *Wise conduct is the key to happiness.*
> *Always rule by the gods and reverence them.*
> *Those who overbear will come to grief.*[77]

Creon's edict was such overbearing.

Creon Comes to America

Creon's ghost is the specter of the conflict between man's law and higher, maybe even unsayable, law which results in a failure of justice.[78] The question of how to resolve the conflict is an ancient one, and Creon provided one answer which, while ultimately fatal, was not irrational. Creon's positivist justification for his law has great resonance today. Law, argue the positivists and Creon, can be identified from its accepted sources or through its accepted conventions. As king, Creon had lawmaking power, and he exercised that power in the name of state preservation. For Creon, as for the legal positivists, there is no necessary connection between man's law and higher law; there is no necessary connection between law and justice. Instead, man's law is either indifferent to moral claims[79] or, to suit state purposes, man's law can incorporate moral claims as needed.[80] Creon adopted the stronger position; he was not indifferent to Antigone's higher law claim—he wanted to extinguish it.

How well does Creon's ghost travel through the centuries and across the seas? Remarkably well as it turns out. So well that *Antigone* can be read as a precursor of American First Amendment jurisprudence. *Antigone* is a cautionary tale about not only confusing the reach of a ruler's authority but also about the dangers of imposing that authority where it does not belong. In the United States today, Creon's ghost lives on and is appearing with greater frequency in contemporary politics.[81]

Man's law can interact with the higher law claims of moral or religious beliefs in one of two ways.[82] First, the state can attempt to interfere with, restrict, or even prohibit the free exercise of religion. Sunday closing laws and the prohibition of Mormon polygamy and sacramental hallucinogens have been challenged as abridgments of the free exercise of religion. Second, the state can attempt to establish its own conception of religion on the polity. Lately the government's attempt to impose particular moral or religious beliefs is expanding. Government opposition to certain forms of stem cell research, same-sex marriage, certain forms of birth control, a woman's right to choose, and assisted suicide, together with the promotion of intelligent design, school prayer, public displays of the Ten Commandments, and state funding of "faith-based" initiatives are the most notorious contemporary examples of the state imposing its set of religious principles on all citizens.[83]

Religion in America presents particularly thorny conflicts about which we are "perennially divided."[84] Our constitutional jurisprudence requires tolerance for free exercise and prohibits the establishment of religion. Nonetheless, accommodations between religion and law are routinely made and are seen as necessary. To put the case simply, public fire protection will not be denied to a burning church.[85] Still, while our First Amendment jurisprudence may not be in "hopeless disarray,"[86] as justice Clarence

Thomas claims, it does reveal the continuing and inconsistent resolutions of conflicts between man's law and the higher law.

Creon's Law Prevails

The Case of Sacramental Peyote[87]

Alfred Smith and Galen Black, members of the Native American Church, participated in a sacred rite during which, under controlled and restricted circumstances, they ingested sacramental peyote. Peyote is a hallucinogenic drug listed as a controlled substance by Oregon's criminal laws. Oregon criminal authorities were unconcerned about Smith and Black and made no effort to charge them with any criminal violation.[88] There were, however, other consequences.

Upon learning of their use of the drug, their employer, a private drug rehabilitation organization, fired them both for misconduct in the workplace. Smith and Black then sought state unemployment compensation which was denied. They challenged the denial in state court as a violation of their First Amendment right of the free exercise of religion. The case wound its way through state and federal courts with the Oregon Supreme Court ruling that although sacramental peyote was not exempt from the criminal statutes, the respondents' free exercise rights, their higher law, took precedence over the criminal law, man's law. The case then went to the U.S. Supreme Court which reversed the state court, reinstating the denial of benefits, in an opinion by justice Antonin Scalia.

Justice Scalia's argument is straightforward. Oregon can prohibit the use of certain drugs as "controlled substances." Oregon could have exempted sacramental peyote from criminal sanction as had Arizona, Colorado, and New Mexico but chose not to do so. In support of the denial of unemployment benefits, Scalia writes that an "individual's belief [does not] excuse him from compliance with an otherwise valid law prohibiting conduct that the State is free to regulate."[89] He quotes justice Felix Frankfurter in an early flag salute case to great effect:

> Conscientious scruples have not, in the course of the long struggle for religious toleration, relieved individuals from obedience to a general law not aimed at the promotion or restriction of religious beliefs. The mere possession of religious convictions which contradict the relevant

> concerns of a political society does not relieve the citizen from the discharge of political responsibilities.[90]

With this language, the Court upheld a state requirement that students salute the American flag in school. It is also strong language to support Scalia's rationale that political society, on occasion, necessarily interferes with religious beliefs and such interference is constitutionally protected. There are two problems with relying on this language. First, the Frankfurter opinion was expressly overturned three years later.[91] Second, the balance Scalia uses to weigh the interests of political society and the individual puts the burden in the wrong place, a point later addressed by Congress.

Scalia's position is that a general law, criminal or civil (think of tax or licensing laws as civil laws which can affect religious organizations), not aimed at restricting religion must be honored. Man's law takes precedence over an individual's belief in a higher law. Here Creon wins. And he wins because individual conduct cannot override the needs of society. Shades of Lord Devlin who argued, famously, that even victimless crimes such as abortion, bigamy, prostitution, and homosexuality could and should be prosecuted so as not to tear the fabric of society.[92] In this vein, Scalia writes, "It may be fairly stated that leaving accommodation to the political process will place at a relative disadvantage those religious practices that are not widely engaged in; but that unavoidable consequence of democratic government must be preferred to a system in which each conscience is a law unto itself. . . ."[93] The skeptic might be forgiven for understanding this passage as holding that minority or marginal religions are just out of luck where free exercise protections are concerned.

Although justice Sandra Day O'Connor joined the majority and agreed with the outcome of the case, she wrote a separate concurrence criticizing Scalia's First Amendment analysis. She directly challenges Scalia's opinion as "sweeping" and "strained." Scalia drew a distinction between belief and conduct that O'Connor rejects: "But a law that prohibits certain conduct—conduct that happens to be an act of worship for someone—manifestly does prohibit that person's free expression of his religion."[94] She also rejects, as unworkable, Scalia's test that a law of general applicability does not violate the free exercise clause while a targeted law does. Clearly, there are any number of generally applicable laws that apply to religious practices. Speeding to church is not a defense. At the other extreme, prohibiting virgin sacrifice must be socially preferred to a "religious practice not widely engaged in."

There is a balance that needs to be struck between society and individual religious belief. The problem that O'Connor had with Scalia's analysis is that instead of making the state show a compelling interest to be protected before interfering with the religious practice, Scalia simply dropped that test in favor of some unarticulated balancing. O'Connor argued that in free exercise cases, the government should bear the burden when the claim is made that religious beliefs are affected. For O'Connor, leaving the matter to the political process is exactly what the First Amendment was designed *not* to do: "[T]he First Amendments was enacted precisely to protect the rights of those whose religious practices are not shared by the majority and may be viewed with hostility.[95]

There is a dramatic postscript to this case. Justice O'Connor's free expression analysis regarding the appropriate burdens and the proper balance persuaded Congress that the Court went too far and reached an unacceptable level of interference with religion. Congress took these concerns seriously and passed the Religious Freedom Restoration Act (RFRA) in response. The RFRA prohibits the federal government from substantially burdening a person's exercise of religion "even if the burden results from a rule of general applicability."[96] The statute was tested and upheld in a case strikingly similar to *Smith*.[97] The RFRA and justice O'Connor's analysis in *Smith* have now become the law of the land. Still, Smith and Black lost their state unemployment benefits as man's law prevailed over their religious beliefs.[98]

The Case of the Ten Commandments

The Texas state capitol building is surrounded by 21 historical markers and 17 monuments, including a six-foot high monolith inscribed with the Ten Commandments. The monument was given to the state by the Fraternal Order of Eagles, a national social civic and patriotic organization, because of their religious beliefs. During frequent visits to the capital, an Austin resident encountered the monument and sought its removal as a violation of the First Amendment establishment clause. The U.S. District Court found that there was a valid secular purpose for having the Ten Commandments on state grounds and the U.S. Court of Appeals agreed. The U.S. Supreme Court, in a 5–4 opinion written by Chief justice William Rehnquist, affirmed.

The district court determined that the state had a secular purpose in displaying the Ten Commandments and that a reasonable observer who is mindful of the history and context of the monument would not conclude that the state was seeking to endorse religion. Rehnquist wrote that Supreme Court cases are not uniform in examining establishment clause controversies. Some cases honor the strong role played by religion in our nation's history. Another set of cases prohibits government interference. These cases conflict, and the area is unsettled.[99] Some cases assist religion by allowing public funds to flow to them,[100] and other cases inhibit its exercise by disallowing practices such as school prayer.[101]

In the Texas case, the Court noted that in the past it ruled that a Kentucky statute requiring the posting of the Ten Commandments in every public school classroom was unconstitutional.[102] The Court reasoned that the Kentucky statute had a plainly religious purpose. In the case before it, however, the Court said that the "placement of the Ten Commandments monument on the Texas State Capitol grounds is a far more passive use of those texts than was the case in *Stone*, where the text confronted elementary school students every day."[103] The Court, rather, saw its inclusion as part of the state's political and legal history.

Justice John Paul Stevens writing in dissent, joined by justice Ruth Bader Ginsburg, saw the case differently. Instead of viewing the Ten Commandments as an example of the political and legal history of Texas, they saw the message written on the monument, "I AM the Lord Thy God." The Ten Commandments had displayed no purpose concerning the formation of Texas. Rather, "the message transmitted by Texas' chosen display is quite simple: this state endorses the Divine code of the 'Judeo-Christian' God."[104] Justice Stevens then argued that there should be a strong presumption against the display of religious symbols and that such metaphysical line drawing should be drawn against the establishment of religion, thus protecting our country's commitment to religious diversity and tolerance.

There are surreal moments in this case. For the lawyers arguing the case of *Van Orden* v. *Perry* and for the justices who had to hear and decide the case, they did so in the Supreme Court's courtroom adorned by a frieze of 18 figures of various lawgivers including Moses holding the Ten Commandments. From the sublime we then go to the ridiculous. The granite monument given to Texas by the Fraternal Order of Eagles was given not only out of the conviction that the Ten Commandments should be known by youth to guide them on the right path of life; the gift was also given in part to promote the movie *The Ten Commandments* by Cecile B. DeMille. As a final note, on the same day that *Van Orden* was decided, the Supreme Court held that the posting of the Ten Commandments in two Kentucky courthouses violated the First Amendment because, despite legislative declarations of secular intent, the displays were for a predominantly religious purpose.[105]

In *Smith* and *Van Orden*, man's law prevails over higher law but not without significant ambiguity. We are conflicted about the proper relationship between man's law and higher law. More specifically, we are conflicted about law's proper relationship with religion. Given this conflict, it is not difficult to sympathize with either side in these controversies.

The state in both instances prevailed for the reasons expressed in the majority opinions, and those reasons are reminiscent of Creon's espoused view that the state needs protection. Yet, the higher law claims are not unsympathetic. Smith and Black lost their jobs and their benefits for taking part in a religious ceremony that is permitted in at least three states and was not going to be criminally prosecuted in Oregon. Visitors to the Texas state capitol grounds will see the Ten Commandments on display proclaiming a Judeo-Christian God's message. While individuals should be unfettered by the state in the sincere expression of their religious beliefs, nevertheless, the state has a general and important interest in maintaining its historic heritage, its criminal laws, and preserving its traditions. After all, surely no one believes that a ritual sacrifice in violation of a general criminal law can be excused on the basis of the free exercise of religion.

Antigone's Law Prevails

The Case of Ritual Slaughter[106]

Well, apparently with all nine justices of the U. S. Supreme Court in agreement, ritual animal sacrifice as part of the ceremonies of the Santeria religion in Hialeah, Florida is protected under the free exercise clause of the First Amendment.

Hundreds of thousands of Yoruba people were brought to Cuba as slaves from Western Africa. With them they brought their religious practices and beliefs which, in the New World, mixed with Roman Catholicism to create the religion of Santeria. Practitioners observe the Catholic sacraments and strongly believe in spirits with whom every member of the church must cultivate a personal relationship. A principle form of nurturing this relationship is through ritual animal sacrifice which is performed on specific occasions such as at births, marriages, deaths, and to cure the sick.

In Cuba, Santeria members were persecuted and the ceremonies could only be practiced in secret. Cuban exiles brought their religion to

South Florida where it is estimated there are at least 50,000 adherents. Ernesto Pichardo, the head of the Church of the Lukumi Babalu Aye, Inc., wanted to bring Santeria into the open and to that end announced plans to construct a church and religious center in the city of Hialeah. He successfully obtained all of the necessary land use and building permits before his plans confronted the citizenry and city leaders. Justice Kennedy's opinion for the Court notes that, "The prospect of a Santeria church in their midst was distressing to many members of the Hialeah community."

The Hialeah city council held emergency public sessions at which they passed a series of resolutions and ordinances which halted the church's plans and led to litigation. The city's ordinances stated that Santeria's practice of animal sacrifice was inconsistent with the traditional police powers of public, health, safety, welfare, and morals of the community and, therefore, was subject to criminal penalties if performed. The church challenged these laws in federal court which ruled for the city, reasoning that the church could practice its religion freely only without the ritual sacrifice and that the city could enforce its criminal laws of general applicability.

The trial court found first that animal sacrifice presented a substantial health risk. Second, the ritual might be harmful to the emotional health of the children who might witness it. Next, the City was concerned about the cruel and unnecessary killing of animals. And finally, the city wanted to place animal slaughter in the proper land use zones. The court of appeals affirmed, and the case went to the U.S. Supreme Court.

Justice Kennedy, adopting the law in *Smith*, stated that the test to be applied was that a law that is neither neutral nor of general applicability which burdens a particular religious practice can stand only if it is supported by compelling governmental interests. The Court found that the city ordinances were neither neutral nor of general applicability and that its asserted interests were not sufficiently compelling. Regarding neutrality, the Court found that "no one suggests, and on this record it cannot be maintained, that city officials had in mind a religion other than Santeria."[107] The Court analyzed the city's compelling interests and found that the ordinances were overbroad in regulating Santeria's animal sacrifice rituals while allowing animal slaughter in other situations such as the preparation for food consumption.[108] Kennedy found that the city ordinances, "had as their object the suppression of religion," "disclosed animosity to Santeria adherents and their religious practices," "targeted this religious exercise"[109] and therefore were not neutral.

The Court's analysis of general applicability follows similar lines. The ordinances intended to be protective of health and to avoid cruelty to animals did not ban other nonreligious conduct as it did Santeria's practices. Regarding general applicability, Kennedy concluded that Hialeah's ordinances were aimed at conduct motivated by religious belief.[110] He further wrote, "The Free Exercise Clause commits government itself to religious tolerance and upon even the slightest suspicion that proposals for state intervention stem from animosity to religion or distrust of its practices, all officials must pause to remember their own high duty to the Constitution and to the rights it secures." Notably, "Legislators may not devise mechanisms, overt or disguised, designed to persecute or oppress a religion or its practices. The laws here in question were enacted contrary to these constitutional principles and they are void."[111]

In *City of Hialeah*, the Court rejected the city's attempt to interfere with or suppress[112] the religious practices of a minority church. Higher law prevailed over man's law. The higher law of free religious belief also prevails in the next case.

The Monkey Case[113]

The infamous Scopes monkey trial in Dayton, Tennessee was high drama, putting Darwin on trial with the testimony of three-time presidential candidate William Jennings Bryan under cross-examination by Clarence Darrow.[114] One would have thought that the issue belonged to history and that science won the day even though Darwin and Darrow lost the case and John Scopes, the teacher, never regained his teaching position. Not so. Today state legislatures continue to champion God over Darwin through legislation directed to what must be taught as science in public schools.

Freedom of religion entails a prohibition that governments may not use law to advance either a religion or a religious practice or belief. Courts will invalidate laws that advance religion such as those requiring the posting of the Ten Commandments in schools,[115] requiring a minute of silence in schools as a subterfuge for prayer,[116] or prohibiting the teaching of evolution.[117]

The Louisiana legislature tried to promote creationism by passing a statute entitled the "Balanced Treatment for Creation-Science and Evolution-Science in Public Instruction Act." Known as the Creationism Act, the law prohibited the teaching of evolution in public schools unless "creation science" was also taught. The legislative hearings attempted to articulate secular reasons for the Act, including broadening the curriculum and exposing students to the science of creationism. At trial, parents and religious leaders sought to have the Act declared an unconstitutional violation of the establishment clause.

The federal district court held that the purpose of the Act was to advance a particular religious doctrine, and the court of appeals affirmed. Supreme Court establishment clause jurisprudence uses a three-part test, infelicitously named the *Lemon* test, to evaluate these cases.[118] The first part of the test is that the legislature must put forward a secular basis for the statute. Louisiana could not satisfy this first prong, and the statute was held unconstitutional.

Louisiana argued that the purpose of the statute was to maximize academic freedom and the effectiveness of science instruction. The Court rejected the claim as a sham because it curtailed teachers who chose to teach evolution. "The preeminent purpose of the Louisiana Legislature was clearly to advance the religious viewpoint that a supernatural being created humankind. The term 'creation science' was defined as embracing this particular religious doctrine . . ."[119]

In his concurring opinion, justice Lewis Powell noted that the sponsor of the legislation was quite explicit about the purpose of the bill and that the legislation was introduced because of "disdain for the theory of evolution resulted from the support that evolution supplied to views contrary to his own religious beliefs."[120] Powell also cited the fact that the original version of the bill defined the "theory of creation *ex nihilo*" as holding that, "the origin of man, and the origin of all things and their process and relationships were created *ex nihilo* and fixed by God." Further, the "creation scientists" that the state relied on in support for its position were all affiliated with either the Institute for Creation Research, an institution directly associated with a Christian college, or with the Creation Research Society which required its members to subscribe to the bible as the written word of God.

The 7–2 majority opinion concluded, "The Louisiana Creationism Act advances a religious doctrine by requiring either the banishment of the theory of evolution from public school classrooms or the presentation of a religious viewpoint that rejects evolution in its entirety."[121] *Edwards's* clear holding is that creationism cannot be taught as science because it is an explicitly religious doctrine.

The clarity of the opinion has not stopped religious enthusiasts who continue to press their claims in state legislatures[122] and local school boards to enact rules requiring the teaching of intelligent design as science.

When a local school board in Dover, Pennsylvania, required that intelligent design be taught alongside evolution, a group of parents challenged the requirement as a repackaged version of creationism.[123] Federal Judge John Jones found that intelligent design was creationism under another name, had no basis in science, that the school board's decision constituted "breathtaking inanity,"[124] and, therefore, the requirement violated the establishment clause.

Imagine now if Antigone were to bring her claim to the U.S. Supreme Court and challenge Creon's edict. Was Creon's law neutral and generally applicable? Or did it target Polyneices' soul? Could Creon successfully assert a sufficient compelling governmental interest? Or could his desire to protect the citizens of Thebes and his throne be achieved in ways that did not burden the free expression of Antigone's law?

The four cases just reviewed demonstrate that the conflict between man's law and higher law is alive and well today. Governments, particularly in pluralistic and democratic societies, cannot avoid these conflicts. Tolerance for one religion can go only so far before it bumps into the deeply held beliefs of another religion or deeply held beliefs not religious in nature at all. Society and religion can, and do, conflict, and decisional rules are necessary for resolving these conflicts. Courts resort to standards, tests, balancing, and other decisional devices, and all are imperfect. This situation is not all bad. These cases present conflicts of laws that must be resolved for society to go on with its daily life. And conflict resolution, even between man's law and higher law, is precisely what the U.S. Supreme Court does. But is conflict resolution justice? I defer answering that question until Chapter 8.

Conclusion

Creon's ghost is a specter that haunts us still. Man's law can and does conflict with higher law and has done so for 2500 years, and the conflicts remain unresolved. The conflicts can be messy, tragic even. Further, the conflict between man's law and higher law is not just an exercise in scholastic metaphysics or modern linguistic philosophy. The consequences are deathly real as events around the world demonstrate daily.

At the heart of the failure to resolve the conflict is the problem of justice. Assuming that we can know and articulate the higher law, how are we to decide to favor one law over the other? When does the higher law trump man's law?

Creon is sympathetic and Creon's law deserves respect because Creon wanted to break away from the law of the gods and to have man's law operate effectively in the world. Unfortunately, he overreached. Creon wanted the law of the land, man's law, to have universal application when it can only have provisional and temporary application. His mistake was a human mistake with fateful consequences nonetheless. Like Creon, we want man's law to bring stasis to a moving world; we want law to bring harmony among men. Unlike Creon, though, we want law to be fair and just. Such is our desire for justice and in *Antigone*, Sophocles demonstrated that man's law must give way to higher law when it is not just. Justice, then, will dictate when higher law supercedes man's law. *Antigone* gives us an example, rather than a complete definition, of the higher law.

Several years after Sophocles wrote *Antigone*, Plato demonstrated that while the ideal of justice is alive in all of us, it is also very, very difficult to realize in our world. Justice cannot be realized without struggle, or as Plato put it, without a struggle between the shadows of belief and the light of the truth. Our reality is that we can only find justice if we engage in that struggle between shadows and light and do so through reason. The struggle is difficult because beliefs are so strong. Nonetheless, beliefs alone are insufficient to ground man's law and expect justice to follow. Our challenge is to find the light of truth in the shadows of belief—for that is where justice resides.

Next, let's see what Plato has to teach us.

TWO

Shadows and Light

The snub-nosed man sat on the edge of his pallet after rising from a gentle sleep where he dreamed of fertile Phthia. He was aroused from his slumber by a friend with a heavy burden. The visitor came to tell the man that the end was near. The visitor also came to persuade the man to flee his jail cell.

The visitor argued that the man should save himself to not embarrass his friends; to help continue to educate and raise his sons; and, to right a wrong that had been committed by an unjust court, applying an unjust law. The friend argued to console himself. The man responded with consolation of his own, the consolation of philosophy,[1] *as the man argued for his own death.*

THE MAN ON THE PALLET, the snub-nosed one, is Socrates.[2] Socrates wrote nothing, annoyed many, and died at the hands of a democratic state, the city of Athens. Three charges were leveled against him. The first charge was that he took money for teaching students how to make the weaker argument the stronger; this old charge could not be sustained. The newer charges were more dangerous. Socrates was charged with corrupting the youth of Athens and for not believing in the gods in which the City believed. For these crimes he was convicted and condemned to death. If we can believe anything about Socrates, it is that he was not guilty of the sophistry of making the weaker argument the stronger because his whole life was devoted to refuting exactly this charge. Just as we can be certain that he was not guilty of the first charge, we can be equally certain that he was guilty of the other two—the charges of philosophy and impiety.[3]

Socrates encounters Creon's ghost when, on his deathbed, he justifies his death sentence through a dialogue with the Laws in which the debate between man's law and higher law is replayed in a different key. Socrates' deathbed dialogue contrasts man's law, here the law of the Athenian jury with the higher law of justice. Although Socrates, like Antigone, meets death for his belief, Antigone's death comes in the name of a higher law to be left alone and to live according to her conscience. Socrates' death comes in the name of the Constitution and Laws of Athens which allowed him to live a life of philosophy. The Laws let Socrates flourish in the City and in the Soul. Socrates desired the unity of man's law and justice. Antigone experienced man's law separately from justice.

Jacques-Louis David's 1787 painting, *The Death of Socrates,* is a powerful image of the philosopher's end. Sitting upright in large chambers in a flowing white robe, Socrates looks to his left with his left arm raised, finger pointing upward in an emphatic gesture.[4] His right hand is reaching for the cup of hemlock that will take his life. To his left, his friends engage their teacher in his last moments of philosophic conversation. To his right, his friends and wife turn away in sorrow, weeping. David captures our sense of Socrates, dignified in death yet leaving us perplexed about his life and his defense of it.[5] How can this man who lived in search of the Good and the Just succumb to what is so obviously an unjust act of law? How can Socrates yield to man's law when he lived by and exemplified the life of the mind, the higher law of philosophy? We will explore these questions through the writings of his most famous disciple, Plato.

Defining Justice

Plato, writing barely 40 years after *Antigone* was first performed, confirms Sophocles' idea that man's law is limited, and there are occasions when the higher law should prevail. Otherwise, people—Antigone and Socrates are prime examples—die because of this conflict of laws. Plato helps us think more deeply about the conflict and suggests a way of living with even if not completely resolving it. His response is to struggle with Creon's ghost as a way of life, as a way of being fully human. Occasionally we win a struggle over the ghost and justice prevails; the struggle for justice is Plato's lodestar. We focus on two episodes from Plato's *Republic,* Book I and the Allegory of the Cave in Book VII, to understand Plato's idea of justice and the role it plays in leading the good life.[6]

The setting for the *Republic* is an inauspicious dinner party at which it seems that once the conversation begins, the guests in the house of Cephalus never make it to the dinner table. Book I opens with Socrates and his friend Glaucon, Plato's brother, leaving the Pireaus, the harbor of Athens, having just offered prayers to the goddess Bendis at her new festival.

As they are about to return to the city, they are stopped when a servant boy grabs Socrates' cloak and tells him to wait for his master, Polemarchus, Cephalus's son. Socrates explains that they are heading back to Athens when Polemarchus tells Socrates to come to dinner with him and his friends. Socrates is reluctant to go, but Polemarchus says that Socrates should comply because Polemarchus and his friends outnumber him. Socrates replies that perhaps there is another way for Polemarchus to convince him to go with them; Polemarchus can use persuasion rather than force.

This opening banter sets a central theme for much of the *Republic*. Is justice to be found in power or persuasion, force or reason? Polemarchus persuades Socrates and Glaucon to attend dinner and enjoy fine conversation after which they can watch a nighttime torch race on horses as part of the festival.

Socrates is warmly welcomed by Cephalus, and they talk about the pleasures of old age, sex, and wealth. Having gotten older and now better able to control that "savage master" of sexual passion, Cephalus can reflect on his life. As part of that reflection, he can consider whether or not he has cheated, deceived, or remains indebted to anyone so that he can correct these injustices. With these thoughts, "What is justice?" is on the table for discussion.

Cephalus provides the first definition of justice: Tell the truth and pay back debts, including giving back things that have been borrowed.[7] Socrates rejects this definition by saying that it cannot be correct because a friend would never return a borrowed weapon if the lender had gone mad and might harm himself with it. Socrates' rejection is hardly persuasive. Rather, it is a routine parlor trick used in law school classrooms everyday. Socrates simply changed the hypothetical by making the lender mad in order to support his argument. Giving back what is owed is a solid conception of the Just; it is not, however, a full concept of justice.

Cephalus leaves Socrates to offer the evening sacrifice, and Polemarchus takes up his father's conversation, offering the second definition. Justice, he says, is, "to give to each what is owed,"[8] with, of course, the exception that it is not just to give a crazy man a weapon. Polemarchus expands this idea by saying that justice is, "doing good to friends and harm to enemies."[9] In this way, then, every man is given his due.

Socrates refutes Polemarchus's definition of justice with two arguments. His first argument is epistemological: How do you know who your friends and enemies are? Is it not at least sometimes the case that we mistake one for the other? If so, this is too weak of a definition because bad or unjust things can happen when mistakes about friends and enemies are made. The second argument is both metaphysical and central to Plato's concept of justice. It is never just to do harm. This radical idea cuts against all morality as the Greeks knew it from Homer and Hesiod through Herodotus and Thucydides. The stories of these poets and historians revealed time and again to the Greeks that the great acts of their gods and heroes were acts of helping friends and harming enemies. Such behavior constituted the good order of the state and the good nature of man even if trickery and deceit were sometimes necessary. How, then, can justice not be defined in exactly these same terms of helping friends and harming enemies?

Polemarchus responds with a clarification: justice is helping true friends and harming true enemies. Socrates will have none of this for while it is a good response to his epistemological argument, it is no response at all to his metaphysical one. Assuming that we can know and discern our true friends from our true enemies, "Can it really be a just man's business to harm any human being?" asks Socrates. In support, Socrates offers the practical claim that harming enemies will make them worse, make them stronger, make them a greater threat, and contribute to making them unjust. This last point is a pure contradiction for Socrates. If justice is a virtue that tends toward just acts, then it cannot be virtuous to do unjust acts or to make people unjust. "Nor is harming, in fact, the work of the good but of its opposite. . . . And it's the just man who is good?"[10] Opposites do not beget each other. Justice cannot be born of injustice—*Quod erat demonstrandum.*

It should not take much reflection on this point to realize the circularity or tautological nature of this question-begging argument. Why is it never just to do unjust acts? Didn't Winston Churchill save England during the Second World War by not warning the people of Coventry about an impending German bombardment, thus concealing that British cryptographers had broken Germany's secret enigma code?[11] Wasn't a great good accomplished by an act of deception? The whole of the *Republic* is a response to this consequentialist problem.

Enter Thrasymachus

Regardless of the power of the Socratic Dialogues, no one can be blamed for finding Socrates exasperating, even rude, which is exactly how another dinner guest reacts to Socrates as he swats away the definitions of justice offered to him. The exasperated dinner guest is the sophist Thrasymachus. He will become familiar to us. His argument will reappear throughout this book.

To Socrates, Thrasymachus is a "wild beast" who has to be restrained from entering the conversation for fear of upsetting it. At a lull in the colloquy with Polemarchus, Thrasymachus "flung himself" into the discussion, "as if to tear us to pieces," frightening Socrates almost into speechlessness.[12] Thrasymachus is aggravated with Socrates' method and message. He thinks Socrates' method is a sham. Thrasymachus cannot abide by the fact that Socrates prefers to reject definitions of justice by exhibiting their weaknesses rather than by offering a definition of his own. He wants Socrates to define justice so they can discuss the matter on an equal basis. Socrates refuses.[13] Thrasymachus is further aggravated by the fact that to him, justice is obvious and easily defined.

Socrates, although frightened by Thrasymachus, steels himself to answer him, replying that he is sincere in his search for justice. This merely elicits laughter from Thrasymachus who scolds Socrates for his "habitual irony."[14] How can Socrates claim sincerity when he refuses to offer his own definition of justice for critique? Socrates responds by telling Thrasymachus that it is unfair to invite him into a conversation and also set the ground rules for that discussion. Thrasymachus cannot ask someone to define twelve and then also tell him that he cannot answer by saying that twelve is two times six or four times three. Socrates can only respond, he says, by telling the truth which to him means continually questioning assumptions, received truths, or accepted pieties.

Thrasymachus takes the bait, telling Socrates that he is prepared to offer a definition of justice better than the others, "I say that the just is nothing other than the advantage of the stronger."[15] Thrasymachus's definition is exactly that of Creon. Both men accept that may be right, but neither adopts such a crude version. Justice is not raw power; it is not Xerxes' justice. Both adopt the need for accepted authority to affirm the assertion of justice. Creon's claims of authority rested on his kingship. Thrasymachus says that regardless of the form of government, the rulers set the rules which define justice even in a democracy. "And each ruling group sets down laws for its own advantage. . . . [I]n every city the same thing is just, the advantage of the established ruling body."[16] Thrasymachus argues that justice is not power alone. Instead, it is based on the claim of those "established in power." Thrasymachus's claim of authority is a claim of legitimacy. This is not Austin's gunman state; it is Hart's conception of law.[17]

Socrates agrees that people act in their own interest. He disagrees that the interest of the stronger is always correct. After all, the strong can make mistakes. Given the possibility of mistake, Thrasymachus makes the same correction that Polemarchus did. Thrasymachus is only talking about rulers when they act correctly in their interest.

Socrates then takes Thrasymachus on a journey through the arts of medicine and seamanship to point out that these experts act not in their own interest but toward other ends. Physicians act in the interests of their patients, and ships' captains act in the interests of their crews. Socrates continues by posing the question, "Is it not the case that, instead of their own advantage, rulers act in the interest of the ruled?" Flummoxed, instead of answering, Thrasymachus asks Socrates if he has a wet nurse. Why do you ask such a question? responds Socrates. "Because . . . she neglects your sniveling nose and doesn't give it the wiping you need. . . ." answers Thrasymachus. Shepherds do not act in the interest of their sheep, says Thrasymachus. They act in their own interest, for profit. The same can be said for physicians and ships' captains.

The notion of connecting profit with justice gets sticky and, unsurprisingly, Thrasymachus's and Socrates' minds do not meet on the proper relationship between the two. For Thrasymachus, profit makes men materially better off and happy which, to him and for many people, are obvious signs of justice. The relationship between profit and justice is a much deeper issue for Socrates because the discussion of profit goes to the metaphysical issue of whether it is ever just to do harmful or unjust acts. Socrates says that unjust acts can never be justified even when they appear to profit the wrongdoer.[18] He deflects talk of profit by saying that while wages are common to all practitioners of the arts, there is nothing distinctive about wages. His more penetrating concern is about the ends of the arts, not their accidents of wages. For Socrates, the benefit of practicing one's art allows one to flourish as a human; money and other material gains are incidental but not central to a concept of justice. For Thrasymachus, moneymaking and material gains evince justice as the successful exercise of power.

Socrates and Thrasymachus then debate whether a life of injustice can and should be preferred to a life of justice. Thrasymachus's point is not without appeal. The strong and the cunning realize gains while the weak and the guileless do not. For Thrasymachus, his definition of justice is proof of strong character—the type possessed by Greek gods and heroes. For Socrates, the connection proves nothing. Socrates and Thrasymachus have completely different reference points. Injustice to Socrates can never signal superior character regardless of what it pays because profit and character have nothing to do with each other. Socrates gets Thrasymachus to admit that justice, rather than injustice, implies superior character.[19] He then wants to demonstrate that injustice brings neither strength nor happiness.

Thrasymachus's patience has reached its end, and he is about to throw up his hands and say, "Okay Socrates. You win. Justice is whatever you say it is." This abdication from the argument is worse to Socrates than a tough battle, and he implores Thrasymachus to continue because the conversation is only getting started. Socrates says they are beginning to reach the heart of the matter, "for the argument is not about just any question, *but about the way one should live*."[20] Thrasymachus and Socrates disagree deeply about how to live one's life. Thrasymachus believes in living the life of reward and recognition. He believes in attaining power in the City and only affecting the appearance of the Soul, not affecting its intrinsic worth.[21] Socrates believes that justice is a virtue affecting the Good in the City and in the Soul.[22] Reward and recognition are for appearances only and of no intrinsic value.

Justice Thus Far

At the end of Book I, Socrates underscores the importance of justice in our lives but has yet to fully make his case. The dinner conversation in which Socrates confronted three distinct definitions of justice is instructive; his critique of each is valid but partial. The proffered definitions cannot be rejected wholesale because each contains some truth about justice. Cephalus's definition is that justice is giving every man his due. Aristotle called this corrective justice.[23] Today we call this compensation. Persons who breach contracts must compensate those that they harm. Tortfeasors must compensate those persons injured as a result of their wrongdoing. Giving people their due is universally perceived as fair and just. It is a form of common morality.[24]

Polemarchus's definition that justice is helping friends and harming enemies is not far from our experience. Reward and penalty are parts of the civil and criminal laws with which we live. Those who follow the law are rewarded as citizens who enjoy the benefits the state has to offer, including the enforcement of one's legal rights. Penalties are assessed for wrongdoing either through civil or criminal laws. Thrasymachus's definition of justice as the will of the stronger is everyday politics.[25] The whole of foreign relations can be perceived as a series of alliances forged on the very premise of helping your friends and harming your enemies.

If it is the case that Socrates' refutation of these definitions of justice did not deal any of them a death blow, then why not? In part it is because the game was rigged as the parties talked past each other. Creon and Antigone talked past each other about their conceptions of law as did Creon and Haemon about reason, as well as Creon and Tiresias about fate. At Cephalus's dinner party, Socrates talks past the other guests about justice. When Socrates asked, "What is justice?" his respondents gave examples of justice in terms of rules or principles of compensation, reward and penalty, and power politics. Socrates, however, was not interested in examples. He was interested in essences.[26] When he asked, "What is justice?" he might have better engaged his dinner companions if he had asked, "What is the *nature* of justice?" Socrates did not want conceptions, examples, or ancillary rules; he wanted to discuss the *concept* of justice. Socrates was interested in the nature of the Good, a concept so ineffable that Cephalus, Polemarchus, and Thrasymachus missed the very heart of the Socratic inquiry. The Good to Socrates is that to which we all aspire. But what drives us to the Good? What exactly is it? Socrates attempts to grasp the Good by trying to understand justice.

Because Socrates was searching for the concept of justice and the others were offering conceptions, it was easy for Socrates to dismiss such sound bites as "injustice pays," the "strong have superior character," or that "the unjust are happier than the just" because these phrases were nonresponsive to Socrates' question. Because he is searching for but does not discover the concept of justice in Book I of the *Republic,* it closes with Socrates noting that while he enjoyed the conversation and like an epicure or gourmand, he could not resist tasting from every dish offered to him, he was still unsatisfied and left the conversation knowing nothing.[27] "So long as I do not know what the just is, I shall hardly know whether it is a virtue or not and whether the one who has it is unhappy or happy."[28]

Later, Socrates will tell us that justice is a virtue, that it will make us happy, and that justice is harmony in the Soul and in the City. These insights do not give us much detailed direction on how we should live our lives. Equating justice with virtue, happiness, and harmony indicates the primacy of justice and its significance for the problem of Creon's ghost. If the conflict of laws is to be resolved, Plato asserts that it should be resolved in favor of justice. Can it be?

If Creon's ghost haunts us through the ages, more haunting still is the death of Socrates.[29] The story outline is familiar enough. The angry state trumps up charges against an irritant gadfly who is then tried and convicted and condemned to die by his own hand from the sleep that comes from drinking hemlock. The familiar story makes Socrates a tragic figure, an innocent man unjustly condemned. This story also misses the deeper significance of Socrates' death for philosophy and for justice.

Socrates' death was tragic not because of his innocence because he was indeed guilty as charged of corrupting the young and impiety toward the City's gods. Socrates did not believe in the same gods in which the City believed, and he was therefore guilty of impiety. Socrates also corrupted the young, for in arguing that they should "question everything," he argued against the order of the state. The meaning of Socrates' death is not that he died a martyr; the meaning of his death resides in his way of life. One must never do injustice or even return injustice for injustice. One must live truly according to human nature and justly for the benefit of City and Soul. And in living the just life, one must live philosophically, questioning everything. But who among us can live a life free of even the slightest corruption or compromise, never afraid of conformity, always questioning, never taking a misstep in the direction of profit rather than sacrifice? Not many. More to the point, even if we desired to live philosophically, how do we do that? Socrates' tragedy lies within us, within the human condition. We desire the ideal of the Good as we experience the imperfections of reality. We need a method to mediate the conflict between experience and desire and we need a path for finding justice. Plato offers us both.

The *Allegory of the Cave*

In a book of many stories, the Allegory of the Cave is the most famous part of the *Republic.*[30] I find that most commentators are content to discuss the first half of the story, the prisoner's ascent out of the Cave into the Sun, and half tell the second half of the allegory—the prisoner's return.[31] In a superb scholarly commentary on the *Republic,* Professor Stanley Rosen writes, "At this point after the prisoner has seen the Sun, Socrates asks us to imagine that the ex-prisoner has descended back into the cave. No reason is given here for this step."[32] Another commentator tells us, "[T]he great messy hairball of the issue that is the philosopher's return to the cave has no clear resolution without importing a great deal that is not explicit in the text, so any answer that is put forward . . . is speculative."[33] To the contrary, Socrates explicitly explains and justifies the prisoner's return. Both parts, the ascent and the return, are necessary for our deeper understanding of justice and of the reconciliation of man's law with it. While the first half of the allegory, the ascent, emphasizes the Good, the second half, the return, emphasizes law and the struggle for justice.

Recall the opening of Book VII where Plato tells us a parable about our enlightened and unenlightened natures. Imagine, he says, living in a Cave, where since childhood, people have been chained in such a way that they cannot move their heads and can only see what is in front of them. So situated and looking forward, the chained men, the prisoners, can see images on the wall directly in front of them. These images of people, animals, and other objects are accompanied by sounds, and the prisoners assume that the sounds they hear come from the images themselves. Socrates asks us to imagine that as the prisoners view the images on the wall, they might even award prizes to those who correctly guess the image that will next appear. They enjoy a life with rewards, not a life of truth. They enjoy a life of profit that Thrasymachus accepts, not a life of philosophy for which Socrates searches.

Ascent to the Sun

From what we have been told, the prisoners know only the images on the wall and the sounds they assume they make. These images and sounds constitute their world. In every way, the prisoners assume that the images on the wall are real. The prisoners are mistaken about reality because they possess a mistaken state of mind called *eikasia*.[34]

Plato then asks us to imagine what it would be like if one of the prisoners was released and then compelled "to stand up, to turn his neck around, to walk and look up toward the light."[35] Certainly, moving after being in chains and then looking into a light would be painful. The prisoner might prefer to turn away and return to his chains, but he is forced to go on. With that pain also comes puzzlement and shock for now the freed prisoner sees what he could not see before. Behind him and the other prisoners is a parapet with a fire burning behind it. Along the parapet, between the fire and the wall of the Cave, men march carrying objects which project onto the wall to make the images seen inside the Cave. The freed prisoner then realizes, at last, that the images are shadows, a puppet show, the prototype movie theater. The sounds are not made by the images the man realizes; they are made by the men carrying the puppets. The prisoner's former reality is exposed to a truer vision. The images are not reality, they are shadows.

There is more. The man has only seen the puppet show, he is still in the Cave; he has not seen reality and he is forced further upward into the sunlight. The sunlight, even more than the fire below, causes such pain that he is temporarily blinded. He slowly grows accustomed to the blinding light of the Sun in the upper world. He first sees foggy images of people and other things before seeing them clearly and distinctly. The prisoner also finds it easier to look at the moon and the stars before looking at the Sun. But look he must, for it is only by contemplating the Sun and its nature that reality is revealed. The light of the Sun reveals the source of the seasons, of time itself, and that it is the cause of all things seen on the wall of the Cave.[36]

Reflecting on his former life and his fellow prisoners, the freed man recognizes his good fortune and their sad plight. The prisoner would prefer to stay in the warmth and the light of the Sun, enjoying a true picture of reality rather than return to the darkness and the illusions of the Cave. Plato asks what would it be like if the prisoner returned? Wouldn't he want to tell his companions about what he saw and, in turn, reveal that the shadows on the Cave wall are not the reality that they believe it to be? How would his companions react to such news? They would laugh at the returning man. They would ridicule him, telling him that he left the Cave and returned without his sight, without his mind. They might even kill him. Imagine—killing someone for describing reality and speaking the truth.

A Very Brief Explanation

After Plato tells Glaucon the allegory, he does something rare in his writings; he explains it. Plato tells Glaucon that the prisoners are us. Next, the allegory is about how we learn, and it continues the teaching about education in the stories of the Line and the Sun earlier in the *Republic*.[37] The ascent upward stands for "the soul's journey up to the intelligible place." Most important, the last thing to be perceived, the Sun, is "the *idea* of the good," and that idea is "the cause of all that is right and fair in everything." The idea or Form of the Good, "provide[s] truth and intelligence—and the man who is going to act prudently in private or in public must see it."[38] The Form of the Good is necessary for without it, "no one can act with wisdom, either in his own life or in matters of state." The City and the Soul are both driven by this Form. The Form of the Good entails the Form of justice as it entails Truth and Beauty.[39] With this insight we can begin to solve, or maybe simply better apprehend, the problem of Creon's ghost. The resolution of the conflict of laws is to prefer the law that furthers justice.

When Plato explains the allegory, he is explaining the situation in which we all find ourselves. We live with shadows, unsure and uncertain about the purposes of life. We should all aim to contemplate the Good, and we can believe that with the Good comes justice. The contemplation of the Good brings wisdom. Is the contemplation of the Good, of justice, even humanly possible? Plato contends that we are all capable of perceiving the Good because it is a sense of the Good which guides us.

The Return to the Cave

Having seen the Sun, the Form of the Good, the freed prisoner would prefer to spend time in divine contemplation in the upper world rather than descend back into the miseries of human life. But then human life is the catch. We are human and not divine, and we lead human and not divine lives. We cannot escape the Cave. It is not that we "return" to the Cave; the Cave is where we live even after having glimpsed or experienced or sensed the Sun. So, while we prefer the upper world to the one we know, we must "return." And when we return we will be, "[C]ompelled in courts or elsewhere to contest about the shadows of the just or the representations of which they are the shadows and to dispute about the way these things are understood by men who have never seen justice itself[.]"[40] Herein lies the Socratic method dedicated to finding justice and resolving the conflict between man's law and the higher law.

The contemplation of the Good is the most desirable way of life, and we must be educated to have the privilege of experiencing philosophical contemplation. In Plato's world we are all capable of making the ascent to the vision of the Good. However, we cannot be allowed to stay there. We are, instead, compelled to return to the Cave and live among the prisoners, to live among and with ourselves. On the matter of forcing someone to return, Glaucon asks, "Are we to do them an injustice and make them live a worse life when a better is possible?"[41]

Plato's requirement that the educated must return to the Cave has troubled some commentators who bristle at the notion of compulsion in satisfaction of the Good. Plato defends the requirement as just and consistent with his program of education.[42] Those who have received a philosophical education are privileged because of it. They should, then, share their contemplation of the Good and contribute to the good of the social order.[43] Plato supports his argument with law because, "it's not the concern of law that any one class fare exceptionally well, but it contrives to bring this about in the city as a whole harmonizing the citizens by persuasion and compulsion. . . ." The return is justified for Plato because individuals cannot, "turn whichever way each wants"; instead they must act for the common good.[44]

There is, though, another argument to be made here. It is not unjust to compel the fortunate prisoner back into the Cave for the very reason that the prisoner never left it. We cannot escape the human condition. Yet it is part of our human nature to think beyond our circumstances, to contemplate the Good, and to seek justice. All of those impulses are in us because we are human, and each soul can be educated to the Good because we are born with a sense of it.

Justice Refined

Socrates confessed ignorance of justice at the end of Book I, yet in Books II through X his statements about justice are stark. Justice in the *Republic* is a virtue, the highest virtue, which applies to the City as well as to the Soul, and at its most fundamental level, justice is captured in the slogan "Mind your own business" which is a shorthand, if crude, way to say that justice is harmony.[45] When all parts of City and Soul do their own job, justice is realized. "Justice is a virtue of the city as a unity, for it required of each citizen a recognition of his or her own role as contributing in some characteristic way to the common good."[46]

Justice, Plato asserts throughout the *Republic*, is better than injustice.[47] Justice is like health. A healthy soul is better than a troubled one, and a healthy city is better than a chaotic or feverish one. Platonic justice is what scholar Gregory Vlastos calls "psychic harmony."[48] Justice is "good in and of itself not merely for its consequences; and it is so great a good that no good securable by injustice could be greater."[49] Plato's harmony in City and Soul will never be realized in the imperfect would in which we live. Still, the contemplation of justice, of the harmony of and in City and Soul, does provide guidance[50] on how we should live our lives, which is the most important question posed by Socrates[51] as the *Allegory of the Cave* instructs.

Law and Justice

The return to the Cave is about the education of the Soul and the governance of the City. The return is also about the relationship between law and justice. Plato tells us that every soul possesses the capacity for education, the capacity to contemplate the Form of the Good. "[T]his power is in the soul of each . . . until it is able to endure looking at that which *is* and the brightest part of that which *is*. And we affirm that this is the good, don't we?"[52]

But there is something tricky here. No human being can actually possess the Good anymore than he or she can look directly into the Sun. Aristotle criticized his teacher's theory of the Forms on this basis.[53] So how is it that we can have the capacity for education and for the contemplation of the Good without being able to look into its light? How can we know justice? How can we know the higher law?

The *Allegory of the Cave* teaches us that our human lives come with illusions. The daily lives we lead are not different from the prisoners in the Cave, and the daily beliefs that we hold are not different from the shadows on the wall. The human condition is that we have beliefs about a wide range of matters, and we are yet uncertain about which beliefs are consistent with justice. There are, nonetheless, other matters about which we are certain and about which we can call just. Let's look at both matters, certain and uncertain.

Can we imagine a time in the history of the United States about which we can now say that society was clearly in the Cave and looking at shadows on the wall rather than at justice? Some obvious cases quickly come to mind. Slavery, racial discrimination, and the disenfranchisement of women are all parts of our history. Today all are considered unjust. Yesterday all were justified by society based on its beliefs in the shadows of racial inferiority and about the "weaker sex." All of those beliefs were enacted into man's law. These shadows have been exposed by the light of the Sun and no longer command respect. About these things we are certain—a just society will not tolerate these shadows of discrimination. A just society knows these beliefs to be unjust. It follows that we do possess a knowledge of justice.[54] But how persistent is our knowledge of justice, and how deeply does it run? How can we transform our knowledge of justice into how we live our lives and how we construct our state today?

Imagining a past time, about which we are now certain that we were wrong about our conceptions of justice is one thing. It is quite another thing to know justice now with certainty. Are we in the Cave today about any beliefs? Put another way, are there issues about which society cannot summon the same confident knowledge of justice that we have about slavery and women's rights? Obviously such matters abound—abortion, the death penalty, same-sex marriage, gay rights, affirmative action, etc. Equally obvious, individuals have strong opinions about where justice falls on each of these matters. For some, prohibiting abortions to save the lives of the unborn is just. For others, protecting a woman's freedom over her body is just. What is painfully clear is that there is no consensus in society on where justice lies on so many issues. We use man's law to make such decisions, and we are frequently uncomfortable on where the lines of the law are drawn.

We have uncovered a conflict between matters that we are certain are just and those we are not. How can it be that we have ascended from the Cave into the light on some things but remain bound in the shadows where our vision of justice is blurred on others? Do we lack any understanding of the Form of justice? Or are all of our opinions merely shadows on the wall? Do all of us always suffer from the mistaken mind of *eikasia*?

The thought experiment reveals that we do have a sense of justice, that somehow and somewhere, maybe only historically and backward looking, we have glimpsed its Form. The human condition continues to plague us such that we do not, and cannot, sustain our sense of justice for long. More important, we cannot even know it without struggle. As Plato teaches us, justice is a matter of haggling over shadows and light. Virgil too teaches us that "to climb back to the upper air–/there the struggle, there the labor lies."[55]

Return to the uncertain matters for a moment, those about which no consensus exists in society. How should we deal with these uncertainties? Do we ignore them and say that sooner or later society will emerge from the Cave and arrive at the just resolution of the debates about abortion, the death penalty, and the like? Perhaps, but that is not what people actually do. Nor is it what Plato prescribes. Debate, instead, and often heated takes place and people retreat to assertions of faith and belief in support of their positions.

When beliefs run deep, the paraphernalia of politics enables decisions on contested matters to be made so that people can go on with their lives. Is justice thus served by a political process? We will return to this question at the end of the book.

Plato suggests another approach. Given the human capacity to know the Good and our capacity for education, we have an obligation to seek out the Good and the just. The return to the Cave comes with an obligation to share that knowledge. That obligation entails a struggle for justice among those who live with shadows rather than with light.[56] Plato also gives us the necessary tool to help with the struggle—reason.[57] More specifically, Plato counsels that the struggle is aided by reason as applied through the dialectic.[58] The dialectic is the process of asking and answering questions about assumptions and beliefs in the search for the nature of reality, in the search for justice. This questioning was the life led by Socrates, led to his death, and is captured by Plato in the Socratic Dialogues. The dialectic in Benjamin Jowett's words is the ideal science which "defines the abstract essences or universal ideas of all things, and connects them; which pierces the veil of hypotheses and reaches the final cause or first principle of all." This science is the "highest process of thought, and may be described as the soul conversing with herself or holding communion with eternal truth and beauty."[59] We must now connect method with substance and dialectic with justice.

Plato's Higher Law

The return to the Cave is the key metaphor for law and justice. The Cave is the world in which we find ourselves, uncertain and unsure of the Good and the just. With reflection and a willingness to exercise dialectical skills through asking questions and positing answers—through philosophical reasoning—we can attempt to reduce these uncertainties at least provisionally. The dialectic is not untethered. We possess a sense of justice like the slave who possessed a sense of geometry in the dialogue the *Meno*. In that dialogue, Socrates poses the question, "What is Virtue?" and in answering it he teaches his theory of recollection. Socrates argues that learning is a form of recollecting what our soul already knows but which must be made conscious by the search for truth.

Learning is like being stirred from a dream and occurs by questioning to recover the knowledge we already possess. Through this process of recollection we learn the "truth of things," says Socrates, because the truth, "is always in our soul." Through continual questioning not only are we continually learning, we must continue to learn to be fully human. We must continue to question even those things we do not think that we know. For that ability to question, Socrates asserts, he would, "do battle for, so far as possible, in word and deed."[60] Socrates lived up to his word, dying for his right to question and to learn. We can recognize our ignorance of justice and still search for it through inquiry, through the dialectic. We have an obligation to search. Bringing the light of justice back into the Cave is for Plato and for us a matter of the higher law. To examine the higher law, we move from the *Republic* to two other Socratic Dialogues.

This chapter opened with the observation that Socrates meets his end as the result of the application of man's law. The Athenian jury found him guilty of corrupting the young and of impiety. We can find that Socrates did violate the express law of Athens; we can also argue that he died for philosophy, for questioning everything. His death is the result of the application of an unjust man's law. Antigone thought Creon's law was unjust and, therefore, no law that she could obey. It was a law that violated the higher unwritten law of the gods and because it violated that law, she had an obligation to disobey it. Socrates does not act as Antigone did. Instead of disobeying what we perceive to be unjust, Socrates follows the law and carries out his own death sentence. How can we understand the apparent unjust treatment of Socrates at the hands of man's law? More to the point, how does Socrates, in his own words, reconcile the conflict between the shadows of man's law and the light of justice?

Crito[61]

The snub-nosed man on the pallet, Socrates, has been tried, convicted, and sentenced to death in an Athenian court, by an Athenian jury, according to the laws of Athens. The rules of judicial procedure entitled him to address the jury, and he spoke to them in defense of the charges against him and about his sentence. Due process, it appears, was accorded the accused and convicted man. These events and his speeches are recorded in the *Apology*[62] and reveal much about his life,[63] the history and government of Athens, and about Socrates' method and his beliefs.

The *Apology* is a central story in the Western Tradition, defending the philosophical act and way of life even as it portrays its dangers. Socrates died in the name of philosophy, and it is the fact of his death that deserves the label unjust. But unjust in what way? Was Socrates unjustly convicted in that he was not guilty of the charges against him? If so, then the injustice we perceive would be a procedural injustice. Or was Socrates convicted according to the proper procedural requirements but convicted by an underlying law that itself was unjust? Was it unjust to stir up the youth by way of philosophy or through impiety? If so, then the injustice is a matter of the substance of the law. A fair reading of the trial of Socrates shows that he received procedural justice. His death occurred because of a lack of substantive justice; Athens could no longer allow this gadfly to upset its settled ways. Socrates died, and philosophy was born.

At the conclusion of the trial, Socrates is sentenced to die by drinking hemlock, and he is sent to prison to wait for the sentence to be carried out. Plato paints a picture of Socrates' last day far different from that of Jacques-Louis David. Where David's portrait is noble, full of light, and situates Socrates in a grand chamber large enough for several of his friends, Plato describes a dark room with a little oil lamp, a bare pallet, a small table, and a stool on which Crito, Socrates' old friend, sits in the early morning while Socrates sleeps.

On awakening, Socrates is surprised to see Crito who bears the bad news that the ship from Delos is expected soon, and its arrival signals the time for Socrates' death. After delivering that news, which does not trouble Socrates terribly much, Crito implores Socrates to avoid execution and save himself. Crito tells Socrates to disobey the order of the Athenian court; he does not come unarmed. He then offers several arguments for disobedience including that it would be easy to bribe the guard, that Socrates owes it to himself to save his own life, that he should do it for the sake of his children, and, Crito does not want people to think badly of him for not saving or trying to save his friend.

Socrates is unmoved by all of these arguments. He recognizes Crito's plea for what it is—an attempted evasion of the law. And it is to this issue—the evasion of man's law—to which he turns his attention. "[W]e must consider whether or not it would be right for me to try to escape without permission of the Athenians."[64]

Socrates' response restates the familiar theme of Book I of the *Republic*, "Then one must never do injustice,"[65] even when one is wronged. Injustice cannot beget justice. Socrates says that it is as wrong to bribe the guard just as it is wrong to breach his agreement with the state. What can Socrates mean here? How is it that Athens can mete out an injustice that

Socrates is compelled to honor? To answer that question, Socrates, in the *Crito*, invokes the "Laws and Constitution of Athens" and engages them in a dialogue.

The personified Laws first reproach Socrates for even contemplating leaving the jail and avoiding the death penalty. "Or do you think that a city can continue to exist and not be overturned, in which legal judgments once rendered are without force, but may be rendered unauthoritative by private citizens and so corrupted?"[66] An obvious response is, "Yes. I do intend to violate the law. Violations happen every day. And, I intend to violate it because I was wrongly and unjustly convicted." Socrates recognizes this possible response, Antigone's response,[67] but returns to his contract with the state. He imagines the Laws to ask, Didn't you agree "to abide by such judgments the City might render?"[68] The Laws remind Socrates that he has enjoyed the benefits that Athens offered, including his own birth by parents whose marriage was sanctioned by the state. His children were educated by Athens as he was. If Socrates is dissatisfied with the laws of Athens, then he should either persuade the leaders to change them in accordance with justice or leave the City. The Laws further argue that they exist for the good of the city as a whole and for the citizens who stay in Athens and enjoy its privileges. The Laws are for the good of the people; they are not savage commands; they are not the threats of the gunman state. Therefore, Socrates can seek to change the law, leave Athens, or obey. Destroying the Laws is a violation of the agreement between citizen and City, between Socrates and Athens.[69]

Socrates obeys the City's Laws because, as he first asserts, the Laws are our guardians; they are our parents, and, therefore, obedience is due to the City for the same reasons that it is due our parents. Next, we have a contractual obligation to obey the Laws. Third, to disobey the Laws is to destroy the foundation of the City. And finally, Socrates would betray his life if he were to disobey the Laws at the end of it. Socrates believed it just to obey the Laws because he both agreed with and benefitted from them. He neither challenged them nor left Athens to live in another city. He staked his life on these propositions.

The *Crito* is Socrates' explanation of the correctness of his concept of the higher law. Socrates accepted his agreement with the City not simply by staying and living in Athens or even by raising his children there but by living in Athens free to do philosophy. To avoid the Laws would contradict the way he lived his life in the search for the Good. Athens allowed Socrates to live his philosophical life. The Laws tell Socrates that he has always believed in the City and its Laws and that the Laws speak the truth. The Laws further say that they are his guardians, and that if he has been wronged he will leave Athens as "the victim of an injustice done at the hands of men, not at the hands of us who are the Laws."[70] Socrates dies as a consequence of man's law, not the higher law. Socrates lived by the idea of the higher law as his dialogue with the personified by the Laws attests.[71] He died, however, by the reality of man's conception of it. He died because of his higher law agreement with Athens and because of his concept of her Constitution and her Laws.[72]

Minos

The brief dialogue *Minos* precedes and introduces Plato's *Laws*.[73] The *Laws* opens by declaring that law comes from the gods, not men,[74] then becomes an extended discussion about politics and the composition of the government of the City. The *Minos* poses the narrow question, "What is Law?" To this question an unnamed Comrade answers, "What else would law be, Socrates except the things that are lawfully accepted?"[75]

Aside from the circularity of that answer, it is logical. The idea of law is generally thought of as being comprised of the accumulation of laws passed by governments. The Comrade continues, "In my opinion at least these official opinions and decrees passed by votes; for what else would one declare law to be? So as a result it's likely that what you've asked about, this whole, law, is the official opinion of the city."[76]

The Comrade adopts Creon's and Hart's legal positivist understanding of law. Law is what recognized and authorized officials promulgate. Socrates presses the Comrade about the relationships between law and justice. At first, Socrates distinguishes the lawful as just from the lawless as unjust. He is still pressing for law's essential goodness. "So then one ought to think about law as being something noble and seek it as a good."[77]

Socrates has moved from conception to concept, and the Comrade does not follow along. The Comrade makes the common, everyday observation that laws vary from place to place and from time to time. Athenians, for example, do not practice human sacrifice because it is impious. Carthaginians, however, do practice it because human sacrifice is an act of piety. Besides, he tells Socrates, the Athenians change their laws every day. Given such variability, it is impossible that all laws are just.

Socrates responds by looking for universal principles. There are, he says, fixed laws of cooking for cooks; of medicine for physicians; and prefiguring Auden of gardening for gardeners.[78] As we read along we can complete the thought, "Then there must be fixed laws for humans." Is law universal and theoretical; is there a higher law as Plato has it; or is law particular and practical; is law equivalent to man's law, as the Comrade sees it?[79] Plato argues for the universal, higher law. "And it is the case to speak universally, that the things that are lawfully accepted as being, not the things that are not. . . . ."[80] For Plato, the concept of law, the higher law, exists to guide human action to the Good.

The Platonic Unity of Law

The slip between cup and lip, desire and experience, and concept and conception can be fatal. Law as concept, as the higher law, can be just and good. But law, as man's law, can fail in conception as Antigone and Socrates realized. *Creon's Ghost* asks whether reconciliation between concept and conception is possible. *Antigone* shows a failure of reconciliation; man's law can be unjust with tragic, deathly consequences. Plato argues that reconciliation is necessary to achieve the Good.

Legal philosophers today continue this disagreement. H. L. A. Hart argues that reconciliation is not possible for two reasons. Theoretically, man's law and the higher law are separate; they serve distinct purposes and rely on distinct vocabularies. Positive, man's law is about ordering society; and justice, the higher law, is about assessing and evaluating the goodness of that society and the laws in it. There are cases for which man's law has no answer, and an answer must be supplied by a judge who must look outside the law for it. There is no necessary guarantee that the judge will find the higher law. The lacuna of the law reveals a lack of unity. Consequently, because of the holes in man's law there is an imperfect fit with justice.

Hart's most notable critic, Ronald Dworkin, argues to the contrary. Both theoretically and practically, hard cases have "right answers," and there is a Platonic Unity to the law[81] because all law is grounded in an identifiable political morality. Dworkin recognizes that finding political morality is no easy task, but looking for it is both worthy and necessary for law to work at its best. We seek Dworkin's political morality, his higher law, because we all share a sense of justice. Just as Creon and Thrasymachus contrast with Antigone and Plato, Hart contrasts with Dworkin.[82] Creon, Thrasymachus, and Hart assert that man's law has its own work to do, and that work may be either just or unjust. Antigone, Plato, and Dworkin assert that imperfect man's law can be corrected or improved by the higher law.

Hart's theory is familiar to any lawyer or law student. In a common lawsuit, the possibility exists that either the precedential cases are in equipoise and support both parties, or there is no precedent. Consequently, prior case law provides no answer. In a statutory lawsuit, the statute can have conflicting provisions or be silent. Again, no answer is available and must be supplied by the judge. In constitutional cases, the language of the Constitution may be so broad as to give little or no guidance so that answers to constitutional questions are supplied by the judge. Admittedly, no judge publicly admits to making law because such an admission runs contrary to the idea of law as objective and neutral. The admission is also not made to distinguish law from ordinary political decisions.[83]

Hart contrasts these two views of law as the Nightmare and the Noble Dream. The Noble Dream is the dream of Platonic Unity in which litigants can expect that "judges should apply to their case existing law and not make new law for them even when the text of particular constitutional provisions, statutes, or available precedence appears to offer no determinate guide."[84] The Nightmare with no determinant answers Hart argues, is the more accurate view of the law. Although litigants may expect judges to apply existing law rather than make new law, often the law is indeterminate. More troubling, the image of a judge as an "objective, impartial, erudite, and experienced declaimer of the law" is an illusion, and expectations to the contrary are doomed to disappointment.[85] Hart does not go on to argue that cases are decided on the basis of a judge's "uncontrolled will" or based on the realist slogan that law is "what the judge had for breakfast."[86] Rather, he says, the judge is constrained by the legal system as a whole yet still exercises considerable discretion.

Hart's position is commonsensical and attractive. Our common experience of law is that gaps exist, and it is an attractive proposition that judges are not wholly unconstrained when required to fill those gaps. Judges must search, instead, for the broad institutional principles and values of the legal system as a whole in reaching their decisions.[87] Hart's analysis does not eliminate gaps in the law; it tells judges how to fill them. The Nightmare may have been reduced to a bad dream or to a sleep disturbance but has not been eliminated entirely.

Dworkin disputes Hart's analysis. For Dworkin, there are no gaps in the law. Therefore, it is wrong to assign judges any discretion to fill them.

Dworkin's career as a legal philosopher has been dedicated to sustaining this position. Dworkin's unitary or holistic concept of law brings us back to Plato and prefigures our discussion of natural law in the next chapter.

Early in his career Dworkin posited that even in so-called hard cases, cases which for all intents and purposes appear indeterminate, judges do not make new law; they find existing law. "It remains the judges' duty, even in hard cases to discover what the rights of the parties are, not to invent new rights retrospectively."[88] Dworkin neither advances any mechanical procedure for judges to do this nor does he assume that judges and lawyers would easily agree about legal answers. He invents, instead, his famous and aptly named Judge Hercules who has the intellectual fire power to develop a "theory of the constitution," a "political theory . . . about what the legislature has done," and identify the "gravitational force of precedent" to decide constitutional, statutory, and common-law cases respectively.[89] Hercules also meets and rebuffs the objection that judges exercise their own personal discretion, thus offending democracy and the rule of law. Judge Hercules identifies a "particular conception of community morality as decisive of legal issues" and applies that conception to the case at hand. Dworkin's political conception "holds that community morality is the political morality presupposed by the law and institutions of the community."[90] Hercules, according to Dworkin, simply applies the law that exists in the community; he does not make it up as he goes along. A community's political morality is guided by a sense of justice and fairness.

The idea that Hercules exists and can find the law was labeled the "right answer thesis," and critics found it implausible. It is not difficult to imagine that different judges would reach different conclusions even applying the Herculean methodology. There is no unique right answer as any lawyer on the losing side of a lawsuit will attest. Philosophers found a lack of logical coherence to the assertion that there are right answers to questions when searching for and deciding matters of value.[91] Dworkin/Hercules responded to these criticisms[92] and refined his right answer thesis as well as his conception of law.

In his most recent publication, Dworkin tries to lay to rest the "farrago" about the right answers thesis. "My thesis about right answers in hard cases is, as I have said, a very weak and commonsensical legal claim. It is a claim made within legal practice rather than at some supposedly removed, external, philosophical level."[93] Dworkin's point is that when lawyers argue, they argue about which answer is correct; when judges decide cases, they offer their opinions as to why their decisions are correct. Because lawyers and judges are claiming "correctness" for their positions, they are then claiming that law supplies a "right answer." This seems to me a weak argument. By arguing that both sides are claiming "correctness," Dworkin is watering down his insistence that law is not indeterminate and that judges do not have discretion to impose their uncontrolled will on litigants. Dworkin still maintains his position that law, in its best manifestation, forms a cohesive whole.

The right answer thesis might well be a farrago, but it is one of Dworkin's own making. Regardless of how much he dilutes it, Dworkin still argues that judges lack discretion to fill in the gaps of the law. They must base their decisions on the law that exists and is waiting to be found. He continues by explaining that judges, in finding the existing law, are operating within some sort of unitary concept of law. Dworkin's refined conception of law in his magisterial book *Law's Empire* buttresses his claim for the Platonic Unity of law by conceiving the existing body of law as consisting of an identifiable political morality.[94]

Identifying the community's political morality and its conforming laws is serious business not to be taken lightly because of the dangers law poses to the people living under it:

> Law insists that force must be used or withheld, no matter how useful that would be to ends in view, no matter how beneficial or noble these, ends, except as licensed or required by individual rights and responsibilities flowing from past political decisions about when collective force is justified.[95]

On the face of it, Dworkin's description does not appear terribly different from Thrasymachus's definition—law is the politically justified use of force. Dworkin, however, throughout his jurisprudence, emphasizes the middle part of the definition—the role of individual rights and responsibilities over and against a utilitarian calculus. Embedded in this notion is a Kantian idea of concern and respect for the individual from which emerges the political morality of the community, including the fundamental individual rights and liberties which law must protect. The use of state power must be justified; it cannot be based on the indiscriminate use of naked aggression against the individual. Where Thrasymachus defined justice as the use of political power, Dworkin justifies law through political morality as a respecter of persons.

Dworkin then argues that his conception of law is contained in the legal practice of the community as interpreted by lawyers and judges. Most important, this interpretation and these practices cohere in his conception of Law as Integrity which he distinguishes from the conceptions of legal conventionalism or legal pragmatism. Law as Integrity "instructs judges to identify legal rights and duties . . . on the assumption that they were created by a single authority—the community personified—expressing a coherent conception of justice and fairness." In this way, then, "propositions of law are true if they . . . follow from principles of justice, fairness, and procedural due process that provide the best constructive interpretation of the community's legal practice."[96] Dworkin's insistence on law's coherence is what gives law its Platonic Unity. For Dworkin, integrity is a political virtue which, although recognizing that compromises are part of everyday politics, contains the notion that our political tradition and past practices constitute an interpretive whole. Law follows this idea and guides us in resolving the controversies that separate us, resolving even the hard cases according to the political morality of the community which is capable of reconciling man's law with the higher law.

Justice in Plato's *Republic* and Ours

The death penalty presents a particularly acute conflict between man's law and higher law for those Supreme Court justices opposed to it. In a later chapter, we will also see how antislavery judges decided cases under Fugitive Slave Laws and the similar crises of conscience that those cases presented.

Since 1976, the constitutionality of the death penalty has been reaffirmed.[97] It is also the case that the issue remains divisive in society and on the Court. A hard challenge exists for anti–death penalty justices who believe that death penalty laws are unconstitutional and contrary to, "evolving standards of decency that mark the progress of a maturing society"[98] but must honor their oath of office to obey the Constitution. What, then, may an anti–death penalty justice argue?

Recently two justices of the U.S. Supreme Court, Harry Blackmun and John Paul Stevens have expressed strong opposition to the death penalty. Both justices, of course, face the problem of existing law, and both thus feel committed to expressing their opposition to the death penalty with arguments grounded in the positive law and not based on their own personal moral sentiments. In the case of one justice, man's law and the higher law remain separate reflecting Hart's positivism; in the other, they are partially reconciled reflecting Dworkin's Platonic Unity or his conception of law as integrity.

The Case of Justice John Paul Stevens

Justice Stevens confronted the death penalty under a specific set of circumstances. In the case of *Baze v. Rees,*[99] several convicted murderers sentenced to death in Kentucky filed suit asserting that the lethal injection drug protocols used by the state violated the Eighth Amendment ban on cruel and unusual punishment. In a 7 to 2 opinion, the Supreme Court upheld Kentucky's method of execution, and justice John Paul Stevens concurred in the opinion. His concurrence, however, expressed great skepticism about the wisdom and continued validity of the death penalty.

The case involved the proper method for administering the death penalty through a three-drug protocol, one of which, pancuronium bromide, can cause excruciating pain if administered improperly. Justice Stevens was of the opinion that the case opened up the matter of the constitutional justification of the death penalty itself. Justice Stevens was critical, in part, of continuing to develop unworkable death penalty case law that was inconsistent and seemed to have no end in sight.

Stevens had multiple concerns with death penalty procedures. He was first concerned that defendants charged in capital cases might be deprived of trial by a jury representing a fair cross section of the community. Capital litigation pays particular attention to jury selection, and the Supreme Court has developed a series of cases to seek a "death qualified jury."[100] Stevens notes that prosecutors are fearful that 12 randomly selected jurors might vote against the death penalty, and thus prosecutors seek to prevent anti–death penalty jurors from sitting. Another concern for Stevens was a risk of error. In cases with particularly aggravating facts, emotion can overtake reason and cloud the identity of the defendant. One example of the use of emotional testimony is that the Court allows "victim impact" evidence relating to the personal characteristics of the victim to be admitted during the sentencing phase, regardless of the fact that such evidence sheds no light on the guilt or innocence of the defendant. The man in the dock will be tainted by such emotion-laden testimony regardless of whether or not it bears on his guilt. Stevens also notes the racially discriminatory impact of death penalty cases in which the penalty was imposed even where the Court recognized the "strong probability that [the defendant's] sentencing jury . . . was influenced by the fact that [he was] black and his victim white."[101] Finally, Stevens is persuaded that the irrevocable nature of the death penalty, coupled with its several possibilities for error, support the argument for its unconstitutionality.

Stevens argues for the abolition of the death penalty for additional reasons. He believes that the death penalty has been retained as a "product of habit and inattention rather than [from] an acceptable deliberative process" which weighs costs and benefits and examines underlying assumptions. Constitutional law holds that there are three societal purposes for administering the death penalty: incapacitation, deterrence, and retribution. Stevens argues that each of these assumptions is flawed. Regarding incapacitation, Steven notes that if given an opportunity, more people would impose the sentence of life without parole rather than death thus not necessarily incapacitating the defendant. Regarding deterrence, Stevens notes the absence of empirical evidence that capital punishment deters potential offenders. In regard to retribution, he talks about the irony that while vengeance indeed is a strong emotion in these cases, society has moved further and further toward a death penalty that is administered through more humane forms of punishment.

In reaching his conclusion, Stevens quotes the earlier words of justice Byron White and argues that his opposition to the death penalty is based on "the pointless and needless extinction of life with only marginal contributions to any discernable social or public purposes. A penalty with such negligible returns to the State [is] patently excessive and cruel and unusual punishment violates the Eighth Amendment."[102]

Having stated his opposition to the death penalty as unconstitutional, Stevens nonetheless concurs with the majority in *Baze* upholding the administration of death by lethal injection by saying that his opposition, "[D]oes not, however, justify a refusal to respect precedents that remain a part of our law."[103] Justice Stevens uses his role as a justice to write a concurring opinion which announces his opposition while allowing him to maintain his oath. At bottom, man's law prevails over the higher law, and yet the higher law makes its presence felt.

American jurisprudence contains a strong strand of legal positivism. Judges must follow the law. Judges must not make the law. Judges must base their decisions on precedent and other legal authorities as they exist on the books. They may not impose their personal morality in deciding cases. Judges who oppose the death penalty have few legitimate avenues open to them to contest its imposition.

The Case of Justice Harry Blackmun

Justice Blackmun's opposition to the death penalty more closely merges man's law with the higher law. His opinion arose in a particular procedural setting which distinguishes his opinion from justice Stevens's opinion. Bruce Edwin Callins was scheduled to be executed and sought relief from the U.S. Supreme Court. The Court's jurisdiction is discretionary, and they declined to take his case. Justice Blackmun was writing in dissent from the refusal to hear the case and, consequently, he was able to argue more broadly about the constitutionality of the death penalty.

Justice Blackmun's opposition, written shortly before his retirement, is strong and explicit, "From this day forward, I no longer shall tinker with the machinery of death."[104] He argues that as a justice on the Court, he has watched death penalty jurisprudence grapple with questions of procedural and substantive fairness, none of which he found convincing. "Rather than continue to coddle the Court's delusion that the desired level of fairness has been achieved and the need for regulation eviscerated, I feel morally and intellectually obligated simply to concede that the death penalty experiment has failed." Blackmun's assertion of moral and intellectual obligation, however, is not to be read as a statement of personal preference.[105] Instead, he goes on to argue, "It is virtually self-evident to me now that no combination of procedural rules or substantive regulations ever can save the death penalty from its inherent constitutional deficiencies."[106] To Blackmun, the constitutional deficiencies are several. There are too many demonstrable cases of arbitrariness and discrimination in its administration. General rules necessarily frustrate the fundamental fairness of individual sentencing. Human error can mean conviction and death to the innocent as the Innocence Project grimly attests.

Most troublesome to Blackmun and others is the pervasive racial and economic discrimination in its application.[107] Blackmun grounds his argument firmly in the Constitution: "Although most of the public seems to desire, and the Constitution appears to permit, the penalty of death, it surely is beyond dispute that if the death penalty cannot be administered consistently and rationally, it may not be administered at all."[108] Blackmun concludes that the administration of the death penalty is so fraught with obstacles, arbitrariness, standardless discretion, and inconsistent objectives, that it cannot be imposed in accordance with the requirements of the Eighth Amendment—our higher law constitutional jurisprudence requires no less than the invalidation of the death penalty.

These two opinions provide clear examples of our discussion. Blackmun's concurrence follows closely the positive law path of Hart's analysis, and Stevens's closely follows Dworkin's path by grounding his dissent in the boarder integrity and political morality of the Constitution.

Conclusion

Plato provides us with a solution to the problem of Creon's ghost. To determine the proper relationship between man's law and higher law, simply answer the question: what is justice? Justice in Plato's world is the highest virtue and, therefore, the highest moral good. Justice is also the end of the Laws. Therefore, to determine whether man's law or higher law prevails, determine the just position. Things are more difficult than that as Plato well knew. To even begin to understand justice, we must first become like Socrates at the end of Book I and admit that we know nothing. As Wallace Stevens wrote, to contemplate:

> *The inconceivable idea of the sun.*
> *You must become an ignorant man again*
> *And see the sun again with an ignorant eye.*
> *And see it clearly in the idea of it.*[109]

Such contemplation is not free from difficulty. First, justice is a Form, and lowly humans cannot know or possess or exactly experience the Form. The best we can do is tap into and try to recollect our sense of justice. To achieve this objective, we must realize that justice is a matter of struggle over shadows and light because we are the prisoners in the Cave. We all suffer from *eikasia*; we suffer from mistaken beliefs about the world; and, according to Plato, we may only find justice through struggle using reason and the dialectic.

Thus, Plato gives us a key insight into the problem of Creon's ghost. There does exist a concept of justice which enables us to make judgments about when man's law is just and when it is not. We can make judgments about whether man's law or higher law should prevail in a given case. These judgments emanate from a process of reasoning which depends on asking and answering questions, a dialectical process. Still, there remains a nagging feeling that we can have a better, clearer understanding of both law and justice. Thomas Aquinas, the "dumb ox," attempts to provide this better understanding in the next chapter.

THREE

Rule and Measure

The portly Dominican friar's schedule of writing, teaching, and preaching at the University of Paris was prodigious, productive, and exhausting. In December, 1273, he took a respite from writing his magnus opus *and returned home to Naples for Christmas. After celebrating Mass on the feast of St. Nicholas, he neither wrote nor dictated another word. When asked why such a prolific scholar had "hung up his writing instruments," Thomas replied "I cannot go on. . . . All that I have written seems to me like so much straw compared to what I have seen and what has been revealed to me." Three months later, in March 1274, fifty years after his birth, he died.*[1]

ANTIGONE'S LAW AND PLATO'S SUN are ideals of justice. When man's law does not satisfy the ideal, it is unjust—so much so that it has been said that "an unjust law is no law at all"—*Lex injusta non est lex.* Both ideals, however, lack definite content, and neither can be fully known. At best, they suggest a sense of justice but provide little guidance about how to actually live our lives justly. The ideals, although not fully knowable, compel us to seek and apply justice in our lives and in the world; they challenge us to seek the higher law.

Antigone and Plato provide specific examples of justice. From Antigone we learn that the higher law requires that bodies should be buried so that their souls can rest. From Plato we learn that justice is harmony, and we learn which specific definitions of justice Socrates rejects as partial. We also learn from the Allegory of the Cave, particularly the prisoner's return to it, a method for thinking about and acting on our innate sense of justice. Persons who have been educated to an awareness of justice and the Good (and we are all capable of such education) are obligated to use the dialectic and to haggle over shadows and light in law courts or elsewhere. This haggling is a valuable tool for our search, but it is untethered to any substantive notion of justice.

The challenge to make clear, concrete statements about justice is not inconsiderable. It is a challenge that the scholar-friar with the mystical experience, St. Thomas Aquinas, undertakes with vigor. Because of Aquinas's deep understanding of human nature, particularly the role of reason, he helps us better understand the problem of *Creon's Ghost.* He confirms Antigone's claim that man's law must not transgress the higher, unsayable law. He also confirms Plato's dialectic as a strong method for discerning the unjust from the just. Yet Aquinas goes further. He gives us a concept of law that fundamentally contrasts with, and provides a powerful alternative to, a positivist concept of law. Further still, Aquinas begins to articulate the substantive principles of the higher law.

Aquinas's concept of law is humanistic and heroic.[2] He tells us that when we act most humanly, we act according to a higher law. Aquinas's genius transforms Antigone's and Plato's abstractions about law into a human and moral force, a force which still attracts and perplexes us. His theory continues to occupy our own discussions about law in the twenty-first century, and today's followers apply their interpretations of Thomistic natural law to today's most difficult and divisive moral and political questions.

Aquinas was born of a wealthy family in the Roccasecca castle in the town of Aquino, midway between Rome and Naples, in 1224. Sent to the abbey at Monte Cassino to begin his schooling, he was later educated at the University of Naples when he entered the Dominicans, the Order of Preaching Friars, to the displeasure of his family who kidnapped him and placed him under guard. Upon his release, he continued his studies at the great universities of Cologne and Paris. Friar Thomas returned to Paris to teach and write what was to become the greatest book of philosophy and theology of the Middle Ages.

Thomas Aquinas is one of those rare world figures whose scholarly output, in excess of ten million words, is daunting because of its magnitude and its complexity. His masterwork, the *Summa Theologiae*, was written for beginning seminarians and can be usefully read as a catechism.[3] His scholasticism[4] can be tedious, yet the dialectic method he uses to establish his principles should be familiar to us from Plato's dialogues. The *Summa* is the culmination of his philosophical and theological thought and is an architectural marvel as each section builds upon another and incorporates much else of Aquinas's work. The majesty of his scholarship dazzles as it poses, then analyzes and answers the grand questions: What is God? What is man? What is happiness? What is law?

Aquinas's *Treatise on Law*, comprising Questions 90–97 of the First Part of the *Summa*, is the central natural law text.[5] The *Treatise* links ancient Greece to the modern world and to the new natural law. Aquinas was a disciple of, and chief expositor for, Aristotle in the Middle Ages. He refers to him as the Philosopher throughout the text, thus reaching back to classical Athens for his philosophical grounding.[6] Today, in no small part because of the human depredations of the twentieth century, natural law theory is experiencing a significant revival as we ask ourselves if universal, inviolable human rights exist?[7] The question calls for a strong affirmative answer, unfortunately, and as we have seen, matters of law resist simple solutions.

The Natural Law Tradition

We can make some broad statements about natural law before narrowing our focus. First, the natural law tradition is a philosophical tradition over 2500 years old and is reflected in the work of Plato and Cicero as well as Aristotle. Aquinas, however, gave natural law its first systematic treatment. Aquinas's debt to philosophy cannot be underestimated. While the general concept of law plays an important role in the *Summa* and in Aquinas's theology, his treatment of natural law can be arrived at independently of theologically revealed truth. Aquinas's theory of law does not depend on scripture; it is derived through philosophical reason.[8] After Aquinas, the natural law tradition continued through Grotius, Locke, Rousseau, and others and continues vigorously today.[9]

Second, as a philosophical tradition, natural law is a much broader discipline than law as we commonly use the word and encompasses moral and political philosophy, epistemology and ontology, moral metatheory, and forms the basis for a significant school of international law.[10] We narrow our focus, however, and concentrate on the impact of the natural law tradition on the conflict between man's law and higher law. Put in other words, we ask whether natural law can serve as the higher law.

Third, and finally by way of introduction, natural law is most often used by way of contrast with positive law. The opposition between natural law and positive law is a familiar one and turns on how each jurisprudential school treats the relationship between law and morality.[11] The inseparability of morality and law is the core concept of natural law theory. It is so much so that Thomist scholar Anthony Lisska writes that Aquinas "provided a theory entailing a denial of the possibility of legal positivism."[12] Aquinas provides an antidote for the weaknesses of the positivist law of Creon and Thrasymachus as he provides support and further understanding for the ideal, higher law of Antigone and Plato.[13]

Aquinas's Concept of Law

Reading natural law and positive law in opposition to each other is a correct, even a definitional reading, but it is a partial reading. Another way to contrast natural law and positive law is to see positive law as descriptive of man's law and natural law as evaluative of it. In this way, the function of natural law is to serve as a commentary on and a normative assessment of the justness of man's law. According to this tradition, when natural law and positive law are aligned, justice is then found. If they diverge, injustice exists. Natural law, then, is a rule and measure of man's positive law. With this reading, natural law and positive law occupy distinct planes of reference. Positive, or human, law describes the legal validity of the rules that govern us. Natural law evaluates and serves as a moral philosophical commentary on these rules.[14] Natural law is Aquinas's candidate for the higher law and serves as the legitimizing source for man's law.

In Question 90, Aquinas provides a general definition of law which serves as the regulative concept of all law.[15] He then applies the general definition to five more specific conceptions of law, including natural law. Aquinas's discussion of the fundamental concept of law and the relationship among the more particular conceptions helps us better understand the conflict between man's law and higher law and helps us better define justice.

Aquinas's concept of law begins with two components: "Law is something pertaining to reason," and "law is a rule and measure" of human acts.[16] These seemingly simple statements belie something deeper. Aquinas speaks of the higher law, a law above man's law, but here we see that law is profoundly human. Law is the product of human reason. Law is neither the result of the king's will nor of faith in the divine. Law "belongs to the reason to direct the end, which is the first principle in all matters of action, according to the Philosopher."[17]

Following Aristotle, Aquinas writes that human reason is always directed to a good end, thus begging the question, what is the good? We will sketch an answer to that question below. What is noteworthy is the stated but unproven and unprovable notion that it is the nature of reason to always act toward the Good. Law, then, is a rule and measure of how reason acts toward that good. As rule, law is something general and prospective. As measure, law is capable of articulation and evaluation. Law guides, by permission and prohibition, human actions, "whereby man is induced to act or is restrained from acting."[18] After grounding law in reason to rule and measure human behavior, Aquinas offers his concept of law. Law is an "ordinance of [1] reason, [2] for the common good, [3] made by him who has the care of the community, and [4] promulgated."[19] Each of these four elements should be familiar. Aquinas's general and regulative concept of law should strike us as pertaining especially to the sort of law we know best—the sort of law that is taught in law school,[20] the sort of law we generally recognize as man's law.

As an ordinance of reason, law is a human product. Reason distinguishes man from beast; reason is essential to human nature. Because of reason and its natural inclination to an end, law is neither naked command nor arbitrary whim. Law is not to serve some personal, private good. Law, instead, is for the common good, echoing Plato's assertion that law is not for any special class; it exists for the good of all classes in the community. Additionally, law cannot be made by anyone. Law can only be made by an authority sanctioned by the community. This authority can be either king or demos.[21] Aquinas makes a clear distinction between ruler and ruled. The obligation to obey the law runs to the ruled. In part, the ruler has a special status as the caretaker of the community. In other part, the ruler has coercive power behind him. Aquinas distinguishes the ruler's lawmaking and law-enforcing authority from the obligation to obey the law by the ruled. Finally, law's legitimacy is derived from its publicity. Promulgated law can serve as a rule and measure of human acts. Law's promulgation enables it to be ruled and measured as just by the human actors. A law must be publicly known to be effectively followed. But more important, law must be publically known to be legitimately enforced.

These elements lead to the conclusion that naked assertions of power by even a recognized authority lack legitimacy. Xerxes' orders did not constitute law. Nor do the orders of a regime that comes to power through violence and intimidation of legislatures and judges to pass laws that deprive some its citizens of property, retroactively validate executions, or proceed to exterminate a religious minority.[22] The purportedly authoritative pronouncements of the Third Reich would not be law for Aquinas, because law has both structural[23] and substantive components. Structurally, law must be general, public, forward-looking, and directed toward the end of human bliss or happiness.[24] Substantively, law has a moral obligatory force because it is directed to an end of common good. Aquinas's concept of law precludes pure legal positivism and precludes justification for the legitimacy of the Third Reich because it asserts that law is to serve an end—the common good. Law cannot be indifferent to the virtue of justice.

Aquinas's Conceptions of Law

Aquinas grounds his theory of law in a moral concept. Human reason defines our nature and it is in our natures, as rational human beings, to act toward an end—pursuing good. The search for good—the common good of society as well as our individual happiness in contributing to that good—defines our moral core as well as the moral core of law. But what is the Good to which action is aimed? His concept of law needs further refinement, and Aquinas provides five more specific conceptions of law. These conceptions contain specific and distinct ends. In Question 91 of the *Treatise*, Aquinas discusses his several conceptions of law as well as the relationships among them. His conceptions of law are the eternal law, natural law, human law, divine law, and the law of fomes (sin) *in that order.*

Eternal Law

Aquinas starts with eternal law which is the law in God's mind and is promulgated in the Book of Life.[25] Eternal law, like Antigone's law, is unsayable and like Plato's Sun,[26] it is not completely knowable. The eternal law is imprinted on us and we know it ("experience it" is a better phrase here) by its effects.[27] Eternal law drives all things to their proper ends. The eternal law acts as the governing force of all things as a matter of God's will. Eternal law is God's plan for the universe and everything in it. "For the universe is no mere jumble but a vast community of beings, indeed a complete community. . . ."[28] That plan extends "to all things and all events in the entire history of the universe," shaping them all to the common good of eternal happiness or bliss.[29]

Aquinas's conceptions of law form two branches after the eternal law. Natural law followed by human law forms one branch and divine law and the law of fomes forms the other. Most important, "[t]he first thing to remember is not to confuse eternal law with divine law."[30] There is no necessary connection between divine law and either natural law or human law. While all law emanates from eternal law, natural law can be derived from reason while divine law is a matter of faith. Natural law and divine law have distinct ends. Natural law and human law are directed to governance and behavior in this world. Divine law and the law of fomes are directed toward happiness in the next. Eternal law moves everything to complete fulfillment of God's will but not by identical paths.

Natural Law

Natural law is man's participation in eternal law; it is how we can come to know the eternal law to the extent that we can know it. Natural law is our ascent out of the Cave. As such, the object of natural law is to discern good from evil through natural reason. Natural law is comprised of very general first principles that find their application in the world through human law. Human nature guarantees that the applications will be imperfect.

Human Law

The human law, which Aquinas also refers to as positive law,[31] is the law most familiar to us. It is as familiar as Creon's edict and it is just as problematic. Human law exists to lead men to the common good and to our happiness. Yet we sometimes (often?) get it wrong and we veer away from the just, natural law. We miss following the natural law because as humans we must make particular decisions and specific applications of general natural law principles, and we simply get things wrong because we apply these principles imperfectly. We may participate in the eternal law through the natural law, but we cannot know either perfectly. Human fallibility precludes such knowledge. Such is the story of the Fall.

Man's mind is imperfect, yet human reason and human nature require that we pursue good, and we do so through the particular applications of human law. Because of human imperfection, we cannot have full knowledge of each single truth, but that deficiency does not preclude striving for good. In other words, the human law has a general sense of eternal law but necessarily fails in its particulars. We have sensed the Sun and are destined to haggle over its shadows and light.

Divine Law

Divine law, the truth revealed in the Bible, is necessary for man to reach his true, last end—salvation. Because human nature is also imperfect and human judgment uncertain, the divine law can help us know right from wrong, especially in our heart and in our conscience. Man is not competent to judge interior motives, particularly of others. Human law cannot reach into the soul, and divine law satisfies this role by punishing sin.[32]

Law of Fomes

The law of fomes, or sin, is Aquinas's last conception of law.[33] Just as man's mind imperfectly perceives and applies the natural law, man's imperfections also include a propensity to do wrong. Our concupiscence leads us to venture into vice, and because all men have this propensity, they behave according to a law.

Aquinas puts high stock in law. He writes that the purpose of law is to make men good. Aquinas contains shades of Plato: both in the City and in the Soul, law should exist to lead men to virtue, to foster the common good, and to habituate men to good works according to eternal justice. His precepts of law, then, are concerned with pursuing the Good, avoiding evil, and permitting the indifferent because of human fallibility. Law regulates human conduct through the fear of punishment because our concupiscence makes us prone to error and susceptible to responding to that fear.

An important moral quality of law is emphasized by Aquinas. He notes that obedience to law is good in and of itself because obedience is a characteristic of good citizenship. He writes that a tyrannical law, one contrary to reason, is not a law but a perversion of the law. To the extent that bad law has the nature of law, people obey even bad laws because law in general seeks to make citizens good.[34] The most significant problem for us mere mortals is aligning human law with natural law. So now we turn to a more detailed look at natural law, human law, and their relationship.

Thomist Natural Law

Natural law serves as a bridge between Creon's law and Antigone's law, between man's law, and the unsayable higher law that even the gods must obey. It also serves as a bridge between Plato's Sun and the haggling over shadows and light. Natural law brings the higher law down to the earth by deeply considering the nature of man and his desire for good. By aligning human nature with the desire for the Good, the natural law can begin to prescribe behavior that we can evaluate as good or bad.

The fundamental problem with Antigone's unsayable law and Plato's Form of justice is that both are without much specific content. Natural law, thus, performs a second complementary function by providing more substance for the higher law. Through his discussion of what naturally drives man, Aquinas develops a substantive conception of justice based on reason connecting man's law with a higher law. His theory of natural law and natural reason generates a set of first and second principles so that we can live our lives justly as individuals and in society to the end of the common good. These principles guide us in developing the positive, human laws by which we live. Natural law serves as a bridge connecting us to the higher law and serves as a rule and measure of the justness of man's law.

These are large claims for any theory of law, and natural law theory does not come without its challenges. The first problem that confronts us is epistemological: How do we know the natural law? Can people differ on what constitutes the natural law? When people do differ, can we eliminate conflicts between and among differing interpretations of natural law? As a philosophical matter, natural law raises problems of knowledge, and our experience tells us that we will perceive and apply the natural law imperfectly. Let's start now with first principles.

First Principles

Reason is central to Aquinas's theory of natural law, and we reason from first principles which are indemonstrable but naturally known; they are self-evident.[35] We apply these first principles through a habit of mind Aquinas calls *synderesis*.[36] *Synderesis* is the "law of our mind," a "habit containing the precepts of the natural law."[37] We naturally apprehend, although imperfectly, the first principles of natural law because we are human, and we cannot do otherwise.[38] This habit of mind, discerning good and evil, has also been called conscience.[39] *Synderesis* drives Antigone to behave according to the laws that even the gods obey.

The architecture of Aquinas reveals itself as he discusses the roles of reason and the ordering of the universal principles flowing from them.

"Now a certain order is to be found in those things that are apprehended universally."[40] Aquinas, drawing on Aristotelian categories, gives us a schematic description of how reason informs the natural law and drives us to pursue good. Speculative reason generates the first indemonstrable principle that "the same thing cannot be affirmed and denied at the same time." This principle is "based on the notion of *being* and *not-being*."[41] It encompasses the idea of noncontradiction; something cannot be and not be at the same time. Additionally and more significantly, this first principle is grounded in the essential idea of being. We act and we must act to an end. These actions and this end cannot be contradictory. Hamlet knew, as a matter of natural law, that he could not *be* and *not be* at the same time. This principle of being is universally true.

Aquinas's sparse statements belie their significance. The first principle of speculative reason, the principle of being, appears commonsensical, but it is profound. Hamlet also knew that being was essential and that it meant that the world makes sense. The universe, to repeat an earlier quotation, is not a jumble. We believe in the principle of being, rather than not being, as self-evident. Yet it is indemonstrable; it is in us as a matter of our nature as rational animals. Surely we can conceive of an *Alice in Wonderland* world that makes little or no sense. We can conceive of a world that has no purpose or end goal. Equally surely, we cannot sustain this thought for very long, and Aquinas rejects it as a matter of first principle.

Speculative reason is about necessary matters, matters in our minds rather than "in the world." To function in the world, we rely on our practical reason. Just as speculative reason is about thought, practical reason is about action. Aquinas makes the observation that we all apprehend being, and that the Good is the "first thing that falls under the apprehension of practical reason." He then derives the first principle of practical reason that "good is that which all things seek after." Aquinas further derives the first precept of natural law that "good is to be done and ensued, and evil is to be avoided."[42] All other principles of natural law are based on these fundamental precepts so that whatever practical reason apprehends as good or evil belongs to the precepts of natural law as to what should be done or avoided.

Germain Grisez, a key figure in the new natural law, argues that Aquinas's formulation to pursue good and avoid evil is dramatically distinct from the imperative, "Do good and avoid evil." Instead of stating a moral command, Aquinas is describing a motivating human impulse to pursue good and avoid evil as a part of our human nature,[43] not as a necessary or morally required reaction to divine edict. In this way, man's nature, imperfections and all, are given full realization. Practical reason still has more work to do before it is manifest in the world. It is about contingent matters; it is about human actions. The first indemonstrable precept of practical reason—humans are naturally driven to seek the good and avoid evil—must be applied through man's law and these applications can be either true or in error;[44] they can be consistent with the natural law or out of alignment.

These two indemonstrable principles of speculative and practical reason construct an important stage on which man acts, and they generate an important role for both natural and human law. Through these first principles, Aquinas's recognition and acceptance of human fallibility is bracing as well as realistic. Human nature, as a matter of natural law, moves us (1) to be and act in the world, (2) in an orderly (noncontradictory) manner, (3) to the purpose or end, (4) of pursuing good and avoiding evil. Even though mistakes are part of our human nature, we cannot act otherwise.

As robust as this description of human nature may be, we cannot help but look for more direction; we cannot help but look for more content in the natural law. Aquinas finds this content in our natural inclinations which themselves are derived from these first principles. Because good is the end of man, then "all those things to which man has a natural inclination are naturally apprehended by reason as being good" and are worthy of pursuit.[45] So the things apprehended by man to be evil are objects of avoidance. We can discern the actions that will lead us to the Good. First, Aquinas writes that as humans, we are naturally inclined to the Good in accordance with the nature we have in common with all living things—preservation of our own beings. We are driven to preserve human life and avoid obstacles to it as a matter of natural law. Next, we have a natural inclination that we share with other animals. We are naturally inclined to sexual intercourse; to educate children; "and so forth." Third, we possess a natural inclination to good according to the nature of our reason. We are naturally inclined to want to know the truth about God, to live in society, to shun ignorance, avoid offending others, and "other such things."[46]

This list of natural human inclinations is not terribly controversial, but it is ambiguous. The ambiguity resides in the matter of specificity. Aquinas says that all of the precepts fall into one natural law, and all the inclinations are reducible to the first precept—pursue good and avoid evil. But how far can we go? How many inclinations can we find? How specific can things get?

Aquinas recognizes that greater detail is problematic,[47] and his response to the problem of specificity is to distinguish between unchangeable first principles and changeable second ones.[48] First principles of natural law are good and unchangeable, but men are imperfect. As we attempt to apply first principles in greater detail to specific situations, we will need to adopt changeable second principles of natural law.[49] Man was born naked in nature, by way of example, but man's art invented clothes, thus adding to the natural law. Aquinas also writes that in nature, man held property in common and had full freedom. Later, man developed private property and slavery by reason, for the benefit of human life.[50] Slavery, especially racial slavery, surely cannot be a first principle of natural law. Assuming that it is a second principle, we can eliminate the positive law of slavery without violating a first principle of natural law.

As if Aquinas's questionable treatment of slavery was not enough, we can identify and discuss a modern moral and legal problem also recognized by Aquinas. In his *Treatise*, Aquinas writes of human nature that "[C]ertain special sins are said to be against nature; thus contrary to sexual intercourse, which is natural to all animals, is unisexual lust, which has received the special name of the unnatural crime."[51] Is this true? Does Aquinas's statement stand up against his own theory of natural law? Is this prohibition against homosexual sex a matter of first or second natural law principles? To assess this claim, we must first acknowledge that Aquinas makes this statement as a matter of practical reason and not revealed truth. Citations to the Old or New Testaments are irrelevant for the purpose of natural law analysis. Yet regardless of what answers we derive; i.e., homosexual sex is naturally immoral or naturally moral, today the problem persists and divides society. We will now discuss, in more detail, this problem in terms of natural law.

The Relationship Between Natural Law and Human Law

After quoting Augustine, "*Lex injusta non est lex*"[52]—an unjust law is no law at all—Aquinas goes on to write that if a human law, "at any point [] deflects from the law of nature, it is no longer a law but a perversion of law."[53] Human law is either just or unjust. It is just when it has, "the power of binding in conscience, from the eternal law [from] whence [is] derived," which is to say in accordance with natural law.[54] Therefore, human law which deviates from reason is "called an unjust law, and has the nature, not of law but of violence."[55] When human law follows the natural law, it is just and morally binding. But what is a citizen to do in the face of an unjust law? Is she morally obligated to obey? Is she legally obligated? Is she acting immorally if she does obey?

Not surprisingly, Aquinas's answers to these questions defy resolution by slogan such as "an unjust law is no law at all." Aquinas argues that natural law and human law are bound to each other through moral obligation. We must examine more carefully the extent of the moral obligation to obey man's law when man's law is unjust, and to do so we must first understand Aquinas's view of human nature. Then we must understand what constitutes an unjust man's law before addressing the extent of this obligation.

Aquinas has a realistic, if hopeful, view of human nature. Man has a "natural aptitude for virtue" but needs "some kind of training" to achieve it. This training comes through the discipline of the laws which can compel men to virtue through fear of punishment.[56] Men may well desire virtue, but they are not strangers to vice, and they can use reason to devise means for satisfying their lust.[57] Human laws help protect the innocent from the wicked and even help protect man from his own evil inclinations. As natural law serves as a rule and measure of human law, human law serves as a rule and measure of human actions.[58]

To monitor and guide human action, human law must be dynamic and adaptable. Human law is detailed and driven by regulating how humans live together.[59] The function of human law is to address particular problems. The human law that an evildoer should be punished derives from the natural law and is just. The human law that the evildoer should spend five years in prison for his crime addresses a particular problem, but we must recognize that the five-year penalty has "no other force than that of human law,"[60] which is to say that the penalty may be just or unjust. A five-year penalty for a first robbery offense may well be just because it is proportionate to the crime. A five-year penalty for spitting on the sidewalk may be a bit too much and can be called unjust.

The purpose of the human law is the common good, and yet the human law cannot reach everything; it cannot prohibit all vices—only those which harm others. Nor can human law further all virtues but only those which further the common good.[61] Human law cannot reach into all matters of the soul, which is the rightful province of divine law. So too, the general principles of Thomist natural law cannot be applied to all men in the same way because of the great variety and diversity of situations in which we find ourselves. Because man's law is human, it contains the imperfections that make us human. Human imperfection, however, does not forgive obligation.

It does not relieve us from the obligation to sometimes obey even unjust human laws.

Aquinas is very much a legal conservative, and he assigns man's law an obligatory force. Law, to be construed as legitimate, must be just as to its purpose, emanate from a recognized authority, and be proportionate to an articulated end. Man's law can be unjust if any one of these three elements is missing and in three parallel ways. A human law is unjust when it is not in accordance with natural law, when it is beyond the lawgiver's legitimacy, when or it is unequally or otherwise unfairly applied. These laws are not morally binding, "except perhaps in order to avoid scandal or disturbance."[62] One might then follow a defective human law to the "extent that disobedience would cause disorder or demoralization . . .or give the kind of 'example' that leads others to wrong doing."[63]

Aquinas's concept of law contains moral obligation because it is in the nature of law to seek good and, in doing so, to make men good. Aquinas does not advocate disobedience as a matter of course. Law, instead, is to be construed to foster obedience and further the good. To understand a human law, one must, "take account of the motive of the law giver rather than his very words"[64] and must provide reasonable, not strained, interpretations in its favor and follow the spirit of the law.[65] Human law must be observed in reasonable, understandable circumstances. In short, Aquinas demands much of citizens. Human law should be followed, reasonably interpreted, and properly applied and obeyed in specific circumstances because the law seeks the common good. Laws are not to be too loosely construed to find injustice. They should not be changed blithely only when evidence exists that there is a benefit to be derived from a change.[66] Aquinas places real moral value in the order and stability of the human law, and human law should be observed as much as possible because the good order of the community is served by obedience. Nevertheless, it will come to pass that even when Aquinas's conditions are satisfied, a law can be unjust. Again the question: must one obey an unjust human law?[67] Again, the answer: not in conscience but only after giving man's law several benefits of the doubt.

The higher natural law serves as rule and measure of man's law. The human law, by its own force, comes with significant moral obligation. When man's law and natural law are aligned, they are bound together by the virtue of justice. Consequently, when man's law asserts its natural law roots, it comes with considerable clout. We should therefore be careful about what counts as an alignment between man's law and natural law—a problem for the twenty-first century.

The New Natural Law

Natural law is broad terrain. It refers both to a long historical tradition and to an important philosophical approach to ethics among other philosophical disciplines. The "new natural law" revives and modernizes the Thomist tradition, and the revival was born of necessity and dissatisfaction.

The twentieth century witnessed the Nazi Holocaust, Stalin's purge, Mao's Cultural Revolution, Pol Pot's genocide, the genocide of Darfur, and other evils. These depredations necessitated asking: Where is law? Are these actions "crimes against humanity"? If so, then are they punishable by law, and what law? Natural law provides a basis for answering these questions by establishing law on human, moral principles. The Nuremberg trials, the International Court of justice, current war crimes tribunals, and the U.N. Declaration of Human Rights are modern examples of the application of the natural law tradition.[68]

The new natural law has also been born from dissatisfaction with modern philosophy, particularly with its analytic, linguistic, and deconstructive turns which keep moral talk at bay. Legal positivism, as an analogue of analytic positivism, can be understood to hold that because of the divorce between law and morality, a "legal" Nazi regime is possible.[69] Analytic philosophy, with its focus on language, similarly prefers to stay away from moral talk as too soft, too mushy, too lacking in precision. For philosophy to advance, the philosophical linguists assert, we must be achingly precise about language and how words are used. Likewise, the postmodern and deconstructive moves in philosophy are aimed at understanding (or reducing philosophy to) the politics of it all. Modern philosophy ends where legal positivism does—by taking little or no stand on moral questions lest the rigor and seriousness of their respective disciplines be corrupted.[70] It also ends in moral and intellectual skepticism and belief in the politicization and transience of truth.[71]

Natural law theory is an antidote to modern philosophy and legal positivism. Natural law jurisprudentially responds to legal positivism by asserting that law cannot be divorced from morality. Morality is what constitutes law; morality is what gives law its obligatory content. People obey law not simply because it wears the label law or simply because they fear its sanctions. People obey law because they *ought* to obey it; social coordination is advanced through obedience as is human flourishing. Moral obligation is part of the nature of law, and. it is also a part of human nature. Natural law philosophically responds to modern theory by positing the existence of human good and of our ability to know and act on it. Human good is a moral concept directed to the moral end of human flourishing. Seeking good is the natural end of man, and good can be sought even in the face of linguistic, analytic, and deconstructive skepticism.

The revival of natural law has generated an impressive amount of scholarship. The new natural law is generally considered to have begun with the work of Germain Grisez and developed more fully by John Finnis.[72] For the most part, the new natural law scholars are engaged in moral and political philosophy as well as the traditional jurisprudential inquiry into the nature of law. Many of the new natural lawyers follow in the Thomist tradition and yet are distinguishable from it in two ways. First, the new natural law delves more deeply into the philosophical premises of the tradition. Second, and I think mistakenly, the new natural lawyers attempt to provide more content and more specific prescriptions for human action. In other words, the new natural law is more politically entangled.

The most controversial and intractable philosophical problem in natural law theory involves the question, how do we know first principles? This simple seeming question involves metaphysics as well as epistemology[73] and has challenged and continues to challenge natural law theorists. Do we come to know the first principles through reason? Emotion? Intuition? Do we come to know them because of the very nature of our human rationality? Or do we come to know first principles by observing how humans behave as a sort of empirical, anthropological morality?

The soundness of natural law theory, primarily as an ethical theory, depends upon how we answer this purportedly simple question. The answer to this question also helps us understand and apply natural law in its evaluative role as it serves as a rule and measure of the human law. If, as a rough example, we hold that first principles are generated from observations about human behavior, then how can we discern good from so much human evil in the world? If first principles are generated by emotion or intuition, then given the diversity and variety of human emotions and intuitions, how can we arrive at any universal first principles beyond banal generalities such as "do no harm"? No, the question about first principles is neither simple nor peripheral. It involves centuries of hard philosophy, and answering it is central to understanding the Thomist concept of law as well as understanding those today who claim to be following in his footsteps.

The philosophical problems animated by the epistemological question about knowing the good were given more specific and technical philosophical formulations after Aquinas wrote.[74] And yet the problem of knowing, defining, and applying a normative value—the good or justice—by observing the facts about what *is* in the world has been with us since the beginning of philosophy.

Aristophanes made much fun of Socrates for precisely this predicament. In his play *The Clouds*, he portrays Socrates as suspended from the earth by a basket, scanning the earth with a telescope and his backside pointed to the skies:

Strepsiades:	Hey, look there: what are those fellows doing bent over like that?
Student:	Those are graduate students doing research on Hades.
Strepsiades:	On Hades: then why are their ass's scanning the skies?
Student:	Taking a minor in astronomy[75]

How can it be, Aristophanes joked, that by examining the bugs and flowers of the earth that philosophers can have access to abstract metaphysical thought about the heavens?

The answer was given by Socrates and Plato as well as by Aristotle and Aquinas. Humans by nature are rational beings. Reason not only distinguishes humans from animals; it enables us to study the world, our place in it; to question the world in which we live, and to contemplate beyond it. It enables us to observe human diversity and attempt its coordination to some end. Reason also tells us that there is some good end to the social order beyond the reduction of violence; there is an end of individual and common good found through human flourishing and fulfillment.

Reason reveals these things to us not as a result of empirical observation or deduction from facts. Instead, reason reveals these things by its very nature. The first principle of speculative reason, the principle of being, is not derived or deduced from anything prior. "Rather, this principle is basic in that it is given to us by our most primitive understanding."[76] The first principle of practical reason that we pursue good is not a formula; it is a way of expressing the intelligibility of the end we seek.[77] As humans we naturally seek to be and seek the good as essential to being.

In the *Treastise*, Aquinas states that these first principles are self-evident[78] and like axioms of geometry are indemonstrable. In Finnis's words, they are self-evident because they are preserved in us (we "sense" them) as part of experience and memory.[79] We come to know knowledge as a good, for example, because of our experience and our hard-wired memory of it. These general principles are powerful and profound. As you read this book, you are (1) behaving according to your human nature, (2) by exercising your rational intellect, (3) purposively, (4) to gain knowledge, (5) to an end of good. We can posit that someone would read this book for some evil motive like plagiarism. Yet, as Aquinas maintains, while human nature does not and cannot preclude bad acts, these bad acts are mistakes we do not and cannot avoid even while seeking good. The plagiarist does the bad act to achieve the perceived good of passing a course or achieving acclaim. These "good" ends, however, are mistaken and natural law principles serve as correctives to identify and rectify these mistakes.

The New Natural Law Applied

The new natural law theorists follow Aquinas only so far when identifying the source of their moral principles. They agree that first principles are exercises of speculative and practical reason and of human inclination. But Aquinas was very general in his specification of first principles and human inclinations. While the new natural law theorists begin with Thomist first principles, they are more specific and more expansive about what constitutes the principles and precepts of their new natural law. Along with the greater specification, they exhibit a greater willingness to discuss and provide answers to, and judgments about contemporary, moral, and political problems, they claim that "Modern natural law has reached a point of maturity where the application of its principles to the particular problems of political society is ripe."[80]

The new natural law philosophers identify sets of basic goods which flow from first principles. Where Aquinas says that we are inclined to preserve life, engage in sexual intercourse, educate our children, to know the truth about God, and live in society, contemporary philosophers expand his list.[81] Basic goods are those "aspects of fulfillment of persons" which "correspond to the inherent complexities of human nature, as it is manifested both in individuals and in various forms of community."[82] These basic goods serve the "ideal of integral human fulfillment" for "all persons living together in complete harmony."[83]

The basic goods for Grisez include self integration, practical reasonableness, authenticity, justice and friendship, religion, life and health, knowledge of truth, appreciation of beauty, and playful activities.[84] John Finnis, in 1980, includes life, knowledge, aesthetic appreciation, play, friendship, practical reasonableness, and religion.[85] In 1996, Finnis adds what he calls, "the marital good."[86] What we see in the new natural law, then, is a more detailed specification of what counts as basic goods and what counts for these natural lawyers as the "fundamental reason for choice and action."[87] These modern authors are not shy about discussing contemporary problems, and their natural law judgments extend to individual matters as privacy, family, and bioethics. They also extend to public matters as legislation, judicial review,[88] and the war in Iraq.[89]

Assuming we can know either the natural law or the new natural law, a second problem arises. As a legal matter, can either be incorporated into man's law through legislation, case law, or constitutional interpretation? Should it be? This problem is neither fanciful nor unproblematic. Incorporating natural law principles into the human law is problematic in a country which prizes the positive law. It is also problematic in a country which prizes the separation of church and state because natural law is generally associated with the religious tradition of Catholicism[90] even though that association is at least misleading if not mistaken. Natural law may share the values of a religious tradition, but natural law is independent of it. "Natural law does not direct man to his supernatural end . . . [because] it is inadequate to do that, divine law is needed as a supplement."[91] Natural law is also problematic because it has something to teach us about justice, but what it has to teach is sometimes unclear and sometimes contradictory.

It is not fanciful to desire to manifest natural law principles in our human laws. In our search for just law, the natural law provides a respectable, but often too general, definition of the higher law. We find, for example, natural law sentiments embedded in the historical and political tradition of the United States.[92] The Declaration of Independence proclaims that people have a right to life, liberty, and the pursuit of happiness according to the "Laws of Nature and of Nature's God."[93] Yet, as a matter of constitutional politics, is it legitimate to use natural law principles as the basis for sustaining or overturning legislation?[94] Should we use natural law to find rules or principles of constitutional or common law? Should natural law serve as a basis for public debate? Let's see what the new natural lawyers have to tell us and how our legal system responds to the particular problem of homosexual sex, a contemporary political and moral issue that currently divides society. The division is reflected in cases, statutes, and constitutional interpretation. This issue also divides contemporary natural law theorists.

Homosexual sex has become more politicized today than ever before. A politician's stand on gay marriage can turn an election. The politician who does not agree that marriage is the union of one man with one woman will likely be out of politics. In the 2006 and 2008 elections, eleven states proposed "gay marriage" amendments banning same-sex marriage, and every one passed. Twenty-six states have constitutional amendments prohibiting same-sex marriage, and 43 states specifically define marriage as the legal union of one man with one woman. Clearly homosexual marriage is unpopular, but is homosexual sex against the natural law as many opponents argue?

Neither the science nor the demographics of homosexuality are uniform or highly reliable.[95] Nevertheless, both point in the direction that homosexuality is a fixed dimension of human nature as distinguished from an intellectual or political choice.[96] While the clear trend is toward greater acceptance of homosexuality in our society, full acceptance is lacking and opposition, particularly toward gay marriage,[97] continues. The continuing conflict involves the roles of man's law and natural law.

The Marital Good

Aquinas was quoted earlier condemning "unisexual lust" as contrary to the human inclination for sexual intercourse and deserving of the name the "unnatural crime."[98] The new natural law theorists, notably Finnis and Robert George, also place homosexual sex in the immoral column of the human nature ledger. Are these condemnations consistent with natural law theory? Or is homosexual sex consistent with natural law theory? In either event, how should man's law respond?

Arguing against same-sex marriage and homosexual sex, Finnis begins his natural law analysis with a "master principle of morality" and imposes upon it substantial requirements. "[I]n all one's deliberating and acting, one ought to choose and in other ways will those and only those possibilities [that are] compatible with integral human fulfillment. . . ."[99] Acting against reason is acting against morality because we are not seeking our fulfillment as humans. What is problematic is not whether natural law is intended to guide human action. Guidance decidedly is its intent. What is problematic is how far the new natural law prescribes specific actions in specific contexts.

Finnis and George, following Aquinas, argue that while sexual intercourse is natural, it does not stand alone unregulated. Otherwise, sexual intercourse is nothing more than unconstrained passion and desire and, therefore, is destructive of human integrity, not conducive to human flourishing, and therefore unregulated sexual activity is immoral.[100] Nevertheless, we start with the idea that sexual intercourse is a matter for the natural law and is justified as an intrinsic human good. Finnis and George then link sexual intercourse to marriage which they also treat as an intrinsic, and thus indemonstrable, basic good. From there, the authors argue that nonmarital sex and homosexual sex violate the natural law and are morally wrong. Finnis further argues that any society that says that nonmarital or homosexual sex is reasonable is "seriously unjust."[101]

Finnis asserts that he is grounding his position in Aquinas. "It is clear," he writes, that Aquinas in speaking of the human inclination for sexual intercourse, is "inviting his readers to think of marriage" and specifically a marriage between a man and a woman. In this form, then, sexual intercourse connotes two lives joining as one in marriage for the procreation and education of children as well as a natural form of friendship.[102] "[T]he intrinsic point of sex in any marriage, fertile or not, is . . .the basic good of marriage itself, considered as a two-in-one-flesh communion of persons that is consummated and actualized by acts of the reproductive type."[103] Robert George concurs that sexual intercourse is a moral good according to natural law as the "two become one flesh" in the circumstance of marriage. Marital sexual intercourse accords with natural law, according to these authors, because it satisfies the inclination of all living things for preservation, and it satisfies the human inclination for sexual activity. It also satisfies the human inclination to live in community and educate our children. Therefore, nonmarital sexual intercourse, including homosexual sex, is not natural and consequently is immoral because it is at best, instrumental to one's pleasure and not intrinsic to the human good of marriage.[104]

There are two key moves to the Finnis-George argument. First, you must accept the "marriage good" as a basic human good which possesses intrinsic, not instrumental value and you must accept that only marital, reproductive-type, sex is also an intrinsic good. Second, in order to accept their argument, you must accept that sex and marriage are indissolubly connected. Both claims are just that—claims. "Intrinsic value, cannot strictly speaking, be demonstrated."[105] As such, these assertions can be rebutted through reasoned argument in the natural law tradition, and therefore they do not hold the intrinsic power that Finnis and George claim for them.

There is a Thomist response to the Finnis-George marital good analysis. First, the marriage good is not a first principle of natural law. Instead, it is a second, and therefore changeable, principle. Second, the Finnis-George marital good makes the mistake of combining sex and marriage as two equivalent, indemonstrable, intrinsic, *and necessarily connected* first principles. We can accept the inclination for reproductive sex as an indemonstrable and intrinsic first principle. How else does the species survive? Such acceptance, however, does not entail the larger claims either that reproductive-type sex is the only moral, natural law purpose of sex or that it is limited to marriage.[106] We can also accept the claim that heterosexual marriage and reproductive sex in it is a valuable social institution. Such acceptance does not preclude the possibility that there are other valuable and morally acceptable forms of marriage and other valuable and morally acceptable forms of sexual expression.

Andrew Sullivan, a British gay Catholic, and conservative writer, offers the following: "I was once asked at a conservative think tank what evidence I had that homosexuality was far more of an orientation than a choice, and I was forced to reply quite simply: my life."[107] Sullivan's personal experience, alone, is insufficient to ground a natural law principle. He continues by saying that the homosexual experience, "occurs independently of the forms of its expression; it is bound up in that mysterious and unstable area where sexual desire and emotional longing meet; it reaches into the core of what makes a human being who he or she is."[108] Sullivan sees it as human to "desire to unite with another: not to possess but to join in some way; not to lose myself but to be given dimension."[109] As Catholic theologian and Thomist scholar Jean Porter writes, "once we grant that sex serves more than one purpose in human life, including the formation and expression of personal bonds, it is apparent that the expression of interpersonal erotic love can readily be interpreted as a natural purpose. . . ."[110]

George addresses Sullivan's case by positing that one might assert that marriage may be a mere metaphor to "describe a relationship marked by more or less intense psychological closeness combined with sexual intimacy and certain sorts of commitments and obligations."[111] George rejects his own counterexample by explaining, "[O]ne either understands that spousal genital intercourse has a special significance as instantiating a basic, non-instrumental value, or something blocks that understanding and one does not perceive correctly."[112]

The argument against sex outside of marriage is grounded in the idea that the marital good (heterosexual reproductive sex) is intrinsic to our human nature, and that instrumental reasons cannot morally validate such acts. Yet the mystery of sex can be both intrinsic and instrumental and knowing when sex is one or the other may not be known to us.

There is no *reason* to deny this claim about one of life's most profound mysteries.[113]

The weaknesses of the marital good argument are apparent. First, the same argument can be made for the contrary position. We can turn George's critique of Sullivan's position on its head and against him. Those who do not accept Sullivan's claim that genuine homosexuality exists and that its expression is fully human "lack imagination"[114] and are not "perceiving correctly." Next, what can it mean to accept the genuine humanness of homosexual orientation and deny its expression? Are homosexuals to be denied the human inclination for sexual expression? Is not such a denial a denial of human personality and, thus, cruel?[115] Finally, why is sexual intercourse a human good only in the reproductive act during marriage even when a couple cannot conceive?[116] The marital good as defined above cures the many ills perceived by some new natural law lawyers. It prohibits same-sex marriage, homosexual sex, sodomy, and nonmarital sex. Does it prove too much? It certainly (and reasonably) seems so.

Aquinas relies on human inclination as revealed by human nature. Once we accept the idea that homosexuality is embedded in human nature, it follows that homosexuality is fully human and natural. Sex is as expressive of love and intimacy as it is expressive of the desire for procreation.

While same-sex marriage has divided the United States' electorate, the same cannot be said for homosexuality. The increasing acceptance of homosexuality is apparent throughout our culture. This greater acceptance is, of course, no response to the Finnis/George argument. Yet one cannot but realize that the "aesthetic"objection[117] to homosexuality is lessening. Does the increasing acceptability mean that homosexuality is at least perceived as natural? How should the human law, the law that governs us in society, respond?

Homosexual Sex in Natural Law and in Man's Law

Following Aquinas, natural law is a rule and a measure of man's law. Natural law is a moral theory and as such, we can use natural law to evaluate and assess the morality or the justness of man's law. In this way, natural law has nothing to do with the *practice* of law. Put in other words, natural law does not have the force of positive, man's law in a legal system. One cannot tell Austin's hangman that he cannot be hanged because of a natural law principle without having the trapdoor release from beneath his feet.

Or if the gallows example is too grim, a lawyer appearing before a judge is better served reaching into her briefcase for a case or a statute in response to a judge's query rather than reaching for a principle of natural law from the *Summa Theologiae* in support of her case.

Having denied the relevance of natural law to the *practice* of law, there are cases argued in the upper register of constitutional adjudication in which we can discern natural law arguments. When the Constitution is too open-ended to decide a case, then we can observe justices making arguments which sound very close to, if not fully based on, natural law arguments. The matter of the legality and the constitutionality of consensual homosexual sex is just such a matter.

Majority Morality

Historically, homosexuality has not only been condemned as immoral, it has been criminalized. Admittedly, laws against either heterosexual or homosexual sodomy were rarely enforced. When they were enforced, they were used as part of the political arsenal of those politicians who believe that imposing a specific set of moral values was the role of law and served as part of their election strategies.

In 1986, the U.S. Supreme Court had before it exactly this type of trumped-up political case. The defendant was tried and convicted of sodomy witnessed by police officers who entered his home to serve a summons on him for throwing out a beer bottle outside the gay bar in which he worked weeks earlier. Ultimately, the case reached the Court to decide the question of whether or not, under a Georgia statute, sodomy was punishable as a criminal act.

The Court held in *Bowers v. Hardwick*[118] that the Constitution does not confer a fundamental right upon homosexuals to engage in sodomy. The Court reasoned that no right, based on either privacy or any other liberty interest, existed to engage in conduct which was neither "deeply rooted in this Nation's history and tradition" nor "implicit in the concept of ordered liberty."[119] The Court also stated that since sodomy was a common-law offense since the Founding and that as recently as 1961, all 50 of the United States outlawed such acts, then criminalization was justified. Condemnation of homosexuality, according to the Court, "is firmly rooted in Judeao-Christian moral and ethical practices."[120]

The Court was simply unwilling to find judge-made constitutional law having, "little or no cognizable roots in the language or design of the Constitution."[121] The Court also rejected the argument that the Georgia statute should be declared unconstitutional because it was based on a moral belief that homosexual sodomy was immoral and socially unacceptable. "The law, however, is constantly based on notions of morality, and if all laws representing essentially moral choices are to be invalidated under the Due Process Clause, the Courts will be very busy indeed."[122] Consequently, the criminal conviction for adult consensual homosexual sex would stand.

Justice Bryon White wrote the opinion for the Court in this 5 to 4 decision.[123] Justice Blackmun's dissenting opinion argued that the case was not about finding a new right to engage in homosexual sodomy. "Rather, this case is about 'the most comprehensive of rights and the right most valued by civilized men,' 'namely, the right to be let alone.'"[124] Blackmun also noted that just because the statute contains a moral principle, moral principles do not control constitutional law. The right of adults to engage in consensual homosexual conduct is protected by the constitutional right of privacy. Blackmun also pointed out that the Georgia statute was not aimed at homosexuality. It was aimed instead at sodomy, generally, and therefore the sex or the status of persons was irrelevant as a matter of the positive law. Blackmun argued that sexual intimacy is so imbedded in the concept of privacy that it is constitutionally protected. Individual freedom means that people are free to conduct their lives as they choose, and the state can only interfere if there is a compelling governmental interest to displace an individual's interest in liberty.

The *Bowers* case was controversial in 1986 as the 5–4 opinion verifies. Yale Law Professor William Eskridge has argued that *Bowers* was "an exemplar of legal homophobia."[125] The controversy, as well as the weakness of the decision, was made perhaps most notable by the report that justice Lewis Powell, the fifth vote for the majority, switched his vote after having been lobbied by Chief justice Rehnquist. He publicly stated later that it was the vote he most regretted. Further, the decision has been soundly criticized as "manipulative, ignorant, inefficient, violent, historically inaccurate, misogynistic, authoritarian, and contrary to precedent."[126] Perhaps the most difficult aspect of *Bowers* was not the assertion that there was no fundamental right to homosexual sodomy but Georgia's assertion that criminalization was rationally related to some public objective went literally unchallenged.

Individual Liberty

The *Bowers* controversy did not die away and was brought back to the Court 17 years later in *Lawrence* v. *Texas*,[127] which explicitly overruled *Bowers v. Hardwick* with a strong statement that "*Bowers* was not correct when it was decided, and it is not correct today."[128] How can it be that within less than two decades the Court could have realized, in dramatic fashion, that their prior precedent was incorrect and was of no further force and effect?

Lawrence is a 6–3 opinion with the majority written by justice Anthony Kennedy. The first sentence of his opinion sets its tone, "Liberty protects the person from unwarranted government intrusions into a dwelling or other private places."[129] That liberty interest also involves autonomy of the self including intimate conduct. The Texas statute criminalized sodomy against same-sex partners. It differed from the Georgia statute against sodomy, generally, because the Texas statute was directed at homosexual behavior. Kennedy's opinion forcefully argues that the petitioners were free as adults to engage in private conduct as an exercise of their liberty protected by the Fourteenth Amendment of the Constitution. Most particularly, the liberty interest protects sexual conduct, including the conduct of nonmarried, same-sex adults.

Kennedy's opinion was grounded in the idea of personal dignity. "When sexuality finds overt expression in intimate conduct with another person, the conduct can be but one element in a personal bond that is more enduring. The liberty protected by the Constitution allows homosexual persons the right to make this choice."[130] Kennedy acknowledges that the *Bowers* Court got its history wrong.[131] The *Lawrence* Court noted that "there is no long standing history in this country of laws directed at homosexual conduct as a distinct matter."[132] Other laws prohibiting sodomy had not been enforced against adults acting in private until the 1970s when states singled out same-sex relations for criminal prosecution.

Justice Scalia's dissent chastises the Court for overruling *Bowers* and for overturning a statute that should be sustained on the basis that prohibiting homosexual sex was rational.[133] Scalia argues that it is irrelevant that statutes criminalizing homosexual sodomy are of recent vintage. Rather what is relevant is that sodomy generally has historically been prohibited. Scalia's opinion argues that the state statute furthers the rational government interest in maintaining that certain forms of sexual behavior are immoral and socially unacceptable. He rejects justice Stevens's dissent which held that "the fact that the governing majority in a state has traditionally viewed a particular practice as immoral is not a sufficient reason for upholding a law prohibiting the practice."[134] Scalia felt that such an abandonment of moral tradition by the Court, "effectively decrees the end of all morals legislation if, as the Court asserts, the promotion of the majoritarian sexual morality is not even a *legitimate* state interest. . . ." He was concerned that if the majority's position about the moral dimension of anti-sodomy statutes could result in their invalidation, then any number of other morality-inspired laws could not withstand rational review despite the fact that it is the job of courts to make such decisions as a matter of course.[135]

Scalia's criticism delves deeper:

> Today's opinion is the product of a Court, which is the product of a law-profession culture, that has largely signed on to the so-called homosexual agenda, by which I mean the agenda promoted by some homosexual activists directed at eliminating the moral opprobrium that has traditionally attached to homosexual conduct.[136]

Scalia argues that the Court has taken sides in a culture war and has ignored democratic opinion. He further argues that the Court has failed to serve as a neutral observer, but then where is his neutrality? He says that Americans should be able to protect their families from a lifestyle that they believe to be immoral and destructive and the Supreme Court ought to uphold the right to discriminate against homosexuals. He goes on to write, however, "Let me be clear that I have nothing against homosexuals, or any other group, promoting their agenda through normal democratic means."[137] It is here, however, where Scalia falls into the same error he did in *Smith v. Department of Unemployment.* Individual belief, behavior, and intimacy cannot be subject to democratic voting. The danger is apparent: Majority morality can annihilate individual liberty. As justice Stevens wrote in his dissent in *Bowers*, "[T]he fact that the governing majority in a State has traditionally viewed a particular practice as immoral is not a sufficient reason for upholding a law prohibiting the practice. . . ."[138] Individual liberty demands protection from democratic majorities.

Bowers and *Lawrence* demonstrate the reach of the natural law into man's law. The Constitution contains no explicit prohibition or approval of homosexual sex between consenting adults. There is no positive law in the Constitution itself on the subject. Statutory law, however, exists, and eventually these positive laws were challenged in the Supreme Court.

The Court, in turn, could not look to the text of the Constitution for resolution. The Court, instead, engages in the process of constitutional interpretation reviewing prior case law, current policies, politics, and attitudes, as well as searching for a sense of the direction of the law. There is no single formula for constitutional interpretation and as revealed in these two opinions, the rationales go beyond the text for justification. Sometimes these justifications resonate with natural law sentiments such as human fulfillment, individual liberty and expression, and tradition and firmly rooted practices. The rub, of course, is that such sentiments support both positions. Natural law arguments can support the Finnis-George-Scalia condemnation of homosexuality as contrary to human society. They can also support the Kennedy-Sullivan-Porter acceptance of homosexuality as an indissoluble dimension of human personality and nature.

Conclusion

Aquinas has advanced our understanding of Creon's ghost. Antigone and Plato spoke to our sense of justice. They addressed our human need for the Good. Aquinas gives us more detail about human good and about the nature of our search for it. We search for justice because it is in our human nature to do so. We cannot, however, rely on our human nature alone because that nature is imperfect; we have been known to yield to our baser instincts, to our lusts. Law, in its various conceptions, aids us in our search. The eternal law of God's mind guides everything and every creature even though the eternal law cannot be fully known to us. Antigone and Plato spoke of the eternal law and were motivated by it. Aquinas makes this unknowable law accessible to us through the natural law. The natural law, by establishing fundamental principles, helps shape our human inclination to good.

Thomist first principles are few and general. They allow for the full diversity of human life while recognizing the imperfections of the human and while allowing for human law to assist us in living together. Aquinas's concept of law is grounded in human behavior in society, and his law has a distinct end, the common good which is attained through law's rules and measures. In society, we must confront innumerable situations and conflicts that call for resolution. No single rule or set of rules can accommodate all of our conflicts, and Aquinas acknowledges human freedom to choose and design the laws we need. Thus, natural law has a double vision. Natural law is both descriptive of the Good, and it acts to evaluate what human law should be. Law performs both internal and external functions that authenticate each other. Law measures itself as either just or unjust and sets rules for living.

Aquinas can be seen as a pre-Renaissance humanist in that he treats law as a fundamentally human discipline. We need the help of law to overcome our imperfections, live in society, flourish as individuals, and move toward the common good. More theologically minded philosophers also assert that natural law helps bring man to God, but Aquinas reserves that role for divine, not natural law. Aquinas's concept of natural law as manifest by the human law is also socially conservative. Law, as law, ought (sometimes) to be obeyed even when imperfect. Those ruled by law should not be too quick to dispatch man's law as unjust. Instead, the benefit of any doubts should be given to the lawgiver. The lawgiver's intent should be interpreted as justifying law rather than overturning it. Even unjust law should be observed if the failure to do so would set a bad example for others or result in a disruption of society. Natural law helps us attain justice through man's law. Can man's law, though, effectively function tied to natural law? Niccolò Machiavelli rejects this possibility next.

FOUR

The Ancient Courts of Ancient Men

At the crest of the road between the Albergaccio on his left and the Taverna on his right, the Exile looks north from Sant'Andrea in Percussina. Ten kilometers away, the Exile can see the orange-red cupola of Santa Maria dei Fiore, Firenze's magnificent Duomo, one of the highest achievements of the Italian Renaissance. Contemplating the Duomo, the Exile recalls the fiery sermons of the ascetic Dominican Fra Girolama Savonarola, and he recalls his equally fiery end.

Living in Percussina in 1513, the Exile desired nothing more than to walk the piazzas of Florence, to enter and be recognized in the great public places, and to have a seat in the center of government, the Palazzo Vecchio. The Exile yearned to participate in the grand events of the day and to be among men of action. The Exile's yearning was not without hope. His plan to return to Florence was carefully executed in Sant'Andrea. After a morning of labor and an afternoon of lunch and games with friends in the Taverna, the Exile would retreat to his villa to "enter the ancient courts of ancient men."[1] *There he studied, thought, and wrote a text dedicated and presented as a gift, as a favor, to the reigning ruler of Florence, Lorenzo, grandson of Il Magnifico.*

THE FAVOR FAILED OF its immediate purpose, and the Exile did not return to public life for several more years and only then at the urging of Medici Pope Clement VII, not Lorenzo.[2] Through the Pope, the Exile received a minor position, one quite beneath his talents, for during his active years in the government, he delivered sound diplomatic advice to Florentine leaders from the great courts of France and Rome. Unfortunately, the Exile never returned to the high status of his former public life. Fortunately, the failed favor, the manuscript *De Principatibus* (*On Principalities*) known to us as *The Prince,* succeeded in its deeper purpose—it changed the way we think about man's law and the higher law. Indeed, the Exile's name—Machiavelli—has defined the modern understanding of the political order since Cinquecento Florence.

The Dangerous Book

The enduring fascination of *The Prince* resides in its stark realism and in Machiavelli's reaction to Savonarola,[3] to other ministers of the Church, and to the great political theorists of ancient Greece and Rome. Whether we read it as a dangerous treatise[4] on politics or, worse, as an evil book,[5] it fascinates precisely because its author dared to express opinions about real world politics that previous authors were too timid to voice themselves. When Plato expressed the triumph of power over the Good, he puts that opinion in the mouth of Thrasymachus.[6] For Plato, as well as Aristotle and the Church Fathers following them, political theory was a theory of the ideal state. Man's weaknesses were explained away as impediments to the Good. Machiavelli simply and clearly rejected the ideal in favor of the real. He sees man's behavior for what it is—flawed, imperfect, and, fundamentally, acquisitive.

The realpolitik[7] of *The Prince* alone cannot explain its endurance or its fascination. Instead, the secret of the book lies in its method as well as its message. Referred to as the first treatise of modern political science,[8] Machiavelli tells us his method in the first paragraph of his Dedicatory Letter to Lorenzo. His favor, Machiavelli writes, is the product of lessons, "learned by me from long experience with modern things and a continuous reading of ancient ones."[9] Machiavelli not only loved the life of action, he loved life to the fullest. One key to understanding the importance of Machiavelli and his contribution to political and moral thought is to see Machiavelli as a Renaissance humanist: "It would not be too much to say, indeed, that he is considered *the* man of the Renaissance."[10] As a man of action and of thought, Machiavelli was aware of and knowledgeable about the classics so admired during the Renaissance. He combined classical knowledge with his diplomatic experiences,[11] and the lessons he learned appear in his plays, histories, letters, and treatise.[12]

The Prince is a revolutionary text coming between ancient Athens and modern America. In the book, Machiavelli merged the ancient and the modern, thought and action, and created a new political theory. The power of the book comes from his observations of the world and for his proposals about how the new learning can be applied by real-world rulers.

Real-world application, Machiavelli asserted, required that ancient learning be separated from modern action by distinguishing the real from the imaginary and by decoupling morality from politics. He believed that it was more important to explain how things work rather than imagine utopias in books no matter how learned.[13] He was concerned with what worked in practice, not with what sounded good in theory. And on this basis, Machiavelli created modern political science. He urged princes to observe what rulers actually did to succeed, and he defined success as acquiring and maintaining power for, "it is a very natural and ordinary thing to desire to acquire, and always, when men do it who can, they will be praised or not blamed. . . ."[14] Instead of contemplating the ideal, Machiavelli argued that princes needed to concentrate on political success instead of recreating the ancient utopias of Plato and Cicero[15] or adopting the ancient virtues of Aristotle.[16]

Machiavelli acknowledges the dark side of human nature, man's fallibility, and the reality that political society necessarily functions with vice as well as, if not better than, with virtue. He understood Thrasymachus, and he understood Creon. Machiavelli would dispute neither Thrasymachus's claim that the stronger define justice nor Creon's claim of human authority to issue his edict.

The political philosophy of Machiavelli is modern and realistic as he believed that "to rule is not essentially to follow the laws of nature and reason but rather to succeed in asserting one's will over others."[17] This formulation of pure politics,[18] of will over reason and over natural law, connects with Thrasymachus's philosophy of power and might makes right. It challenges older notions of the relationship of law, justice, and morality as Machiavelli urges us to rethink these relationships in light of power politics.

Machiavelli inverts shadows and light. The men who see the shadows of power on the wall of the Cave see reality more clearly than those who contemplate the light of the Good. The men in the Cave do not suffer *eikasia* as Plato has it; the philosophers lost in thought do. While the Form of justice is a pretty idea, law, morality, and justice are to be used at the will of the prince as he sees fit to acquire and maintain power. Defenders of natural law, classical political philosophy, or Renaissance Christianity are simply foolish to believe that in the real world of politics, successful princes can afford to observe moral niceties. If they did so, they would sooner be the ruled rather than the rulers. The moral or good man can certainly be admired—as a man but not as a prince.

Direct words and actions are preferred by Machiavelli to rhetoric and sentimentality.[19] Princes do not have time to indulge in fine speeches unless fine speeches advance their acquisition and maintenance of power. The ancients used fulsome phrases to convince and construct ideal states. The modern prince has neither need nor time for such constructions; he is too busy living in the world of action. Inattention to that world and the treachery in it will lead to a prince's demise as history tells repeatedly. While Machiavelli's message is direct and *The Prince* is a short treatise, it is a mistake to neglect its nuance and complexity. Though *The Prince* demystifies law, morality, and justice, it is a mistake to diminish or dismiss the significance of the book on these matters. *The Prince* can be read as an exemplar of the realist view of man's law and the consequences of that view for the higher law of justice. We can treat Machiavelli, then, as the first legal realist.

The Prince can be neatly divided into five sections: the Dedicatory Letter, a description of the types of principalities, a description of the types of armies available to a prince, the identification of the characteristics of good princes, and a commentary about the possibility of a new, unified Italy. Each section references the ancient and the modern to tell its story. More subtlety, and more important, each section explores the psychology of man—ruler and ruled. While the Dedicatory Letter has the distinct ring of a job application to Lorenzo, together with all of the other sections of the work it dramatically breaks away from what had historically passed as political philosophy. Although the book appears to be a manual for princes or advice to would-be rulers, it constitutes a radical theory that commands our current understanding of politics.

The Dedicatory Letter

Machiavelli, always of modest means, had little of material value to offer Lorenzo. He had neither horses nor arms with which Lorenzo could add to his might. Nor could he give cloth of gold or precious stones which Lorenzo could add to the Medici treasury. Even so, Machiavelli offered his homage and with it a special gift. He offered his "knowledge of the actions of great men"[20] based on his direct experience and scholarly study. In the opening paragraph, Machiavelli recognizes the things of the world that a prince needs for success, yet he proffers something more valuable—the lessons of power that have come down through the ages from the ancient to the modern.

This slender volume, Machiavelli tells Lorenzo, is a distillation of his many years of diplomatic service including its many dangers and hardships. Machiavelli relies on Lorenzo's humanity to accept and learn from this book written by a man of lowly station who dares to discuss matters of state and the rules of government with a prince. Machiavelli at once tries to respect Lorenzo's position while earning his respect:

> For just as those who sketch landscapes place themselves down in the plain to consider the nature of mountains and high places and to consider the nature of low places place themselves high atop mountains, similarly, to know well the nature of people one needs to be a prince, and to know well the nature of princes one needs to be of the people.[21]

Machiavelli attempts to persuade Lorenzo of the worth of his project, yet there is more here. He tells Lorenzo that while people are ruled by princes, good princes must learn from the people. Machiavelli does not see himself as subservient to Lorenzo; he sees himself as his equal, maybe even his superior. To avoid any such brash reading, however, Machiavelli closes by telling Lorenzo that if he diligently considers the book, then he will "arrive at the greatness that fortune and your other qualities promise you."[22] And, as a final plea if favor is granted, Machiavelli's undeserved bad fortune can be corrected.

The Dedicatory Letter, in three brief paragraphs, establishes the significant themes of *The Prince*. The wisdom of the ancients must be tempered by the necessities of the moderns. The prince can rule successfully only if he understands the people by coming down from his princely heights. And success will be had only by some combination of talent and fate, of virtue and fortune. Success lies not in the ideal world of the clever political theorist; success lies in the real world of people and princes.

Of Principalities

Nearly half of *The Prince* is reminiscent of Aristotle's *Politics* in that both authors provide definitions and a taxonomy of government types. Reading these chapters for the first several times may not be either pleasant or particularly illuminating. How is it that this great book reads with such a dry scholasticism?[23] There must be more here than taxonomy. And there is. In these chapters, Machiavelli teaches[24] through history as well as experience and through human psychology as well as common sense.

Machiavelli's taxonomy of principalities is more than a list of the kinds of governments available to princes; he also explains the psychological nature of princes, people, and the rules by which they live. By describing the various types of principalities together with their strengths and weaknesses, Machiavelli establishes the context for the central message of the book which is to explain princely success. Success in *The Prince* is simply and clearly defined as acquiring and maintaining princely power.[25] The type of principality most desirable is the one that can be successfully acquired and successfully maintained. Some principalities are easy to acquire but difficult to maintain while others are difficult to acquire but easier to maintain. Success in either case turns on the prince's actions and virtues.

The Prince almost luxuriates in dualities.[26] "All states," writes Machiavelli, "are either republics or principalities." Principalities, in turn, are "either hereditary . . . or they are new." New ones are either "altogether new . . . or they are like members added to the hereditary state. . . ." Finally, principalities are acquired either by a prince's own arms or the arms of others, and they are acquired either by fortune or virtue. These pairings of principalities prefigure the pairings of Machiavelli's virtue to come.

The prince needs more than knowledge of the categories of government to succeed. Starting with Chapter II, Machiavelli's taxonomy elides into social and individual psychology as he concentrates on the difficulties of acquiring and maintaining these different principalities while saying nothing about the structure of government within any. With his discussion of principalities, Machiavelli begins his explanation of the psychology of human nature. He starts with general observations. It is easier to maintain hereditary states than new states as commonsense would tell. New states are difficult to maintain because of their inherent instabilities, but the new states are more attractive as a prince expands his territory and, therefore, new states are more important.

New states come with particular psychologies. Men who live in new principalities are conflicted and untrustworthy. First, they "willingly change their lords in the belief that they will fare better. . . ." If they have changed princes once, they will not be reluctant to change again. To reduce such a risk, the new prince must offend some of his new subjects: "So you have as enemies all those you have offended . . . and you cannot keep as friends those who have put you there because you cannot satisfy them. . . ."[27] The new prince must act strongly and decisively in limiting the risks inherent in acquiring new territories. If, for example, a new prince acquires a new state with the same language, then he has two immediate concerns: "one, that the bloodline of their ancient prince be eliminated; the other, not to alter either their laws or their taxes. . . ."[28] To make his point, Machiavelli tells the story of how Alexander conquered Asia, died shortly thereafter, and yet Asia was maintained by his successors because of his complete routing of Darius and the elimination of his bloodlines—shades of Michael Corleone at the conclusion of *Godfather I.*

New principalities are difficult to hold, particularly if the prince must introduce new orders and new laws. As Machiavelli notes: "And it should be considered that nothing is more difficult to handle, more doubtful of success, nor more dangerous to manage, than to put oneself at the head of introducing new orders."[29] He writes that it is easier to persuade people initially about a new order than to keep them persuaded. To keep them persuaded, force is required, and successful princes must have sufficient arms to maintain their principalities.

In the beginning of the book, Machiavelli mixes history and psychology, learning and experience. But so far, nothing particularly revolutionary emerges. As the book continues, the taxonomy becomes unfamiliar and with that unfamiliarity comes the Machiavellian revolution. Machiavelli's new politics is directed to a specific end. While he is mostly concerned with the acquisition of new principalities, he is not interested in acquisition for acquisition's sake. At the end of the book, Machiavelli urges Lorenzo to acquire the new principality of a liberated and unified Italy. While knowledge of the sorts of principalities is insufficient to master them, knowledge of the most difficult principality, the new principality is necessary for the new prince.

In Chapter VI we are introduced to his special conception of virtue because once a new principality is acquired, it can only be maintained by virtue. To begin his explanation of virtue, Machiavelli discusses the "most excellent" princes: Moses, Cyrus, Romulus, and Thesus—the founders of the kingdoms of Judea, Persia, Rome, and Greece. While we might easily perceive Moses as virtuous, how is it that all of the other conquerors could be similarly understood? Machiavelli says they all should be considered together because each had the opportunity to rule a new principality, and those opportunities enabled them to exercise their virtues: "Such opportunities, therefore, made these men happy, and their excellent virtue enabled the opportunity to be *recognized.* . . ."[30] We are beginning to see that "virtue" is used in a different way from which we normally use it, and it is certainly used differently from how Aristotle or the Church Fathers wrote about it. Virtue in *The Prince* is directly connected with successful acquisition and maintenance, not moral goodness. Each of the princes Machiavelli mentions successfully acquires his principality and demonstrates an excellence of virtue in maintaining them; each one is recognized as a grand and noble leader.

Girolamo Savonarola provides Machiavelli with a counterexample of princely excellence. The friar had the fear of God to motivate and control the people of Florence, but he could not maintain his rule. Savonarola's downfall was that he convinced the people that a new order was needed, specifically that France was about to invade Florence and as a result, the Medici would be out of power; however, Savonarola had no second act. "He was ruined in his new orders as soon as the multitude began not to believe in them, and he had no mode for holding firm those who had believed nor for making the unbelievers believe."[31] Savonarola had his "principality" but had no idea of what to do with it, especially after he lost favor with the pope. He was out of favor and out of power. Having failed to keep the people persuaded, the good citizens of Florence tortured Savonarola into a confession, then a recantation, and finally a hanging followed by his own personal bonfire of the vanities.

To explain how new principalities are more easily acquired by fortune but maintained with more difficulty, Machiavelli tells the contrasting stories of Francesco Sforza and Cesare Borgia. Sforza was a private citizen, not a member of the ruling elite, who through great guile and hard work acquired Milan. He was able to acquire and maintain his principality because of his great virtue. By contrast, Borgia acquired then lost his principality in the Romagna through the fortune of his father, Pope Alexander VI, yet exercised great virtue in its maintenance.

For Machiavelli, Borgia is the exemplar of the modern prince. Machiavelli writes that he could not give "better teaching . . . to a new prince than the example of his actions."[32] He says that if he "summed up all the actions of the duke, [he] would not know how to reproach him. . . ."[33] Borgia should be imitated for his virtue in maintaining the Romagna. His downfall came due to Alexander's death and his own bad health.

Borgia began his maintenance of power early. When first confronted by his enemies, the Orsini family, he displayed great virtue in dispatching them. He started his acquisition of power by bribing many of the Orsini "gentlemen," and once weakened, the Orsini agreed to meet with Borgia at which time they were all murdered. To solidify his control, Borgia needed to subdue the Romagna and did so through two acts. First, he placed his lieutenant, Remirro de Orco, "a cruel and ready man," in charge of the Romanga to do his initial bidding. De Orco achieved a peace of sorts through fear and intimidation of the citizens. Then, after his reign of terror, Borgia distanced himself by setting up civil courts in each province. More graphically, to demonstrate that de Orco's actions were not his own, Borgia had him placed in a piazza in two pieces with a piece of wood and a bloody knife beside him. "The ferocity of this spectacle left the people at once satisfied and stupefied."[34]

Praising the cruel Cesare appears strange. How is it that Machiavelli can call him virtuous? And how can Borgia serve as a model of the successful prince? Borgia is the perfect foil for Machiavelli as he introduces realism into politics by redefining virtue. Machiavelli proclaims Borgia's virtues and uses them as a prelude to the heart of the book:

> So whoever judges it necessary in his new principality to secure himself against enemies, to gain friends to himself, to conquer either by force or by fraud, to make himself loved and feared by the people, and followed and revered by the soldiers, to eliminate those who can or might offend you, to renew old orders through new modes, to be severe and pleasant, magnanimous and liberal, to eliminate an unfaithful military, to create a new one, to maintain friendships with kings and princes so that they must either benefit you with favor or be hesitant to offend you—can find no fresher examples than the actions of that man.[35]

Cesare was not so good of a man, yet Machiavelli praises the reproachable Borgia together with the most excellent Moses. Are we to equate these two men? Moses and Borgia successfully acquired and maintained new principalities. They differed, however, in their virtues. Moses possessed the virtues of the ancients. Borgia required new virtues, the virtues that Machiavelli invented for modern politics. In the quotation above, he attributes those characteristics to Borgia which, later in the book, are the "virtues" a prince needs to succeed.

If we do not share Machiavelli's assessment of Borgia's virtues, things get even stickier when he discusses princes who have acquired their principalities through crimes. The "hero" of that tale is Agathocles who, in his quest to become king of Syracuse, invited all of the senators and the richest people in town to a morning announcement. Once assembled, they were all murdered by his soldiers. Of Agathocles' exploits,

Machiavelli writes: "Yet one cannot call it virtue to kill one's citizens, betray one's friends, to be without faith, without mercy, without religion; these modes can enable one to acquire empire, but not glory." Nevertheless, he praises Agathocles for the strength and greatness of his spirit.[36]

How is it that Agathocles lacks virtue *and* possesses it? How is Agathocles different from Cesare Borgia? Machiavelli does not deny that Agothocles possessed the virtues he recognized and praised in Borgia. But Agothocles' excesses prevented him from attaining glory. To fully succeed, a form of moderation is required, as Machiavelli distinguishes cruelties badly used from those well used: "Those can be called well used (if it is permissible to speak well of evil) that are done at a stroke, out of the necessity to secure oneself, and then are not persisted in but are turned to as much utility for the subjects as one can. Those cruelties are badly used which, though few in the beginning, rather grow with time than are eliminated."[37] There are limits to the use of the virtues one needs to acquire and maintain power. Evil cannot be used for evil's sake.

Machiavelli ends this part of *The Prince* with a brief discussion of two other principalities—civil and ecclesiastical. Both are outside of his primary concern, which are the city-states of Italy such as Florence, which are controlled by princes such as Lorenzo. A civil principality is a loose democracy. The prince accedes to power through the support of his fellow citizens who may be either the people or the great. While it is easier for a prince to come to power through the great, it is more difficult to maintain his rule. It is better to have the support of the people.

The Prince concludes Machiavelli's discussions of principalities with a principality of a special and unique nature—ecclesiastical principalities. There is only one ecclesiastical principality—Rome. And Rome posses a special attribute. "[O]nly these principalities are secure and happy . . . they subsist by superior causes, to which the human mind does not reach . . . for since they are exalted and maintained by God, it would be the office of a presumptuous and foolhardy man to discourse on them."[38] But discourse on them he does cleverly and politically sensitively.

Machiavelli is politically sensitive given the family relationship between the Medici and the Papacy, for Lorenzo's uncle is the reigning Pope Leo X, also son of Il Magnifico. Machiavelli knows that however much he desires to criticize the Church of Rome, the political reality is that the Church has mixed the spiritual with the temporal, just as the House of Medici in Florence is mixed with the House of God in Rome. He is clever as well. Rome's power may well come from God; more important though, it comes from its temporal might. Popes Alexander VI and Julius II, who succeeded him, built Rome into a political superpower. As Machiavelli recounts, Alexander prevailed with "money and forces,"[39] and Julius "found the path still open to a mode of accumulating money, never used before Alexander."[40] We can thank Julius for the Reformation because his moneymaking scheme was selling indulgences.[41] Rome was strong not only with God on its side but with its armies and its treasury. Machiavelli closes by saying that Pope Leo X inherited great power and that together with his great virtue, could make Rome, "very great and venerable."[42] We will see that Machiavelli wrote a part in this greatness for Lorenzo. Flattery may not be a virtue of princes, but it is of authors.

Princes and Arms

We have been introduced to a new vocabulary of politics and a new way of thinking and talking about how we live in organized society.[43] Machiavelli's taxonomy not only lists the sorts of princely states, he lists the natures of the rulers and the ruled who inhabit them. This new politics continues as *The Prince* discusses the types of arms a prince can use to acquire and maintain a principality. Again, Machiavelli uses no ordinary taxonomy. He notes, instead, that a prince must have "good foundations," otherwise he will be ruined. The principal foundations are good arms and good laws because "there cannot be good laws where there are not good arms, and where there are good arms there must be good laws. . . ."[44] Machiavelli tantalizes us with law and while he does not expressly say much about it either here or throughout the book, he has a deep and sophisticated appreciation for the roles that law plays in principalities. When Machiavelli uses the word law, he is only referring to man's law, not the higher law. He would accept Hart's paraphrase of John Austin that laws are simply "orders backed by threats."[45]

Machiavelli's greater concern is arms because without suitable arms Italy cannot be united. The greatest failure of Italian princes was their inability to give arms sufficient attention. While there are four types of arms—a prince's own, mercenary, auxiliary, or mixed—the only dependable armies are a prince's own. Machiavelli supports this point through historical examples and human psychology. "[W]ithout its own arms no principality is secure; indeed it is wholly obliged to fortune since it does not have virtue to defend itself in adversity."[46] The arms of others will either fail a prince or betray him.

The preeminence of arms is stressed by Machiavelli: "A prince should have no other object, nor any other thought, nor take anything else as his art but that of war and its orders and discipline; for that is the only art which is of concern to one who commands."[47] More specifically, the prince must attend to the art of war through study of the ancients and constant training. The single measure of any prince is whether he can assemble an army to fight and win any battle.[48] Arms are a necessity of princes without which they can achieve nothing.

Machiavelli's *Virtù*

Machiavelli's analysis of virtue, to be renamed *virtù*, forms the core of *The Prince*[49] and contains its most familiar passages. Harvey Mansfield defines *virtù* as, "a prudent or well-taught combination of vice and virtue in the old meaning."[50] Quentin Skinner defines it as "that quality which enables a prince to withstand the blows of Fortune, to attract the goddess's favor, and to rise in consequence to the heights of princely fame, winning honour and glory for himself, and security for his government."[51] These definitions of *virtù* are indifferent to moral content.

At one level these chapters read like a modern leadership manual. At another, they have transformed political theory. This central section is introduced by the two rich paragraphs of Chapter XV. Machiavelli explains that many have written about political leadership—Plato and Cicero come to mind—and although he does not want to be seen as presumptuous, it is his intention to, "depart from the orders of others. . . . to write something useful to whoever understands it [and] . . . go to directly the effectual truth of the thing than to the imagination of it."[52] He addresses Lorenzo about how people actually live and how princes actually rule, not how ancient theorists imagine the ideal state or the good life to be.

While Machiavelli understands talk of the Good; he also understands its risks. A man can propose to be good and lead a good life, but he will come to ruin at the hands of those who are not. *"Hence it is necessary to a prince, if he wants to maintain himself, to learn to be able not to be good, and to use this and not use it according to necessity."*[53] Machiavelli is very careful. He states that a prince must learn to be "not good."[54] He does not say that a prince must learn to be evil. A prince must learn to use evil and to be "not good" when necessity demands it and for no other reason. Machiavelli will not countenance evil for evil's sake any more than he will countenance good for good's sake. Evil and good, virtue and vice, exist to be used and even manipulated by the prince, "when forced by necessity."[55]

Chapter XV also previews the list of character traits that a prince must have to succeed and which Machiavelli discusses in the following chapters. He acknowledges that it would be "praiseworthy" if a prince possessed all of the character traits people perceive as good without the vices, but "human conditions do not permit it."[56] The prince must use vice as well as virtue to maintain his state.

Before Machiavelli, writers listed those traits or habits of character that we recognize as virtues. For Plato, the virtues of wisdom, courage, and temperance formed the virtue of justice. For Aristotle, the virtues when habitually used built character. And for Aquinas, the virtues were faith, hope, and charity. For each thinker, the virtues were equated with the Good, and to possess these virtues meant that a person possessed goodness.

Reading *The Prince,* one is tempted to distinguish evil princes like the sadistic tyrant Agathocles the Sicilian, from morally worthy leaders like Alexander the Great and Moses. This temptation must be resisted to appreciate and understand the book. Morality instead goes on holiday. Machiavelli consistently rejects classical and Christian conceptions of virtue and consistently distinguishes them from success in politics which constitutes Machiavelli's *virtù.* Isaiah Berlin argues that Machiavelli simply exchanges older pagan or Roman virtues for the then-contemporary Christian virtues, and therefore, he never abandons virtue.[57] We can read *The Prince* differently though. Machiavelli does not desire excellence in a prince as a man; he rather defines excellence as political success apart from any specific set of virtues, Christian or pagan.

Machiavelli warns that the labels virtue and vice are illusory in the search for power. To emphasize his point, he lists the qualities that bring either praise or blame to princes. At first glance, his list appears to form contrasting dualities:

Liberal	Mean
Giver	Rapacious
Cruel	Merciful
Breaker of Faith	Faithful
Effeminate and Pusillanimous	Fierce and Spirited
Humane	Proud
Lascivious	Chaste

Honest	Astute
Hard	Agreeable
Grave	Light
Religious	Unbelieving[58]

These traits, though, do not fall into strict opposing categories. Neither column can be labeled all good nor all bad. In the first column, for example, a person could be religious, but not cruel, or honest but not lascivious simultaneously, which is precisely Machiavelli's point. These are human characteristics to be used by the prince in the service of power as necessity demands.

With his discussion of *virtù*, Machiavelli probes more deeply into the psychologies of ruler and ruled. A prince may desire to be well-regarded, but such regard in and of itself is of no value. It may even be harmful. A prince should not fear a reputation for meanness because it is "one of those vices which enable[s] him to rule."[59] A reputation for liberality, to the contrary, can lead to contempt and undermine the prince and the state. A prince should desire a reputation as merciful but not to the point of losing control of the people. He can keep the people in check through cruelty and fear. While people desire the Good, they desire property even more. While people can be motivated by love, fear motivates more surely and more reliably because fear is controlled by the prince whereas love, often fickle, is given by the people.

While a prince should strive to appear to have all of the good qualities, it is appearance more than possession that matters. The reason for such duplicity is simple. Men, Machiavelli says, are "ungrateful, fickle, pretenders and dissemblers, evaders of danger, eager for gain."[60] Men will lie, cheat, and steal unless checked by a prince who recognizes human nature for what it is and is not afraid to be not good even using fear instead of love to gain men's respect. What people respect one day in a person, for example, religiosity, they will despise another. Results matter, not intentions. As long as the prince succeeds in maintaining his principality and the people are secure in it, he will win the people. "[W]here there is no court to appeal to, one looks to the end. So let a prince win and maintain his state: the means will always be judged honorable and will be praised by everyone."[61]

Machiavelli's *virtù* is of a different order of excellence.[62] *Virtù* is not a list of traits or habits that culminate or lead to the Good. Instead, *virtù* is an attitude about men and behavior, about fortune and freedom which leads to state stability. Machiavelli is living in and concerned about the temporal world, not the next one.[63] For him the common good is a temporal condition, not a spiritual one.

Machiavelli introduces us to an entirely new political world in which the morals of the classicists and of the Church are stood on their head by being intentionally undermined. There is nothing "higher" than or "above" politics. There is only the successful exercise of power through *virtù*. Machiavelli decoupled morality from politics and in turn decoupled man's law from the higher law. The *deus ex machina* for the decoupling was *virtù*. Machiavelli is not the first person we have met to assert that virtue has nothing to do with justice. The honor goes to Thrasymachus in Plato's *Republic*. However, Machiavelli was the most notable writer to claim that position as his own, and he did so at the height of the Roman Church's power. Machiavelli earned the labels evil and dangerous because he ejected morality from the public sphere of politics contrary to the teachings of the great theologians and moral philosophers.

Unifying Italy

Throughout *The Prince*, Machiavelli mentions fortune and, in the penultimate chapter, says that this "violent river" accounts for half of man's actions with free will counting for the other half. The successful prince is a man of action and although he may not be able to control all events, he can develop the *virtù* necessary to respond to fortune when it calls on him. *Fortuna* affects man, no doubt, but *virtù* can affect fortune as well. Man can control that impetuous force through the conscious application of *virtù*, "because fortune is a woman; and it is necessary, if one wants to hold her down, to beat her and strike her down."[64] Machiavelli is creating not only a new prince, he is creating a new man—a man who can look *Fortuna* in the eyes and contend with, if not control, her.

The last section of *The Prince* is Machiavelli's call for the new man, the new prince who can unite Italy. He rebukes those princes of the city-states who failed to keep the kings of France, Spain, and Germany as well as Rome, outside of their borders. Uniting Italy is the task for a great prince, Lorenzo perhaps. The prince who learns Machiavelli's lessons can consolidate his new principality with "good laws, good arms, good friends, and good examples. . . ."[65] This new prince can also learn to avoid the mistakes of the lords of Naples and Milan and others who never secured adequate arms to maintain their principalities.

The Prince closes with an exhortation about the need for a new prince, "someone prudent and virtuous"[66] to introduce a new form of government to liberate Italy, as Moses liberated the people of Israel and Cyrus liberated the Persians. Lorenzo, with his fortune and his *virtù* and the support of God through his uncle Pope Leo X, is just such a person. Lorenzo and his illustrious house can initiate new laws and new orders to his great glory as Machiavelli closes with lines from Petrarch:

Virtue will take up arms against fury,
and make the battle short,
because the ancient valor in Italian hearts
is not yet dead.[67]

Machiavelli's taxonomy of governments, his psychology, his manual of power politics, and his redefinition of virtue are all used in the service of creating a great republican Italy. The new prince will need strength and guile enough to overcome popular pieties and to confront the challenges that *Fortuna* brings with her. Machiavelli knew that this was no easy task because those popular pieties were deeply embedded in thought and behavior. To shake people away from old habits required an audacious assault on Christian morality—a task Machiavelli engages with relish.

Machiavelli and the Church

The convent of San Marco lives as a symbol of Quattrocento Florence and of Machiavelli's world. In 1436, Cosimo the Elder commissioned his favorite architect, Michelozzo, to design and build the convent as a gift to the people of Florence. Today, the convent stands as a serene retreat from the busy streets of *centro storico* as it served Cosimo di Medici as a retreat from his banking empire. San Marco is a square two-story structure with the world's first public library attached to it. The first floor, adorned with meditative frescoes, encloses a garden as the downstairs loggia offers relief from the summer heat and the elements of the other seasons.

The living quarters on the second floor are entered by a large staircase leading to a small landing. Turning right on the landing, there is a set of seven steps and, with each step, more is revealed of Fra Angelico's *Annunciation*, a fresco of such stunning luminescence that it captures the luxury as well as piety of the Renaissance. The main halls of the second floor contain the monks' cells, also decorated with Fra Angelico frescoes. At the end of one corridor there are richly decorated rooms and a chapel for Cosimo. At the other end of the building is Savonarola's austere, unadorned cell.

The contrasts between indulgence and piety, patron and friar, City and Soul are unmistakable. These contrasts provided Savonarola with fodder for his sermons which captivated the Florentines and led to the temporary fall of the House of Medici and to Savonarola's own rise to power in 1494.[68] Ironically, Savonarola had been summoned to Florence by Il Magnifico, Lorenzo di Medici, in 1490. Story has it that Savonarola refused to meet with, and pay homage to, Lorenzo on his arrival. On Lorenzo's deathbed in 1492, the story continues: Savonarola refused to bless Lorenzo until he promised liberty for the people of Florence. While apocryphal, the tale defines Savonarola.

Florentines experienced the vast wealth held by the Medici and other merchant and banking families. The people of Florence worked for these families and could see the accumulation of riches and the power that they wielded over their lives. Savonarola railed against the material excesses of the rich, preached that Florence was doomed in the eyes of God, and that only by ridding Florence of such ostentation could the city be saved. His children's army was pressed into the service of relieving Florentines of their material excesses such as finery, jewelry, paintings, and other valuables that were burnt on Savonarola's bonfires of the vanities.

Machiavelli had a jaundiced view of Savonarola. While he recognized Savonarola's accumulation of power as a feat worthy of any natural prince, he also recognized that Savonarola's actions were based on a falsehood. Machiavelli had heard Savonarola's sermons and observed that "he had persuaded a 'vast' number of Florentines 'that he spoke with God.'"[69] The wise prince uses religion to pacify the people. The wise prince does not confuse God and man; he does not confuse Soul and City. Rome's greatness and its hypocrisy were based on combining the temporal with the spiritual. Savonarola was guilty of the same hypocrisy, and that sin caused his own downfall.[70]

Rodrigo Borgia, Pope Alexander VI, watched Savonarola's growing popularity. Even though Alexander was no friend to the Medici, he was more fearful that Savonarola's criticism of the Florentine leaders would have the same powerful effect when the criticism was trained on a Rome guilty of the same excesses of the Medici, Pazzi, Pitti, Tornabuoni, and other rich Florentine families. To prevent Savonarola from turning his attention to Rome, Alexander had him excommunicated in 1497. This was a clear signal to Savonarola's enemies that Rome would not stand in their way of ridding Florence of the bothersome monk. In 1498, Savonarola was tried in Florence, tortured, hanged, and then burned on the same spot of his own bonfires in the Piazza della Signoria.

Machiavelli criticized Savonarola for his inability to sustain the power he had accumulated. He could not endorse exalting God while exercising political power. This hypocrisy was too much even for Machiavelli who wanted us to understand the divorce between morality and politics, a divorce that Savonarola did not recognize. His criticism of Savonarola mirrored his criticism of Rome. Machiavelli's antipathy toward the Church was based not on its spiritual might; rather his disdain was a criticism of the Church's accumulation of temporal power which came at too high a price for him. While he admired the acquisitive success of the ecclesiastical principality, he believed that the Church's efforts contributed to Italy's weakness and its inability to unify.

Machiavelli understood the role that customs such as morality and religion play in society. These customs comfort man and can be used to maintain the state. Princes cannot be "without faith, without mercy, without religion" and attain glory.[71] A successful prince must at least appear faithful, honest, and religious.[72] Roman Catholic morality is to be used by the prince for his political ends; it has instrumental value which can be used to acquire and maintain power and secure the stability of the state.

The Machiavellian Paradox

Machiavelli deeply affected political thought in two ways. The more visible transformation was turning virtue into *virtù*. The second, but not less significant, transformation was the separation of morality from politics. Morality, as the end of political man, was the last thing that Machiavelli would advocate. It is also doubtful if he would advocate the moral life as the end of man in any respect. Once a friend confided his marital infidelity to Machiavelli and said that he was troubled by it. Machiavelli replied that he believed what "Boccaccio says is true: it is better to act and repent than not to act and regret."[73] More poignant is Machiavelli's deathbed story in which he professes to prefer hell to heaven for hell is where he is more likely to find his friends, great thinkers, and the Great Conversation among the famous men of Antiquity including Plato, Plutarch, Livy, and Tacitus. Regarding the blessed poor, he says that he is, "not tagging along with those ragbags to go to paradise." He prefers to stay, "with that other company, to talk about the state, and go to hell.[74]

The central claim of *The Prince* is that Christian morality should play no more than a supporting role to politics. The divorce between politics and morality, between City and Soul made the term Machiavellian a term of opprobrium, not honor. Today this divorce remains troublesome as we continue to debate the role of and the extent that morality should play in government and in our law. We suffer from the Machiavellian Paradox. We accept Machiavellian rulers who act in ways that violate common morality. And we accept the rationale that they do so for "political" reasons. As a society, we tolerate and excuse much public wrongdoing as long as we are safe from terrorists, enjoy a vibrant economy, or have the benefits of health, jobs, and education. At the same time, we yearn for more morality in our society and in our law. We want our law to reflect our values even as we contest and debate which values the law should reflect.

The first leg of the Machiavellian Paradox is power politics. We are familiar with and do not shy away from its use. In the halls of government, in corporate board rooms, indeed even in academic institutions,[75] power politics is understood as the way of the world. The first principle of United States' foreign policy is "advancing our security and political interests. . . ."[76] which receives widespread nonpartisan support. While it is true that we prefer a morally good leader, moral goodness is secondary if not incidental. We tolerated one president's sexual peccadilloes and another's lack of candor about war and the economy. Our desire for order, protection, and self-preservation is primal and not surprising. What is surprising is our continually felt need to justify that desire with moral claims which constitutes the second leg of the Machiavellian Paradox. We struggle with the conflict between man's law and the higher law, a conflict that posed no struggle whatsoever for Machiavelli.

For Machiavelli, private life can well attend to moral concerns; public life cannot afford to do so and survive. Princely behavior ignores accepted morality. Yet, instead of extracting morality from politics, people desire its inclusion.[77] Here Machiavelli is most instructive. The Machiavellian Paradox is that we accept the amoral or immoral use of power while we want our laws to be moral and just. The conflict between desire and experience exposes the dual sides of princely authority and our responses to it. Princes must learn to be not good and people must learn to accept it even though we reserve the right to criticize the prince's bad actions. The Machiavellian

Paradox is that, as citizens, we want it both ways. We want law to be used instrumentally to protect us, and we want our laws to be intrinsically moral and just.

We must be careful, though, about confusing desire and experience and about mixing man's law with the higher law. The quest to import the higher law into man's law or to import morality into the prince's public policies can weaken the state if the prince ignores the distinctions between them. Machiavelli was critical of ecclesiastical principalities for mixing the temporal with the spiritual. As a result, their mission became confused, and the principalities were weakened. His core claim is that politics is a distinct realm of behavior and that a prince must use his *virtù* to maintain that realm. The prince who mixes the higher law with man's law does so at a risk to his rule.

Man's Law and the Higher Law in the Machiavelli

As a work of modern political science, *The Prince* says remarkably little, at least directly, about either law or justice. Law is mentioned a dozen times and justice half of that. Law and justice are treated like morality and religion as having instrumental, not intrinsic, value. In this way, the prince is unconstrained by either the authority of the law or by the moral virtue of justice. Machiavelli's principality prefigures the Hobbesian world of struggles among men over power.[78] Machiavelli's prince appears like Creon or Hart's Rex I, a leader who defines law as those orders that his subjects obey without questioning his legitimacy[79] because law is backed by sanctions.[80] When necessity demands it, the prince must breach the law or ignore justice to maintain power. This description of law in *The Prince* is Machiavellian in the common but incorrect understanding of the term, but it is too thin and inadequate for Machiavelli's philosophy.

Machiavelli's references to the law are more complex and revolutionary. He is a "revolutionary," according to political philosopher Leo Strauss, because he is "a man who breaks the law, the law as a whole, in order to replace it by a new law which he believes to be better than the old law."[81] Note what Strauss says here. From the misused term Machiavellian, we might conclude that Machiavelli dispensed with the law entirely when it suited a prince's purposes. This understanding is wrong. Law in *The Prince*, and in Machiavelli's *Discourses on Livy*,[82] exhibits several significant and complex functions: (1) law connects the people to their history and to their customs;

(2) law brings order to society because the majority of men favoring stability follow it;[83] (3) law controls men through fear of sanction;[84] (4) law makes men good by controlling their base instincts;[85] and (5) when the prince follows the law, he sets a good example thus controlling men, maintaining order, and gaining a favorable reputation.[86] Law plays an important, even necessary, role in a principality, but law is not autonomous. "For Niccolò, then, law is not self-nourishing. Apart from an ecology of custom, arms and religion, it withers on the vine."[87]

Law, however, still possesses a fair measure of force. Machiavelli warns the prince not to alter existing laws[88] because law is needed, has the respect of, and is relied upon by the people. In principalities with laws of their own, the prince should let the people keep their laws[89] not only because people are comfortable living with them but also because new orders upset social stability and are difficult to maintain.[90]

Law also has a distinct relationship with arms. "The principal foundation[] [of] all states . . . are good law and good arms."[91] Are good laws necessary for good arms? Or do good arms support good laws? Both relationships are possible as arms and laws function together and support each other. Good arms enable acquisition and maintenance of the principality. They check mercenaries who threaten the state,[92] and good laws thwart conspirators.[93] Laws and arms must both be used in the maintenance of power:

> Thus, you must know that there are two kinds of combat: one with laws, the other with force. The first is proper to man, the second to beasts; but because the first is often not enough, one must have recourse to the second. Therefore it is necessary for a prince to know well how to use the beast and the man.[94]

While laws have force for Machiavelli, they may not have force enough; therefore, arms supplement laws. The prince must be lion enough to frighten away wolves who threaten the state and fox enough to avoid the snares of those who would depose him. Arms and laws help him accomplish both.

The prince is ultimately not constrained by law and must break it when necessary. He must not waiver when forced to breach his faith with his people and break treaties and promises when necessary, for a prince never lacks, "legitimate causes to color his failure to observe faith."[95] Even though the prince can break the law, he must stand ready to explain the breech because of the respect that the people have for law.[96] Machiavelli concludes his reference to law when he tells Lorenzo, at the end of the book, that good laws can help unite Italy, and that Lorenzo is the right prince to establish the new laws and new orders.

Justice, certainly as compared with Plato's *Republic*, is mentioned briefly, but it is not absent from *The Prince* and certainly not absent from Machiavelli's thought.[97] His explicit references to justice are pointed. Justice can be used by princes to be held in high esteem.[98] More important, however, "great justice" comes in redeeming Italy as he implores Lorenzo.[99] Like law, justice is to be used, not venerated by successful princes.

Princely *virtù* uses law and justice to further the common good. "The greatest lawgivers, he has shown, are those who have understood most clearly how to use law in order to advance the cause of civic greatness."[100] Stability and the common good form Machiavelli's concept of justice.[101] His reading of the ancients and his observation of the moderns revealed to him that Italy needed a new man, a new leader—the new prince. The new prince will discard theoretical and idealistic political and moral pieties and will substitute princely *virtù* in the service of the state, its stability, its unity, and its freedom.

Is justice so conceived foreign to us? Or is it familiar? The Machiavellian Revolution is the realization and acceptance of the idea that to achieve political ends, the new prince must learn to be "not good" in exercising the art of the state.[102] For Aristotle and Plato, virtue is a matter of consistent character that leads to justice and to the Good; in Machiavelli, *virtù* is variable and supports power. The virtuous prince uses man's law and the higher law to a specific end—political power. In this way, Machiavelli stood Christian virtue on its head. *Virtù* for him is the human capacity to do human things; it is neither divinely inspired nor spiritually useful in the political world in which we live. Machiavelli has nothing to say about the Good as commonly understood by the Church at the time, by the ancient political philosophers or, as commonly understood today. Just as Machiavelli redefines virtue, he redefines and distinguishes law and justice.

The First Realist

Machiavelli's insight is that classical and Christian political thought are about imagined, unreal worlds. These worlds are foreign to and unobtainable by political man. In fact, these worlds are impossible to model given the human condition. As a prince, it is folly to try to create a government on such imaginings for such efforts are doomed to fail. Machiavelli could easily have mimicked Hume and said that since life is nasty, brutish, and short, we should not bother to capture heaven on earth; rather, we should live within the human condition and set rules to minimize human disruption, thus maximizing what we can accomplish by way of living together. The matter of the Soul is a matter for God; the matter of the City is a matter for man.

What is central for Machiavelli is the decoupling of the higher law from man's law. What is central for us is to recognize and acknowledge the distinction for the better attainment of both. The strongest statement that we can make about legal positivism is that law has, and should have, no necessary connection with morality. The more realistic statement is that we often confuse man's law with the higher law as we saw in our discussion of First Amendment religion cases in Chapter 1. Our confusion is pervasive because our desire for the Good is strong. It is so strong, in fact, that Dame Iris Murdoch famously argued that the Good is more prevalent in societies than God.[103] Nevertheless, understanding the distinction between man's law and the higher law is necessary to understanding Machiavelli, and the argument goes that it is a valuable and even necessary condition for understanding the proper role of law in society and the proper relationship between law and justice.

The standard reading of *The Prince* is that Machiavelli is advocating the exercise of political power in the face of claims of law or of morality or of justice. This reading leaves the prince unconstrained. A better reading is that the new prince is not unconstrained. Rather he is restrained by *virtù*, and he must use his *virtù* nimbly. He cannot do whatever he wishes for the sake of exercising power. Power must, and should only, be used in acquiring and maintaining a principality. If the prince takes a man's property, patrimony, or women, he risks losing his rule, and he has not exercised his *virtù* well.[104] While the prince is not completely constrained by law or justice, he is constrained by the prudent exercise of *virtù*.

Man's law enables certain actions—and enables states and their modern princes—to further a specific common good which is the stability and security of the state. Law, then, is an instrument of the prince's political power although it is wrong to say that law exists at the prince's whim.[105] Law emanates from explicitly political institutions which exist for any number of political ends,[106] not for the single purpose of achieving a single Good.

Man's law is about what is, not what ought to be. Man's law helps the prince administer his principality; it allows the state to function.

Law, then, can be considered as a behavioral or social science, the science of furthering the ends of the prince or the ends of the state. Laws which keep society stable rather than corrupt and which keep the prince strong and in power, rather than weak and deposed, are the good laws not necessarily the laws of the Good. Law and justice can both be used to mollify the people; the prince should appear to honor both; and, both can be breached as necessity demands. The wise prince would do well to study the laws of the great leaders as much as he studies the tactics of the great generals.[107]

The Legal Realists, like Machiavelli, saw their brand of jurisprudence as a descriptive, purposive enterprise rather than as an idealistic one. They wanted to understand and explain how law actually operated in the world, not how it should ideally be used. So conceived, law could be analyzed apart from its morality or justice. Legal realism, like legal positivism to an extent, separates morality from law yet it looks somewhat differently at law by focusing on its political and policy dimensions. While rejecting overarching claims for *The Law*, the Realist movement had two distinct dimensions. First, Legal Realism was critical. Next, it offered prescriptions for how law could better function stripped from its airy pretensions.

The realists were a self-described rag-tag group of scholars[108] writing primarily in the 1920s and 1930s through a series of books and articles, no one of which attained the canonical status of *The Concept of Law* for example.[109] The Realists developed a set of principles which continue to occupy our jurisprudential thoughts today whether we see these principles as pragmatic amplifications of how law "really" works in society or as critical precepts to be applied when legal theory becomes too abstract and unconnected from the business at hand.

Legal realism had specific targets. The law, as Oliver Wendell Holmes, Jr. would have it, is not a "brooding omnipresence in the sky"[110] waiting for judges, Herculean or otherwise, to find the right legal answer to the questions before them. The idea that law is a whole, providing determinate answers to legal disputes is "transcendental nonsense."[111] Law, so conceived, is based on a misconception. "The law always has been, is now, and will ever continue to be, largely vague and variable."[112] Law resides in facts on the ground, not in theories in the air.

The Legal Realists were reacting to late nineteenth century jurisprudential thought that the rule of law could be scientifically understood; that a legal system could be logically constructed from those rules; and, that once constructed, legal questions could find determinate answers. In rejecting these propositions, Holmes's aphorism that law is not based on logic, it is based on experience,[113] could not be more true.

Experience taught the Realists that law posed open-ended questions; that legal formalism and autonomy were chimerical; and, that judicial decision making was less predictable, more susceptible to policy and politics, and more quixotic than their predecessors posited. These Realist beliefs, however, did not necessarily collapse into cynicism. The law was not measured by the length of the prince's foot. Rather, the open textures of the law allowed law to serve its social purposes. Law was not infinitely elastic; but it was elastic enough to establish rules and principles for economic growth, social coordination, political participation, individual liberty and freedom, and other recognizable "felt necessities."[114]

Accepting the reality that not all legal questions have answers in existing legal materials raised difficult and troublesome questions. If there were no determinate legal answers to specific legal questions, then how do judges decide cases? Realists offered several responses, none of which satisfies any desire for law's unity or wholeness. Judges could decide cases based on personal or political biases or hunches,[115] or judges could hypothesize some method such as situation sense,[116] for deciding cases. As justice Benjamin Cardozo writes: "Every judge consulting his own experience must be conscious of times when a free exercise of will, directed of set purpose to the furtherance of the common good, determined the form and tendency of a rule which at that moment took its origin in one creative act."[117]

The Realists were concerned with what appeared to them as the false notion that law could be mechanically applied. Today we can update mechanical jurisprudence[118] through the image of a computer. Imagine a computer fully loaded with all the extant legal materials in all the world's law libraries. Our imaginary computer would contain all of the cases, statutes, constitutions, and legal commentary ever written about law. So loaded, it would seem, that we could input a question into our law computer and receive in a matter of moments a legal response after our Pentium processor scanned our universal law library. While it may well be the case that most questions will receive reliable answers, there will always be those cases, sometime called hard cases, which do not. Sometimes hard cases pose questions of fundamental human importance; other times the hard cases are fundamentally prosaic. Panels of judges have disagreed about how to interpret the phrase, "navigable waters,"[119] while other panels have disagreed about whether same-sex marriage is constitutionally protected.[120]

For the Legal Realists, indeterminacy begged not only questions about how to decide cases, it begged questions about the end or ends of law. If law is to be used incrementally,[121] then to what end? Presumably to the good end of a better society. But that end was too grand, by half, for the Realists. The Realists offered no good answer to this grand question beyond expressing the desire to better understand how judges decide cases and to debunk the illusion that the law was a reliable whole and an end in itself. Realism was a method[122] guided by some sense of arriving at just outcomes[123] and for furthering such polices as improving commercial transactions, mediating corporate power, and rationalizing the administrative state—good ends, indeed, but not claiming too much for law.

Legal Realism is in many ways a transitional jurisprudence. In its two modes of criticizing grand theories and proposing effective methods for delivering law, the Realists moved law out of the nineteenth century and made possible the jurisprudential movements of the twentieth. Legal Realism rejects formalism and acknowledges pragmatism while it also rejects scientism and accepts policy science. Philosophically, Legal Realism takes legal positivism a step further. It accepts the separation of law and morality, yet where positivism purports to offer a concept of law, legal realism dispenses with this aspiration. Realism and its incandescent cousin, critical legal studies,[124] link law to politics with all of its variability. There is, however, a danger in too much politics. Full acceptance of the vagaries of politics precludes the formation of a stable and reliable concept of law. The Realists tempered their political critique of formalism by arguing that policy analyses could make positive contributions to society through the thoughtful use and application of law as a social science discipline, not as a handmaiden of political ideology.

Machiavelli would have found the Legal Realists boon companions. The Realists would understand Machiavelli's instrumental use of law for state stability just as Machiavelli would have understood the Realists desire that law be used to advance sound social policies. Grand theories of either law or justice might have served the ancients well. We moderns, however, live in a complex, technical, and uncertain world where the tool of law can be usefully applied to ease our way in it. If these laws also serve justice, then all for the better. A better world, however, cannot be found if some unrealistic idol of justice blinds us to the necessities of our lives and our societies. Such is the Realist legacy.

Machiavelli's *Prince*

The popular reading of *The Prince* conjures up the image of Tony Soprano, Michael Corleone, Jeffrey Skilling, or Dennis Kozlowski as examples of the modern prince. Such images can hardly be faulted given Machiavelli's homage to Cesare Borgia. These are Machiavellian images rather than the image of Machiavelli's prince. For Niccolò, Michelangelo's *David*, not a Mafia don or a corporate raider, would serve well as the ideal prince. *David* was the prince that Italy needed in the early sixteenth century.

With the exile of the Medici in 1494 and with Savonarola's demise in 1498, Florence had a chance of republican government under Piero Soderini, Machiavelli's patron and employer. To inaugurate the new, youthful Florence, Soderini lured back to Florence from Julius II's Rome a sculptor who had previously enjoyed the early patronage of the Medici. In 1501, Michelangelo, then 26 years old, was commissioned to create a public sculpture for the new Florence, a sculpture which would capture the city's new found exuberance, strength, and vitality.

From 1501 to 1504, Michelangelo worked on the brilliant *David*, a youth whose strength is captured in his oversized hands alone—a youth whose pride became the pride of Florence. A youth of biblical proportions who defeated Goliath as the people of Florence defeated the old tyranny of the Medici. A youth who would be prince enough to understand the times and have the political skills necessary to breathe new life into a country divided by fractious city-states and mean rulers. A youth unafraid to use force, violence even, to destroy an enemy and save a people rather than turn a Christian cheek and seek glory in Heaven.

Upon completion, the seventeen-foot *David* was placed for all of Florence and for all of the world to see in the Piazza della Signoria at the entrance to the halls of government in the Palazzo Vecchio. Machiavelli, secretary to Piero, would see *David* every time he set foot into the Palazzo. *David* reigned in the Piazza for over 350 years before being removed to the Accademia Gallery for its protection. *David*'s sheltered presence in its new home does not diminish its power. Even today *David* instantly recalls Florence on the edge of greatness on September 8, 1504 when it was first unveiled; it instantly recalls a prince of great and glorious *virtù*, as well.

David has guile as well as vitality. He could be a prince every bit as cultivated as Il Magnifico as well as free from Il Magnifico's old family ways and old family ties. Machiavelli, and all of Florence, could see the power of a new prince for a new state in Michelangelo's masterpiece.[125] Where Cesare Borgia exhibited princely *virtù*, *David* exhibited princely glory to be celebrated among the most excellent men.

Michelangelo's genius was never more on display than in *David*. *David* stands alone, naked, free. There is no evidence of his adversary—no Goliath's head as in Verrocchio's *David with Head of Goliath*. This *David* remains poised for any enemy with his right hand strongly curled around a rock and his left hand casually touching his sling. Approaching this statute directly from the front, *David's* profile is one of serene confidence. Approaching from the left, his face changes to an intense watchfulness. From this perspective, the viewer can see *David's* furled brow and his concern and determination. *David* possesses the princely *virtù*—power, magnificence, pride, austerity, pursuit of glory, vigor, and discipline[126]—that will make Florence and Italy great. *David* is Machiavelli's ideal prince, Machiavelli's new man.

Machiavelli's *David* and neither the Machiavellian Corleone nor Agathocles has the sense of justice necessary for the world of men. *David* is capable of the guile of being not good when necessity calls. *David's* law, Machiavelli's law, is realist but not evil. It is used as an instrument to preserve the political power necessary to maintain the state and satisfy the people in it. *David*, no less than Machiavelli's great treatise, lives the life of a prince who knows the nature of people and lives enough among them to know the nature of princes.

Machiavelli's solution to the problem of Creon's ghost is *David*. *David* rules with vitality, with strength, with *virtù* not to the ends of the ancients, but to the ends of the moderns. Machiavelli entered the ancient courts of ancient men not to follow them, their ancient gods, or their ancient virtues but to learn from them to enter into the modern world, into the world of modern men and their politics. If love and virtue are the instruments of the ancients, law and *virtù* are the instruments of princes. So teaches Machiavelli's *The Prince*.

Conclusion

Halfway through our journey, we find ourselves in the dark woods. Well, our situation may not be Dante's visit to hell, but there is an analogy. Dante had come to a point in his life at which the demands of reason failed to bring him the harmony and satisfaction he craved. He then turned to faith.

We find ourselves in a similar conflict between man's law and the higher law; between the desire for a moral and just law and our experience of unfair and unjust laws. We cannot reconcile the desire for the higher, just law with the many imperfect faces of law in action. We desire law to provide determinate answers to the conflicts that find their way to courts, and in turn, we desire judges who apply the law instead of making it out of whole cloth. Yet we know that any body of law based on past disputes cannot have answers for the new disputes that new technologies and new politics create. All of these tensions reveal that it is impossible to reconcile desire and experience into a single, unitary concept of law.

There are, instead, two conceptions that compete for our attention and occupy our thoughts about law and justice. One conception is positive and descriptive, the other is normative and evaluative. The conception of law posed by Creon, Thrasymachus, Hart, and Machiavelli is based on the exercise of man's power by legitimated authority. Morality is either irrelevant, incidental, or incorporated into that conception. Regardless, morality is not necessary for law to operate. The competing conception of Antigone, Plato, Aquinas, and Dworkin, while also exercising legitimated power, is guided to an end such as justice, the Good, or integrity.

Machiavelli offers theoretical and practical reasons for understanding and using law separately from justice. Theoretically, Machiavelli, like Thrasymachus before him and Hart after him, decoupled law and morality in the service of realpolitik. Law and morality have distinct ends. Where law exists to keep peace among men, morality exists to bring men to God. For Machiavelli, Plato's attempt to merge virtue in the City with virtue in the Soul fails. In modern liberal democracies committed to tolerance of a variety of religious, moral, and political points of view, there can be no single viewpoint that can or should take precedence over others. Hans Kelsen's pure theory of law makes exactly this point. "In view of the extraordinary heterogeneity, however, of what men in fact have considered as good and evil, just or unjust, at different times and in different place, no element common to the contents of the various moral orders is detectable."[127]

How does Machiavelli's new politics bear on the problem of Creon's ghost? Does the conflict between man's law and higher law even bother Machiavelli? Or is the matter simply irrelevant to him because power, its acquisition and maintenance, is the proper end of political man? The higher law, the moral law, and God's law do not matter to Machiavelli as ends in themselves. But they can and should be used to the prince's advantage for that is what men do; it is in their natures.

This is not the cynic's response, it is the realist's. This answer bears on the problem of Creon's ghost by falling on the side of the human law as the law that controls men and brings stability to their states. Although the higher law may well save our souls, law only matters to the extent that the princess maintains her principality. For Machiavelli,"[a] good society is a society that enjoys stability, internal harmony, security, justice, a sense of power and of splendour. . . ." like Athens, Sparta, and the Roman Republic.[128]

In *The Prince,* Creon's ghost, the conflict between man's law and higher law, is played out as a conflict between ancient virtue and modern *virtù.* Machiavelli saw Creon's ghost clearly and dispatched it. He was neither afraid of nor perplexed by the conflict of laws. He was exasperated that classical and Christian thinkers and leaders did not address the reality of human political power more directly and more forcefully. Machiavelli dispatches the ghost not by ignoring it but by recasting the problem that it posed.

Machiavelli's solution to the conflict between man's law and higher law is as simple as it is direct and revolutionary—avoid the conflict by redefining virtue and its true end. We live with the Machiavellian Paradox of wanting our law to be moral and therefore just, while wanting our laws to ignore morality, especially the moral principles with which we disagree, in the service of security. That we cannot have it both ways is just another version of *Creon's Ghost.* Our desire for the Good conflicts with our desire for security and stability. Our desire for moral law conflicts with our desire for effective law. Our desire for man's law to prevail conflicts with our desire to honor the higher law. All of these desires confront our experience of not attaining the Good.

Machiavelli teaches us that these desires are inconsistent and irreconcilable: he teaches us that we must choose among these conflicting desires. And he teaches us that in the world of men and action, only one choice is available to us—relying on man's positive laws to save the City; the salvation of the Soul will occur in other precincts.

Machiavelli's conception of law, even if we reject the less nuanced notion of Machiavellian power politics, leaves us wanting. How, if law and justice are separate, are we to evaluate law's content? Racial slavery is and always was unjust. Yet racial slavery and its more modern Jim Crow counterparts were law. Can we afford to live in a society which legitimates slavery and racial segregation and in which law pays little or no attention to justice? Do we wish to live in such a society? Failure to answer these questions led to the bloodiest war in our nation's history and to another conception of the higher law.

FIVE

Law Breaking

The National Underground Railroad Freedom Center is situated on the Cincinnati side of the Ohio River. Looking south from its grand hall, one can view the Suspension Bridge linking Covington, Kentucky and Cincinnati, Ohio. The bridge will be familiar for it was the prototype for the Brooklyn Bridge. Construction was begun in 1856 and halted in 1858. Various reasons for the stoppage are given including financial necessity, the threat of war, and fear of the flight to freedom undertaken by fugitive slaves.

The memory of the partially completed bridge serves as powerful symbol and metaphor. For not only did the uncompleted bridge slow down the movement from slave-soil to free-soil, it symbolized our country's deep divide over the "slavery question." Today, the memory serves as a metaphor for our own incomplete conversation about race and our incomplete reconciliation with its legacy, a legacy involving the conflict between man's slave law and a higher religious law.

THE UNDERGROUND RAILROAD and the fugitive slaves who traveled on it have become part of America's historic past and part of our current consciousness—a consciousness which embodies myth and reality, symbol and sin. The Underground Railroad was neither as organized nor as extensive as the mythology may wish, nor did it transport as many slaves to freedom as might be hoped.[1] Nor should the mythology of abolitionist whites working on the railroad overshadow the courage and heroism of the fugitive slaves who risked life and family for liberty.[2] And yet the Underground Railroad, the conductors that operated it, and the fugitive slaves that it transported constitute an essential story of the conflict between man's law and higher law; it is a story about how a higher, religiously inspired, law expiated the sin of slavery contained in man's law.

The story of the conflict will be told through three episodes from *Uncle Tom's Cabin.*[3] Upon meeting Harriet Beecher Stowe at a White House reception, the story is that President Abraham Lincoln greeted her by saying, "So you're the little woman who wrote the book that started this great war!"[4] The anecdote has some substance to it because the book had a powerful impact throughout the country. Southern politicians and preachers excoriated *Uncle Tom's Cabin* as an untrue and scurrilous picture of life in the South for the free and slaves. Northern politicians and preachers cited it in their crusade for justice. And the book was widely read, selling over 2 million copies in the 1850s and selling more copies than any other book in the nineteenth century.

Stowe, daughter, sister, and wife of ministers were all influenced by the Protestant evangelism of the Second Great Awakening which fueled the Abolitionist Movement. She "breathed the doctrinal air of sin, guilt, atonement, and salvation since childhood."[5] While resident in Cincinnati, Stowe witnessed the depredations of slavery and the flight of the fugitives firsthand. These experiences informed her book and strengthened her religious message. Religion and the religious devotion to a higher law contribute to Stowe's sentimental novel and to the social and political transformation that occurred. Religion, however, had to confront and combat man's law.

A dark reality of our history involves the role of man's law in creating, sustaining, and perpetuating slavery. Man's law, the law of slavery, the law of treating human beings as property, was legitimized by our Constitution and shaped our constitutional history and jurisprudence. Whether we choose to accept the Constitution as, in William Lloyd Garrison's words, a "covenant with death and an agreement with hell,"[6] or if we accept the Constitution as a temporary expedient necessary for creating the Union,[7] man's law entrenched this peculiar institution into our country's politics and history. Whether we treat the Constitution as either a Faustian bargain or as a political compromise, the Constitution legitimized racial injustice. It took nearly three generations, from the Founding to the Civil War, for slave law to be overturned and injustice righted. Man's law of slavery had to be broken time and again, in many ways, and with much bloodshed before the higher law prevailed. Lawbreaking consisted in not only a series of individual acts of civil disobedience or even the flight for freedom by the fugitives; lawbreaking constituted one of the few true constitutional moments in our history as we broke from the Founding to create the Reconstruction.

Prelude to a Novel I—The Declaration of Independence and the Constitution

American slavery began with the arrival of 20 black Africans in Jamestown, Virginia in 1619.[8] From the first settlement through Emancipation and Reconstruction, slavery was a constitutive part of our legal system. Even our sacred scripture, the Declaration of Independence, was not unsullied by this institution. The Declaration's remonstrances against King George III calling for equal liberty were cloaked in the language of the "Laws of Nature and of Nature's God"—"We hold these truths to be self-evident, that all men are created equal, that they are endowed by their Creator with certain unalienable Rights, that among these are Life, Liberty and the pursuit of Happiness." Stirring language and yet omitted from the Declaration was any remonstrance against slavery although Thomas Jefferson did offer complaints against England's slave trade.

Jefferson's draft included a charge that King George, "waged cruel war against human nature itself, violating its most sacred rights of life & liberty in the persons of a distant people who never offended him, captivating & carrying them into slavery in another hemisphere." The king was accused of incurring the miserable deaths of the slaves during the long passage. This Christian king was charged with engaging in the "execrable commerce" of the slave trade with its "assemblage of horrors," and he was also charged with the responsibility of inciting the slaves to murderous riot.[9] Jefferson's indictment against the slave trade was eliminated to satisfy South Carolina and Georgia who refused to consent to the Declaration as long as those charges were included.[10]

The hypocrisy of the Colonists blaming George III for the slave trade without admitting their own complicity became more apparent in the drafting and passage of the U.S. Constitution. The Constitution contains up to 10 references to slavery.[11] Most prominent among them is the three-fifths clause which treated slaves as three-fifths of a person for purposes of counting representatives and direct taxation without any corresponding rights of citizenship.[12] The Constitution further specified that slave importation was to end in 1808.[13] The most disastrous provision, however, was the Constitution's fugitive slave clause which reads: "[N]o Person held to Service or Labour in one State, under the Laws thereof, escaping into another, shall, in Consequence of any Law or Regulation therein, be discharged from such Service or Labour, but shall be delivered up on Claim of the Party to whom such Service or Labour may be due."[14]

Notice that the Fugitive Slave Clause, like the rest of the Constitution, never uses the word slave and yet its intent is patent and demonstrates how fully entrenched slavery was in the culture.

The Constitution's fugitive slave clause was not self-executing and, on its face, left room for abolitionists and free soilers to maneuver against slavery. The clause does not limit the judicial process to be used to affirm or contest a person's status as slave or free. Nor does the clause prohibit allowing fugitives to exercise due process rights such as a right to counsel or a right to trial by jury. Abolitionists could use the open-ended clauses of the Constitution to provide slaves with legal protections. These weaknesses, however, were remedied by the passage of the Fugitive Slave Act of 1793.

Prelude to a Novel II—Constitutional Interpretation

The 1793 Act arose as a result of a controversy between Pennsylvania and Virginia. The governor of Pennsylvania sought the extradition of three men who had kidnapped a black man from Pennsylvania. The Virginia governor refused to send the kidnappers back to Pennsylvania, arguing that Virginia was entitled to the return of any fugitive slaves. The 1793 Act allowed for the rendition of slaves who could be seized by the owner or his agent or attorney. The Act required the claimant to appear before a federal or state judge, and upon affidavit of title, the magistrate was to provide a certificate giving title to the claimant. The Act contained no provisions for a slave to offer evidence on his own behalf. More onerously, criminal penalties would be imposed on anyone obstructing the capture of or aiding fugitives.[15] The Fugitive Slave Act of 1793 worked well for a short period of time, until free states began to pass laws providing escaped slaves with some due process rights to contest their rendition. Further, as the country expanded west, anti-slavery forces fought hard to keep the slaves states from outnumbering free states.

The U.S. Supreme Court entered the fugitive slave fray in 1842 with an opinion by justice Joseph Story in the case of *Prigg v. Pennsylvania.*[16] The case involved Margaret Moran, a slave, who escaped from her owner, Margaret Ashmore. Moran fled from Maryland into Pennsylvania in 1832. Prigg had been hired by Ashmore to capture Moran. Pennsylvania had a statute which provided fugitives with due process rights, including the right to a judicial hearing before they could be ordered to be returned. When Moran was brought before the justice of the peace, the officer refused to take action.

Nevertheless, Prigg took Moran and her children back to Maryland, where Prigg was arraigned, charged, and convicted of kidnapping in Pennsylvania. Prigg challenged the legitimacy of the conviction.

Justice Story was avowedly anti-slavery,[17] yet in *Prigg* he granted relief to the slave catcher and in doing so enshrined slavery into the Constitution and into our constitutional history. Writing that without the fugitive slave clause, "the Union could not have been formed,"[18] Story's opinion goes further. Not only was the fugitive slave clause of the Constitution necessary for the formation of the Union, Story argues in *Prigg* that it was necessary for its preservation. His opinion strips away states' authority to impose procedural safeguards in favor of runaway slaves. The clause, he reasons, was intended to give slave holders the "positive, unqualified right"[19] to recapture their slaves. According to Story, the "true design [of the fugitive slave clause] was to guard against the doctrines and principles in the non-slaveholding states, by preventing them from intermeddling with, or obstructing, or abolishing the rights of the owners of slaves."[20] Owners had more rights to the bodies of slaves than the slaves did in their own bodies.

Story's opinion discussed the earlier British law on slavery—*Somerset's Case*—which recognized that slavery was prohibited in England. James Somerset was a slave owned by Charles Steuart, a British Customs Officer, stationed in Boston. When Steuart brought Somerset to England, Somerset fled and his cause was taken up by abolitionists who argued that he was emancipated because he was on free soil. In an opinion by Lord Mansfield, his freedom was sustained. Mansfield wrote that while there is no natural right to slavery, slavery can be established by man's law. "[T]he state of slavery is of such a nature, that it is incapable of being introduced on any reasons . . . but only by positive law. . . . It is so odious, that nothing can be suffered to support it, but positive law."[21] Man's law can trump natural law. England, however, as a sovereign nation, was not obligated to respect the positive slave laws of another country—the United States.

Justice Story was well aware of this precedent and drew a distinction between the law of nations and the law of federalism in the United States. While he could agree that two nations do not have to respect the laws of one another regarding slavery, the Constitution established the law for the relationship among the several states. The Constitution provided for the resolution of fugitive slaves cases by giving slaveholders a right to the return of runaway slaves by empowering the federal government to pass laws so that one state could not thwart the rights of another state all in the name of Union.

Prigg had severe constitutional consequences for the anti-slavery movement. First, it constitutionalized the fugitive slave clause more firmly than it had been. Now the federal government could pass a stringent fugitive slave law as an aid to the preservation of the Union. Second, it reinforced the rights of slave owners. The southern states were assured that their property rights in slaves would be protected. Further, *Prigg* recognized no rights for fugitive slaves, and it reduced the sovereign power of the northern states to offer legal protections for the fugitives, thus making them accomplices in the slave trade. These constitutional lessons were well-learned by legislatures and courts. So too, did these lessons have bloody consequences.

Prior to *Prigg*, several states had passed personal liberty laws providing fugitive slaves with procedural rights to contest their slave status, often resulting in their freedom. After *Prigg*, several northern states passed new personal liberty laws as abolitionists were outraged by the specter of disrupting families, while slave owners violently captured escapees even after the fugitives enjoyed years of freedom. Slaveholders argued that they were losing their property,[22] and the federal government responded with the Fugitive Slave Act of 1850 to rebut the new personal liberty laws.

The1850 Act was part of the Great Compromise on slavery in the West, greatly strengthened the 1793 Act, and was notorious because of its ugliness. Slaves were taken from their homes and from their work; were taken from their children and from their spouses; and were beaten, tortured, and murdered in the process. The most odious fact is that all of these travesties were accomplished under color of man's law—a point not lost on Harriet Beecher Stowe.

Fugitive slaves caught in the net of these laws were subject to a series of deprivations. Slaves, fugitive or free, found in the North could be captured by owner, agent or slave catcher for rendition to the South without protection of rights: to counsel, to jury trial; to have charges made against them, to speak in their own defense, to cross-examine or know the evidence against them, to a hearing to determine their status as free or fugitive, or to other protections such as the right of habeas corpus that we collectively know as due process.[23] Federal officials had a duty to arrest runaway slaves and any official who did not capture a runaway was liable for a $1,000 fine. Also, any person aiding and abetting a runaway slave was also subject to a $1000 fine. The most pernicious provision of the Act involved compensation. If a magistrate held in favor of the slave owner, their compensation was $10. If they held in favor of the slave, they were compensated $5.[24]

The Act worked as intended. During the decade of the 1850s, 332 slaves were returned and only 11 were declared free.[25] The Fugitive Slave Act of 1850, the Compromise of the same year, and the Kansas-Nebraska Act of 1854, all heightened national attention on and agitation about slavery. If it were in the mind of the founders that slavery would go out of fashion in a generation, they were mistaken. The opposite was the case as free soilers and slave soilers fought for every inch of land in the West and for every new state in the Union on the very matter that threatened the Union's existence.

Uncle Tom's Cabin

Prior to writing *Uncle Tom's Cabin*, Harriet Beecher Stowe was a successful author. She was also at the center of the Abolitionist Movement. Harriet Beecher moved with her family to Cincinnati in 1832 when her father, Lyman Beecher, became president of the Lane Theological Seminary, an institution with abolitionist sympathies. Harriet married Calvin Stowe in 1836 and resided in Cincinnati until he was transferred to Bowdoin College in 1850. These were indeed formative years for the city as well as for the country. Cincinnati had experienced significant race riots, Harriet herself participated in the Underground Railroad, and the increasing abolitionist activism informed her work—so, too, did the Fugitive Slave Act of 1850. Upon its enactment, her sister wrote, "Hattie, if I could use a pen as you can, I would write something that will make this whole nation feel what an accursed thing slavery is." To which Harriet replied, "I will if I live."[26] Harriet was led to the conclusion that all Americans were complicit in the sin of slavery, and she resolved to use her pen for the Abolitionist cause.

Before beginning the serialized novel that became *Uncle Tom's Cabin*, Stowe had been writing for Abolitionist journals including the *National Era*. In the August 1, 1850 edition she published a story about a runaway slave family and the Christian anguish that their capture and return caused. Entitled *The Freeman's Dream: A Parable*, the story begins with a northern planter on a fair summer evening, enjoying his estate and giving thanks to God, "with a full heart."[27] The farmer was also enjoying the pleasure of his family's company when he was approached by a "poor black man, worn and wasted." The man was accompanied by his family and begged for food and shelter if only for one night. The farmer, Stowe tells us, was not hard and yet when he thought of the human laws of his state and nation, he "hardened his heart, and set his face as a flint, and bade him pass on, and trouble him not." Shortly thereafter, the farmer watched slave catchers capture and bind the man and his wife and take them away.

That night the farmer dreamed that he sky grew dark and the earth "rocked to and fro, and the heavens flashed with strange light in a distant rush." Then, the Son of Man appeared and the farmer was called to judgment before Him where he felt himself, "standing alone and trembling before that all-searching Presence." The Lord then spoke verses from the New Testament and accused the man of failing to give him meat when he was hungry, drink when he was thirsty, or the shelter that was most needed. There then appeared before the farmer the fugitive slaves who he had denied, the very brethren who he did not help, therefore, failing Jesus.

Stowe ends her parable with what was to become a central theme in *Uncle Tom's Cabin*. "Of late, there have seemed to be many in this nation, who seem to think that there is no standard of right and wrong higher than an act of Congress, or an interpretation of the United States Constitution." Stowe wrote that it was humiliating to think that there were Christians who could not put the higher law of Christ, "above human laws which come in conflict with them." Black or white, slave or free, deserved to be treated equally because Christians know, "Inasmuch as ye did it not to the least of these my brethren, he did it not to *me!*"

In this parable, as in the novel, Stowe recapitulates the problem of *Creon's Ghost* as the conflict between man's law and higher law. In Stowe's particular case, the higher law is Christianity. "The great object of the author in writing [*Uncle Tom's Cabin*] has been to bring this subject of slavery, as a moral and religious question, before the minds of all those who profess to be followers of Christ in America."[28]

"In Which It Appears That a Senator Is But a Man"[29]

In our search for the higher law, religion offers its candidacy as the way to overturn slavery. More particularly, Stowe's Christianity is derived from the core of the Abolitionist movement. Not so parenthetically, though, it is also central to the southern defense of slavery.[30] Religion, particularly in a pluralist democracy and one dedicated to nonestablishment, is problematic. Our First Amendment jurisprudence precludes any sectarian religious tenet from being absorbed directly into the positive law. Yet our politics is not so precise. Our politics virtually requires that our leaders display devotion to religion and its values. If politics absorbs but does not require religion, then how secure are nonestablishment principles? In other words, can the positive law be insulated from religion? *Uncle Tom's Cabin* demonstrates how both propositions are true as anti-slavery, religious sentiments found their way into constitutional law. Slavery engendered a constitutional crisis as well as a civil war, but neither Christian principles nor natural law were directly used in the law courts to overturn the fugitive slave laws. Nevertheless, the politics of it all was not unaffected by religious anti-slavery fervor as Stowe demonstrates.

The first episode begins in the warm Ohio household of Senator and Mrs. Bird. Stowe's book is replete with the politics of gender and domesticity, in addition to her attack on slavery which add force to her religious arguments for human equality.[31] As the senator enters his house, Mary, his wife, asks, "and what have they been doing in the Senate?" Stowe writes that "it was a very unusual thing for gentle little Mrs. Bird ever to trouble her head with what was going on in the House of State." And yet we know full well as did Mrs. Bird, what was going on in the House of State. The legislature, the Christian legislature, had passed a Fugitive Slave Law forbidding the very Christian admonition to, "give meat and drink" to people in need. The law was directed specifically at the slaves coming into Ohio from Kentucky at exactly the place where the Suspension Bridge stands today. Senator Bird thought the fugitive slave law was necessary because of the actions of the "reckless Abolitionists that have stirred up their brethren in Kentucky." The senator was not immune from religious meaning. He saw the fugitive slave law as Christian, in much the same way that the southern churches saw the law, because it is aimed at quieting the excitement.[32] Mrs. Bird challenges the senator on his reading of the Bible by telling him that Christianity requires charity toward the suffering. The senator's response, "that would be aiding and abetting you know," thus implicating even sympathetic northerners in the institution of slavery under threat of criminal prosecution.

Stowe paints Mary Bird as a "timid, blushing little woman" who could only be aroused or provoked by "anything in the shape of cruelty [which] would throw her into a passion." The Fugitive Slave Law aroused exactly that passion, and she directly questions her husband as to whether or not he thought such a law was Christian. John admits that in his mind the law is Christian as he draws a distinction between his private feelings and his public obligations. "[T]here are great public interests involved,—there is such a state of public agitation rising, that we must put aside our private feelings."

Politics may not always be the last refuge of a scoundrel, but it does allow us to disassociate our private selves from our public selves. Mrs. Bird attempts to demolish that disassociation through religion. "Now, John, I don't know anything about politics, but I can read my Bible. . . ." Mary does not conflate the public and the private arguing that "Obeying God never brings on public evils. I know it can't. It's always safest, all around, to *do as He* bids us."

For the senator, neither religious sentiment nor the Bible can refute the national necessities of state, an argument Mary rebuffs by saying that the senator can argue all night but could not convince her that even he would turn away a "poor, shivering, hungry creature" from his door. Mary assails John by telling him that he would never put a woman out in a snowstorm, which is a reference to a historic incident upon which the story of Eliza is based.[33] John is not finished trying to convince Mary of her duty, a word that Mary rejects like she rejects his reasoning. The senator's position is exactly that of Creon's defense of his rule. Man's laws are passed for reasons of state and for practical reasons; they are not passed for either personal or religious sentiment. "I hate reasoning," Mary tells John because she fears that bad reasoning is used by politicians to avoid doing the right thing.

After this exchange, Eliza appears at the house with her young son Henry, seeking shelter from a storm and help on the Underground Railroad. Eliza sits in the kitchen, "A young and slender woman, with garments torn and frozen, with one shoe gone, and the stocking torn away from the cut and bleeding foot. . . ." The senator then softens and helps arrange clothes and comfort for Eliza and her child.

Eliza escaped into free soil Ohio across an ice-strewn river. It was the peculiar insult, not only of the fugitive slave laws but of our constitutional jurisprudence that even once on free soil, safety was not assured. *Somerset's Case* established the proposition for England that once a slave was voluntarily brought onto free soil, they were emancipated. But the 1771 precedent was exactly what the Fugitive Slave Clause of the Constitution sought to avoid and exactly what *Prigg v. Pennsylvania* prohibited. Instead, once across the Ohio River, it was necessary for Eliza to proceed to Canada to receive the protection of another country's laws before her freedom was secure.

After a brief rest, Eliza tells her story of escape across the ice. She also tells the senator that she was a slave to a "kind master" in Kentucky. The man and his wife both treated her well, but the threat of losing the last of three children was unbearable. When she overheard plans to have young Henry sold downriver with Uncle Tom, she knew that she must flee.

In this brief vignette, Stowe explodes the myth that southerners treated their slaves well for even without beatings, they were never safe from having a family destroyed in the name of profit. Throughout the book, Stowe does not let her reader forget the degradation of chattel slavery where blacks are property, not people. For though Eliza thought well of her owners, their need for money compelled the sale of Uncle Tom and threatened the sale of Henry. Eliza's story is intensified when she tells the senator that her husband, George Harris, belongs to another man who treats him hard and who himself has run away to Canada.

Senator Bird knows that the slave catchers are on the trail not so much for Eliza but for Henry, and that immediate action is necessary. He is also concerned about his own liability and reputation but nevertheless is willing to lend aid—Christian aid. Senator Bird has an old client who was now part of the Underground Railroad, and he agrees to take Eliza and Henry there that night and then taken North to Canada.

Stowe plays out Senator Bird's predicament, "What a situation, now, for a patriotic senator, that had been all the week before spurring up the legislature of his native state to pass more stringent resolutions against escaping fugitives, their harborers and abettors!" Patriotism becomes the dominant motif for man's laws which conflict with the higher law. And yet Stowe notes the human side, the Christian charity side, of the political man "He had never thought that a fugitive might be a hapless mother, a defenseless child . . ." Indeed, "The Senator Was But a Man."

The senator's midnight carriage ride will be a way for him to expiate his sins. Through the woods, over creeks, and finally to the farm house of John Van Trompe, former farmer and slave owner from Kentucky who had freed his slaves. Stowe tells us that even southerners and former slave owners can see the light of the higher law. Van Trompe had witnessed and rejected the "workings of a system equally bad for oppressor and oppressed." Van Trompe saw not only the light of humanity, he also saw the light of Christianity once he found a minister to preach the Gospel against slavery rather than in favor of it.

Stowe's use of Christianity is as pointed as it is critical. The Christian Gospel was not owned by the North and served as justification of slavery by southern churches. She was well aware of the many churches with their many resolutions which favored slavery for explicitly political reasons. The Gospel in the City of God should not interfere with politics in the City of Man. The disassociation between our public and private selves was given sanction not only by arguments of political necessity but by arguments from the Gospel itself.

Stowe believed that the clergy were a powerful political force on both sides of the issue, so much so that "no statesmen would ever undertake to carry and measure against which all the clergy of the country should unite."[34] The problem, of course, was that there was no unity among the churches of America. Stowe quotes the resolutions of southern churches which acknowledge both the institution of slavery as fully within human history as recounted in the Bible, and therefore, slavery as an institution to be respected. At the same time, the Gospel compels believers to render to God the things that are God's and render unto Caesar the things that are Caesar's to effect and bless the separation of God and man.[35] From the Harmony Presbytery of South Carolina she quotes, "Resolved, That as the kingdom of our Lord is not of this world, His church, as such, has no right to abolish, alter, or affect any institution or ordinance of men, political, or civil, &c."[36] To similar effect, the Charleston Union Presbytery adopted a resolution reading in part that "slavery, as it exists among us, is a political institution, with which ecclesiastical judicatories have not the smallest right to interfere. . . ."[37]

Some churches went further to declare that slavery was not a moral evil in the attempt to bolster their argument that slavery was a matter for civil society, not for religious community. The Charleston Baptist Association did not believe that "the Holy Scriptures have made the fact of slavery a question of morals at all."[38] Even further, some churches saw slavery as a moral good, "sanctioned by Scripture and capable of producing a Christian social order based on the observance of mutual duty, slave to master and master to slave."[39] Thus, the use of church authority reinforces the distinction Senator Bird made between public and private feelings. Private feelings may conflict with but must give way to public need. Our moral feelings and our religious beliefs save our souls but not the state.

Stowe argues that northern churches were of a different mind. They saw slavery as evil and immoral, and they saw persons who favored the fugitive slave laws as, "guilty of a great sin, and ought to be dealt with as for other scandalous crimes."[40] To Stowe, those laws which prohibited the education of slaves were particularly immoral and pernicious. Stowe recognizes the moral goodness of educating children, a Thomist principle of natural law. "To prevent their being taught to read was cruel, and would prevent them from obtaining as much knowledge of the laws of Heaven as otherwise they might enjoy."[41]

Stowe's argument from church authority is centrally critical about using humans for financial gain. She asks: "Did Christianity abolish slavery as a matter of fact?" Her answer is as short as it is emphatic, "We answer, it did."[42] Her recommendation, then, is clear: "The thing to be done . . . is, that the whole American Church, of all denominations, should unitedly come up, not *in form*, but *in fact*, to the noble purpose . . . to seek the *entire abolition of slavery throughout America and throughout Christiandom.*"[43] It remained, for Stowe, that "every Christian ought seriously to examine the extent to which our national government is pledged and used for the support of slavery."[44]

The Abolitionist fight against slavery from Stowe's point of view and the theme of *Uncle Tom's Cabin* is that the struggle is religious to its core. The law of Christianity should supercede that of the national government. Fugitive slave laws should be overturned, and slavery should be abolished as a matter of the higher law.

"The Property is Carried Off"[45] and "Select Incident of Lawful Trade"[46]

"*Uncle Tom's Cabin* insisted that slavery was a national sin, to be eradicated only when Christ's love and higher law triumphed over men's customs, economics, and legislation."[47] Stowe's Christianity informed her religious argument against slavery because of its dehumanizing treatment of people as property. "Uncle Tom,"especially since the Black Power movement in the mid-1960s, has become a term of opprobrium because of the passive way in which Tom accepts his fate and, ultimately, his Christ-like death. Tom is removed from his family, sold downriver to New Orleans, and ultimately beat to death by Simon Legree, a transplanted northerner. Throughout his physical and spiritual crises, Tom carries his Bible and preaches its lessons of the acceptance of God's will with its reward of everlasting salvation.

As Tom looks at his children for the last time, he tells his wife that in the South ,"There'll be the same God there, Chloe, that there is here." Chloe rejects Tom's religious acceptance as she worries about what will happen to him to which Tom responds, "I'm in the Lord's hands . . . nothin' can go no furder than he lets it. . . ." We know that Tom will go as far as death and even then, he expressed thankfulness for the fact that he was the one sent down South instead of either Chloe or his children. Tom thanked God for the mercy shown to his family as the family is destroyed and as Tom accepts his martyrdom.

Tom is the sentimental heart of the novel for many readers. His acceptance of a pejorative form of "slave religion" that forces acceptance rather than resistance is seen as reinforcing and perpetuating the peculiar institution.[48] Yet as passive as he is, it is hard not to read Tom with his Christ-like symbolism as a rebuke to this institution of slavery. Tom, a strong and powerful figure with Christ's love in his heart, is torn from his family and will meet his death as inevitably as Jefferson did in a *Lesson Before Dying*.[49] Being sold down South meant near-certain death and, in any case, was the most fearful possible future for a slave. It is that threat, Stowe writes, that emboldened slaves to flee northward, even from good masters. As Tom sits for his final meal with the family, Chloe ruminates about their future. Tom may have accepted his fate in order to save the family, but what future was there for them when they can be sold as property at any time?

The cruel justification for treating human flesh as a commodity is to dehumanize people and turn them into animals. Tom, with all his strength and loyalty, is treated exactly that way. "He's the faithfullest, best crittur . . ." says a blacksmith on seeing Tom shackled for the journey with the slave trader. As chattel or animal, owners then had the legal "property right" to sell a person in a market for profit or in the satisfaction of a debt.

Repeatedly throughout the novel, Stowe exposes the multiple hypocrisies of the many sides of the slave issue. The false idealization of a good master is exposed in the sale of Tom. Tom's master, George Shelby, became indebted to the slave trader Haley, and rather than lose his farm, sold Tom and tried to sell Eliza's son, Henry. Tom was loyal to the Shelbys and befriended by their son, George. As Tom is driven away by the slave trader Haley, George castigates the trader for his unsavory business to which Haley replies, "So long as your grand folks wants to buy men and women, I'm as good as they is . . 'tan't any meaner sellin' on 'em, than 't is buyin'!"

As Haley and Tom proceed, Haley becomes slightly more comfortable with Tom and less fearful that he will run. Even so, Haley can only think of Tom in one way: "he thought first of Tom's length, and breadth, and height, and what he would sell for, if he was kept fat and in good case until they got him into market." Men, women, and children were market commodities fettered like animals. For his part, though, Tom continued to meditate on the Bible, seeking happiness in the next world if not this one. As they ride on, Haley learns of a slave auction that he will attend in order to put together a gang of slaves to be sold down the river, telling Tom that the other slaves will make good company.

At the auction, Haley walks up to a group of men, picks a particular individual, "felt of his teeth," and asked him to perform various exercises. The slave auction repeats the pattern of breaking up families, selling women and children separately. At the next stop, Haley buys a woman, Lucy, with her child. The woman is incredulous believing that her master would ever sell her as he does. To prove his ownership, Haley brings out a bill of sale and has it read to the woman. This paper, this legal document, confirms the sale and justifies this human transgression in the eyes of the trader because the trade is "legal."

Haley gets into a conversation with a stranger on the boat taking them South and negotiates for the sale of the child. The conversation is overheard by Lucy. When the boat docks in Louisville, Haley takes the child from his sleeping mother and gives it to the stranger. When Lucy awakes, Haley tells her that he sold the child, and that he will have a better life in Louisville than he would down South. Stowe comments, "The trader had arrived at that stage of Christian and political perfection which has been recommended by some preachers and politicians of the north, lately, in which he had completely overcome every humane weakness and prejudice." Justification for slavery, even in the North, has now been complete with the political justification outstripping morality. Stowe continues, "You can get used to such things, too, my friend; and it is the great object of recent efforts to make our whole northern community used to them, for the glory of the Union." Lucy's anguish, then, was nothing more than a necessary consequence of an unsavory but legal trade—a trade with the beneficent purpose of Union.

Tom has witnessed the whole incident with horror, sick to his soul. Stowe sarcastically chastises Tom for not understanding the argument of "certain ministers of Christianity" but merely points out that the separation of mothers and children is an everyday incident of a lawful practice that supports an institution about which some American ministers find no evil whatsoever. All Lucys are nothing other than what law, "coolly classes with the bundles, and bails, and boxes, among which she is lying." That night, Lucy is driven to suicide by jumping overboard to her death. When Haley learns of the suicide, he is neither shocked nor overly concerned because he accepts such consequences as in the ordinary cost of doing business.

Stowe points out, again, the hypocrisy of slave trade. For those who condemned the slave traders must only ask themselves Haley's rhetorical questions: "But who, sir, makes the trader? Who is most to blame? The enlightened, cultivated, intelligent man, who supports the system of which the trader is the inevitable result, or the poor trader himself?" Stowe hopes that there are legislators with some shred of humanity, and yet she is critical of the national Congress which protects and perpetuates the slave trade. At least the international trade is roundly condemned, hypocritically so. "Trading Negroes from Africa, dear reader, is so horrid! It is not to be thought of! But trading them from Kentucky,—that's quite another thing!"

Opposition to slavery did not admit of any single or easy solution. Both the North and the South were guilty of perpetuating slavery; northern and southern churches were either in denial, negligent, or complicit, and the politics and constitutional history of the country had already invested heavily in the institution. Abolitionists were not of one mind about slavery. Some wanted to have the slaves colonized in another country. Some wanted slavery to end immediately. Stowe's father, Lyman, seemed to be of both minds—he was a colonizationist and an abolutionist.[50] Others sought a gradual accommodation between North and South for the protection of the Union. The mix of politics and religion did not yield a reliable strategy to end the practice. Other approaches and arguments, however, were available.

"In Which Property Gets Into an Improper State of Mind"[51]

Mrs. Bird and Uncle Tom offer two distinct religious arguments against slavery. While both arguments are grounded in Christianity, each reads the Gospel slightly differently and with different consequences. For Mrs. Bird, the institution is immoral and its immorality is obvious because it degrades God's creatures. Her reading of the Gospel compels action through either law reform or civil disobedience. For Tom, the institution is immoral for what it does to people and their families, yet slaves can act morally within that institution. Tom believes that while slavery should be abolished, the message of the Gospel tests God's creatures, God does not abandon them. Tom's reading of the Gospel leads to acceptance, acceptance of the Word, and acceptance of the faith in salvation. While neither argument alone changes the course of events, both contribute to a rejection of man's law and its replacement with a higher law.

In addition to these religious attacks on slavery, there is another higher law argument to be made—a natural law argument. Human equality is part of our birthright, it is part of our social contract, it may even be a part of our political morality, and the higher law can be pursued even if it means breaking the human law.[52] This nineteenth-century natural law argument is made by Stowe through the story of Eliza's husband, George Harris. Uncle Tom's religious passivity lies in stark contrast to how George Harris chooses to live his life. Like Tom, George is property. Unlike Tom, George does not find comfort in religion nor did he look South for his future. Instead, he will stake his life moving North to Canada on the Underground Railroad for his and his family's freedom.

Stowe plays out the scene of George's escape on his way into Ohio and on to Canada in the warmth of a northern Kentucky tavern. One of the patrons, Mr. Wilson, has his attention drawn to a handbill which advertises a reward for $400—dead or alive—for the runaway George Harris. The handbill paints a handsome portrait of George, "six feet in height, a very light mulatto, brown curly hair; is very intelligent, speaks handsomely, can read and write. . . ." It also paints an ugly portrait, for George is "deeply scarred on his back and shoulders; has been branded in his right hand with the letter H."

The conversation in the tavern over the handbill underscores the hypocrisy of slavery. Upon reading the handbill, one of the customers spits a mouthful of tobacco juice into the fire saying, "Any man that owns a boy like that, and can't find any better way o' treating him, *deserves* to loose him. Such papers as these is a shame to Kentucky. . . ." The customer's ire is not directed against the institution of slavery, it was directed at the negative attention slavery drew to the South. The customer then brags about how well he treats his own slaves, arguing that if you treat them like men rather than like dogs, they will return the favor with the work of men and not the work of dogs. Mr. Wilson acknowledges that he knows and thinks highly of the advertised George Harris. In fact, George is an inventor, but the patent he developed was held by his master. Conversation then turns to discussing the value and risk of having intelligent slaves.

A stranger then enters the tavern. "He was very tall, with a dark, Spanish complexion, fine, expressive black eyes, and close-curling hair, also of a glossy blackness. His well-formed aquiline nose, straight thin lips, and the admirable contour of his finely-formed limbs, impressed the whole company instantly with the idea of something uncommon." And uncommon George Harris was. After a few moments, Wilson recognizes George and George invites him to a private conversation. While George acts calmly, Mr. Wilson is nervous and agitated, fearful of aiding and abetting. Wilson, Stowe writes, was "divided between his wish to help George, and a certain confused notion of maintaining law and order."

Wilson is so concerned about man's law that he feels it is his duty to tell George that he is, "setting himself in opposition to the laws of your country."

Wilson continues by saying that even if George is willing to disregard man's law, he should follow the Bible and return to his master, to which George responds, "don't quote Bible at me that way, Mr. Wilson." George is not denying his belief in Christianity; it is wrong-headed Christianity, Tom's Christianity, that upsets him. George then questions Wilson by asking him how he would react if he were taken prisoner, away from his wife and children, and condemned to hoe corn for the rest of his life. Would he think this was the meaning of divine providence? Still, Wilson continues to warn George about the risks he is taking—a risk which George freely acknowledges and willingly undertakes. George will not suffer going down South; he would rather face death.

Wilson then says, "Why, George, this state of mind is awful; it's getting really desperate, George. I'm concerned. Going to break the laws of your country!" George's response to Wilson's charge that he is about to break the laws of his country recalls Socrates' argument in the *Crito*.[53] Socrates refused to escape his death sentence. He drank the hemlock as part of his bargain with Athens. He had agreed to abide by the laws of Athens because he had benefitted from them. To disregard his bargain would give lie to his life, something Socrates could not do.

Although differently situated, George is compelled by the same principle. The slavery laws of the country are not George's laws. He had no hand in making them. This is not George's country. Canada may well be. "What laws are there for us? We don't make them—we don't consent to them—we have nothing to do with them; all they do for us is to crush us, and keep us down." George tells Wilson that he should listen carefully to the speeches that are delivered on the Fourth of July; government should, "derive their just power from the consent of the governed." If these words are true then George cannot be bound by any obligation to a country which denies him any participation in lawmaking; lawbreaking, then, is a legitimate alternative as well as a moral imperative.

George's response to Wilson recalls Shylock's speech, "Don't I sit before you, every way, just as much a man as you are? Look at my face,—look at my hands,—look at my body, why am I *not* a man, as much as anybody?" Individual equality is the essence of human nature; it should be the essence of the human law—its absence releases George from obedience.

George's story is all the more poignant because he was born of a white father, a Kentucky gentleman. Unfortunately, his own father did not think enough of him to have him kept from being sold as his dogs and his horses were sold to satisfy his estate. George saw his own mother sold on the auction block with each of her seven children going to different masters. George heard his mother beg his buyer to buy her as well only to be kicked away with his heavy boot as George was tied to a horse's neck to be carried off. His master did buy his sister and George was sorry for it because her whipping seared George's memory, for "it seemed as if every blow cut into my naked heart, and I couldn't do anything to help her; and she was whipped, sir, for wanting to leave a decent Christian life, such as your laws give no slave girl a right to live . . ." George's sister was sentenced to New Orleans, sold downriver, and he never heard from her again.

George is taken away from his job, taken away from the factory in which he worked, and taken away from his wife and children all in the name of the law of Mr. Wilson's country, not George's. He will find his own country, Canada, a country whose laws he can obey because they are laws to which he gives his consent, and they are laws that make him free: "Because I'm a *freeman*. . . . Yes, sir; I've said Mas'r for the last time to any man. *I'm free.!*" George and Wilson end their conversation imprecating God and by Wilson telling George to trust in God for the good, if not of this life than of the next, to which George responds, "I'll *think of that.*"

The story of George Harris contains a nascent constitutional argument. The Declaration's dedication to equal rights, the Constitution's "We the People," and the nature of the Founding all speak to individual dignity and equality in the spirit, if not in the letter of the law. This is a natural law argument and was part of the education and understanding of the Founders and, therefore, was part of the political morality of the country. Unfortunately, that interpretation of history and of constitutional law was over a century away.[54] Judges charged with the responsibility of interpreting and applying the fugitive slave laws, instead, felt overwhelmingly constrained in what they could and could not do. What they could not do, at least as their opinions demonstrate, was ignore or sidestep the law through strained interpretations. What they could do was either resign from the bench or apply the law as they understood it giving legal force to the property rights of slave owners.

Thomas Sims and Lemuel Shaw

The infamous case of Dred Scott is particularly poignant. Scott had been a slave who had accompanied his master to live in the free state of Illinois and then in the Wisconsin territory which was also free. After his master died,

Scott returned to Missouri and sued his master's widow claiming his freedom because he was voluntarily taken to live on free soil. Scott's claim adopted the reasoning of *Somerset's Case* that once a slave was voluntarily taken to free soil, then freedom attached. Scott's suit found its way to the Supreme Court where he was not only denied the right to sue on his own behalf, he was stripped of all civil and political rights solely because of his race.

The *Dred Scott*[55] opinion remains the ugliest stain on our country's constitutional jurisprudence. The opinion held parts of the Missouri Compromise unconstitutional with the consequence of allowing slavery in the federal territories north and west of Missouri. The Court also held that Congress had no authority to outlaw slavery in the territories even though they had done so in the Articles of Confederation and in the Northwest Ordinance of 1787. Most pernicious, the Court held that free blacks, even in northern states, would never be considered citizens of the United States or protected by the Constitution. Chief justice Roger Taney's words continue to sting as he wrote that black persons were "so inferior that they had no rights which the white man was bound to respect."[56] By denying blacks citizenship, the Taney Court denied them any recourse to constitutional rights.

Taney's opinion was steeped not only in the racism of the times but also in a theory of law that prevented either the religious sentiments of the abolitionists or the natural law aspirations of the Founding to play any role in the interpretation and application of the Fugitive Slave laws. Taney argued that the Declaration of Independence and the Constitution intentionally disenfranchised blacks and intentionally relegated them to the status of property, the status Stowe abhorred. "[T]he right of property in a slave is distinctly and expressly affirmed in the Constitution. The right to traffic in it, like an ordinary article of merchandise and property, was guaranteed to the citizens of the United States. . . ."[57]

As evil as *Dred Scott* has been called[58] and as significant a contribution as it was to the Civil War,[59] the case of Thomas Sims sharply highlights the problem of Creon's ghost. *Sims's Case*[60] also sharply reveals the dilemma of the American judiciary committed to the rule of law even when a judge's moral sympathies lay elsewhere. The judge's oath to uphold the Constitution and the laws of the states meant that he may be, and several judges found that they were, obligated to enforce an odious, immoral law such as the Fugitive Slave Acts. Given the dilemma between an oath of office and an immoral and unjust law, how should a conscientious judge act?

In *justice Accused*, the late Yale scholar Robert Cover examines the role of judges like Joseph Story in *Prigg v. Pennsylvania* and Lemuel Shaw in *Sims's Case.* Unlike Taney, a pro-slavery southerner, Story and Shaw were pro-freedom, anti-slavery northerners. Yet all three judges upheld the "right" of slave owners to their property. Cover argues that anti-slavery judges had four options before them: (1) apply the positive law against conscience, (2) apply conscience against the positive law, (3) resign, or (4) cheat.[61] In each instance the judges did not resign, did not engage in acts of civil disobedience under the last three options, and did apply the positive law—sometimes against conscience—thus perpetuating the institution of slavery.

Sims's Case was the first and most authoritative case to examine the Fugitive Slave Act of 1850 and its decision was handed down by Chief Judge Lemuel Shaw, a noted abolitionist and father-in-law of Herman Melville. Shaw upholds the Fugitive Slave Act, thus going against his convictions. In this decision, he is likened by Cover to Captain Vere in Melville's *Billy Budd.* Vere condemned Billy Budd to death under the Mutiny Act even though he knew him to be innocent. Vere's conflict of conscience between upholding man's law against his own sense of justice was played out by Shaw in *Sims's Case.*[62]

The facts of the case are straightforward, but what transpired in Boston and in the courthouse there were not. Thomas Sims, a former slave living in Boston, was captured and imprisoned as a fugitive slave by Charles Devins, an agent of his master. Boston may well have been a hotbed of Abolitionist feeling; it was also "warming toward Southern interests" as southern cotton and northern manufacturing became increasingly profitable.[63] Bostonians in 1850 had several choices before them for addressing controversies involving fugitive slaves. They could choose among individual liberty for the fugitive, preservation of the Union, personal conscience, or prevailing politics. Professor Leonard Levy's account of *Sims's Case* draws out this conflict by noting that two months prior to Sims's arrest and imprisonment, a group of abolitionists broke into the Court House and freed a captured fugitive named Shadrach. Daniel Webster, then serving as secretary of state, reacted to that act of abolitionist self-help by calling it an act of treason that threatened the Union. *Sims's Case,* according to Levy, gave Boston "an opportunity to make good on its promises of loyally enforcing the Fugitive Slave Act"[64] to counter the charge of treason and to demonstrate its patriotic commitment to the Union.

Upon his arrest, under the stealth of night, "while the city slept, the Court House had been barricaded. . . . Under the direction of City Marshall Francis Tukey, iron chains had been girded entirely around the building."[65] The metaphor of a courthouse enslaved by chains could not have been more pronounced; it would only get worse. This lone alleged fugitive slave had bound the entire city in his drama. The Court House was also surrounded by the full police force and supplemented by special law enforcement officers to ensure that Sims stayed put. Longfellow, upon hearing of the goings on, decried the events, "O city without soul! . . . Shame the great Republic, the 'refuge of the oppressed,' should stoop so low as to become the Hunter of Slaves."[66]

In order to enter the Court House, lawyers, clients, and others had a choice—enter under the chains through the front door or sneak in the back. Shaw, not one to sneak around anything, entered through the front but "the great Shaw, venerated for his wisdom and for his advanced age, was among the first that morning to stoop beneath the chains" to enter his own court.[67] The metaphor is complete. Not only was the Court House bound, justice Shaw, too, bowed beneath the chains of slavery.

Sims filed a *writ of habeas corpus* seeking his release from prison. He claimed that he was a free man, not a slave, and that he was legally entitled to his liberty. The Abolitionist attorneys for Sims argued that the writ should be granted as a matter of right and that Fugitive Slave Law was constitutionally defective. Sims's lawyers argued that the commissioners who were given authority to order rendition were not constitutional judges. They also argued that Sims was not afforded the right to be heard and contest his case and was therefore denied his due process rights. The lawyers also pressed the claim that the commissioners' compensation scheme favoring slave owners was unconstitutional. None of these arguments was successful although they were available and were professionally and constitutionally respectable and could be used by Shaw as the basis for overturning the Fugitive Slave Law.[68] Shaw, instead, denies the writ, resulting in Sims's return to slavery.

Shaw begins his opinion by recognizing his "deep sense of responsibility," as by way of apology, then he develops his legal analysis. Before a *habeas corpus* hearing could be held, the petitioner must show sufficient probable cause of wrongful detention. Then, if cause is shown, a writ would not be granted if it appeared that the prisoner would likely be remanded after the hearing. To have a hearing, the prisoner had the burden of showing that the imprisonment was illegal *and* that he was likely entitled to discharge.

He then noted the possible conflict between state court and federal court jurisdiction. The Fugitive Slave Law was a federal law and it could be argued that suits brought under the law should be heard in federal court. He went forward with the state court suit, however, and considered the constitutionality of the Fugitive Slave Act in two respects. First, was the

Fugitive Slave Act of 1850 constitutional? Second, did that act violate any of the petitioner's constitutional rights? To answer these questions, Shaw examines the constitutional history of the Fugitive Slave Clause in Article IV because, "its history is too deeply interwoven with our whole social system, to be disregarded. . . ."

The country's independence from Great Britain and the original Articles of Confederation resulted in a set of sovereign states whose unity was fragile. This fragile political network was deeply divided on the matter of slavery. Some states such as Massachusetts considered slavery abolished as part of its state constitution; others openly trafficked in human bodies. A country divided by slave and free states could not hope for Union without compromise. "If two states bordered on each other, one a slave state and the other a free state, there would, of course, be a constant effort of slaves to escape into the free state, and a constant temptation to slave owners to follow and recapture them, which must be done by force. . . ." In such circumstances, border wars between sovereign states without a treaty to bind them would be inevitable. And such border wars must be avoided, Shaw reasoned.

Shaw's political and sociological history brings him to the conclusion that a constitutional agreement on fugitive slaves was necessary and that it would, "be in vain for the government of the free state to insist that they would enter into no such compact, because slavery is wrong and unjust. . . ." He feared a Hobbesian war of all against all with no fugitive slave compact. With this background, Shaw finds, "the absolute necessity of forming a more perfect union, in order to secure the peace and prosperity of all the states." Such peace and prosperity could only be accomplished by several states renouncing portions of their sovereignty to the others in a constitutional convention.

Next Shaw examines the Fugitive Slave Clause and finds that it intended that no state could serve as an asylum and sanctuary for fugitive slaves and that the clause was intended for the peaceful and expeditious return of escapees.[69] The Fugitive Slave Act of 1793, the first law to implement Article IV and passed so shortly after the Constitutional Convention, convinced Shaw that it was, "entitled to the highest respect." More particularly, according to Shaw, the "manifest intent" of the 1793 Act was to allow a claimant the use of judges and magistrates of another state to "exercise his right" to his property in prompt and summary proceedings. After reviewing several state and federal court opinions, Shaw found that the Fugitive Slave Act of 1793 was constitutional, and that the provisions of the 1850 Act that were being contested, i.e., allowing a summary proceeding by judicial officers who were not Article III judges, had been constitutionally established. Therefore, the Fugitive Slave Act of 1850 was constitutional and Sim's writ had to be denied, thus guaranteeing his rendition.

Even though Shaw was not reluctant to have a state court grant a *writ of habeas corpus* against a federal magistrate, he would do so only when it was, "necessary to the security of personal liberty from illegal restraint." Sims, he reasoned, was restrained, but not illegally, because there were competent judges of the U.S. courts to entertain their own *habeas corpus* hearings. Not so ironically, this is exactly the same argument made by the Bush Administration in denying *habeas* relief to prisoners held at Guantanamo Bay.[70]

Shaw concludes that he is bound by a series of legal precedents which were, "absolutely necessary to the peace, union and harmonious action" of the state and federal governments and were, "regarded by the framers of the constitution, and has ever since been regarded as essential to the peace, order and prosperity of all the United States." Shaw felt himself bound by man's law. "[H]owever odious we may consider slavery and the slave trade, however abhorrent to the dictates of humanity and the plainest principles of justice and natural right . . . each nation has a right . . . to allow or prohibit slavery . . . established by positive law. . . ." The positive law of slavery trumps the natural law of liberty and the higher law of justice.

The necessity of Union for Shaw was paramount. Otherwise, the situation between slave and free states would lead to a, "war likely to be perpetual, or perhaps to a still more disastrous result—that of some states being subjugated by others of superior physical strength, in a contest in which right and wrong would be disregarded, and violence and brute force would supercede the government of law and the reign of peace." This was the Hobbesian world Shaw said that the Framers feared and intentionally avoided through devilish compromise. It was also the Hobbesian world of brother against brother that the country would soon encounter in Civil War. For Shaw, matters of political necessity take precedence over matters of personal moral preference in the name of state sovereignty. For, as Creon stated, the ship of state needs some pilot.

Shaw concludes his opinion with a curious apologia. "The constitution, therefore, is not responsible for the origin or continuance of slavery." Instead, Shaw writes, the Constitution is an adjustment of conflicting rights and claims in the name of harmony to avert violence and war. His attempted exoneration of the Constitution does not succeed. The Constitution cannot be both absolved from the continuance of slavery and complimented for its Faustian compromise with it. With his apologia for the Constitution, Shaw is attempting his own one because the Constitution's compromise and Shaw's oath of allegiance to it allowed Shaw to do his job rather than resign because it is the "duty of all judges and magistrates to expound and apply these provisions in the Constitution and laws of the United States. . . ." The conflicting loyalties embedded in the Constitution between slave and free states were replayed in the conflict in Shaw's own temperament between his allegiance to the positive law and his belief in a higher one.

Nomos

From the period 1850–1852, we move forward 20 years to 1870. We leave behind the Fugitive Slave Act of 1850, *Sims's Case,* and *Uncle Tom's Cabin.* By 1870, the Civil War with its 650,000 dead had been fought; the Emancipation Proclamation of 1863 had been issued; and the Thirteenth Amendment outlawing slavery, the Fourteenth Amendment guaranteeing equal rights, and the Fifteenth Amendment guaranteeing the right to vote to formerly disenfranchised citizens had created the Reconstruction, a transformative moment in our constitutional history. The restructured Constitution not only broke the Founders' agreement with hell, it replaced it with the reconstructed promise of freedom and equality. To be sure, racist sentiments behind the earlier laws resurfaced in Jim Crow legislation, and the badges and incidents of slavery are still identifiable today. Nevertheless, man's law of slavery had been replaced through politics, violence, and a new Constitution all driven by the higher law.

The higher law, the "idea that the universe contains an ultimate, fundamental law to which all human laws must conform in order to be legitimate,"[71] is no one thing. Rather, the higher law during this period was comprised of Christian evangelism,[72] Enlightenment natural law,[73] and the "higher law" of the Constitution.[74] Together, these elements were transformative because they embodied a moral universe, a *nomos*, in which we chose to replace the Founding with the Reconstruction.

Such a universe was best described by Robert Cover:

> We inhabit a *nomos*—a normative universe. We constantly create and maintain a world of right and wrong, of lawful and unlawful, of valid and void. . . . No set of legal institutions or prescriptions exists apart from the

> narratives that locate it and give it meaning. For every constitution there is an epic, for each decalogue, a scripture. Once understood in the context of the narratives that give it meaning, law becomes not merely a system of rules to be observed, but a world in which we live.[75]

Cover's jurisprudential insight is that law contains within it normative meaning; it cannot be otherwise. Cover knew that the meaning we derive from law may not always be congenial. There will be laws which are viewed as profoundly unjust or immoral by some. His analysis of Shaw's opinion in *Sims's Case* demonstrated that the constitutional *nomos* of the time entrenched, it did not vanquish, slavery. Shaw's commitment to legal positivism and his perceived obligation of fidelity to the Constitution and its precedents prevented him from finding any way around the demands of the Fugitive Slave Act to summarily return runaway slaves.

The conception of a *nomos* containing unjust laws such as racial slavery is dark and disheartening. Such a conception cannot sustain a society for long before it implodes. Most important though, an unworthy *nomos* can be salvaged and Cover promises a way. His conception of *nomos* contains the promise of the Good. He invites us to see both the reality of evil in the law and the redemptive possibility of the Good even when the Good can only be achieved through struggle, even violence.

Law and the *nomos* it inhabits, for Cover, is an evolving institution. Law contains "history and destiny, beginning and end, explanation and purpose."[76] We live with evil, violent laws because such is the human condition. That admission, however, does not mean that we are condemned to live there always. Rather, precisely because law constitutes a narrative of our lives together as social and political beings, it also contains the possibility of reform, perhaps redemption. Today we acknowledge the universal immorality and injustice of racial slavery which had been such a long part of our history—but it was not always so. Slavery was abolished nearly a century after we had declared the all men were created equal and endowed by their Creator with certain unalienable rights. Indeed, it is a principle theme of this book that it will always be the case that moral conflict is imbedded in human law.

The world of law entails myth and history, reality and vision.[77] Because these several impulses are contained in the law and in the normative world in which we live, the law is a dynamic, not static, institution; therefore, law can create a new future.[78] As Cover writes, the law "looks to the future and to a better world and a higher law might trump inferior man's law is not to accept Utopia, rather laws create a force and will generate multiple visions of the future as even alternative stories will provide normative basis for the growth of distinct constitutional worlds . . ."[79]

Cover is not naive about the dangers involved in turning the higher *nomos* into new law. This transformation takes "place in a field of pain and death."[80] A judge who sentenced a criminal to death, like the judge who ordered a fugitive slave return to his master, effects death through the word. Such acts of violence are not limited to the pronouncements of a single judge. They can attend a constitutional regime for generations before change occurs, and the change can be painful—"revolutionary constitutional understandings are commonly staked in blood."[81] Our Founding was an act of rebellion as was our nineteenth-century Reconstitution. Is it not the case, then, that man's law can be oppressive to the point of death and yet contain the seeds of its own redemption? Can it not be the case that our *nomos*, with its prophetic force, can be transformative?

For Cover, the fugitive slave laws and the efforts of the abolitionists to overcome them, had a biblical force,[82] and yet the religious impulse alone was insufficient to transform the law, to give law it's prophetic moment. Throughout the first half of the nineteenth-century, especially during the 30 years preceding the Civil War, Enlightenment natural law arguments grew in importance. The natural rights identified by Hobbes, Locke, Montesquieu, and others[83] were familiar to the Founders and were an essential part of their political discourse and of their argument against the king. The divine right of monarchy had long since passed to be replaced with a social contract through which individuals choose their own government. King George denied the colonists this choice and the colonists, as a matter of natural right, choose for themselves.

The idea of slavery as metaphor was a part of the colonists' fight with the king. The colonists would not be held in slavery to George III. The "Laws of Nature and of Nature's God" meant, quite simply, that individuals possessed natural rights of liberty and equality against the monarchy and in favor of a new republic. Admittedly, those rights were skewed toward white property-owning men and away from women, Native Americans, and slaves. But those natural rights sentiments could not remain limited for long before the natural law rhetoric was taken up by abolitionists wishing to obliterate the hypocrisy.

The choices for slavery's opponents were limited roughly to three. The religiously inspired Abolitionist movement could seek to redesign the social order for the salvation of all. Abolition has been called the first great era of religious activism in American history and it was played out on a constitutionally historic stage.[84] Or one could understand the Constitution and the cases and statutes which followed it as a Garrisionian agreement with hell to be denounced, disobeyed, and destroyed. Or, one could attempt to change the law as the "radical constitutionalists" attempted to do.[85] None of these paths alone was successful, but together they were revolutionary.

The church-fed Abolitionist movement was inadequate to overturn the Constitution's racist compromise in the face of the positive law and in the face of arguments for the preservation of the Union. Garrisonian civil disobedience had minimal effects as the number of successful fugitive slaves was marginal. And constitutional law reform, as argued in the courts and in the Congress, faced insurmountable hurdles. Judges acculturated to be faithful to the rule of law felt duty bound and constrained by the positive law on the books and refused to negate the fugitive slave laws. Together, however, these three options changed history because the conflict between man's law and the higher law became intolerable.

Anti-slavery forces could no longer accept the positive law; the dissonance was unbearable. They would be forced to either accept slavery or give up their vision of freedom, an option they would not accept. Instead, in Cover's words, "The vision of slavery destroyed by the power of law require[d] for its fulfillment the participation of the larger community that exercises state power."[86] The Constitution had slavery encrusted in it; rebellion either in the name of the Union or in opposition to slavery was the only path left open to sustain, then fulfill the vision. The higher law *nomos* of the 1850s lead to lawbreaking through acts of civil disobedience and war, and ultimately lead to breaking the original Constitution.

The conflict between man's law and the higher law was painfully apparent when Shaw bowed beneath the chains to enter the Court House. Through that act, he became a symbol to the abolitionists. He bowed before the chains, Cover writes, because "his only choice was between accepting the yoke of office or resigning it. The sense of overwhelming and external compulsion and the subjugation of deep personal instinct to social necessity were symbolized by the justice's acceptance of the chains."[87] This personal journey of a judge symbolized the journey of a country although when the judge bowed beneath the chains, the country refused.

Instead of bowing, the country revolted and transformed itself from a Founding based on slavery to a Reconstructed Union which abolished it. The Reconstruction is an example of a Lockean Revolution in which one government is dissolved because of a breach of trust to be replaced by a new "legislative."[88] The Founders dissolved their relationship with England because of a breach of trust. King George denied the colonists participation in government and attempted to tax them into subjugation. The Reconstruction dissolved the agreement with hell because of a breach of trust that the slave trade would end in a generation.

Both the Founding and the Reconstruction were radical changes in government.[89] Both were deeply grounded in the rule of law and both were accompanied by bloody revolts. Together law and revolution accomplished constitutional transformations, and neither element can be ignored. In the 1850s, the country was more deeply divided than since the Founding, and the division was only getting worse. The Civil War, politics by another name, became inevitable as the slave issue dragged past the middle of the century with no resolution in sight. Chief justice Shaw saw the fugitive slave laws as necessary for the preservation of the Union even though that meant that individual states had to yield some of their sovereignty against their collective wills. What he failed to see was that while sovereignty could be given up in the name of peace, it must be freely given. The fugitive slave laws forced the free states to accept the will of the South against their own wills. Any peace founded on the logic of *Sims's Case* was fragile indeed.

The war came and the Union survived. It survived because the country, its leaders, its politics, and its citizens persevered in a process of higher lawmaking which involved breaking away from the law of the past. Professor Bruce Ackerman argues that the Thirteenth and Fourteenth Amendments are part of the Constitution because they weathered a modern constitution-making process; they are not part of the Constitution, "by virtue of Antietam and Gettysburg and the war power."[90] His emphasis on lawmaking, however, cannot ignore the lawbreaking that necessitated it. Amending the Constitution took place in the bloodless halls of politics, but constitution drafting was preceded, and necessitated, by the bloody fields of war.

The act of rewriting the Constitution in a radically new way should be taken as a story of our commitment to and experience of the higher law which encompassed the wide and broad support of the citizenry.[91] The elements of the higher law—religion and rebellion, natural law, and constitutional law—were forged into an irresistible *nomos* which violently destroyed the seemingly impenetrable man's law of slavery. The Civil War may have been a necessary condition for a new constitutional moment, but it was insufficient. The formal legal processes of constitution-making were also necessary. Reconstruction not only eliminated slavery, it constituted a dramatic change in the structure as well as the substance of the Constitution.

This legal transformation is the pride of a country built as a constitutional democracy. The codification of higher anti-slavery law into man's law does not, of course, prevent future conflicts; it does, however, transform them. In this way, the Lockean Revolution is fulfilled and the disintegration of the state was prevented.

Conclusion

For many, religion constitutes the higher law. In the United States, however, from the very beginning, religion occupies a delicate position.[92] In a country with a jurisprudence committed to separation and nonestablishment, religion cannot be directly incorporated into the positive law. We struggle mightily to maintain a balance and a reasonable separation between our religion and our law. We believe that there ought to be a separation between church and state. We also believe that no religion, nor religion *tout court*, should garner government favor. And we also recognize that the influence of religion cannot be, and for many should not be,[93] extracted completely from politics. Religion, instead, continues to be an essential and often- contentious element in our politics.

During the 2008 campaign, President Barack Obama brought these themes of religion, law, and politics—of man's law and higher law—together in an eloquent speech. He was harshly criticized for the racist and anti-American statements made by his former black minister Rev. Jeremiah A. Wright. Addressing those statements, the "nation's original sin of slavery," and the continuing racial divide in the country, Obama spoke of a higher law. In spite of being a flawed document, he said, "[T]he answer to the slavery question was already embedded within our Constitution—a Constitution that had at its very core the ideal of equal citizenship under the law; a Constitution that promised its people liberty, and justice and a union that could be and should be perfected over time." Barack Obama stood Chief justice Shaw's argument on its head.

President Barack Obama's commitment to the higher law of the Constitution was forged in faith–"But I have asserted a firm conviction—a conviction rooted in my faith in God and my faith in the American people—that working together we can move beyond some of our old racial wounds, and that in fact we have no choice if we are to continue on the path of a more perfect union."[94] Obama more than echoes, he reiterates, the theme of *Uncle Tom's Cabin*—our religious impulses inform our understanding of the higher law and those impulses are felt in our politics. They can also make their way into our law but not directly. Rather, they become part of our *nomos* that informs our law.

Uncle Tom's Cabin was driven by a religious fervor to end slavery, yet that fervor gained no victories in courts of law. The positive law of the country, including the silence of the Declaration of Independence, the accommodations made in the Constitution, and the Fugitive Slave Laws enacted by Congress perpetuated a system of slavery that become intolerable to many and threatened the Union for all. The lesson of *Uncle Tom's Cabin, Sim's Case*, and the Reconstruction is that man's law stands strong against religion's claims, but is not impenetrable. The higher law, including its religious sentiments, can be ignored only at great price, a lesson eloquently taught in Lincoln's Second Inaugural Address:

> If we shall suppose that American slavery is one of those offenses which, in the providence of God, must needs come, but which, having continued through His appointed time, He now wills to remove, and that He gives to both North and South this terrible war as the woe due to those by whom the offense came, shall we discern therein any departure from those divine attributes which the believers in a living God always ascribe to Him? Fondly do we hope, fervently do we pray, that this mighty scourge of war may speedily pass away. Yet, if God wills that it continue until all the wealth piled by the bondsman's two hundred and fifty years of unrequited toil shall be sunk, and until every drop of blood drawn with the lash shall be paid by another drawn with the sword, as was said three thousand years ago, so still it must be said "the judgments of the Lord are true and righteous altogether."

The constitutional moment of Reconstruction embodied several impulses of the higher law. We applaud this achievement as a validation of our constitutional government and the values our founding documents contain. Is this commitment to these higher law impulses sustainable? justice Oliver Wendell Holmes Jr. thinks not.

SIX

Law's Practical Theory

The main hall of the red brick building was filled to capacity on a cold January 8. Outside, the day was cloudy with snow threatening. Inside, the room was warm and the crowd was drowsy after an hour of welcoming remarks, prayers, and a glee club recital. The state court judge moved to the podium, prepared speech in hand, intent on rousing the audience from its "poisoned slumber."

The audience politely listened as the judge read his speech honoring the dedication of a new law school building. Mostly, the audience heard what they might have expected to hear as the judge exhorted the students to study hard and learn the law. The audience might not have expected to hear the judge tell the students that to best understand the law they must study law as if they were bad men. Studying law with the bad man in mind, he told them, is the best path to the law. The judge's remarks seem not to have roused the audience from its slumbers on the January 8th of 1897. His remarks, however, have roused us from ours and resonate over one hundred years later.[1]

THE OLD JUDGE WHO wished to rouse the audience from the "poisoned slumber"[2] was completing his fifteenth year on the bench of the Supreme Judicial Court of Massachusetts and was five years away from his appointment to the Supreme Court of the United States where he would sit for 30 years. Oliver Wendell Holmes Jr. occupies a unique place in legal history. Lawyer, teacher, scholar, and judge, he has been labeled liberal and conservative, cynic and saint, positivist and realist.[3] Regardless of the label, his place as a jurisprudential Olympian is sound.[4] Holmes was aristocratic, cosmopolitan, literary, and distinctly American.[5] His Boston Brahmin upbringing put him in contact with the great minds of the turn of the twentieth century and those experiences meaningfully shaped his philosophy of law.[6]

Holmes began to draft his speech for the dedication of a new law school building at Boston University in the fall of 1896. His remarks were untitled.

He wanted his speech to fit the occasion and as he wrote to Lady Castleton, he described his topic as "Legal Education" or his "Theory of Legal Study."[7] The speech acquired the title, *The Path of the Law*, upon publication, and it remains one of the great documents of American jurisprudence. Holmes intended to provoke, and today scholars and philosophers continue to engage and argue about his jurisprudence in general and this speech in particular.

Another Walk Down *The Path*

Law professor Tom Grey writes that *The Path of the Law* is a cohesive whole and is thoughtfully connected to Holmes's broader philosophy.[8] He also writes that the speech, with all of its prescriptions for law study, reveals Holmes's romantic, grand quest for the law.[9] Holmes had great ambitions for law. He was a consummate insider who practiced, taught, and wrote about law. His devotion to law and his capacious intellect married grand ambition with deep inside knowledge as they culminated in what is the most widely subscribed-to jurisprudential school today—legal pragmatism.[10]

The Path is a look at law from the inside;[11] it is an examination of how law should be studied and practiced.[12] Concentrated study and deep understanding will greatly benefit law practice and the society it serves as we learn how to best apply law to achieve socially useful ends. Law study and practice are purposive. We need to seriously engage both so that the policies of the law and law's direction can be understood for future application, not for the purpose of "striving for some useless quintessence of all systems."[13] Law, as Holmes's "brooding omnipresence in the sky," can be studied from the outside as a subject of historical, sociological, or anthropological curiosity. While informative, these external approaches do not illustrate the best picture of law. Holmes could not believe otherwise for that is where his life in law was situated. Not only did he know the inside perspective, the inside perspective fit his grand vision of law. In short, the object of Holmes's study and theorizing was man's law, not something higher.

Introduction

The Path starts with law study, ranges over law practice, and culminates with a practical theory of law. Holmes links study and practice in the first sentence of *The Path:* "[W]hen we study law, we are not studying a mystery but a well known profession."[14] As lawyers, we advise clients and appear before judges. As judges, we manage and decide cases. As legislators, we debate and promulgate law. As executive branch officers, we observe and enforce it. And as citizens, we sometimes test and sometimes disobey the law. All of these figures are insiders to the law, all are involved with this well-known profession, and all engage man's law.

At bottom, as insiders, we are concerned about the power of the state. Sometimes we care to keep the power of the state at bay. Other times we care to apply law to our benefit or regulate its use. Regardless of perspective, we should all share an understanding of the law. *The Path* sketches such an understanding and leads us to Holmes's legal pragmatism.[15]

Law study starts with the mundane, with the cases and statutes of the common law running back hundreds of years. We study law so that we can make accurate and reliable predictions about legal sanctions. As students of law, we can make more accurate and reliable predictions if we theorize about law, the policies it contains, and about its best practical applications. Law study thus encompasses a historically developed body of doctrine with an eye toward its future development. With these opening paragraphs, Holmes sketches the whole of his speech[16] in which he wants to identify first principles and weave them into "an ideal which as yet our law has not attained."[17] Holmes's first principles are anchored in the study of a system leading to practice and its improvement, then leading to what he will later refer to as a "hint" of the universal law.

The Limits of the Law

Holmes intended to shock his audience with his first first principle. He told his audience that law and morality are, and should, be kept separate. He recited this positivist canard because he wanted to "dispel a confusion between morality and the law." Holmes's point is a simple one. The languages of law and of morality overlap and led to unnecessary confusion, particularly when first studying law. This first principle is troubling as Holmes recognizes in his speech because separating law and morality has never been popular for the familiar reason that immoral laws are unjust laws, and unjust laws sustain an unjust society.

Holmes, though, is on solid ground. We should think of law and morality as distinct ways of thinking, talking, and behaving in the world. The Kantian categorical imperative or the Golden Rule is widely accepted as moral principle: we should not do unto others what we do not want done unto us. Morality may well benefit society; it certainly influences law. But morality is not coextensive with law. Morality guides the inner life, the life of the conscience. Law guides our outer life, our sociopolitical arrangements. The moral command *Be Nice* cannot attain legal status. We may have a moral duty to *Be Nice*; we do not have a legal duty to do so. What is so often overlooked in *The Path* is that Holmes repeatedly qualifies his statement about separation. The separation between law and morality is necessary for the study of law; the separation is necessary to understand the limits of the law; the separation is the first step on the path. Later, after we at least learn to identify and name the law, then we can return to and assess the relationship between law and morality. Moral principles may teach us about law's limits and about law's justness. Moral principles may inform and evaluate law—they cannot and should not define it.

In support of his separation argument, Holmes invokes the infamous bad man. Holmes's bad man is the perfect foil for testing law's limits as well as for accomplishing Holmes's central purpose—the "right study and mastery" of the law.[18] The bad man looks to law's material consequences and does not look for reasons outside of law to obey. Holmes intends neither moral pronouncement nor grand theory by his separation thesis. Holmes argues that moral language simply, and singularly in his mind, confuses the matter of learning, understanding, applying, and, ultimately, building a theory of law. Holmes does not deny that immoral laws are on the books and are enforced, but he emphasizes the positivist point that immorality neither negates a law's validity nor invalidates its sanctions for disobedience.

Holmes's bad man simply wants to avoid fines, penalties, and jail time. The bad man wants to avoid liability, a liability that can only be imposed and enforced by the state. How, then, should the bad man behave to avoid sanctions? We begin by separating the language of morality from the language of law. To prove his point, Holmes gives the example of the efficient breach of contract.[19] "The duty to keep a contract at common law means a prediction that you must pay damages if you do not keep it. . . ."[20] Keeping contracts may well be a morally worthy thing to do. It may also be a socially nice thing to do, but the law does not think so. Keeping contracts just for the purported moral goodness behind the idea is not legally required.[21] The legal actor here, the bad man, or the efficient homo economicus, honors contractual obligations to avoid sanction. Holmes ends this first principle with the challenge that if we could banish from the law every word of moral significance, then our study and understanding of it would improve.

Holmes's separation argument is a warning about confusing legal duty and moral obligation and confusing the future development and application of law. This confusion must be dispelled if one is to study and know the law on the books before applying it in the streets. The bad man (and the student of law) cares not a whit about grand theory, she rather needs to know, "[t]he prophecies of what the courts will do in fact, and nothing more pretentious. . . . "[22] Holmes's grand positivist prediction thesis may be lightly sketched. It may not bear empirical scrutiny and it may not congeal into a satisfying grand theory of law.[23] Still, for a few paragraphs in a speech at a building dedication, it captures our continuing attention and resounds throughout the century. More important, the prediction thesis has identifiable legal consequences. Clients go to lawyers to predict when the state may impose or refuse state power. Legislators and presidents pay at least occasional attention to constitutionality and judicial review. Judges pay attention to how their decisions comport with existing and developing law. Even Supreme Court justices read the newspapers. All of these activities involve legal predictions of what courts (and legislatures) will do.

Even here, when he intends to shock by banning moral talk from law talk, Holmes claims the higher law ground when he writes that law is the "witness and external deposit of our moral life;" and is the "history of the moral development of the [human] race." Holmes even believes that the observance of the law, "tends to make good citizens and good men."[24] With these clearly moral sentiments, Holmes touches familiar ground for his audience, and he sounds very much like a natural lawyer.[25] Law and morality may be related, yet the relationship should not come at the cost of a better understanding of law and of building a better legal system. To understand the law and to study it and practice it, one must first learn what the law is rather than what it ought to be. Evaluative judgments can be made later.

Logic and the Law

Our understanding of law benefits from recognizing that law is limited in its scope and intent. Some of these limits are realized when we remove moral talk from law. Others are realized when we free law from the strict application of logical rules. Just as law is not to be confused with morality, it is not to be confused with logic.[26] Holmes's second first principle distinguishes law from logic because law is not a purely deductive system of rules derived from axioms. Yet if we successfully separate law from both morality and logic, then what determines law's content and growth? Law has its own rules for its growth and development, and those rules are rooted in experience and practical application. Holmes's great aphorism from *The Common Law* that "the life of the law has not been logic, it has been experience,"[27] is revived in this speech and is a central tenet of his pragmatism.

Holmes believed that law forms a more or less cohesive whole; law has "some order, some rational explanation."[28] As a more or less cohesive whole, law can be studied, understood, and applied in the world in service to clients and in service to society as law grows and develops by it own internal logic and demands. Law does not follow Christopher Columbus Langdell's dark science through which law generates fixed legal rules to be deductively applied without consideration of consequences.[29] Law cannot be, "worked out like mathematics from some general axioms of conduct,"[30] otherwise, how would legal disagreement be possible? And legal disagreement, particularly the haggling over the shadows and light of justice, lies at the heart of law practice.

Lawyers are trained in logic but lawyer logic is inductive as well as deductive; it is logic by analogy, comparison, categorization, and discrimination.[31] Law cannot be a pure deductive system because law is a fully human enterprise. It is intended to serve human needs as it not only helps people avoid the strong arm of the state; it also helps people achieve their goals and aspirations. Holmes's bad man seeks to avoid sanctions. We can easily posit a Holmesian good woman who wishes to start a business, provide for her children, or establish a charitable foundation. She can accomplish all of these goals through law because law has a power-conferring dimension as Hart taught. Strict logical rules get in the way of human experience and desire as Holmes knew and warned. "[C]ertainty generally is illusion, and repose is not the destiny of man."[32] Legal rules and decisions are imprecise because human nature is imprecise and incapable of "exact quantitative measurement, and therefore not capable of founding exact legal conclusions."[33]

Holmes knew that logical rules, deductively applied, would hinder the development of law because law does not only look backward for the resolution of a case. Legal thinking looks forward in anticipation of the best rules to be applied in a changing society. Yes, past disputes must be resolved, but must they be resolved by ancient legal rules that have not adapted to the times? Not for Holmes. The legal thinker asks: What is the point of a legal rule? What are the purposes and policies for applying any specific rule? What are a law's "legislative grounds?" These policy questions have more relevance for the future than for the past because they are about how well law functions and develops.

Holmes was anything but naive. He acknowledges that decision makers often decide cases on unconscious or inarticulate grounds. The day-to-day business of the law does require lawyers and judges to move cases along, and reliance on established rules is a part of law practice. Still, the conscientious lawyer and judge must inquire about the purposes of a legal rule because clients and cases demand new applications of law as novel situations arise. When lawyers and judges make such inquiries, they look to the panoply of legal and nonlegal materials available and they also, says Holmes, attempt to follow the practice of the community regarding appropriate policies. In addition to being variable, legal decisions are intentionally provisional. They are intended for the society in which the conflict arises. And they are open always, "for reconsideration upon a slight change in the habit of the public mind."[34]

In *The Path*, Holmes warns against an unreflective reliance on morality, logic, and past law. This openness does not mean either that anything goes in the law or that law lacks some cohesion or direction. Instead, the reflective practice of law considers moral, logical, and historic influences together with society's needs and the law's own internal structure and institutional values. Such reflective practice allows law to adopt ways that refine and improve it. While Holmes would feel comfortable with legal realist views about the need for understanding law's policy content, he would not go as far as the critical legal studies slogan that "all law is politics" (and nothing but).

Holmes gives examples of legal rules and exposes the policy preferences behind them. Certain statements are privileged, for example, so that the information contained in them is revealed without fear of liability or compromise. A business which may impose external social costs upon neighbors may be created in the spirit of free competition is another example. As Holmes did with contracts earlier in the speech, he does with torts at this point. He notices that tort suits involving railroads, factories, and the like are ultimately lawsuits about liability and damages. "The public really pays the damages, and the question of liability . . . is really the question how far it is desirable that the public should insure the safety of those whose work it uses."[35] Common law suits are grounded on policy decisions about economic costs and benefits.

Tort rules are neither purely logically derived nor normative truths; they are provisional policy preferences. These preferences reveal legislative conflicts which do not admit a deductive resolution. Holmes makes no claim as to the truth value of these rules or as to the clear wisdom of the policies behind them. He never goes so far as to assert that a pragmatist judge can simply substitute her policy preferences for those contained in the law. His point is that it is necessary to study and practice law to understand what the policies are. If "interstices" of the law appear, then a judge may be called upon to fill them when issuing a ruling, but those are not run of the mill cases.

Holmes was a half century or more ahead of his time. He recognizes that legal decisions are fundamentally about social, and most frequently economic, policies. Yet he is cautious about the role that judges should play. Holmes says that judges, "have failed adequately to recognize their duty of weighing considerations of social advantage."[36] Ideally, judges should have the intellectual capability to understand and assess the legislative reasons behind the statutes that they are required to interpret and apply. If judges were more open and accurate about the reasons for their decisions, then perhaps they might better understand the choices available to them. Judges should hesitate to take "sides upon debatable and often burning questions."[37] They should not hesitate to articulate the policies behind the law. Judges should hesitate to legislate. They should not hesitate to apply legislation modestly and correctly. Holmes did not want them to substitute their own policy preferences, which they might well do if they were unreflective about the basis of their decision. His concern was that if a judge was not reflective and aware, he might decide a case on the basis of some inchoate fear such as a fear of socialism or of the labor movement. If decisions are so made, then the purposes and the policies of the law are not served.

The Present Condition of the Law

Holmes's view of man's law had one eye on how law is practiced and the other eye on law's ideal, an ideal Holmes knew had not been reached. He recognized that law as practiced in the Anglo-American legal profession had been developing, mostly unconsciously, for hundreds of years. While unconscious development is a natural tendency—we adopt the legal rules of our parents and our neighbors—law will better develop when a legal rule is "referred articulately and definitely to an end which it subserves, and when the grounds for desiring that end are stated or are ready to be stated in words."[38]

Of first importance, then, is to understand the purpose of a legal rule. We can, and do, look to history and tradition for clues. "The rational study of law is still to a large extent, the study of history."[39] But history is only a part of rational study; it should lead to enlightened skepticism and to reconsideration in light of present and future conditions. Holmes writes that the man of the present is the black letter man, and it is necessary for all who study law to start with the black letter rule and test it against society's needs with the best social science tools available. Holmes then says that the man of the future is a master of statistics and economics. He uses the "future" metaphorically. The "future" is not meant to be some distant time; rather the future is now after the black letter rule has been learned, the policies behind it understood, and as the application of the rule is contemplated. Can the social sciences assist us in this process? Holmes says yes. Social science can improve the current application of and the future development of law.

To make his point that we should have a better reason to apply a rule than it "was laid down in the time of Henry IV,"[40] Holmes tests this theory against the criminal law. Does it really matter, he asks, that when property is taken whether the taking falls under the label of larceny, trespass, or embezzlement? In each case, a person's property has been taken, and a loss has been suffered. Are the definitions of these crimes tight enough so that miscreants pay for their crimes? Or, as he implies, are these age-old legal categories so porous that injured persons are left uncompensated? Holmes makes two points. First, he asks whether historic legal categories are functional and should be retained. His second concern is whether the focus in these cases should be on compensating losses rather than finely defining crimes. Holmes then asks another more penetrating question about criminal law to make his point. Does criminal law work? Not only should the punishment fit the crime, the punishment should be administered to some useful end. Does punishment deter? Does it rehabilitate? Does it satisfy society's yearning for retribution? What do sociology, criminology, and statistics tell us about the administration of punishment and its effect on criminals and its consequences on society?

The present condition of law is always evanescent as today elides into tomorrow. What is troublesome to Holmes about the present condition is that law will stagnate if we have no reason other than history and tradition for applying its rules. To ensure that law does not stagnate, we must ask about law's purpose and function, and we can use the tools of social science to assist us. In that way, once we uncover the purpose of the law, we can ask how best that purpose is served by applying a rule to decide a case with an eye on the future development of the law.

The Future Study of Law

Holmes greatly respected legal history and the contributions made by nineteenth-century legal thinkers, yet to supplement the learning of the past, Holmes urges the study of economics, particularly political economy, to "consider and weigh the ends of legislation, the means of attaining them, and the cost."[41] Holmes's desire to use cost-benefit analysis is consistent with his pragmatic theory of balancing and weighing competing interests, and of looking backward for clues about the future.

Beyond economics, Holmes urges the greater study of jurisprudence as he brings his speech to a close. *The Path* opens with the bad man and the black letter study of law as prelude to understanding law's nature and law's aspiration. By jurisprudence, Holmes did not intend to create unified and theoretically cohesive philosophical constructs. He refers, instead, to the process of generalizing the rules of law into a coherent body of doctrine to see what holds them together so that they can be usefully applied. His examples from torts, contracts, and criminal law are intended to force us to think about the concepts which hold each legal category together. Further, the common law is not best perceived as a series of discrete legal categories. Instead, common-law categories are connected by broader, more overarching concepts such as liability and compensation rather than a morally ambiguous concept such as fault. Searching for, finding, and articulating these concepts is the work of jurisprudence. The generalizing dimension of jurisprudence will help the lawyer make better predictions.

Holmes saw law study and practice as the use of "enlightened instrumental reason."[42] While law may well be experience, it employs reason and logic to help it with its work. Neither reason nor logic serve law as intrinsic goods; they serve law instrumentally. Morality and logic, reason and experience have little or no value to the law apart from the usefulness of the results that they generate. Similarly, law's history and its future must be connected to some useful, practical purpose. The purpose is partially found in the law itself and in the felt needs of society. It is the obligation of practitioners of law, including judges, to understand and articulate these purposes and those needs. In this way, law can be more accurately applied and encrusted legal rules can be recognized as such and reformed or deleted as necessary.

Holmes advises students of law—and all participants in the legal system are students of law—to start by understanding doctrine, generalizing legal rules through jurisprudence, uncovering the purpose of the law through history, and then conclude by asking what purpose the rule is to serve, the reasons for this end, and the cost of accomplishing it.[43] Through this process, Holmes's path reveals his pragmatic approach to and his ideal of man's law.

Conclusion

Holmes closes his speech with the exhortation that if one studies law along his path, not seeking $50,000 but instead seeking intellectual nourishment, then the student can become a great mistress of law. More ambitiously, if the student follows her path, she can connect her "subject with the universe and catch an echo of the infinite, a glimpse of the unfathomable process, a hint of the universal law."[44] This remarkable offer is more remarkable still when we realize that Holmes is still speaking from inside the practice of law.

He believes that the student who delves deeply enough into doctrine and looks forward enough to its proper application will have the majesty of the law revealed to her. A student's library cubicle can make one little room an everywhere.[45] In his conclusion, Holmes reveals the breadth of what he meant by the study of law. It is not confined to textbooks or rules; it expands to their application in the world, and it expands even further to understanding the nature of man's law. A student of law will never become master or mistress until he or she can theorize about the law. A theory of law is not the antithesis of its practice; it is its apotheosis because it is a theory drawn deeply from the inside. The end of mastery is not money; it is the life of the mind and the contribution a lawyer can make to society and to intellectual culture.

Holmesian Pragmatism

Holmes has been criticized for his failure to develop either a full theory of law or a theory of judging.[46] Both criticisms miss the mark.[47] Holmes was not an abstract system builder; he did not construct a unified or closed theory of law.[48] Instead, Holmes's pragmatism is based on his experience, practice, and reflection about law. When Holmes uses the architect as metaphor in *The Path*, the architect is someone who designs a building to serve a purpose. The architect is not a workman who constructs a building perfectly according to a set architectural rendering. He is a craftsman, a jobber[49] who designs creatively and practically. So, too, must lawyers perform creatively and practically. Legal behavior cannot conform to a set theory. It must be open to a range of influences. Outsiders need systems to understand phenomena. Insiders cannot be constrained by them. Holmes, the insider, the judge of one-half century, knew law was guided by general principles, one of which is flexibility. Law is a dynamic social institution driven by a variety of social, political, and moral forces that change with history and culture. Nevertheless, law is the stabilizing counterforce to these influences even while this counterforce must be adaptable to serve society and anticipate, rather than dictate its direction.[50] Holmes's pragmatism is defined by how law manages the reality of flexibility and the necessity for stability. Holmes looked to history and social practices to begin to understand the purposes of the law, and he looked to modern social sciences such as economics and statistics to assess and fit the rules to the needs of the times[51] Holmes's jurisprudence, then, had its own two faces. Jurisprudence serves to help practitioners understand law from a broader perspective while serving as a stabilizing force. A pragmatic approach to law enables jurisprudence to evolve more toward the potential majesty of man's law.

Legal practitioners know two things about the law: law is messy, and law should serve a social purpose. Law is messy because it is embedded in history and culture; is expressed in general and imprecise language; is expected to be objective and neutral; and in reality, serves conflicting needs and masters and values. Law must serve the purpose of enabling people to achieve their dreams and avoid their fears. It also serves the purpose of empowering the state to create social institutions such as markets and political processes for its growth and stability so that its citizens can flourish. None of these goals flows in one direction only.

Holmes acknowledged that law practice has its own inherent limitations. "Practices are not only habitual and largely unconscious; they are mainly collective in origin."[52] Unless the context and conventions in which a rule of law was born are uncovered and evaluated, law may be wrongly and ineffectively applied. The conscious and reflective practice of law can cure these defects. So conceived, law practice can serve to resolve the conflicts that confront it, react to the need for clarity and stability for law's future application, and respond to the desire for a better future.

Consequently, to manage law's messiness and purposefulness, no single theoretical construct, certainly no construct based on a set of scientific principles to be logically applied, can function. Rather, law must be fluid and adaptable with an eye on what law does best—solve problems and resolve conflicts. But law must aspire to do more than that; otherwise it will stagnate.

Holmes does not assert some overall scheme for his judicial philosophy, nor does he proclaim a set of social ends for the betterment of mankind. His lack of a full-scale and external theory of law and his reluctance, skepticism even, to articulate a social program is completely consistent with his pragmatism. Law practitioners work from the inside. They respect the law and believe that man's law is valuable in and of itself. While law is certainly influenced by moral and political values, it is not the purpose of the law to advance any particular comprehensive world view. Law, including its conflicting goals, should be made as clear and predictable as it can be without sacrificing the flexibility and dynamism that law needs to grow and improve. The Holmesian pragmatist, thus, adheres to judicial precedent for stability and defers to the legislature for change.[53] By paying attention to the social institution of the law, it can evolve by looking backward and looking forward with the intent of enhancing predictability while maintaining institutional integrity.[54]

Holmesian pragmatism does not urge wholesale judicial legislation; it urges wholesale judicial understanding of the best use of existing rules in light of new and changing circumstances. Context and purpose, neither history nor predetermined theory, point the direction of the law.[55] Law practice is to serve society, not satisfy a philosopher's theory. At the same time, practice can improve the law when applied articulately and clearly. The ideal of law fits no specific philosophical or jurisprudential school. It is neither Kantian nor utilitarian, formalist nor realist. Instead, the ideal of law is found in its rational and instrumental functioning. In other words, law is ideal when it works.

Law works best by following Holmes's principles. Law's practitioners begin their study from (a) the perspective of the bad man, (b) who predicts what the courts will do, (c) for the purpose of assessing sanctions, (d) eschewing formal logic and deduction, (e) while appreciating history and culture, (f) while formulating a general theory, (g) for the purpose of identifying the policies behind the law, (h) to be applied to contemporary conflicts with the aid of the social sciences which, (i) when the applications work, (j) improve the legal system. In short, steps (a) through (j) constitute the Holmesian pragmatic path of the law.

Posnerian Pragmatism

Judge Richard Posner of the United States Court of Appeals for the Seventh Circuit is today's leading legal pragmatist. Sitting on the bench as well as professing in the classroom, Judge Posner is our most prolific legal scholar and has written extensively about pragmatism. There is no basic principle of Holmesian pragmatism with which Judge Posner would disagree. He does diverge from Holmes, however, in the application of the principles of legal pragmatism. Where Holmes adheres closely to precedent and legislative intent, Posner is more willing to venture beyond both to find the "best" answers to legal conflicts. Posner recognizes the distinction between them, noting that pragmatism is expansive enough to include legalist judges who believe that "the best results would be produced if the judges . . . simply applied the rules."[56]

Like Holmes, Posner's view of legal pragmatism is an inside view of law. Law "is better, though not fully, described as an activity of the licensed professionals we call judges."[57] Posner bases his pragmatism on the idea of law as a profession.[58] Although he cites *The Path* for its criticism of the orthodox and formalist view that tomorrow's law should not emanate from yesterday's, he goes further than Holmes did. Posner writes that "the law is merely a transitional phase in the evolution of social control."[59] Consequently, law is not an end in itself; it is a human instrument to be used to advance human ends. For Posner, as for Holmes, law can only mean man's law.

Posner defines legal pragmatism broadly as a "disposition to ground policy judgments on facts and consequences rather than on conceptualisms and generalities."[60] From this 30,000-foot level, his definition must be qualified and explained. Posner provides a dozen additional details for what he means by legal pragmatism;[61] all of these details contribute to a theory of law as law practice.

To Posner, the legal practitioner must do the best job that she can. As office lawyer, the legal pragmatist must advise clients about the best (e.g., the most reliable, least costly) way to go about their businesses. As advocate, the pragmatist lawyer must make the best legal argument available, which means staying within the substantive and interpretive rules as best she can and putting forward novel arguments when they have the best chance of winning. As legislator, the legal pragmatist must draft statutes in the best way possible. A well-crafted statute will satisfy constitutional requirements, fit within existing statutory law, and achieve the policies that it is intended to achieve. As judge, the legal pragmatist writes opinions that resolve past disputes and can be meaningfully applied to the next conflict while advancing the direction of the law. Judicial opinions cannot be *ad hoc* nor should a legal pragmatist judge decide only the case before her. Every case is retrospective insofar as a conflict is resolved, and almost every case must fit into existing jurisprudence as well as look forward for its best future application. The backward/forward view of a case allows the judge to take into consideration the systemic and institutional consequences of a decision.[62]

Sometimes, although rarely in Posner's view, the rules can be applied formally to resolve a case. While all relevant facts and circumstances are considered, they must be considered reasonably within the context of the dispute.[63] There is no mathematical formula for applying reason to cases. Law is not a system of logical deduction. Existing legal materials, the needs of society, the continuing vitality of then-current rules of law, and even a judge's own ethical and policy preferences,[64] are all incorporated into the decision process. Pragmatic legal reasoning is based on reasonableness and rationality. It is also based on empirical data and can employ all rational decision procedures such as cost-benefit analysis, risk-benefit analysis, public choice, and the like, as fair procedures for judicial decision making. Deciding a case, then, means that "all things [are] considered."[65]

The most distinguishing characteristic of legal pragmatism is that it rejects legal formalism[66] as the defining decisional rule. Holmes made the point in *The Path* that simply because a legal rule has been applied for centuries, tradition, in and of itself, is no reason to apply it again. Past decisions provide valuable and *maybe* conclusive information about a legal rule and its application. But past decisions alone do not constitute law. Posner, more so than Holmes, is willing to jettison past cases for new and improved rules.

Pragmatism, Posner writes, is not hostile to all theory; it is only hostile to using abstract moral or political constructs or principles as the determining basis for deciding concrete cases, particularly ones that would be better decided on narrow grounds. There is no higher law for Posner; there is only man's law.[67] The pragmatist judge has an eye on the consequences of the decision, but this does not make her a consequentialist judge who attempts to fit a decision into a predetermined philosophy. A pragmatist judge deciding a case about market share liability can consider the consequential effects on tort law without reaching the consequentialist conclusion that market share liability is good (or not) because it is based on utilitarian grounds.

The pragmatist judge seeks a decision that fits best with present and future needs. In making that decision, the judge must consider, weigh, and balance doing substantive justice in the case at hand and honoring the need for certainty and predictability for law as a social institution.[68] Law as an institution can best serve its purposes through flexible, pragmatic adjudication that requires rules to function on these multiple levels if they are to function well.[69] Legal pragmatism appears to ordinary observers to be what Posner calls "everyday pragmatism."[70] Legal pragmatism is not an academic abstraction reinterpreting the epistemology, metaphysics, or political theory of philosophical pragmatism. Legal pragmatism is functional and based on common sense, practical reasoning, expertise, and special (legal) training.

Special legal expertise sensitizes the practitioner to the ways of the law. Legal expertise does not bestow upon lawyers a special and unique way of reasoning. Instead, legal reasoning becomes a matter of habit which instills in practitioners an understanding of the principles and institutions of the law. Legal education and training also vest practitioners with a specialized vocabulary so they can speak a common language to address the diverse problems that law must confront. Legal pragmatism is not wed to any particular analytic method nor is it wed to any particular moral or political philosophy. Legal pragmatism is intended to decide cases and to work effectively in the world.[71]

Largely because of its open refusal to subscribe to a set methodology or philosophy, legal pragmatism is not free from criticism. Critics argue that if a pragmatist judge can wander far from the rule of law on the books, then there is no clear or necessary stopping point for a legal decision. Nor can a pragmatist judge wander too far from the forms of law without getting lost in a judge's personal presuppositions and loose law's power of predictability.[72] If all methods of analysis are available, there is no sure guide. If all jurisprudential theories are available, there is no coherence. If all methods and theories have informational or decisional value, there is questionable reliability. How does legal pragmatism avoid being nothing more than a judge's "gut reaction"? Is it the case, then, that there is no content to legal pragmatism because all data, from the case at hand to facts in the world, and from public opinion to the social sciences, are all available for judges to use? If so, then is legal pragmatism contentless and, therefore, indeterminate?[73] A further criticism is that legal pragmatism is question-begging. To the extent that legal pragmatism is about applying or fashioning the "best" rule, then what counts as the "best" without have some sort of moral or political philosophy?

Because these criticisms aim at abstractions, including truth,[74] they miss pragmatism's core insight. Legal pragmatism is about how law is practiced and how it can best be practiced. Legal pragmatism is neither contentless nor indeterminate because for it to be applied in the world, it must be applied with a sense of fit. Pragmatist law practice fits what came before it and what will come after. It accommodates the cases at hand as well as the larger institutional concerns of the legal system. Good, effective lawyers and judges do not wander aimlessly in the world of facts or in the fields of philosophy, moral theory, or public opinion. Reasonableness and relevance are fundamental for legal pragmatism. No legal pragmatist would decide an antitrust suit based on a client's white hat.[75] Instead, the behavior of a legal pragmatist is cabined by experience and insight, training and education, and a sense of what works and fits into the traditions and institutions of the legal system.

While legal pragmatism is more coherent than its critics suggest, and while any number of legal scholars and jurists may find themselves labeled as such, it does not lead to single determinate results, as we will see in a moment.[76] Morality and experiment are not antithetical to legal pragmatism but are a part of it. Politics and policy do not determine outcomes; they inform the decision maker. The pragmatist judge must confront and engage existing legal materials which together with the degree and amount of flexibility the judge enjoys, determine the outcome of a case.

Judge Posner has written that precedent, statutes, and even constitutional texts are not determinative of lawsuits. They are "sources of potentially valuable information" and act as "sign posts" for decision. He writes that these internal 'authorities' are merely sources of information and are only limited constraints on a judge's freedom of decision; the judge does not depend on them to supply the rule of decision for the "truly novel case."[77] It remains for us to determine what constitutes the "truly novel case" and then to determine how flexible and novel precedents, statutes, and constitutional texts truly are. Can the legal pragmatist justify any outcome? Or if that question is too broad, can the legal pragmatist justify different or opposing outcomes? Further, what is the question-begging "best" outcome? Let us look at just such a novel case.

A Truly Novel Case?

The following discussion is based on the facts of the case of Boumediene v. Bush[78] *and I then suggest how our two pragmatist judges would decide it. The petitioners are detainees being held at the U.S. Naval Station at Guantanamo Bay, Cuba, and they argue that they are being held illegally and seek a writ of habeas corpus. Their case was heard, and their claims were denied by the United States District Court and the United States Court of Appeals for the District of Columbia. Petitioners then sought review in the United States Supreme Court. In the original proceeding, the Court declined to hear the case. In the usual course of Supreme Court business, such denials are simply reported without comment. What was a bit unusual about this case is that four justices issued written comments about the denial, leading commentators to suggest that at least some of the justices were waiting for the right set of facts to hear this type of case. In Supreme Court Term 2007, the Court heard that case on the merits. Let's imagine now how our pragmatist justices, Posner and Holmes, would decide.*

The Facts

Khalid is a foreign citizen being held as an enemy combatant at the U.S. Naval Station in Guantanamo, Cuba. He has been in prison for over six years without charges having been filed against him, and he seeks a federal court hearing through the writ of habeas corpus. Through the habeas process, Khalid, at the least, wants to know the charges against him to prepare for his defense. At best, he wants his immediate release.

Khalid appeared before a military tribunal at Guantanamo for the purpose of determining whether or not he should be labeled an enemy combatant. The military tribunal determined that he was an enemy combatant, thus leaving him with little or no due-process protections. Khalid then filed his petition for habeas corpus relief in the federal district court. The government opposed Khalid's petition, and the lower court sided with the government.

On appeal, the Court of Appeals dismissed Khalid's habeas corpus claim on the express grounds that Guantanamo Bay was not part of the sovereign territory of the United States but, rather, was land that the United States leases from Cuba. Consequently, the federal court of appeals held that the *writ of habeas corpus* did not extend to the naval station at Guantanamo Bay. There, then, sat Khalid and others similarly situated.

Posner, J.

The threat of international terrorism is real. The United States has been the target of repeated acts of violence against its embassy, its navy, and most frightfully, our own shores. The wanton destruction of the Twin Towers of the World Trade Center on September 11, 2001 is evidence of not only pernicious evil in the world; it is evidence of unprecedented methods for spreading violence. The world has indeed changed. Technology has made it easier to spread hateful ideologies. And as the world shrinks, terrorism is easier to export. The United States is more vulnerable to greater dangers. We hold dear the liberties on which our country was founded. Yet liberty without security is worse than foolhardy, it is useless. In a time of national emergency, our country is called upon to test not only the limits of liberty and security but to test the proper relationship between the two.

The case before us requires us to understand that relationship and settle a delicate controversy. To help us accomplish both tasks, this Court has before it existing case law, including our recent decisions, and statutory law, as well as history and tradition and knowledge of the current conditions in the world. All of these materials are sources of useful information. None of these sources, however, is determinative. There is no one single set standard for balancing the correct amounts of liberty and security in our democracy. Instead, as the needs of society change so must the balance. Ultimately, recalculating that balance means making marginal adjustments in rights and liberties.[79] Shifting the line between liberty and security extends even to constitutional claims, including this petition for a writ of habeas corpus.

The petitioners argue that they are entitled, at a minimum, to a federal court hearing on the basis of the habeas corpus clause of the Constitution which reads in full: "The Privilege of the Writ of Habeas Corpus shall not be suspended, unless when in Cases of Rebellion or Invasion the public Safety may require it."[80]

Were this an academic conference, we might carefully parse this clause and ask several questions: Does the writ apply to foreign citizens? Does it apply outside the territory of the United States? Has the United States been invaded such that Congress has the authority to suspend its application?

While each of these constitutional questions is important, each is off target. Briefly, we can conclude (1) the writ does apply in appropriate circumstances to foreign citizens;[81] (2) the writ applies to the leased naval base in a foreign country regardless of the lower court's opinion that the writ applies in sovereign territories only;[82] and (3) the United States is not in rebellion, and while clearly invaded on 9/11, is not under invasion today. Consequently, we can assume that habeas corpus protections apply and that the writ is not suspended.

Because Congress has enacted protective statutes for detainees, I decide this case on the basis of these statutes and, therefore, need not reach the constitutional matter of the reach and scope of habeas corpus. In brief, the petitioners have been afforded sufficient habeas protections by statute. Therefore, I find that the petitioners' request for habeas corpus relief must be denied for two reasons. One reason speaks to the individual rights of the petitioners and their liberty interest. The other reason speaks to the institutional competence of all three branches of government and their respective roles in preserving national security.

Liberty

The situation of imprisoning an individual indefinitely, without charges and with limited opportunity to consult legal counsel, is not ideal. Such constitutional protections are guaranteed to our citizens, and in times of peace such protections are granted expeditiously. In times of national emergency, however, when we do not know who our friends are and when terrorism wears many faces, it is neither irrational nor unconstitutional to be cautious and treat foreign citizens differently from our own. United States citizens are certainly not immune from their own violent terrorism as the Oklahoma City bombing attests. Equally certain, foreign citizens have offered their lives for our protection as the deaths of British and other soldiers in Iraq attest. Nevertheless, to draw a constitutional law line between citizen and alien is perfectly defensible and legitimate.

I would decide this case differently if the petitioners were denied any hearing whatsoever. They were not. The petitioners were afforded a hearing and federal appellate court review. Petitioners specifically requested an initial federal court hearing and Congress has foreclosed that avenue first with the passage of the Detainee Treatment Act of 2005, Pub. L. No. 109-148, 119, Stat. 2680 (2005) (hereinafter DTA), and then with the passage of the

Military Commission Act of 2006, Pub. L. No. 109-366, 120 Stat. 2600 (2006) (hereinafter MCA). Admittedly, these statutes were passed at the urging of the Bush administration in response to this Court's rulings in *Rasul v. Bush*, 542 U.S. 466 (2004) and *Hamdan v. Rumsfeld*, 548 U.S. 557 (2006) and were intended to restrict federal court jurisdiction in these cases.

The MCA and the rules and regulations in force at Guantanamo Bay afford the detainees sufficient due process protection so as not to run afoul of our sense of constitutional values or of fair play. The petitioners received individualized determinations by a military Combatant Status Review Tribunal (CSRT) and were found to be enemy combatants. That determination is subject to review in the U.S. Court of Appeals for the District of Columbia Circuit under the DTA. These petitioners have failed to avail themselves of that federal court review.

While I have previously opined in a nonjudicial writing that a *judicial* determination would be appropriate habeas corpus procedure, that opinion was expressed before the MCA was law. Now that the opinions in *Rasul* and *Hamdan* as well as *Hamdi v. Rumsfeld*, 542 U.S. 507 (2004) have been questioned by Congress, the subsequent legislation should be given time to operate and be tested.[83] We can assume that the petitioners have habeas corpus rights. I find, however, that those rights have been protected because the petitioners have been shown to be detained by a tribunal of competent jurisdiction.[84] Petitioners may appeal to a federal court of appeals for judicial review of the application of the CRST's determination. The constitutional safeguards of habeas corpus require no more. A military tribunal's determination, together with federal appellate review, provides adequate habeas corpus protection by neutral decision makers.

Security

As I noted in the beginning of this opinion, the world has changed as it always does, and its change after 9/11 has profound consequences on the society in which we live and on the laws by which our lives are governed. A generation ago, Congress and the judiciary sought to circumscribe the reach of the executive branch in matters of national security. Abuses by the Federal Bureau of Investigation involving the domestic surveillance of our citizens and even surveillance directed by the White House resulted in legislation, *see, e.g.*, War Powers Act, Pub. L. No 93-148 (1973) and judicial opinions, *see, e.g.*, *United States v. Nixon*, 418 U. S. 683 (1974) favoring individual liberty against claims of national security.[85] Perhaps the balance struck in that legislation and precedent was the right one and both liberty and security were, if not optimal, then constitutionally correct. Assuming that the balance between liberty and security was constitutionally correct in the 1970s, there is no reason not to reassess that balance against current circumstances. Most specifically, the claims of national security made over 30 years ago were claims specifically about domestic threats. Today, while we may not have less reason to fear our own citizens, we definitely have more reason to fear foreign terrorists. The claims of national security confront a more mobile, more dangerous enemy than imagined when those restrictions on the executive branch were imposed.

How, then, should we balance the inevitably competing claims of individual liberty and national security? This is a question to which I have paid considerable attention. *See e.g.*, RICHARD A. POSNER, NOT A SUICIDE PACT: THE CONSTITUTION IN A TIME OF NATIONAL EMERGENCY (2006) and other writings.[86] I have reluctantly come to the conclusion that as a judge, I am not in the best position to assess the national security side of this equation even after substantial study and reflection which has been open to public scrutiny through publication. As judges, we deal with matters of rights and liberties on a regular basis, and consequently, have a propensity for deciding cases by favoring liberty over security.[87]

Tipping the balance in that way raises a question about institutional competence.[88] Judges routinely decide cases of individual claims such as a claim that a criminal was denied a specific constitutional safeguard. Occasionally judges are called upon to determine matters involving a social institution such as a school or a school system, a prison or a prison system, or a hospital or the health-care system. We do less well managing such institutions. Rarely, and thankfully, are judges asked to assess matters of national or international security. The imponderables of today's terrorism are many and, quite frankly, their assessment is beyond the competence of any individual, let alone judges who are trained to resolve concrete disputes with determinate facts placed into evidence before them.

Perhaps assessing terrorism is ultimately an impossible task. Nevertheless, it is a task that must be addressed, and as judges we have the competence to and the responsibility for determining which branch of government is best suited to make at least initial determinations about how to address terrorism, including how to treat detainees. The Congress and the president have developed a scheme of law, rules, and regulations, for doing precisely that—addressing terrorism and treating detainees. If given the responsibility, perhaps I would write a different law. But I serve as a judge and as neither a legislator nor chief executive.

The other coequal branches of government are more politically sensitive than the judicial branch as is the intent of our constitutional scheme of government. They are more sensitive to our nation's needs and its place in this new, more violence-prone world. The political branches, by design and necessity, must take the pulse of the domestic and world situations and prescribe the best treatment they can. It is our job, as judges, to let the political branches do theirs. The political branches have spoken. Our constitutional values are not violated. The petitions are denied.

Holmes, J.

While I agree with much of what justice Posner has written, the petitions for habeas corpus relief must be granted. Times certainly change; it cannot possibly be otherwise. Still, *plus ça change, le plus c'est la même chose.* Today, our country is assailed by the War on Terror, if, indeed, it is properly called a war. Two generations ago, we were assailed by the Communist threat; a generation before that, the Red Scare; and, a generation before that by outside labor agitators. Today's terrorists are yesterday's anarchists.

It is also true that technologies change such that weapons are smaller and more destructive and that their delivery can range more widely and travel faster. Yet an anarchist's bomb or a rioter's club kill and maim in the same ways. Today's religious fanatics that swear "Death to America" are not so distinct from yesterday's political ideologues sworn to enslave America and replace our cherished democracy with communist control. Times change. History changes. Culture changes—but not enough to abandon the principle of the constitutional liberty which forms a bedrock value of our country and which has served our national security needs for over 200 years.

Liberty

Justice Posner correctly writes that as judges we cannot slavishly adhere to precedent, statutes, or even constitutional texts. He also correctly writes that we must balance the decisions of the past against the needs of the present as we anticipate the future. This balance includes balancing the needs of liberty and security. I respectfully disagree, however, that the balance he struck today against granting habeas corpus relief to these petitioners is simply a marginal adjustment of constitutional protections.

His core claim is that the petitioners' liberty interests are adequately and constitutionally protected because the petitioners were afforded a hearing by a legitimate military tribunal and, if dissatisfied with that determination, are availed of federal appellate review. He concludes, then, that the Constitution's habeas corpus provisions are satisfied. However, both hearings were dramatically attenuated and therefore constitutionally infirm.

Habeas corpus relief is among the oldest protections held by an individual. The Great Writ grants the right of the imprisoned to ask the king or president: "On what authority do you hold my body?" Blackstone traces the writ to the reign of King Edward I and others back to Henry II. I have written that there must be more reason to apply a rule of law than that it was laid down in the time of Henry IV. Still, this petition clearly demonstrates that the reasons for habeas corpus relief in the thirteenth century continue to exist in the twenty-first.

The petitioners were arrested by Bosnian police in October 2001 on suspicion of attempting to commit international terrorism.[89] There was no basis for the arrest, and the authorities were acting under pressure from the United States. After a three-month investigation, Bosnian authorities concluded there was no evidence for the prosecution and, subsequently the Bosnian Supreme Court ordered the petitioners released with the concurrence of the Bosnian prosecutor. As the petitioners were being released, Bosnian police, again at the insistence of the United States, seized and shackled the petitioners in a rendition process which ultimately landed them in the naval station at Guantanamo Bay where they have been ever since.

Petitioners, now in their sixth year of confinement at Guantanamo, are imprisoned in $8' \times 6'$ concrete and steel cells. A fluorescent light stays on above each man's bunk for 24 hours a day. Petitioners have suffered up to 15 consecutive months of solitary confinement as well as sleep deprivation and extreme temperature conditions. They have not been charged, and the term of imprisonment is indefinite. Before the petitioners filed for habeas corpus relief in federal district court, they were given a hearing by the Combatant Status Review Tribunal (CSRT). Upon arrest, the petitioners were labeled enemy combatants for the explicit purpose of denying them prisoner of war status to which certain due process rights attach by domestic and international law. In response to this Court's ruling in *Hamdan v. Rumsfeld*, 548 U.S. 557 (2006), the CSRT process was instituted precisely to review enemy combatant status determinations.

The CSRT hearing was conducted by three commissioned U.S. military officers. The petitioners were denied legal counsel and the right to view any classified evidence offered against them. Although petitioners were allowed to introduce testimonial and documentary evidence on their own behalf, such evidence was restricted to evidence that the CSRT concluded was "reasonably available." In practice, that standard excluded much evidence including documents already in the government's possession and the testimony of witnesses who are easily located. One glaring example of excluded evidence, under the reasonably available standard, was the Bosnian Supreme Court's determination that the arrests lacked any evidentiary support. The CSRT refused to introduce that court's determination as not reasonably available even though the government already possessed a copy of the Bosnian Court's order.

Compounding the evidentiary weaknesses, the CSRT was allowed to consider any evidence it decided relevant, including hearsay and evidence produced by torture and coercion. The CSRT applied a rebuttable presumption in favor of the government's case.

Appellate judicial review is more limited still and ends in the *Twilight Zone*. The MCA allows for only circumscribed review of CSRT proceedings. Petitioners are limited to the already attenuated record compiled in the CSRT; they may not contest that process or introduce new facts or evidence in rebuttal. The statute limits the court of appeals review to whether the CSRT complied with its own standards, and it appears whether the use of those standards is constitutional. While a constitutional challenge can cure many defects, it cannot clear an infirm record. Worse, the statute cannot fix the CSRT's *Alice in Wonderland* practice of convening a new CSRT determination hearing for prisoners for whom the CSRT had first determined they should not be detained. In other words, it is the CSRT practice that if a determination is made that a prisoner is not an enemy combatant, another CSRT tribunal is impaneled until the desired enemy combatant determination is made.

Limited judicial review of a constrained hearing by a military tribunal does not satisfy habeas corpus requirements.

When a nation is at war, constitutional rights guaranteed in times of peace must be reviewed and, if necessary, adjusted. *Schenk v. U.S.*, 249 U.S. 47 (1919). Yet there are some constitutional rights that endure regardless of historical or political circumstances including war. *See Schaefer v. U.S.*, 251 U.S. 466 (1920) (Brandeis, J. dissenting with Holmes, J. concurring); *Gitlow v. New York*, 268 U.S. 652 (1925) (Holmes, J. dissenting). The Constitution may well be an experiment in political democracy, but it is an experiment that does not allow a statute such as the MCA to eliminate minimal rights and liberties.[90] *Abrams v. U.S.*, 250 U.S. 616 (1919) (Holmes, J. dissenting). Habeas corpus relief and the due process protections that attach to it is one such right. Assuming we are at war, a proposition I find dubious, we are not in a state of rebellion or invasion, and the suspension clause cannot save the MCA.

Security

Justice Posner correctly writes that a case is decided not only by the individual facts before the judge but also by the systemic or institutional effects the decision may have. Resolving past disputes is the proper province of a court. So too is a court's obligation to peer, no matter how briefly, into the future. Our Court's limited docket attests to the fact that our decisions are often more forward-looking than retrospective. Consequently, as we decide the petitioners' claim for habeas corpus relief, we should properly consider not only the roles of the judge and the judicial branch, but we should also properly consider the roles of the political branches.

Before I reach these institutional considerations, I need to dispose of an argument that the lower court weighed heavily and upon which it based its disposition. The Court of Appeals ruled that habeas corpus relief is constitutionally limited to the sovereign territory of the United States and, therefore, does not extend to military land leased in Cuba. *Boumediene v. Bush*, 476 F.3d 981 (D.C. Cir. 2007). While I would enjoy debating the finer points and niceties of property law, justice Kennedy has forcefully made the point that the United States exercises exclusive control over the U.S. Naval Station at Guantanamo Bay. *Rasul v. Bush*, 542 U.S., 466, 487 (2004). Our landlord, Fidel Castro, or his successor, will not successfully evict our navy. Our Court has spoken. Tenuous land tenure arrangements will not defeat petitioners' habeas corpus right to be heard.

Justice Posner writes that because judges are biased in favor of individual rights and liberties and less knowledgeable in matters of national security, they therefore should defer to the more political branches. I agree that judicial deference to the combined will of Congress and the executive branch, especially in trying and challenging times, is most often a wise path to follow.[91] Yet, the problem with the political branches is that they are political. They must respond to the felt necessities of the times and to the intuitions of public policy. Judges must be sensitive to how current politics may affect the institution of the law. In the present circumstances, the war in Iraq appears to have been waged on faulty data and predictions, with no clear end in sight, with a set of legal weapons that have been found questionable by this Court and others including the government's legal counsel,[92] and in the face of diminishing public support. While it is not the job of this Court today to comment upon, let alone decide, the wisdom of the war or its prosecution, it is incumbent on this Court to acknowledge that the vision of the political branches on this matter is less clear-sighted than we might desire. If the record of the political branches on this matter of national security, which admittedly deserves great respect and ordinarily great deference, is murky, then the role of the judiciary increases in importance. Admittedly, I would be the first to concede that I do not have a solution to the matter of intelligence and national security and were it a question of whether I agreed with the theory of the war's prosecution, I would desire to study it further and long before making up my mind. *Lochner v. New York*, 198 U.S. 45, 75 (1905) (Holmes, J. Dissenting).

Fortunately, I do not have to comment on national security policy. I do, however, have to decide whether or not a constitutional provision applies in this case as against a statute that attempts to restrict its scope. The tasks of constitutional interpretation, statutory construction, and the application of precedent to a concrete case is wholly within the competence of a judge and within the proper function of a court. Deference to the political branches, in a matter of concrete and constitutional cases and controversies, is an abdication of the judicial function. The systemic and institutional interests of all three branches and the rule of law itself is ill-served in this case by allowing petitioners to sit one more day in the confines of an $8' \times 6'$ steel and concrete cell with no charges, for an indefinite period and with increasingly restricted access to legal representation.[93] The purported substitute for habeas corpus relief provided by the MCA and DTA is no substitute at all. The hearings afforded under those statutes are a subterfuge, and, consequently, I vote to grant petitioners requests for a writ of habeas corpus.

Case Commentary

This moot court exercise contains a double irony. First, both judges are committed pragmatists but they arrive at opposite conclusions. Second, both judges are playing against type.

Posner's writings about national security are notably deferential to the executive branch, and this position runs directly contrary to his scholarship on pragmatist adjudication. Posner has a muscular theory of judging, and he does not shy away from judicial decision making. He views an expansive role for the legal pragmatist judge to craft opinions in ways that advance a rule of law and the policies it contains. Holmes, to the contrary, is more differential to Congress and the executive, yet he is famously known for his opinions upholding individual free speech liberties against claims of national security. While Posner's legal pragmatism should lead him to grant the petition, he defers to Congress and the president while he denies relief. Where Holmes's legal pragmatism should led him to defer to the other branches, he grants the habeas corpus relief as a result of his analysis and rejection of the government's statutory arguments. Thus, both decisions go against each judge's articulated position on legal pragmatism in their other writings. Still, both would claim that legal pragmatism is broad enough to justify both opinions.

We find, then, two pragmatist judges at war with themselves and at war with each other. If each had adhered to his personal brand of legal pragmatism, he would have reached conclusions opposite from what he did reach. One might also assume that each should reach the same conclusion because each applied the same decisional methodology.

Is the variability and flexibility of legal pragmatism a strength or a weakness? It depends upon who you ask. Critics argue that the antitheory theory of legal pragmatism is too open to application and, therefore, cannot be taken seriously as a theory of law. If you ask virtually every Supreme Court nominee over the last two or more decades, you will hear some version of legal pragmatism as no one of the nominees risked being pinned down to a set theory of law or a theory of judging. Pragmatism's openness and flexibility may be a vice for those who desire a cohesive theory of law but for those seeking the bench, openness and flexibility, indeed, constitute a political virtue. And for lawyers, legal pragmatism allows them to advise clients and fashion arguments based on what makes sense and what works best. To outsiders, pragmatism's openness and flexibility reveal its weaknesses; to insiders, pragmatism's openness and flexibility reveal its practical and instrumental strengths.

Conclusion

For 50 of his 94 years on this earth, Oliver Wendell Holmes Jr. was a judge. Serving on the Supreme Courts of Massachusetts and of the United States,

Holmes lived within the practical needs of law and lived with a deep desire for a life of the mind. His mind was capacious, his writing elegant, and his profound yearning to participate in and have an impact upon intellectual culture was restless. Holmes's critics, of which there are more than a few and whose criticisms come in varying degrees of sharpness,[94] argue that Holmes was unsuccessful in reconciling his roving intellect and his practical reality into a theory of law. Yet "reconcile" is exactly the wrong word as Holmes knew and told us—certainty is an illusion and not the repose of man. Holmes did not seek to design an airtight, cohesive theory of law; he sought to describe a theory of best legal practices.

For a thinker accused of aphoristic and epigrammatic thinking, his consistency in inquiry yields a coherent practical theory of law. More precisely, Holmes has left us a theory of law as it operates in the world, not as it might or even ought to operate in another more theoretical, more academic, or more philosophical world. Holmes has delivered to us, the practitioners and participants in law, just as he delivered to the law students and the distinguished guests at Boston University's school dedication, a map—*the path*—for doing and appreciating the practice of law, for doing and appreciating man's law while pragmatically eschewing the higher law.

We can accept the criticism that Holmes had no grand or unified theory of judging or of law—that he never articulated such a theory is precisely consistent with his thought. His conscious reluctance to articulate a theory of judging confirms his theory of law as a necessary practical exercise of social life. We, as part of our human nature, cannot avoid haggling in law courts or elsewhere. If we are to live in society, then conflict is inevitable. The law mediates those conflicts. The lawyer counsels and advocates for persons caught in conflict. The judge is assigned the responsibility for resolving them. How else can a judge resolve conflicts other than by balancing competing claims and interests, by balancing them against the past and the future, by balancing them against the law on the books and against what the law can and should become, and by balancing them against society's needs and the institutions society establishes for its own good?

The Path of the Law has taken us from the mundane law in the books to the sublime "echo of the infinite, a glimpse of its unfathomable process, a hint of the universal law."[95] As our docent, Holmes's approach to the study and practice of law revealed the pragmatic dimension of this social institution. As lawyers, we do practice with the mundane, and we must be watchful for law's possibilities. Our inside perspective requires us to know the details of the law so we can advise, apply, advocate, and judge the legal controversies that confront us. Yet at the same time, we cannot afford to be ignorant about law's larger possibilities. Law is a dynamic process, rooted in history, applied in the present, and will change as the future greets us. Only by understanding the historical, jurisprudential, and other social forces that comprise or contribute to those changes can we participate, perhaps even greatly, in the law.[96]

Legal pragmatism of either the Holmesian or Posnerian varieties is an attempt to improve upon man's law. It does not for once and for all times define what the higher law is or even what it should be. In this regard, the expectations for law are lowered from what Antigone or Plato or Aquinas may have wished for law's grand ambition. Legal pragmatism sees man's law as occasionally defective, in need of repair and refinement, and offers a method for doing so. The Holmesian *Path*, also followed by Posner, bets that legal pragmatism will improve law, make it more useful, and better serve society. Both jurists believe that grand theories of law cannot be blindly or formulaically followed and that pragmatism is the most sound approach to law practice and law theorizing. It may well be possible for the Holmesian pragmatist to craft an over-arching theory of law, but such a construction is unnecessary and may be cumbersome. Instead, the Holmesian pragmatist can become mistress and guardian of the law when she best serves the law through reflective application of craft.

Legal pragmatism, then, is concerned exclusively with man's law, having no use for the higher law in the sky. The pragmatists rebelled against formalism as too restrictive and against high-brow theory as too airy. Neither formalism nor abstract theory advances our understanding of law in action. If the pragmatists jettison the higher law, then where does justice reside? For Holmes and Posner, justice resides in the best application of the craft of man's law. In the next two chapters, reliance is placed elsewhere. Martin Luther King Jr. relies on democratic processes and Stuart Hampshire relies on procedural justice as the best approximations of the higher law.

SEVEN

Timeliness and Justice

The man, a man of the cloth, sat on the edge of a cot in a municipal jail cell. Instead of his usual dark business suit, he wore a work shirt, crisp new blue jeans and a pair of clodhopper working shoes. The man had been arrested for violating an unjust law, a law that would later be upheld against him by the Supreme Court of the United States.

While in his cell, the man began to write a response to his recent critics. He wrote on the edges of newspapers, on scraps of paper, and finished his writing on a legal pad. The man entered that cell with some doubt about the proper timing of his cause for justice and yet the man could foresee what the world would see in a few short weeks—fire hoses aimed at and police dogs charging children, a scene which galvanized attention on what was then one of our nation's most segregated cities.[1]

THE MAN OF THE CLOTH is Martin Luther King Jr. The time is Easter 1963. The city is Birmingham, Alabama. And the writing is the *Letter from the Birmingham Jail*. In this chapter, we look at a new approach to defining the higher law. In many ways, the March on Birmingham was a turning point in the period of the civil rights movement that started after *Brown* v. *Board of Education*[2] in 1954 and led to the passage of the Civil Rights Act of 1964 and the Voting Rights Act of 1965. King and other civil rights leaders were emboldened by *Brown's* constitutional right to an equal education. They were simultaneously frustrated by *Brown's* admonition to wait for justice as school desegregation was to proceed, "with all deliberate speed."[3] Their frustration led them to search for the higher law.

This man of God inspires a commitment to social justice. King is also an inspiration for a powerful secular political morality that endures. The *Letter from the Birmingham Jail* is rich in theology, philosophy, and social commentary. The *Letter* is as prophetic as it is historically grounded, and it is as secular as it is religious. It is also rich in a vibrant and essential political theory that can instruct any movement for civil, political, and human rights.

At the heart of the *Letter* is a strategy for democratic participation open to all individuals regardless of race, gender, or other characteristics which can be, and have been, used by the many to diminish the few.

A strategy of democratic participation is distinct from an attempt to define substantive justice in terms of essential or fundamental values.[4] King relied upon proper and legitimate political procedures as the means to racial equality. As a man of religion, King's faith easily leads him to believe in the sinfulness of segregation; as a man of politics, he must find a remedy for this injustice in a pluralist democracy. Instead of defining justice in specific, substantive terms compatible with his religious faith, he turns to the political idea of democratic participation, where every individual is accorded equal concern and respect, for relief. In this chapter, we examine the question: can a substantively just outcome result from an unjust process? Late in the *Letter,* King quotes T.S. Eliot's sentiment that "The last temptation is greatest treason: To do the right thing for the wrong reason." Expediency, political or otherwise, even one which results in a just outcome, must be avoided. Thus, for King, as for Eliot, and in a democracy, the answer must be, "No." Echoing Plato, injustice cannot yield justice. In the next chapter, we will explore the opposite question: can a substantively unjust outcome be legitimized by a just process?

The March on Birmingham

The dramatic event that publicized the injustice of segregation and publicized the beginning of a new era was Rosa Parks's refusal to sit in the back of the bus. Her arrest triggered the Montgomery bus boycott of 1955 and King's involvement with it.[5] Freedom rides, voter registration, lunch counter sit-ins, and other civil rights efforts after Montgomery then led to Albany, Georgia where the civil rights efforts stalled. In Albany, the intention was to desegregate the entire city and, with resources spread too thinly, the Albany civil rights movement faltered in the summer of 1962. The movement then went from Albany to Birmingham where, through the auspices of the Southern Christian Leadership Conference and Rev. Fred Shuttlesworth's Alabama Christian Movement for Human Rights, a plan aimed at the Birmingham business community was drafted.

Birmingham was generally recognized as the most segregated city in the United States. Birmingham Negroes were unemployed at higher rates, received lower pay, were born and educated in Jim Crow hospitals and schools, and had only a fraction of the franchise to which they were entitled. Birmingham Negroes could work in the white stores but could not eat at white lunch counters. Most stultifying, Birmingham segregation was controlled by an avowedly racist city government which included the infamous Eugene "Bull" Connor, who held the title of Commissioner of Public Safety but who aspired to become mayor of Birmingham on a racist ticket. The mayoralty race in early 1963 threatened to upset the movement's plans for that city.

King, Shuttlesworth, Ralph Abernathy, and others began what they called Project C, standing for Confrontation. Protesters would begin with a selective buying campaign and boycott white businesses during the Easter season, the second largest shopping season of the year. The campaign would culminate in a civil rights march held on Good Friday. The religious symbolism could not be missed.

Project C was a strategy to fill the jails until they overflowed with protesters. The architects of the plan hoped that the media would broadcast the images of the arrests, sit-ins, and kneel-ins which would shock the rest of America and pressure the Kennedy administration to move forward with civil rights legislation. While displaying some sympathy for the civil rights movement, President Kennedy was caught between a debt to black voters in the 1960 election and the need for votes from segregationist southern Democrats for the 1964 election. He and his administration would stay in close contact with Martin Luther King Jr. but would not lead a confrontational effort on behalf of the civil rights movement.

Movement leaders believed that by concentrating on a business boycott, their chances of success improved over the strategy in Albany, and yet in Birmingham they met another set of challenging complications. Birmingham was in the midst of a mayoral race among Albert Boutwell, Bull Connor, and Tom King. Although King and Boutwell ran as moderates, they were segregationists nonetheless. The mayoral election, held on March 5, ended with no clear winner, and required a runoff between Boutwell and Connor just before Easter. The runoff election was held during the first week of April, one week prior to the planned march. In the white community sympathetic to civil rights, the public sentiment was one of wait and see. If Bull Connor were to lose to Albert Boutwell, the cautious argued, then peaceful negotiations could take place rather than a protest which was sure to become violent.

King, Shuttlesworth, and Abernathy struggled with the decision to press forward with Project C during Easter week. The dilemma, on the one hand, was that the business boycott would be most effective if held during that time because media attention would be optimal. On the other hand, if the civil rights advocates were too vocal, they risked pushing the election in Connor's favor, and the racist practices would continue unabated. They decided to move forward but other troubles were on the way.

Boutwell won the runoff election, but Bull Connor neither disappeared nor stayed silent. The election meant that Connor's term as safety commissioner would end shortly, but he contested whether or not he could legally be removed from office immediately. In addition, Connor, with the acquiescence of Governor George Wallace, raised the bond for release from jail for protesting from $300 to $2500. If the bond was low, then hundreds of protestors could "suffer" incarceration knowing that their sojourn in prison would be short if not sweet. If the bond was raised high enough, then the number of those willing to spend a longer time in the Birmingham jail would diminish significantly, thus reducing the impact of publicity.

Police and civic leaders understood the civil rights leaders' strategy—to a point. They paid attention to other civil rights actions in other cities and were particularly impressed by how Albany Police Chief Laurie Pritchett exercised restraint and controlled the demonstrators without provoking media attracting violence. Connor's police force would be visible but would not provoke. But Connor was not done trying to frustrate King and company. Connor adamantly refused to grant requests for a parade permit, saying that he would "picket you over to the City jail" before issuing one. He then sought and obtained an *ex parte* injunction from a state court enjoining any protests whatsoever.

At this point, the planners had serious issues to resolve. Their intent was to fill the jails. Protesters would expect to spend two or three days in jail and then seek release on bond. The problem was that with bond prices significantly raised, bail money was in short supply. King was reluctant to go forward with the Good Friday march because of a fear of violence at the hands of Bull Connor's police and because of the possibility that there would be too few willing to go to jail and too little bail money for those that did. But failure in Birmingham would have been disastrous. King, after discussion and reflection, and against the advice of his father and others, decided to go forward.

On Wednesday, April 10, two days before the march, the deputy sheriff presented the *ex parte* injunction to King, Shuttlesworth, and Abernathy, ceremoniously, in the restaurant of the Gaston Motel. Among other things, the injunction prohibited King and the demonstrators from engaging in street parades, picketing businesses, boycotting, or kneel-ins. The legal battle lines were drawn. The demonstrators were denied a parade permit and were under a state court order enjoining exactly the scheduled parade. Arguably, both the permit denial and the court order were unconstitutional. Yet, those under a legal ruling must challenge the ruling or risk jail or fine or both. King and company chose to proceed with the march instead of challenging either the ordinance or the injunction in court, a decision that would later subject King to return to the Birmingham jail by order of the U.S. Supreme Court.[6]

On April 12, protestors and police, in kabuki-like action, played out their roles as King and about 40 others began the Good Friday march. As they marched toward the city, the crowds swelled singing and cheering their progress. The police, under Bull Connor's directions, were ready and blockades were set up with motorcycles and squad cars at the ready. As Taylor Branch writes, "the pageantry of confrontation played out abruptly. Giving no warning, a detective seized King by the back of his belt, lifted him to his toes, and shoved him toward a paddy wagon."[7] Ralph Abernathy followed soon behind while 52 others were arrested. The arrests took place but not exactly as planned. According to King, "we did an audacious thing, something we had never done in any other crusade. We disobeyed a court order."[8] This ruling, the order of a state court judge, pits man's law against the higher law as precisely and starkly as it presented Creon's law against Antigone's.

The Birmingham Jail

In jail, Martin Luther King was separated from the other prisoners and held in solitary confinement. He was released from solitary only after a phone call from President Kennedy to his wife, Coretta Scott King. In addition to his release, King had other surprises awaiting him that weekend. On Saturday April 13, eight white Alabama clergymen published a statement in the newspaper about the Good Friday demonstrations. This statement prompted the extraordinary *Letter from a Birmingham Jail*.

King's Critics

In a few short paragraphs, the clergy argued that racial justice should be pursued peacefully in the courts and that decisions of those courts should be peacefully obeyed. Negotiations, not demonstrations, should be the order of the day. The clergy positioned themselves as responsible citizens in Birmingham willing to work toward racial harmony and that "recent public events," the election of Albert Boutwell over Bull Connor, had given them hope for a new constructive dialogue. Then the clergy expressed their dismay at "a series of demonstrations by some of our Negro citizens, directed and led in part by outsiders." Recognizing the "natural impatience" of people who had been denied their rights, the clergy nonetheless believed that the demonstrations were "unwise and untimely."

The clergy preferred local black leadership to King and his group of outsiders. Local clergy, they noted, had called for open and honest negotiations and had asked that white and black leadership cooperate to "find proper channels" to discuss racial issues. The white clergy condemned hatred and violence, "however technically peaceful those actions may be" and continued to believe the demonstrations were extreme measures and unjustified. The statement closes with the clergy commending the community, the local news media, and law enforcement on the calm manner in which they handled the Good Friday demonstrations. Finally, they wrote that they "strongly urge our own Negro community to withdraw support from these demonstrations" and seek relief in courts, and through negotiations, and not in the streets. The clergy urged King to obey man's law now and delay the coming of the higher law.

The statement from the clergy against the demonstrations, in favor of local negotiations and in favor of judicial relief, struck notes of division. Not only did the letter criticize the strategy of Plan C, it sought to divide King from local leaders and to divide the black community against itself. King not only reacted to the attempt to divide, he reacted to the very theological, moral, and political bases for the clergy's message.

King's Letter

King's open epistle[9] serves as a coda to *Creon's Ghost* as it searches for the higher law. King's *Letter* looks backward over the many characters and issues discussed in this book and it looks forward to a new democratic politics of racial inclusion. King's democratic politics offers a way of reconciling man's defective, segregationist law with the higher law of racial justice.

The *Letter* opens by assuming the sincerity and good faith of his critics as King expresses his willingness to respond to their concerns. The clergy expressed opposition to King as an outsider who came into their community with disruption in mind. This language about outsiders echoed the outside agitator language of the earlier era of communist scares. King responded that he had ties to Birmingham through the Southern Christian Leadership Conference and its affiliate, the Alabama Christian Movement for Human Rights. He told the clergy that he was in Birmingham because he was invited there, but more important, he was in Birmingham because "injustice is here." By identifying injustice, King also identified with St. Paul's mission to carry the Gospel of freedom into Birmingham. For King, it is not a case of the "outsider" fixing a problem for other people because all communities are interrelated and "[i]njustice anywhere is a threat to justice everywhere." More important, as a citizen of the United States, racial injustice in Alabama is a threat to the justice of all citizens because citizens were caught in an "inescapable network of mutuality."

The clergy deplored the violence of the demonstrations, but they misunderstood it completely. King writes that he agrees with the white clergy that it is unfortunate that the demonstrations are taking place, "but it is even more unfortunate that the city's white power structure left the Negro community with no alternative." King explains how meticulous the demonstrators were in pursuing a Gandhian nonviolence campaign. Direct action, the demonstrations, the boycotts, and the other activities, were the conclusion of a thoughtful process, not the beginning. Fact finding and negotiation preceded direct action. No less important, self-purification also preceded direct action. Demonstrators needed to be educated about nonviolence and about restraint, and they had to be taught a willingness to take the violent blows aimed at them.

The black leaders of Birmingham did their fact finding and their negotiating before direct action and the negotiations failed. As a result of negotiations with the white business leaders, promises were made. Jim Crow signs were to be removed from the stores, and as a result of that promise, a moratorium was called on the business boycott and on all demonstrations. Jim Crow signs were removed for a short period before the signs returned. The promises were broken. After finding the facts of injustice, after negotiating, and after suffering broken promises, direct action was necessary as the demonstrators would present their "very bodies as a means of laying [their] case before the conscience of the local and the national community" and as symbolic of the spiritual revival of Easter.

King was not unaware that even nonviolent direct action would create tension. He saw nonviolent tension as necessary and refers to Socrates as his authority. Socrates, he wrote, would create a "tension in the mind so that individuals could rise from the bondage of myths and half truths. . . ." With this allusion, King returns us to Plato's Cave, and the struggle between shadows and light becomes authority for the civil rights struggle. King and the demonstrators knew that they had seen the light of racial justice and tolerance. They also knew that the white power structure in Birmingham remained fettered to a segregationist past. More pointedly, King tried to educate the white clergy and tell them that they continued to see the racist shadows on the Cave's wall instead of seeking the light of justice.

There is perhaps one word, more than any other, that provoked outrage in Martin Luther King—"wait." The clergy wanted King to wait to give the new city administration time to act; to wait to give the protesters time to negotiate; to wait to let the courts do their work. But King saw Boutwell as much as a segregationist as Connor even if Boutwell was more genteel in his demeanor. Further, even if Boutwell, as an individual, believed in desegregation, the system would not allow him to act on that belief. Nor would the courts preserve individual rights as the *ex parte* injunction against the parade demonstrated. King knew that "freedom is never voluntarily given by the oppressor, it must be demanded by the oppressed." King knew that the word "wait" meant "never."

For a document which resounds with memorable phrases and poignant moments, there is no more heart-rending paragraph in the letter than that which closes the section on timeliness. King personalizes the indignity of what it means to live in Birmingham in 1963. After 340 years in America, Negroes still had not received their constitutional and God-given rights. They could not have a cup of coffee at a white lunch counter. They could not be educated to the same degree as white citizens. They could not vote as was their constitutional right. Instead, they had seen mobs lynch mothers and fathers; they had seen racists drown, beat, and kill their brothers and sisters. They suffered these tragedies as millions of Negroes lived in "an airtight cage of poverty in the midst of an affluent society." A father could not tell his daughter, as King could not tell Yolanda, that the local amusement park, Funtown, was closed to black children. He could not explain to his son why white people treated him meanly, why he was humiliated daily, or why he was unable to sleep in a motel. How do you explain to your children that "when your first name becomes 'Nigger,' your middle name becomes 'boy' . . . and your last name becomes 'John;'" that you are "harried by day and haunted by night by the fact that you are a Negro, living constantly at tiptoe stance, never quite knowing what to expect next, and are plagued with inner fears and outer resentments; [and that] you are forever fighting a degenerating sense of 'nobodiness.'" When they understand those depredations, he writes to the white clergy, then they might understand why it is unacceptable to wait. Waiting is no longer an option. And still, the tactic of nonviolent demonstrations appeared to need further justification as the next theme of King's letter addresses the relationship between law and justice.

Nonviolent direct action need not break any laws. Peaceful protests, public prayer meetings, even asking to be served at a segregated lunch counter need not be violent nor a violation of the law. Still, marching on Good Friday in 1963 in Birmingham, Alabama without a parade permit and in violation of a state court injunction is clearly a violation of man's law. But is it just?

King directly confronted the apparent inconsistency of threatening to disobey the court's injunction when he had earlier advocated obeying *Brown*. How could he advocate breaking some laws and obeying others?

King begins by recognizing that there are two types of laws—just and unjust. Then he answers his own question: "I would be the first to advocate obeying just laws. One has not only a legal but a moral responsibility to obey just laws. Conversely, one has a moral responsibility to disobey unjust laws." With these two sentences, King presents us with a schematic for thinking about the relationship between law and justice. First, he recognizes the natural law idea that one has both a legal and a moral responsibility to obey just laws. Next, he recognizes that conscience, like the consciences of Antigone and George Harris, may compel someone to disobey an unjust law. Therefore, there are laws which we must legally *and* morally obey and those which our conscience compels us to disobey—which, though, are which? Our inquiry has only begun. Before we can know which laws to obey or disobey we must define just and unjust laws. King gives us a way of thinking about the difference between the two. His analysis spans the secular and the religious, the past and future, and the philosophical and the political.

King starts by adopting the Thomist position that we can identify an unjust law as a human law that is rooted neither in the eternal law nor the natural law. More specifically, "[a]ny law that uplifts human personality is just. Any law that degrades human personality is unjust." King acknowledges that segregation is an unjust law which "distorts the soul and damages the personality." King then quotes Martin Buber and Paul Tillich in support of the proposition that segregation is not only "politically, economically, and sociologically unsound, it is morally wrong and sinful." King's first definition of justice is grounded in the religious tradition in which he and the clergy he addresses were educated. It is a tradition familiar to all Americans, and it is a tradition that brought King and the country to that place at that time.

King's spiritual definition of justice seeks to reaffirm the soul and promote the personality. Yet soul and personality are difficult to identify and define, so King provides us with a more concrete definition of justice. "An unjust law is a code that a numerical or power majority group compels a minority group to obey but does not make binding on itself. This is *difference* made legal." With this move, King transforms his spiritual definition into a secular one, into a definition of justice comfortable in the political realm, a realm of individual equality and fairness, a realm in which minority and majority share a common view of their political selves.

King is more precise with his next example. "A law is unjust if it is inflicted on a minority that, as a result of being denied the right to vote, had no part in enacting or devising the law." Political equality must be manifest in some way and it is best manifest through democratic participation in the political process. The promise of representative democracy now confronts the segregationist policies, strategies, and tactics used throughout Alabama and the South to disenfranchise black Americans and keep them in bondage. Segregation is exposed for what it really is—injustice. Segregation laws are unjust because they are enacted without the full voice of the people. Still, even with a voice, a law can be unjust if it is applied unjustly. King accepts the reasonableness and legality of a parade permit requirement. He disagrees when the parade permit is routinely denied and made impossible to obtain as it was in Birmingham in 1963.

King recognizes that civil disobedience is not to be undertaken lightly. King's *Letter* honors the spirit of Ghandian nonviolence, and his justification for direct action draws on religion, philosophy, and politics and in a memorable phrase, "[o]ne who breaks an unjust law must do so openly, lovingly, and with a willingness to accept the penalty." There, then, is the tradeoff. One has a legal and a moral obligation to obey just laws. And one has a moral obligation to disobey unjust laws *if they willingly and lovingly accept the penalty*. In this way, an act of conscience may arouse the conscience of the community and may demonstrate the highest respect for man's law. This act of conscience is the lesson that King took from the biblical story of Shadrach, Meshach, and Abednego. It is the philosophical lesson he took from Socrates. And it is the political lesson he took from the cries of "no taxation without representation" heard at the Boston Tea Party.

King's call to justice is a universal call; it cannot be fractured or marginalized without undercutting its power. While King's response to his critics is decidedly political, it is a matter of political morality, not of expedient partisanship. His response is critical of those, black and white, who seek to serve local self-interest rather than universal human justice.

King writes that he has been, "gravely disappointed with the white moderate" even more than with the White Citizens Committee or the Ku Klux Klan. For King, the white moderate would rather have order than justice and be satisfied by a superficial sense of peace to avoid tension. Law and order for King were good and valuable goals but only in the service of justice; law and order failed justice when it silenced the voices of the oppressed. The calls for law and order and the calls to reduce tension were attempts, King believed, by the white moderates, "to blame African Americans for their own plight." More specifically, King criticized the charge that black citizens were responsible for the violence that they themselves had suffered. "Isn't this like condemning a robbed man because his possession of money precipitated the evil act of robbery?" King asks. Blaming the victim is like condemning Socrates for his philosophical inquiry and blaming Jesus for doing his father's will.

From King's perspective, the white moderate confuses time and freedom. Equal rights will not "eventually" come without struggle, without voice. Time alone is neutral, King writes, it is what we do with it that matters. Sitting by and avoiding struggle not only delays justice, it denies it. King's argument recalls Martin Niemöller's poem, "[T]hey came for me,/ and by that time there was no one/ left to speak up for me."[10] For King, Birmingham 1963 was the time to speak up, it was the time to fulfill the promise of democracy, it was the time for nonviolent direct action.

King was labeled extremist because of the tension that was created and the violence that erupted. The charge of extremism was one to which he was sensitive because he believed he stood in the middle of two forces in the black community. One was a force of complacency which had adjusted to segregation or had achieved some degree of economic security. The other force was Elijah Muhammad's condemnation of the white man as the devil and his advocacy of hate and violence without negotiation. King believed there was middle way between the "do-nothingism" of the complacent and the hatred of the black nationalist. He found that way through democratic participation. He also found that way through the creative tension of nonviolent direct action. King's middle way was intended to achieve justice and avoid a "frightening racial nightmare" born of black nationalism. Through this middle way, black citizens could exercise their voices, could participate in the struggle, and could participate in the democratic experiment.

Nonviolent direct action was a channeling mechanism, and if it had to bear the label of extremism, King was willing to bear it. As he called down religious references to Jesus as an extremist for love, Amos as an extremist for justice, Paul as an extremist for the Gospel, and Martin Luther as an extremist for his religion, King also called down political references of Abraham Lincoln and Thomas Jefferson as extremists for equality. Throughout the *Letter*, King continually brings together the religious and the political as sources of inspiration and asks, "not whether we will be extremists, but what kind of extremists we will be?"

King expressed special disappointment with the white religious leadership of Birmingham. He was appalled that many ministers argued that the struggle for racial justice was a social issue about which the Gospel was not concerned. He wondered aloud what was said in those white churches when Governors Barnett and Wallace cried for segregation and hatred. Still, King declares his love for the church, his commitment to it, and his hope that the scars he identified would be healed. He believed the witness and true meaning of the Gospel could still be achieved. In closing his letter, King expresses the expectation that "[w]e will reach the goal of freedom in Birmingham and all over the nation, because the goal of America is freedom."

His final criticism was to chastise the white clergy for commending the Birmingham police for keeping order. Shortly after the Good Friday march, the Children's Crusade began with horrific consequences. In the weeks following, fire hoses would be turned on children, police dogs would show their fangs, women would be brought to the ground with police knees at their throats, and houses and churches would be bombed for all the world to see. King knew that the Good Friday march was peaceful because the local police did want to draw attention to Birmingham; it was not peaceful because of Birmingham's commitment to justice. Instead of praising the Birmingham police, King writes his critics that commendations should have gone to the demonstrators, to those who participated in kneel-ins and sit-ins for their "sublime courage, their willingness to suffer, and their amazing discipline in the midst of great provocation." Those were the real heroes—the James Merediths, the Rosa Parkses, the freedom riders, the voter registrants, and the young students willing to suffer violence, even death, and those willing to go to jail for conscience. He ends his letter with a call for fellowship among the clergy and signs his letter in the name of peace and brotherhood.

From the Religious to the Political

King's *Letter* blends the religious and the secular. The civil rights movement, as most certainly exemplified by King, was born in black churches. Accordingly, King's *Letter* is steeped in theology and uses his theology to criticize the go-slow strategy of the white churches and the white moderates. Yet progress could not be made without rousing the consciences of the white majority, if not in Alabama, then throughout the rest of the country and the world. If the churches were going to remain segregated and if the message of the Gospel was inadequate to rectify 300 years of racial discrimination, then another avenue must be found. The genius of King's *Letter* lay in not only using theology to argue that the white clergy had been corrupted and co-opted away from the struggle of justice, it lay in the argument that segregation was the result of an unjust political system which contravened the fundamental principles of our government. If racial justice was to be realized it could not be found not only through the Gospel, it had to be found through the Constitution. King's antidote to racial segregation was participatory democracy. Once democratic participation becomes a reality, King hoped, then equality could prevail and racial segregation would fall as a matter of law.

The march on Birmingham was pivotal to the civil rights movement. It brought the Kennedy administration onto the stage when, before, they had been reluctant actors waiting in the wings. In June 1963, Kennedy introduced what would become the Civil Rights Act of 1964[11] after a heroic struggle by Lyndon Johnson.[12] The Act was aimed at outlawing discrimination in hotels, restaurants, theaters, and other public accommodations. The Act prohibited the unequal application of voter registration requirements and encouraged the desegregation of schools among other provisions. The Act, however, did not go far enough in ensuring equal voting, and in the following year, the National Voting Rights Act of 1965 was passed.[13] The Voting Rights Act outlawed literacy tests and gave the Department of justice significant authority to oversee the voting rules in states that had curtailed voting along racial lines.

The matter of voting rights should appear simple, and yet its history continues to be contested because voting is central to the partisan political process. The simple principle of one person, one vote[14] had been difficult to establish. In the past, the franchise was denied to women and racial minorities. While, these forms of blatant discrimination have been eliminated, voting rules continue to disadvantage some citizens. Because we are a representative democracy, voters often do not elect candidates directly. Instead, we vote for electors for the president of the United States,[15] and we vote in districts for our representatives. Consequently, drawing voting district lines becomes a very contentious matter as the party in power has an opportunity to draw those lines favorably to themselves. The difficult issue, of course, is whether gerrymandering is done on the basis of race rather than party affiliation[16] or whether voter registration requirements adversely affect racial minorities. These controversies continue despite the voting gains made by the civil rights movement.[17]

Voting, then, is the most obvious form of democratic participation, and it should be available to all qualified citizens regardless of race. Voting alone, however, is insufficient to remedy the ills King witnessed in Birmingham and throughout the country. Poverty needed to be eliminated and health care, jobs, and education needed to be provided in order to ensure full participation in the democracy. How can democratic participation respond to those needs?

Democracy and Distrust

King's *Letter* is explicit about the matter of participatory democracy: "A law is unjust if it is inflicted on a minority that, as a result of being denied the right to vote, had no part in enacting or devising the law." He argues that justice can result only through full and equal participation in the political process. His theory is a powerful one as it takes us in a different direction in our search of the higher law. Instead of identifying the fundamental values which constitute justice, democratic participation is a process intended to distribute the political rights through which justice can be sought. One problem with a democracy is the threat of tyranny of the majority. Democratic participation, to be effective, must articulate a theory which allows the majoritarian democratic process to function while affording minority protection. In his 1980 book, *Democracy and Distrust*,[18] then–Harvard Law Professor, John Hart Ely, offered such a theory one which also contains a set of political values congenial to King's *Letter*.

Searching for Fundamental Values

Ely, like Holmes and Posner in the last chapter, is skeptical about finding and articulating fundamental values or the higher law. Nevertheless, Ely's theory of democratic participation, which he calls representation-reinforcing, has a specific political and historical relationship to justice. Ely recognizes the predicament of trying to name substantive values in a pluralistic democracy. In a pluralist society, where faction fights faction, it would seem logical that "if we are willing to wheel and deal, we can usually protect ourselves pretty well politically."[19] The problem, however, is that throughout history, "minorities that the rest of us have insisted on seeing as 'different' . . . have thus been rendered unable to participate effectively in the usual pluralist give and take."[20] Ely echoes King's sentiment that justice is absent when difference is made legal. The problem remains, however, how to cure that defect.

The analysis of democratic participation by Ely begins with a footnote and ends with great skepticism. As our country reaches 300 million citizens, and as technology challenges us both domestically and globally, we ask much of our government. The administrative state must respond to multiple demands and must be able to operate fairly fluidly. One way to assist the fluid operation of government is to allow legislators and government agencies to pass and implement laws that are rationally related to the goals these laws set out to achieve without having to undergo searching judicial scrutiny. If a legislature, for example, chooses to prohibit the interstate shipment of filled milk as a health measure, then so be it as long as the law is rational. Two things should stand out. First, such a statute is the product of interest group lobbying and as long as multiple interest groups contest for the distribution of government largesse, we should achieve a rough fairness as James Madison argues in Federalist Paper No. 10.[21]

The second observation is less obvious. Thin judicial scrutiny, which holds that as long as a law is rational it is constitutional, should not be applied when it directly impacts and negatively affects the individual rights and liberties of minority groups. Justice Harlan Stone recognized this danger in the famous footnote four in *Carolene Products.*[22] While the rational basis test may be sufficient for distributional issues involving goods and resources, a more "searching judicial inquiry" may be necessary when reviewing statutes, "directed at particular religious . . . or national . . . or racial minorities . . . [and when] prejudice against discrete and insular minorities may be a special condition, which tends seriously to curtail the operation of those political processes normal ordinarily to be relied upon to protect minorities. . . ."[23] At one level, the issue that Ely writes about is a matter of constitutional interpretation, in particular which standard of review courts should use in different sorts of cases. On another level, though, the issue is straightforwardly political. There must be some way to check majority tyranny.

Ely's argument, like King's, is that political participation is essential and necessary in a democracy. And his goal, like King's, is racial justice. Ely's problem, unlike King's, is skepticism. He posits that while as individuals we might feel strongly that racial justice is a fundamental value, locating it in a constitutional democracy is tricky, and the road to democratic participation is hardly smooth. Ely uses his skepticism about finding fundamental values to articulate and justify his robust theory of political representation.[24] Ely first argues that there is no sure path for discerning fundamental values (or the higher law) in a pluralistic democracy, and he leads us down several before reaching a political process solution which he argues is firmly grounded in the Constitution.

In a constitutional system, we might let a judge's own values determine what counts as fundamental. Of course, the judge would be educated, familiar with political and legal institutions that govern the country, familiar with legal texts and the democratic values and principles contained therein, and would be charged by law with the responsibility to decide hard cases. We might also posit that the judge sees herself as objective and neutral, constrained by precedent, and ultimately committed to decisions that fit neatly into the fabric of the law as it has been written and as it is developing. The judge will still encounter cases in which both sides of the argument are at equilibrium, and she must choose between one or the other. Let's further posit that the judge is of the exemplary character of Dworkin's Hercules, and that she actually arrives at the "right" answer. Or we can posit that the judge is an exemplary Holmesian or Posnerian pragmatist.

In each case, the fatal flaw in using a judge's own values resides less in the fact that she will have a broad discretion to decide cases than it lies in the fact that the judge comes from a narrow spectrum of our society. Even a modest judge recognizes that she is the product of certain experiences, including education and professional training and practice, and she subscribes to a relatively narrow set of values. For if it is not the judge's personal values that are being called upon to identify fundamental constitutional principles, then it will be the values of her class and not the values of the broader, democratic society.

Ely then suggests that we might look to natural law, and yet our earlier study of natural law indicates that Aquinas spoke of this ideal in only the most general terms. If natural law is too narrow at one end, it is too broad at the other, as anything can qualify as natural law. Ely argues that what passes for natural law today is more a product of a particular political persuasion than it consists of the Thomistic concept of first principles. Natural law is a compelling idea as we contemplate identifying universal human principles. Even assuming that we can arrive at reliable universal principles of human nature, the difficulty lies in not only articulating those values beyond generalities but locating them in the Constitution.

Another approach discussed then discarded by Ely is Herbert Weschler's "neutral principles" analysis. Weschler posited that all cases should be decided on the basis of neutral principles such as the requirement that like cases be decided alike.[25] Weschler feared two enemies. By using neutral principles, he argued, a judge was immune from the criticism that he was taking a substantive or partisan position when deciding a case. Instead, a neutral-principles judge was objectively and neutrally applying the law. His other enemy was *ad hoc* decision making. He feared that without the application of neutral principles the law would not cohere. He preferred, then, to rely on the objective (and neutral) legal process for the good of the constitutional order even in cases affecting individual rights.[26]

Weschler would rail against the notion that a judge's own values can determine an outcome of a case, let alone find our fundamental values. To Weschler, a judge who "simply lets his judgment turn on the immediate result may not, however, realize that his position implies that the courts are free to function as a naked power organ,"[27] a principle anathema to our jurisprudence. Weschler's target was judicial decision making which was based on outcomes rather than "neutral" analysis. He argued that judicial decisions should rest on "reasons with respect to all the issues in the case, reasons that in their generality and their neutrality transcend any immediate result that is involved."[28] Fair enough. But Wechsler does not persuade.

Weschler's skepticism about unconstrained judicial decision making, in favor of what he termed "principled adjudication," also applied to minorities seeking the equal protection of the laws. Weschler thought that *Brown* "stirs the deepest conflict"[29] for his thesis but did not refute it. He would have preferred it if the *Brown* Court addressed the question of whether integration "forces an association upon those for whom it is unpleasant or repugnant"[30] instead of concerning itself with whether it is a "denial of equality to the minority against whom [segregation] is directed; that is, the group that is not dominant politically and therefore, does not make the choice involved."[31] In other words, Weschler is asking the Court how it chose to apply the principle of equal protection over the principle of freedom of association in deciding the *Brown* case. Why should the Constitution favor racial equality over a citizen's right to associate with whomever he chooses for any reasons racial or otherwise?

Weschler does not escape his own criticism. His choice of the legal principle of freedom of association over the legal principle of equal protection reveals the fatal flaw in his argument—a choice between legal rules and substantive outcomes must be made and no one choice is neutral. The decision maker who chooses equal protection will arrive at an outcome that condemns racial segregation, and the decision maker who chooses freedom of association perpetuates it. Again, a choice must be made and the claim of neutrality does not insulate the decision maker from making a substantive choice. Worse still, neutrality can serve as a mask for other political interests.[32] In other words, under the mask of neutrality, partisan politics can easily enter the judicial decision-making process. In short, no decision maker, judge or otherwise, can decide anything without one eye on outcome and the other on process to see if both conform to each other.[33]

Ely then suggests that reason might serve us well in finding our fundamental constitutional values, yet reason generates as much diversity as do the passions. More precisely, Ely points out that reason is only a method relative to connecting premises to conclusions; it does not dictate which premises to choose with which to start analysis nor does reason lead to particular substantive outcomes or positions. He then argues that those who suggest we reason our way to constitutional values are really asking us to engage in moral philosophy. And moral philosophy, as we well know, is no one thing. It is rather any number of philosophies often justifying a philosopher's specific point of view. Or, as Nietzsche said of moral philosophers, they are "cunning pleaders for their prejudices," and their philosophy becomes an involuntary and unconscious memoir.[34]

Ely ends the opening section of *Democracy and Distrust* by suggesting other candidates for finding fundamental values—including tradition or consensus or predicting progress—and finds that all are wanting. People read tradition differently. They see future progress differently, and consensus is exactly what we are trying to avoid when we try to avoid tyranny of the majority. For Ely, there is no sure path to the substantive fundamental values of the Constitution and, consequently, no sure path to the higher law because pluralism and diversity preclude finding one overarching world view.

Democratic Participation

Ely's catalogue of methods for finding fundamental values reveals the difficulty, and for him, the futility of such a project. Perhaps we can avoid the search for fundamental values completely and simply decide cases on an *ad hoc* basis. After all, *ad hoc* decision making is the stuff of common law. Two problems should be apparent. The first problem is that if every decision is truly *ad hoc*, then there is nothing to rely upon when planning for the future. A judicial decision today can be overturned tomorrow. To remedy such fluctuations in decision making, we can adopt a rule of *stare decisis* or precedent. We might adopt Weschler's rule that like cases should be treated alike. The problem with justice, however, does not disappear. Under a rule of precedent, a decision that separate is equal and that the races must travel in segregated rail cars should then also means that school segregation is constitutional. There are several reasons that precedent is valuable, but it does not serve as a substitution for justice. Our search continues.

Ely's approach moves us away from searching for substantive fundamental values, and instead we look for the procedural values of the political process as a second best solution to finding justice. He relies on the words and structure of the Constitution to sustain his argument. In particular, he sees a connection between political activity and the proper functioning of democratic processes.[35] It is his thesis that the Constitution justifies the internal "'participational' goals of broadened access to the processes and bounty of representative government."[36] He focuses his attention not on whether any "substantive value is unusually important or fundamental but rather on whether the opportunity to participate either in the political process by which values are appropriately identified and accommodated, or in the accommodation those processes have reached, has been unduly constricted."[37]

He takes us on a tour of the Constitution and points out something which may be obvious but is often neglected. The Constitution is a document more concerned with political processes than with specified rights and substantive values.[38] The Constitution establishes our representative democracy, contains the separation of powers inherited from Locke and Montesquieu, reinforces that separation through a system of checks and balances, and honors the federal system apportioning power between the states and the central government among other procedural devices. The document is also grounded in a sense of democratic majoritarianism which acknowledges that various interests will compete for power and privilege.

Because the majority can exercise its will on the minority and because interest groups can gain advantages not allowed to other individuals, individual liberties and rights are protected in the Bill of Rights as well as, according to Ely's argument, by the structure of the Constitution itself. The Bill of Rights is also protective of a political process that ensures citizen voices are heard. The Constitution, Ely writes, leaves the selection and accommodation of substantive values, "almost entirely to the political process and instead the document is overwhelmingly concerned, on the one hand, with procedural fairness in the resolution of individual disputes . . . and on the other . . . with ensuring broad participation in the processes and distributions of government."[39]

Ely is describing a system of constitutional law which preserves processes of government and at the same time attempts to assure fairness through general values such as individual liberty, equal protection, and due process. It is the function of the Constitution, then, to charge the judiciary with monitoring the political process and ensuring that representation is fairly available to all citizens rather than having the courts "find" and announce fundamental values.[40] He furthers his argument by noting that judges are particularly suited to assess process arguments. They are by training, and hopefully by temperament, certainly more suited to assess process and procedure than they are at finding fundamental values for the citizenry. "[L]awyers do seem genuinely to have a feel, indeed it is hard to see what other special value they have, for ways of insuring that everyone gets his or her fair say."[41]

The role of the judiciary, then, is to police malfunctions. Ely identifies two of them. The first malfunction is when the "ins are choking off the channels of political change to ensure that they will stay in and the outs will stay out," and the second is when the effective majority systemically disadvantages "some minority out of simple hostility or a prejudiced refusal to recognize commonalities of interest, and thereby denying that minority the protection afforded other groups by a representative system."[42] This last malfunction clearly prefigures the case of *Romer* v. *Evans* in which a Colorado state constitutional amendment made it more difficult for gay and lesbian citizens to petition the government for redress. The Supreme Court recognized this constitutional impediment and struck down the amendment.[43] To be sure, Ely's conception of political participation is grounded on certain conceptions of equality and liberty. Individuals must be treated equally in the process, and they must have the political liberty to participate.

Recently, justice Stephen Breyer has articulated a position similar to Ely's. In his book, *Active Liberty*[44] Breyer describes the process of constitutional interpretation as essentially grounded in democratic participation. He writes, "[L]iberty means not only freedom from government coercion but also freedom to participate in the government itself."[45] Active liberty consists in sharing a nation's sovereign authority among its citizens. It is Breyer's thesis that courts should take account of the Constitution's democratic structure when they engage in the process of constitutional interpretation. Like Ely, Breyer finds the search for substantive constitutional values problematic except for the value of democratic participation which is embedded in the text and structure of the Constitution itself.[46]

The notion that liberty to participate in government serves as a second best substitute for defining fundamental values or justice has appeal. King's demand, like Ely's, for democratic participation in the processes of government is a minimal or thin theory. It does not, for example, state the requirements for that participation. Actors in the political system are not constrained and do not have to participate under this thin theory, nor does the theory require that a certain type of reason be given in the political arena. There are theories of deliberative democracy which require that certain types of reasons be given in public debate so that citizens can be persuaded to favor one value over another as a matter of proper political participation.[47] We will see a version of this higher requirement for democratic participation in the next chapter.

Is Ely's theory of political participation enough to eradicate racial discrimination? He cautions that equality of access to the political process is not to be confused with equality of distribution of the goods and services of society unless they are "essential to political participation or explicitly guaranteed by the language of the Constitution."[48] A legislature which denies racial minorities the vote or places roadblocks in their way to the polls, or to effective participation in the political or economic marketplace, has violated the fundamental nature of our government. Is there something other than access to the political process that might be necessary to engage democratic participation in an effective and meaningful way?

Affirmative Action

Birmingham, Alabama was the scene of fire hoses and police dogs, murders and lynchings all aimed at preventing blacks from securing the vote to end racial segregation. Voting may well be a necessary condition for democratic participation, but is it sufficient? A constitutional amendment that outlawed slavery, legislation to overturn Jim Crow, and legislation to secure voting rights were not enough for full democratic participation. Lyndon Johnson may always be remembered for the bungled war in Vietnam, but he should more appropriately be remembered for his delivery of civil rights which cost the Democratic party the South for a generation and most likely led Johnson not to seek a second term as president. The struggle for civil rights in this country cost the ultimate personal sacrifice for King and large sacrifices for Johnson, and for so many others named and unnamed.

Johnson recognized that legislation alone banning racial discrimination was insufficient to achieve equality. He believed that the Voting Rights Act of 1965 was not the end of but the beginning of equal justice. On June 4, 1965, the president delivered the commencement address at Howard University entitled "To Fulfill These Rights." In that speech, Johnson recognized that "Freedom is not enough. You do not wipe away the scars of centuries by saying: Now you are free to go where you want, and do as you desire, and chose the leaders you please. You do not take a person who, for years, has been hobbled by chains and liberate him, bring him up to the starting line of a race and then say, 'you are free to compete with all the others,' and still justly believe that you have been completely fair."[49]

He also argued that it is not just liberty but opportunity; not just legal equity but human capability that was needed before racial equality could be achieved. Johnson's dream of the Great Society was a dream in which all citizens had equal opportunities and that the two worlds—one black, one white—were no longer separate.[50] In his Howard speech, Johnson saw these two separate worlds. He saw the corrosive differences between them, and for him the differences were, "the consequence of ancient brutality, past injustice, and present prejudice. . . . For the Negro they are a constant reminder of oppression." Johnson knew that simply freeing a man from his chains did not give him equal status in society, and the lack of equal status restricted equal opportunity. The oppressed must be affirmatively assisted out of their oppression.

The challenge Johnson posed is formidable. If the sin of segregation is racial classification, then how can new racial classifications in the name of affirmative action expiate that sin? Ely wrote that if, "we are to have even a chance of curing our society of the sickness of racism, we will need a good many more minority-group members in the professions and elsewhere in society's upper strata."[51] He also recognized that social equality was unlikely to occur unless race was taken affirmatively into account so that weighing race "necessarily means that others are going to be denied the opportunities in question because they were not born black."[52] Johnson's metaphor supports Ely's point—no one can start a race in leg irons. For the promise of democratic participation to deliver liberty and equality for all citizens, that participation must be meaningful. If citizens are guaranteed an active liberty by our Constitution, then inclusion, not exclusion, becomes the test of participatory democracy.[53]

Democracy and Education

Since the Common School Movement in the nineteenth century, through John Dewey's philosophy of education, and then through *Brown* and its progeny, education has been considered a "necessity of life"[54] just as the denial of education was a necessity of slavery.[55] As voting is a necessary condition for participation in politics, education is necessary for participation in civil society.[56] Full and effective democratic participation anticipates that citizens can act in the political and economic marketplaces.[57] As King wrote, economics and politics are inextricably linked, and that linkage is bridged through education. He desired democratic participation as the means to enable voice in politics as well as to remove the stain of prejudice which was tightly wrapped in the pain of poverty.

The link between politics and education is not ephemeral. Writing for a unanimous Court in *Brown*, Chief justice Warren stated, "Today, education is perhaps the most important function of state and local governments."[58] Warren noted that education is required in order to perform our most basic public responsibilities. He wrote that it is the foundation of good citizenship, and is the principle instrument instilling cultural values in our children, preparing them for professional training, and helping children to adjust normally to their environments.[59] Warren concludes: "In these days, it is doubtful that any child may reasonably be expected to succeed in life if he is denied the opportunity of an education."[60] When public education is involved, it is a right which must be made available to all on equal terms so that the promise of democratic participation can be fulfilled. The idea, then, of not only outlawing segregation but moving affirmatively to promote inclusion was both logically consistent and just. Universities in particular embraced this idea but not without continuing resistance.

The Court first addressed racial preferences in higher education in 1978. Writing for a plurality of the Court in *Bakke*,[61] justice Lewis Powell held that racial preferences for medical school were permissible if their purpose was to improve diversity among students as long as no minority quotas were established. Race was to be counted as one factor among many. The *Bakke* case has generated controversy that exists to this day surrounding the evils of "reverse discrimination." Since *Bakke*, the political movement against ridding government—including institutions of higher education—of racial preferences has grown as legislation is passed and court cases are pressed.[62]

The matter of racial preferences in higher education again reached the High Court in 2003 with two companion cases from the University of Michigan involving its law school and its undergraduate program.[63] The argument against racial preferences in the name of reverse discrimination has a certain logic to it. Ely identified the problem in his early work on affirmative action. He recognized that the fact that some persons may be denied opportunity because they had been born white or because they had been born black was a "wrenching moral issue."[64] Should our constitutional law tolerate racial preferences of any kind or should the Constitution be color-blind? Should a white student be denied admission to a school of her choice, like Barbara Grutter, in order to give a preference on the basis of race to another student? The unfairness seems patent, but the arguments against racial preferences are not airtight, nor are they as unjust as their opponents insist. King's *Letter* and Ely's jurisprudence demonstrate why.

In *Grutter* v. *Bollinger*, the University of Michigan Law School adopted a policy to achieve racial diversity in its student body. The school evaluated the applicants' academic ability together with an assessment of their talents, experience, and potential and required an essay describing how an individual would contribute to the life of the law school and to the law school's diversity. The law school attempted to enroll a "critical mass" of underrepresented minority students, and in doing so, treated race as a plus factor in the admissions process.

The law school's admissions policy contained a racial preference, and the Court had previously held that racial preferences would be strictly construed and upheld only after a showing of a compelling state interest. The "strict construction" test is a formidable one, and it has been said that strict scrutiny is strict in theory and fatal in fact because almost no interest has been deemed sufficiently compelling to justify disadvantaging a suspect class,[65] including a member of the white majority.

The burden, then, was on the University of Michigan Law School to demonstrate a compelling interest for its racial preferences. The law school looked backward as well as forward for its justification. In *Brown*, in a famous and contested footnote, the Court recognized that psychological data demonstrated the sense of inferiority attached to the racial segregation suffered by black children.[66] Fifty years later, the Michigan Law School relied on contemporary empirical data that demonstrated the positive gains to be made by minorities as a result of diversity in higher education. Quite simply, the law school argued that educational benefits flow from a diverse student body. The Court agreed as justice O'Connor wrote for the majority, "the Law School has a compelling interest in obtaining a diverse student body"; the admission policy promoted racial understanding together with the breakdown of racial stereotypes.

The Court paid particular attention to the assertions made in the briefs filed by a group of private corporations and the military. Both sectors argued that diversity was a necessity, not a luxury. To compete in the global marketplace and to ensure a stable military, both the business and military worlds needed diverse and educated students. The military especially noted that they could not have an officer core that was highly qualified and racially diverse unless the service academies engaged in race-conscious recruiting and admissions. Education and career, and political and economic participation, are directly connected.

Justice O'Connor referred back to *Brown*, noting the relationship between education and citizenship, and she referred back to *Sweatt v. Painter*,[67] recognizing the role that universities play in training and educating our nation's leaders. "In order to cultivate a set of leaders with legitimacy in the eyes of the citizenry, it is necessary that the path to leadership be visibly open to talented and qualified individuals of every race and ethnicity."[68] For O'Connor, "[e]ffective participation by members of all racial and ethnic groups in the civic life of our nation is essential if the dream of one Nation, indivisible, is to be realized."[69] O'Connor's opinion noted that it was 25 years since *Bakke* and she wrote, "[w]e expect that 25 years from now, the use of racial preferences will no longer be necessary to further the interest approved today."[70] We will see shortly that the legacies of *Brown*, *Bakke*, and *Grutter* remain and they continue to be scrutinized and debated as our country continues to struggle in the matter of race, as it will perhaps do so for more than the next 25 years.

Affirmative action opponents, including the dissenters in *Grutter*, argue that racial preferences constitute invidious discrimination, that the

Constitution should be color-blind, that quotas are anathema to higher education, and that the "educational benefits of diversity" are chimerical. In his *Grutter* dissent, justice Scalia makes all of these points, chiding his colleagues for upholding an elite law school's political agenda. "[T]he University of Michigan Law School's mystical 'critical mass' justification for its discrimination by race challenges even the most gullible mind."[71] Scalia and others seek the high ground by adopting justice Harlan's dissent in *Plessy* v. *Ferguson* and by waving the flag of color-blindness.[72] They attempt to champion racial equality regardless of the effects or consequences on minorities of continuing racial inequities. They fail to acknowledge that Harlan's dissent was about exclusion, the exclusion of persons from civil society for reasons of race. Harlan's dissent did not extend privileges to the white majority; it restricted them for minorities.

Justice Scalia is also critical of the university's assertion about the educational benefits of diversity writing that "If properly considered an 'educational benefit' at all, it is surely not one that is either uniquely relevant to law school or uniquely 'teachable' in a formal educational setting."[73] One might respond that, of course, such values are teachable.[74] Affirmative action and diversity education are necessary, in Martha Nussbaum's phrase, for "the cultivation of humanity."[75] Diversity allows us to think beyond our boundaries, beyond our experiences; it allows us to think about the other and about others. More important, diversity allows us to recognize the world and our place in it. It enables democratic participation more fully than racial exclusion allows.

Another more germane response to justice Scalia is that his criticism ignores the argument for the social inclusion necessary for full and effective political participation. And it is the fear of inclusion that motivates the opposition to affirmative action. Inclusion is the most threatening and difficult aspect of affirmative action because affirmative action is about political participation, and political participation is about sharing wealth and power. In Lani Guinier's words, university admissions are, in fact, "political acts" and democratic ones at that.[76] Nevertheless, affirmative action in education is the fulfillment of King's dream of political participation and satisfies Ely's theory of political representation.

We have not reached the end of controversies surrounding race and education. Just over four years to the day that *Grutter* was decided, the Supreme Court ruled in the case of *Parents Involved in Community Schools* v. *Seattle School District 1*[77] that two public school districts could not voluntarily use racial classifications to desegregate primary and secondary schools. In those cases, parents argued that allocating children to different public schools based solely on race violated the Fourteenth Amendment, and the Court agreed. Writing for the Court, Chief justice Roberts said that racial balance could not be achieved for its own sake.[78] In support of his conclusion, the chief justice quotes the plaintiff's brief in *Brown* and says that the heritage of *Brown* could not be clearer that "'[T]he 14th Amendment prevents states from according differential treatment to American children on the basis of their color or race.'"[79] Roberts argues that all classifications of persons must be color-blind.

The theme of the color-blind Constitution is heard most forcefully in the concurring opinion by justice Clarence Thomas. "Disfavoring a color-blind interpretation of the Constitution, . . . would give school boards a free hand to make decisions on the basis of race—an approach reminiscent of that advocated by the segregationists in *Brown*. . . ."[80] Both Roberts and Thomas base their color-blind arguments on *Brown* and on the dissenting opinion of justice Harlan against the separate but equal doctrine in *Plessy* v. *Ferguson*. Both justices are wrong. Either their arguments, particularly quoting the plaintiff's in *Brown*, are grossly disingenuous, are based on poor readings of constitutional history, or both. *Brown* and Harlan's dissent addresses racial exclusion and support arguments for racial inclusion in society to remove the bonds of racial inferiority. Roberts concludes his opinion with the slogan that "the way to stop discrimination on the basis of race is to stop discrimination on the basis of race"[81]—an attractive but simplistic and ahistorical principle.

How can it be, then, that racial classifications to achieve diversity, to enhance the educational experience of all students, and to further the promise of political participation is valid in 2003 and invalid in 2007? Justice Breyer's answer from the Bench, when he read his *Parents* dissent, is searing: "It is not often in the law that so few have so quickly changed so much."[82] The post-2003 addition of Chief justice Roberts and justice Alito to the Court changed the law of affirmative action in education.[83] The constitutional law of affirmative action changed because partisan politics intervened.

Breyer's dissent adopts his concern for active liberty and democratic participation: "[T]he Constitution creates a democratic political system through which the people themselves must together find answers. And it is for them to debate how best to educate the Nation's children and how best to administer America's schools to achieve that aim. The court should leave them to their work."[84] In other words, Breyer argues that majority elected school officials developed the desegregation plans at issue and that democracy requires that those plans be allowed to operate. In support of his argument, Breyer refers to the Court's earlier holding that racial inclusion and diversity prepares students to live and participate in a pluralistic society.[85]

Breyer offers three arguments for his dissent. First, Supreme Court precedent supports his argument that racial classification can be used to include people, and he relies on *Brown, Bakke, Swann,* and *Grutter* among others.[86] Second, he asserts that his theory of active liberty is the proper reading and interpretation of the Constitution. The desegregation plans under review, according to Breyer, provide opportunities for all children and "includes an effort to help create citizens better prepared to know, to understand, and to work with people of all races and backgrounds, thereby furthering the kind of democratic government our Constitution foresees."[87] And, third, democratically elected school boards should be allowed the discretion to fashion their school districts to remove the stain of racial segregation. A majority should not be fettered in imposing some burden on itself.[88]

His opinion also echoes Martin Luther King's *I Have A Dream Speech* in which King said that America has defaulted on its promissory note and has failed to live up to the promises contained in the Constitution and the Declaration of Independence. "Instead of honoring [its] sacred obligation, America has given the Negro people a bad check, a check which has come back marked 'insufficient funds' . . . we refuse to believe that there are insufficient funds in the great vaults of opportunity of this nation."[89] Similarly, Breyer concludes by writing that to invalidate the school desegregation plans under consideration is to "threaten the promise of *Brown*. The plurality's position, I fear, would break that promise. This is a decision that the Court and the Nation will come to regret."[90]

The fight over *Brown* and its progeny is a fight over color-blindness. For the opponents of affirmative action and reverse discrimination, the surest way of avoiding a political tangle about race is a bright-line prohibiting all racial classifications whatsoever. The problem with the bright-line is that it is too bright by half. *Brown, Bakke, Grutter,* and *Parents* are all cases about inclusion, not exclusion. Racial classifications imposed by the majority *on themselves*[91] intended to eradicate past evils and further racial equality, and aimed at inclusion do not constitute invidious discrimination. Instead, they honor the promise of equality and honor the ideal of democratic participation embedded in the Constitution as read by King, Ely, and Breyer.

Conclusion

King chastised the white clergy for telling him and his followers to wait for justice. Waiting meant denial because history had stacked the political deck against black Americans. Black Americans had been dealt out of the political process and, as a direct result, dealt out of society and dealt out of the marketplace. Inclusion is all-important, and it must be defined as not only lowering barriers to political participation but also providing the necessary rights so that political participation can be full and effective. Affirmative rights, however, threaten the existing distribution of power and wealth and are resisted with arguments that strain our constitutional jurisprudence. Still, the call for justice, for a higher law, is strong.

King's call for democratic participation has substantial theoretical support. Ely's analysis, like Breyer's, supports the idea that the Constitution is to be read to foster participation in government and in society. Education, no less than voting, is a necessary precondition to full, active involvement in society, its politics, and its markets. And yet we struggle to find democratic participation fully granted. The Supreme Court cases of *Grutter* and *Parents* reveal that the democratic concern for racial equality is not fully realized. These decisions further reveal that the struggle will continue; the time for justice has yet to come. Man's law remains imperfect and inferior, falling short of the higher law, falling short of justice.

King and Ely present us with a procedural approach to justice, and we may well find that approach wanting. Political participation without additional affirmative rights may not grant equal representation to all citizens. Procedural justice, as distinct from substantive justice, may well be an idea that deserves further scrutiny. The next chapter explores the philosophical underpinnings of procedural justice with a curious outcome. The argument made by British philosopher Stuart Hampshire in favor of procedural justice depends on the use of an accepted and legitimate political institution. The exemplary institution he points to is the U.S. Supreme Court, exactly the institution that gave us the conflict between *Grutter* and *Parents*—exactly the institution that has told us that desegregation is not quite timely.

EIGHT

A Poet Dies

"Life is the woman who loves you, the wind through your hair, the sun on your face, an evening stroll with a friend. Life is also a woman who leaves you, a rainy day, a friend who deceives you. I find the idea of dying horrible. But what is left to me is no longer a life."

The Italian poet, Piergiorgio Welby, suffered with muscular-dystrophy for 40 years and at 60 years old did not believe that it was natural to have a "hole in the belly that fills it with fat and proteins . . . [or] a hole in the windpipe and a pump that blows air into the lungs." Nor did he believe that it was "natural to keep a body functional with the help of artificial respirators, artificial feeds, artificial hydration, artificial intestinal emptying, or death artificially postponed." Piergiorgio went to the Italian courts with a request to allow his doctor to sedate him and remove him from his respirator. While the court recognized the right to refuse forced medical treatment, it also upheld the law that death could not occur with the help of another. The Italian court denied his request, so he wrote to the President of Italy for relief.

SHORTLY AFTER HE SENT his letter to the president, Piergiorgio, with the assistance of his doctor, was sedated and the respirator was removed; his life then ended.[1] Piergiorgio's story is neither uncommon nor settled. Physicians, patients, and families confront the question of how to end a life with dignity daily. Piergiorgio's decision could have been made privately through a conversation between him and his doctor. Instead, he publicized his desire, and his request became a matter of politics and law as well as of public morality and religion. The Italian government, the Catholic Church, the Italian legal system, and the public all played roles trying to define the legitimacy of physician-assisted suicide.

Physician-assisted suicide vexes our judges and our politicians as well. At bottom, the legal system is asked to decide the practical problem of how to respond to a request to die with dignity. The legal system is also asked to decide a deeply moral and political question that may involve a fundamental conflict between man's law and something higher. How perplexing and frustrating it is to realize that law's answers to questions about life's end involve conflict rather than consensus and that determinant answers elude us.

As individuals, we may hold a strong moral opinion about physician-assisted suicide. In the broader society, however, there is no clear moral answer, let alone even a temporary consensus, about whether or not terminally ill or physically degenerating but mentally competent patients can end their lives with the help of a physician. Yet these conflicts are regularly brought before the law. How should the law proceed to address issues that are morally indeterminate either because we lack enough knowledge or information to arrive at a sound conclusion or, in what is actually the same problem, where a final decision cannot be made because there are two or more equally viable moral alternatives? Without moral consensus, how do we achieve justice?

We can adjust downward our desire for either perfect justice or a happy marriage between man's law and higher law by aiming to reduce, rather than eliminate, conflicts between them. We can reduce conflicts though sleight of hand and a bit of indirection. Instead of arriving at a consensus agreement about what constitutes substantive justice, we develop rules of engagement for the resolution of the ubiquitous matters of moral and political controversy. It is better to develop rules of procedure for conflict resolution, even for the resolution of problems with significant moral content such as conflicts over life and death, than to have those conflicts fester in society. Good and fair procedures may be the best that man's law can offer and in so doing, law, on occasion, may reach for and may well attain, substantively just results. Here we examine the matter of procedural justice, the rules by which the game of law is played.

This chapter, through a reading of Stuart Hampshire's *Justice Is Conflict*,[2] offers a procedural solution to the problem of the conflict between man's law and higher law. Hampshire's theory does not purport to provide definitive or permanent moral or political answers. Instead, he recognizes that multiple answers are possible and reasonable. He then provides a temporary political and legal response to Piergiorgio's request and to equally morally vexing or divisive questions like abortion, same-sex marriage, the death penalty, and the like. Our discussion of procedural justice builds on the idea of political participation addressed in the last chapter. Dr. King's letter moved our discussion of man's law and the higher law in a decidedly political direction. King's theory of political participation promised that through law, all individuals would be accorded equal dignity and respect. Justice requires no less. King's model of political participation, though, only half delivered on that promise because the political process can still disadvantage individuals and marginal groups. Can Hampshire's theory of procedural justice deliver more?

Justice as Procedure

The central problem for procedural justice is whether even agreed-upon, legitimate and fair procedures can sustain an unjust outcome.[3] Socrates was tried and convicted by a jury after being given the procedural rights to cross examine the prosecution's case, argue his defense, contest his sentence, and propose alternatives. Was his conviction procedurally just? Was it substantively just? We know that there are cases in which the guilty go free and the innocent are convicted. Are these cases just? Good procedures can produce bad results, and it is impossible to justify unjust outcomes by fair procedures. Still, we cannot function in the world without procedures. Fair procedures are necessary but insufficient conditions for justice. We will see that procedures do not exist in a vacuum; instead, good procedures are influenced by norms of substantive justice. Procedural justice and substantive justice are not separate circles in a Venn diagram. Instead they overlap and the greater the overlap, the more justice a society will enjoy. Note, however, they will never overlap completely because rules of general applicability will inevitably confront an individual case which they do not fit and justice will not be served.

We might try to imagine a system of "perfect procedural justice" in which a desirable outcome is known and then once the stated procedures are applied, justice results because the specified just outcome is always reached. John Rawls offers the example of dividing a cake among several persons with the object of arriving at equal shares for all. The perfectly just procedure is that one person cuts the cake and takes the last piece thus insuring that the shares will be equal.[4] Rawls has little hope for perfect procedural justice, "Pretty clearly, perfect procedural justice is rare, if not impossible, in cases of much practical interest."[5]

By contrast, he then suggests that we might also define a system of "pure procedural justice." In such a system, there is no identified outcome, but once the stated procedures are applied, then any outcome is, by definition, just.[6]

Rules of games—chess will do—serve as an example of pure procedural justice. Chess players observe the rules and (skill level aside) whoever checkmates an opponent is the just and fair winner. Perhaps. Shortly, I will argue that "pure procedural justice" is not so pure nor is it unconnected to substantive justice. I would extend Rawls's critique of perfect procedural justice to include pure procedural justice as well. Neither perfect nor pure procedures will lead to justice in any meaningful way, and neither form of procedural justice alone will help us resolve the conflict between man's law and higher law. Still, Rawls's analysis helps us understand the connection between procedural and substantive justice. Procedure alone, unmoored to any sense of substantive justice, has little or no place in the world, even in the world of games, and it certainly has no place in the game of law. Let's see why.

Can a coin toss serve as a procedure to dispense justice? Not without further specification. Imagine agreeing to a coin toss to decide which of two persons will win a prize. One might agree to let a coin toss decide the matter, but one might not agree if the rule of the coin toss is, "Heads I win; tails you lose." The unfairness of such a rule is patent. The fair rule, of course, is, "Heads I win; tails you win." But why, exactly?

Let's look at other procedures that appear to be, and are generally considered to be, fair. Pick the letter closest to A in the alphabet, then you start with a double word score in the game of Scrabble. If your roll of the dice yields the highest number, you play first in a board game. Cut a deck of cards to the highest card and you deal first in poker. And correctly call the toss of a coin, and you can choose to receive or kick off in a college football game. Each of these recognized procedures appear, and are accepted as fair, even though no particular outcome is specified. Whichever player or team wins the game under those procedures is accepted as the fair or just winner.

Among Scrabble players, poker players, and football teams, it is completely undetermined who will start or win the game. Yet regardless of who starts or who wins, the outcome will be accepted as fair all for the same reason—each player has the same chance to pick an A, cut to an Ace, or correctly pick heads or tails. And following the start of the game, all players (skill levels aside) have an equal or fair chance of winning.

The concept of procedural justice appears promising because it appears to relieve us from the need to articulate any conception of substantive justice. There are two problems with procedural justice so conceived. First, the procedural rules we have discussed are neither so pure nor so perfect as these descriptions might suggest. These rules, instead, contain an element of substantive justice without which they cannot be accepted as fair. Second, following Rawls, rules of simple procedure are not of much practical interest because simple procedural rules do not travel well and do not extend to complex games, let alone extend to the rules of law by which societies are governed.

While the procedural rules above are considered fair and just, they are not independent of a substantive conception of justice. Choosing a Scrabble letter, rolling dice, cutting cards, or tossing a coin appear neutral, but they are accepted as substantively fair and procedurally just to the extent that they: (1) are agreed-upon procedures, (2) known to voluntary participants, (3) who each have an equal chance (again skill level aside), of (4) achieving the agreed-upon end of starting and then playing a game to a conclusion. These rules of procedure are recognized and accepted as fair precisely because they have a direct connection with substantive justice. The moral autonomy of individuals is recognized and honored because all players are given an equal chance to start and to win a game. The procedural rules are indifferent to the outcome as to who starts or who wins the game, but the rules are not indifferent to the outcome that the playing field is level for all players. The justness or fairness of the rule depends upon the substantive ideas that all participants are playing on the same field and have an equal chance of winning.

The simple procedural rules described above do not have much shelf life and do not extend to more complex games. Let's look at gambling for a moment, the type of gambling that occurs either in Las Vegas or on Wall Street. Playing at the casino or in the market appears to satisfy the definition of pure procedural justice because voluntary players receive their just desserts, and the rules are fairly applied to all players. Yet the casino takes its cut. Special rules against card counting, for example, are applied when circumstances warrant, and there are information distortions such as information about the accurate odds at Las Vegas tables or insider trading information on Wall Street. Everyone does not have an equal chance of winning in either town. Other rules are needed such as correcting information asymmetries by providing gaming information in Las Vegas and information disclosure through stock registration on Wall Street. These more complex rules level the playing fields and are grounded in substantive considerations such as maintaining the integrity of the games themselves, maintaining the institutions that support them, and valuing the players in them.

Let's raise the stakes. How should we determine guilt or innocence in a criminal matter? Will simple rules suffice? Tragically, our criminal justice system is historically based on simple rules. While we might imagine someone cavalierly agreeing to double down on a coin toss over paying a parking ticket, can we really imagine a society determining criminal sentences with Scrabble letters? Which, by the way, is not to say that we have not come close.[7] Dunking witches, ordeals of hot iron, fire, boiling water, and cold water[8] were all procedures used to determine the truth, more specifically the guilt or innocence of criminal defendants. These procedures properly strike us as archaic. We prefer to find guilt or innocence through individual trial-like adjudication. Nevertheless, we continue to return to procedure to help us find justice.

Today we determine guilt or innocence by heavily relying on procedures including rules about how to conduct a criminal trial, rules of evidence, presumptions of innocence, rules about the ethical responsibilities of prosecutors and police and defense attorneys, and rules for appeal, among others. We need procedures which allow for the weighing of evidence, the assessment of fact, and the application of law to determine guilt or innocence. Still, even more complex and layered rules of criminal procedure often fail us. To date, the Innocence Project has been responsible for the release of over 200 men on death row because of faulty criminal procedures.

If procedural rules do not necessarily yield justice in the case of a single individual, they do not fare better in more complex political systems which make distributional decisions for the whole of society. We can start with democracy and set up a system of government for the distribution of wealth and political power according to the democratic principle of majority rule. Everyone votes and the majority rules. Yet justice is not necessarily achieved. The civil rights movement proved that majority rule and political participation can dispense tyranny as well as justice.

Let's try to move away from procedural justice by assuming that we can identify, with a high degree of confidence and a high level of consensus, *injustice*. Having identified injustice, we can then pass laws designed to avoid it, thereby achieving some semblance of justice. However, we cannot abandon the notion of procedural justice entirely for two reasons. The first reason is epistemological—even if we can recognize injustice, we, too often, do not know of what justice consists. Our handhold on justice is weak. The human condition is imperfect and fallible. The data that we need to make decisions is often not fully available. We often confront reasonably competing and equally strong alternatives; sometimes we lack the necessary will to choose. And attitudes change with the circumstances. Our judgments are neither uniform nor are they complete, and we are often uncertain of our choices and about the future applicability and desirability of the decisions we do make. The theory of procedural justice acknowledges that substantive justice is difficult to define, most likely illusive, and most often transitory as it differs over time and place and culture.

The second and related reason to rely on procedural justice is necessity. Decisions must be made in the face of political, moral, technological, and economic uncertainties; society cannot wait for all of the needed information to accumulate. We cannot avoid the necessity of daily decision making on all varieties of subjects including life and death and political and economic distributions. If we either lack perfect information or the confidence in knowing the outcomes we most desire, then we can fall back on procedural justice so that decisions can be made and life can go on. These decisions affect not only commerce and markets; they affect the moral and political controversies that most deeply perplex us.

Piergiorgio's publicized dilemma demonstrates why fair procedures are necessary but not sufficient conditions for justice. There is no consensus about the moral correctness or political acceptability of physician-assisted suicide yet decisions must be made in the face of uncertainty, and we look to and rely upon political or legal processes to arrive at these determinations. We may either agree or disagree with the Italian court's denial of his request, and yet we may also find that it is worthy of respect. Fortunately, answers have been given to Piergiorgio's problem. Unfortunately, man's law and procedural justice provide conflicting ones.

Justice is Conflict

The connection between procedure and justice has occupied much thought during the last half of the twentieth century both in legal philosophy and jurisprudence[9] and in political and moral philosophy. The late British philosopher Stuart Hampshire addressed procedural justice in his Tanner Lectures on Human Values at Harvard University in 1996. Those lectures were later published in a short and provocative personal book, *Justice is Conflict.* In many respects, *justice is Conflict* returns us to Plato, where we began our story of justice, as Hampshire criticizes the first philosopher. Hampshire's strong assertion for a procedural resolution of moral and political conflicts, instead of a definition of substantive justice as harmony, provides us with a different way of thinking about the relationship between man's law and higher law.[10]

Stuart Hampshire was the last of an influential group of British analytic, moral, and political philosophers. Together with J. L. Austin, A. J. Ayer, A. D. Woozley, and Isaiah Berlin, Hampshire was Oxford-educated during the Great Depression and before the Second World War. Their experiences shaped their philosophy as well as their politics. This is especially true in Hampshire's case where his experience during the war played a particularly poignant role in his life as a philosopher.

Hampshire witnessed evil firsthand when as a British Intelligence officer, he interrogated Nazi officers. The experience changed his attitude toward both politics and philosophy.[11] "The National Socialist movement in Germany is an instructive case for moral philosophy, as a historical embodiment of pure evil both in aspiration and accomplishment,"[12] Hampshire says, and would tell an anecdote about that experience. Toward the end of the war, Hampshire interrogated a French traitor who refused to answer his questions unless his life was spared. Hampshire knew that the traitor was condemned to death, yet he needed the information to protect the lives of Resistance fighters. Should Hampshire lie about saving the traitor's life and get the necessary information or tell the truth and risk French lives? His response to this moral dilemma: "If you're in a war, . . . you can't start thinking, 'Well, I can't lie to a man who's going to be shot tomorrow and tell him he isn't.'"[13] The desire for moral consistency confronts the necessities of realty and must, on occasion, yield. This lesson bears directly on Hampshire's theory of procedural justice.

Hampshire opens his book with an epigram from Heraclitus in Greek. Mark Lilla, in his review of the book, supplies a translation: "one must realize that war is common and conflict is justice and that all things come to pass in accordance with conflict."[14] At first glance, it may appear odd to equate justice with conflict. Clearly, conflict like war is common, but how is it justice? Equally clear, Hampshire is being provocative. His book would be more accurately but less interestingly titled *justice is Conflict Resolution.* Hampshire argues that the political and moral conflicts which plague the world—most notably problems of evil—must be addressed, but no matter how hard we try, we cannot develop any single justice solution. Given the diversity of human nature, more particularly the diversity of the human imagination, multiple and conflicting approaches to justice are inevitable.

His opening sentence is disarming. He writes: "At least since 1970, I had been convinced that it was a mistake to look for a moral theory, or a set of propositions, that could serve as a justification, or foundation, of my political loyalties and opinions, which were, and which remain, the opinions of a democratic socialist."[15] If my personal moral code or political beliefs, he posits, cannot win the day, I am duty bound, certainly as a philosopher and as a citizen, to wonder why and to suggest an alternative. Hampshire argues for a procedural approach to conflict resolution even for political and moral conflicts because he came to the realization that there is no single conception of the Good.[16] His preferred politics of democratic socialism, which Hampshire can defend in moral terms as well as political, will not, in his opinion, prevail in Britain. Instead, it is quite likely that other, equally deeply held moral and political beliefs, will govern. Given a plurality of deeply held moral and political beliefs, how then is justice to be found? His answer is through procedural justice containing a bare minimum of morality.[17]

To support his conception of justice as conflict resolution, Hampshire turns to Plato's *Republic* both as a point of departure and as a point of disagreement. Hampshire acknowledges Plato's brilliant analogy between justice in the City and in the Soul. It is Hampshire's position, as it was Plato's, that reason operates similarly in the City and in the Soul. Yet Hampshire parts ways with Plato in three significant ways. Hampshire argues that Plato is simply wrong that harmony is, or ever can be, the object of justice because conflict is inevitable. Next, he rejects Plato's preference for reason over passion. Finally, he rejects Plato's idealization of the state. Hampshire connects these three points by constructing his theory of procedural justice.

Harmony, to Hampshire, is twice an impossibility because human nature manifests itself in great diversity and variety not in a single moral view of the world.[18] This is so because of reason and imagination. Individual reason leads to a variety and diversity of reasoned opinions about the world. Next, and more deep and mysterious, individuals fashion individual and personal conceptions of the good life—the life each person should lead to achieve personal fulfillment—by way of imagination. Individual conceptions of the Good are infinitely various because imagination is somehow distinct from, no matter how enigmatically related to, reason. Hampshire argues that the multiplicity of our conceptions of the Good are "rooted in the imagination and in the memories of individuals."[19]

Going deeper, diversity arises because reason has been taken hold of by the passions. Following Hume, Hampshire accepts the proposition that "reason both is, and ought to be, the slave of the passions." While we all reason alike, we all imagine differently. Hampshire says that emotion and imagination inform our conceptions of the Good which reason cannot fully explain. Hampshire concludes that, when defining the Good, passion is the "true stopping-point."[20] It is not simply difficult—it is impossible—for any individual to successfully employ reason to justify one's most deeply held beliefs because beliefs are formed by passion, emotion, and feeling. Consequently, multiple conceptions of the Good can neither define nor result in substantive justice in the City even if a person can fashion an individual conception of the Good for the Soul because the multiple conceptions have equal claims to our attention and must be given honor and respect.

Reason, then, performs only a portion of the mind's work; imagination the other. Beauty, art, and aesthetic claims, according to Hampshire, are independent of and gain nothing from "any argumentative procedure."[21] While law, logic, mathematics, and natural sciences need rational argument to prosper; painting, poetry, and music do not. Reason requires uniformity; imagination generates diversity and that diversity is manifested in our moral and political conflicts. This last point may appear curious. After all, we use reason to understand, compare, and test moral and political claims. Yes, but only to a point. "Each side in [an] argument invents a philosophy of mind . . . designed to support its thesis about justice, and consequently the argument goes round and round in a circle."[22] We can reason ourselves to the different moral and political conclusions that our imaginations devise.

Reason and passion, intellect and imagination inform an individual's conception of the Good. Through diverse passions and imaginations, individuals make themselves individually known in the world and, as a result, conflict is inevitable and harmony unachievable.[23] The resulting conflicts are about the Good and the moral and political foundations of the societies in which we live. The existence of a diversity of beliefs and values can bring havoc unless checked. Those conflicts must be managed and resolved, if only temporarily, if violence is to be reduced and if we are to live together. Conflict resolution, Hampshire holds, is ingrained in the human mind and spirit, and he goes on to argue, "fairness in procedure is an invariable value, a constant in human nature."[24] Through harnessing this human constant for fairness and by managing and resolving conflict, justice is achieved.

Hampshire also argues that Plato is wrong to give primacy to reason over passion to achieve justice. "[I]magination and intellect should be considered as equals in the context of ethics and politics."[25] Plato argues that City and Soul can be governed and harmony can be achieved through reason whereas Hampshire argues that reason is an insufficient tool. "Rationality is a bond between persons, but it is not a very powerful bond, and it is apt to fail as a bond when there are strong passions on two sides of a conflict."[26] Rationality is bound to disappoint us, recalling Holmes's quip about the illusion of certainty.[27]

Finally, Hampshire criticizes Plato's description of the ideal state. He says that the best the state can do is to attempt to reduce evil. Conflict resolution, not harmony, is necessary for any semblance of justice because societies are not ideal; they are all too real and all too violent. Even at the level of ordinary politics, social democrats confront their conservative adversaries over any variety of policy options, including the role of government in the distribution of wealth. Should government play an active, redistributivist role as the social democrats would have it? Or should government protect property and markets, as the conservatives prefer, so that individual initiative and drive are amply rewarded? Hampshire argues that, clearly, redistribution is morally justified, but he cannot deliver the knock-out punch to his conservative opponents. He acknowledges instead that both sets of arguments are deeply held moral preferences not amenable to change by reason. Political confrontation, then, must be managed since it cannot be permanently resolved because it involves conflicts between irreconcilable conceptions of the Good generated by diverse imaginations; political confrontation, he argues, is not the result of rational analyses.

Hampshire writes that the most disturbing problem today is the conflict between democratic and pluralistic societies that welcome diversity and those societies which are bound to the one, true conception of the Good. Hampshire's target is monotheism, "Those who accept . . . monotheism will believe that all mankind is subject to the same moral constraints, and that only one conception of the good is finally acceptable."[28] Modern democracies reject such a belief because individuals with various moral and political preferences are unlikely to share a single conception of the Good. Contrast pluralist democracy with a society that pledges allegiance to a single conception of the Good for religious, moral, or political ideological reasons. A clash of civilizations is inevitable[29] and can be deadly as 9/11 has taught us. The stronger claim is that moral and political diversity is a good, healthy state of affairs. The stronger claim will be made shortly.

Hampshire's conception of procedural justice combines conflict and passion, reason and reality. His theory incorporates multiple conceptions of the Good, honors the history and traditions of a society, and recognizes that there are a variety of conflict resolution mechanisms available. Hampshire imbues his theory of procedural justice with some substantive content. "There is a basic level of morality, a bare minimum, which is entirely negative, and without this bare minimum as a foundation no morality directed towards greater goods can be applicable and can survive in practice."[30] Hampshire's bare minimum is that evil must be eliminated. He is referring back to his war experience. The pure evil of Nazism went beyond physical human degradation because its aim was to, "eliminate all notions of fairness and justice from practical politics, and, as far as possible, from persons' minds; to create a bombed and flattened moral landscape, in which there are no boundaries and no limits. . . ."[31] The minimal morality of procedural fairness is intended to curb the great, perennial evils such as the "mutilations of war, tyrannies, massacres, and starvation"[32] through conflict resolution so that greater Good, the higher law, has a chance to survive.

Central to his theory is the "indispensable procedure" of *audi alteram partem—hear the other side.* Adversarial reasoning, the balancing of pros and cons, occurs within any individual making even the most personal choices. Procedural justice is grounded on the idea that both sides are heard, that evidence is weighed, and that even under conditions of uncertainty, decisions are made not on the basis of some simple procedure but on the basis of a procedure connected to fairness. Hampshire maintains that this principle is a universal moral virtue shared by all individuals in all societies over human history. He also shares this principle with Plato because adversarial reasoning, the dialectic, is what Plato tells us that the prisoner uses upon his return to the Cave.

Hampshire's adversarial reasoning takes place under two conditions. First, majority rule must yield to minority or individual protection such as through the safeguards contained in the Bill of Rights.[33] To counteract the problems of majority tyranny, individual rights can be protected by constitutional provisions. The second condition is that institutions which employ adversarial reasoning (and there are many) must possess a degree of legitimacy. Legitimacy, in turn, is obtained by the regular use of recognized procedures[34] by the institutions which are formed by recognized habits and customs such as "law courts, parliaments, councils, political parties and others."[35] Adversarial reasoning, then, takes place within a society's accepted institutions which have earned respect through history and tradition.[36]

There is something compelling in the moral principle of *audi alteram partem.* If moral and political conflicts exist and their management and resolution are valued, then the struggle for justice is a matter of arguing over shadows and light just as Plato told us. More to the point, and it is the point we identified about games, procedural justice is not devoid of some substantive content. Procedural justice takes place within these institutions and through these processes that individuals accept as fair. Further, the processes and institutions used for conflict resolution accord individuals basic liberty and equality as participants.

Hampshire's procedural justice is tied to substantive justice in two respects. First, all individuals must have access to the decision making institutions so that the rights of minorities are protected, and individuals are afforded equality of treatment. Second, the decision-making institutions have public acceptance through history and tradition, thus capturing some of the substantive values of a society, or capturing what Dworkin calls political morality.[37] Admittedly, there is not much substantive justice spelled out in detail, thereby raising the questions: Is Hampshire's theory robust enough to sustain vigorous and well-established liberal democracies such as the United States? Is such a theory of procedural justice strong enough to resolve moral and political conflicts? Can this theory determine matters of life and death?

Justice as Fairness

We can compare Hampshire's theory of procedural justice with that of John Rawls. Published in 1971, John Rawls's *A Theory of justice* is the canonical text of political philosophy in the twentieth century. Rawls constructs a sturdy, complex edifice of substantive justice built on procedural foundations such as his famous "original position," "veil of ignorance," and reflective equilibrium. Rawls spent the rest of his career refining his theory and responding to his critics. Like Hart's *The Concept of Law*, *A Theory of justice* sparked a conversation that endures and continues. Hampshire's *justice is Conflict* is testament to Rawls. Rawls's testament to his critics is his willingness to engage them and to correct and refine his theory as he has done in his last book, *justice as Fairness: A Restatement.*[38]

Hampshire and Rawls share several points and diverge on others. Both philosophers concentrate on conflict resolution in the design of their respective theories of justice. Both recognize that individual liberty and equality are essential starting points. Further, both recognize that there is no single conception of the Good, especially in modern, pluralistic liberal democracies. Neither a political system nor a theory of justice can be based on a comprehensive doctrine derived from dogmatic morality, religion, or philosophy. Finally, although in different ways and in different degrees, both recognize the necessary role of reason for achieving justice.

Where Hampshire rejects the notion of an ideal state, Rawls utilizes the idealization of the well-ordered state[39] as a goal of his theory. Where Hampshire treats reason as a universal method of conflict resolution, it is also subordinate to passion. Rawls gives reason primacy over passion but also limits the statements that count as public reason to support his political theory of justice. Where Hampshire is agnostic about moral theory and antagonistic toward monotheism, Rawls assigns a role, albeit a restricted one, to morality in his theory.

Rawls's idealized well-ordered state is fundamental to his theory of justice because he hypothesizes, like Plato, that everyone shares the same perception of justice.[40] Consequently, as citizens discuss the state that they wish to form and the principles of justice that they wish to guide them, they can assume that they are all starting from the same position of equality. They all have a desire to create the best state that they can to enable human liberty and social justice to flourish.

Rawls also employs a different use of reason than Hampshire. Hampshire's principle of *audi alteram partem* is how we reason both privately and publicly. By weighing data and arguments, by balancing pros and cons, we can arrive at private decisions about which car to buy or even whom to marry. We use the same reasoning process for public decision making about distributions of wealth and power or about establishing rights and liberties. Hampshire puts no apparent limits on what counts as acceptable reasons in political discussion. Rawls limits reason in two ways. First, Rawls is describing public reason only, the sort of reason used in public debate to establish public policies.[41] Next, public reason must contain only political arguments; it cannot resort to dogmatic arguments from morality, religion, or philosophy unless those arguments are contained within an overlapping consensus shared by all citizens.[42] Individuals can, of course, resort to any of these or other arguments in private as they form their own comprehensive doctrines and their own life plans. Publically, though, moral, religious, and philosophical arguments are not available because Rawls's theory of justice is a political conception of the community, not an individual and personal world view to be imposed on anyone else let alone upon society as a whole.[43] Comprehensive dogmatic arguments are, therefore, excluded from Rawls's public reason.[44]

Thus, Rawls's conception of procedural justice is thicker than and amplifies Hampshire's theory. With his theory, Rawls sets out to tame two political problems: First, how can we find the justice principles with which to resolve the conflicts found in pluralistic societies engendered by competing philosophical and moral doctrines, each specifying their own notions of liberty and equality? And second, how should liberty and equality be ordered?[45]

Rawls believes that a system of justice, based on identifiable, substantive principles, can be created that enables people to flourish and develop their own individual conceptions of the Good according to their own comprehensive views.[46] Rawls's theory of justice is ambitious as he tries to establish both a substantively just society and a socially harmonious environment which encourages a diversity of moral and political points of view. He starts with the idea of free and equal persons each possessing two moral powers. Every person has a capacity for a sense of justice to guide them as they go about constructing their state and go about defining justice. This sense of justice is something we have seen in Plato and Dworkin. Additionally, people have a capacity for their own conception of the Good which will generate great diversity among individuals all for the common benefit.[47] Through these two moral powers, people develop their private conceptions of the Good and engage each other in public conversation about the goodness and justness of the state. In other words, the moral powers enable political development leading to the specification and ordering of basic liberties.

From this system, Rawls specifies and rank orders his basic liberties as: "political liberty, the right to vote and to be eligible for public office together with freedom of speech and assembly, liberty of conscience and freedom of thought, freedom of the person along with the right to hold (personal) property, and freedom from arbitrary arrest and seizure as defined by the concept of the rule of law."[48] These basic liberties are derived from his two famous principles of justice—the liberty principle and the difference principle.[49]

Given such specification, Rawls also differs from Hampshire. Hampshire is content to have a system of justice that resolves conflicts with the aim of reducing evil in the world. His position is based upon his resignation that his moral world view will not necessarily prevail over other equally viable ones. Rawls argues that under his constraints, primarily his veil of ignorance and his commitment to individual equality, individuals in society will gravitate to a set of universal, just principles which maximize individual liberty while taking care of the least well-off in society.

Rawls's theory tracks Hampshire's in an important way. Formal justice, according to Rawls, requires at a minimum that the rules of the institutions and dispute resolution mechanisms that we rely upon be impartially and consistently observed as a kind of equality.[50] Similarly situated persons are treated similarly. Such procedural equality and loyalty to institutions, however, is no guarantee of substantive justice. Procedural justice requires principles of substantive justice to accomplish that end.[51] "In general, all that can be said is that the strength of the claims of formal justice, of obedience to system, clearly depend upon the substantive justice of institutions and the possibilities of their reform."[52] Additionally, individuals must be treated with equal dignity and respect so that they can participate in the political and legal systems and so that the rule of law can be honored and executed.

The rule of law is also valued and depends on a degree of liberty so that the power of the state is not indiscriminately applied nor harshly used. The expectations created by law must be reasonable, persons subject to law must know that laws have been enacted in good faith, that they can be reasonably acted upon, that laws are interpreted and publically justified reasonably and consistently, and that the legal system operates under rules to ensure its integrity.[53] Under these constraints, people can rely on law, relate to each other, and perpetuate law's existence as a social mechanism that intends to further justice because the procedural justice of the rule of law is dependent upon the institutional arrangements that provide for liberty and equality.

Rawls's theory of justice, like Hampshire's, values law, procedure, and stable and reliable institutions. His theory moves beyond Hampshire's with Rawls's willingness to identify, order, and justify the liberties necessary for his substantive political conception of justice to develop. Rawls's reliance on procedural justice plays a significant role in his broader project while underscoring the necessary connections between substance and procedure. If Rawls has only one thing to teach us, it is that procedure alone is insufficient for justice to exist. The procedural safeguards of man's law are necessary but insufficient conditions for the higher law to thrive.

There is an interesting point of agreement between these two political philosophers. Both hold out the U.S. Supreme Court as an institution that fits their respective theories of procedural justice. Hampshire says of the Court that it is the institution in the United States that resolves, "very bitter conflicts of moral principle, involving substantially different conceptions of substantial justice."[54] Rawls, in a similar vein, says that the Court is the "exemplar of public reason"[55] charged with interpreting and applying the "higher authority of the will of We the People"[56] to satisfy the public ideal of a people governing themselves in a certain practical way. This institution, steeped in history and tradition, is also one which enjoys acceptance among citizens. The dilemma of Piergiorgio, and others similarly situated, is: if we are uncertain, or conflicted, about the morality of physician-assisted suicide, then how should decisions be made? The U.S. Supreme Court is exactly the institution asked to decide such questions, and the Court enjoys the support of our two theorists. Does the Court merit that support?

Procedural Justice in the Supreme Court

Until 1935, the U.S. Supreme Court met in various places including inside the Capitol building. The Court sat literally under the feet of the legislative branch. In 1929, Chief justice William Howard Taft persuaded Congress to authorize a permanent home. Today, the gleaming Marble Palace occupies its rightful place in Washington, D.C. aligning the Court with the Capitol and the White House. Cass Gilbert, the Court's architect, designed the majestic structure to symbolize the Court's coequal role in our tripartite government while emphasizing the independence of the judiciary.

Looking up from the street, the white marble structure with its Corinthian columns is imposing. The inscription over the main entranceway to the Court—*Equal justice Under Law*—acknowledges the importance of fair procedure in our system of government. The main corridor of the Court, the Great Hall, leads from the doorway into the courtroom. Once inside the hallowed Chamber, the noisy echoes of the marble floor disappear as quiet settles on the bench, on the podium, on the counsel tables, and on the annoyingly uncomfortable rows of spectator seats. While grand, there is something remarkably intimate about the Court Chamber, there is a human dimension to it. The majesty of the building seems to condense into a room in which it is easy to see and hear lawyers argue their cases before the nine justices of the U.S. Supreme Court. The Chamber encompasses both majesty and dignity while lawyers and judges participate in the ritual of procedural justice.[57]

The majesty of the building and the intimacy of the Chamber mirror the challenges of the justices. These nine women and men are not the Platonic Guardians of the U.S. Constitution although they are, on occasion, called upon to decide the impossible. To be sure, much of what confronts the nine justices on the Court is mundane, involving matters of ordinary law.

What does this statute mean? How should it be applied? Who or which institution of government is the best decision maker for a particular legal controversy? Many, if not most, of these questions can be (and are) answered by bright, recent law school graduates. I sometimes wonder if instead of tributes to Moses, Hammurabi, Justinian and the like that adorn the frieze in the Chamber that the Court should rather have a statute of Jocko Conlon in its Great Hall. Conlon, a Harvard graduate, played one year of Major League Baseball before becoming a Hall of Fame umpire. For in truth, most of what the Court does is umpireal; it sorts out who the proper decision makers are for the various legal problems that come to it.

The justices earn their modest salaries, however, not for the mundane. They earn their salaries, and more important, the respect (and criticism) of the nation, for those few cases which each year make headlines and stir our political consciousness. Cases about the death penalty, presidential elections, affirmative action, abortion, or voting rights define who we are as a nation at any particular time in our history. We look, as do Hampshire and Rawls, to the Supreme Court to decide as a matter of man's law, the political and moral conflicts that perplex and divide us. We also hope that the Court's decisions sometimes touch the higher law. Uncertainty and indeterminacy are inevitable in this vale of tears, but indecision in the Supreme Court is not an option. We expect our justices to decide the most delicate and controversial issues of morality and politics including the legitimacy of physician-assisted suicide. It is no wonder then that the justices often proceed to decide delicate cases on procedural rather than substantive bases.

United States Supreme Court cases can involve high ritual and familiar procedure as well as controversies that are sometimes common and sometimes intractable. The matter of making life ending decisions after consultation with a personal physician captures that drama of an intractable moral and political problem. In recent years, the Court has been asked to address this issue twice. In the first case, *Glucksberg v. Washington,*[58] the Court upheld a Washington state statute which made it a felony to cause or aid another person's suicide attempt. The Court was well aware of the delicacy of the matter as noted in an initial question to the lawyers from the High Bench: "[T]here are people who are just totally opposed and people who are totally in favor of [laws prohibiting physician-assisted suicide]. So you're going to have those factions fighting it out in every session of the legislature, how far can we go in regulating this?"[59] The question about the extent to which government can go to regulate this behavior is exactly the right question. The answers to it, however, are less clear.

In *Glucksberg*, the Court did not decide the issue of whether an individual liberty interest in physician-assisted suicide existed. Instead, the Court decided the case by relying on a procedural rule. The decision regarding the legitimacy or illegitimacy of physician-assisted suicide was a matter for the states and their democratically elected legislatures. The Court did not attempt to answer for the nation as a whole whether a right to physician-assisted suicide existed or not. The Court sent the matter back to the states with these words: "Throughout the Nation, Americans are engaged in an earnest debate about the morality, legality, and practicality of physician-assisted suicide. Our holding permits this debate to continue, as it should in a democratic society."[60] The procedural rule chosen here, deference to state legislatures, clearly is one with substantive impact. The people in New York and Washington chose to prohibit physicians from helping competent patients die at their own request by criminalizing their conduct and the Court upheld the prohibitions against physician-assisted suicide. The people in the states of Washington and New York have spoken.

The people of Oregon have spoken but to opposite effect. In 1994, Oregon voters, alone among all of the states, approved a ballot initiative that established the Oregon Death with Dignity Act[61] legalizing physician-assisted dying. Later, the Oregon legislature attempted to repeal the act. The voters rejected that attempt. The Act itself sets out specific requirements. An adult Oregon resident who has been diagnosed by a physician with a terminal illness that will end their lives in six months may request a prescription for a lethal dose of medication. The request must be confirmed by two witnesses, and another physician must examine the patient's medical record and confirm the diagnosis among other regulations.

The second case, *Gonzales v. Oregon*, reveals the distorting effects that procedural rules have on substantive legal questions. Ultimately, litigants in these cases want to know whether physician-assisted suicide is legal or not. But here is how the Court framed the question before it, in *Gonzales*:

> [W]hether the Controlled Substances Act allows the United States Attorney General to prohibit doctors from prescribing regulated drugs for use in physician-assisted suicide, notwithstanding a state law permitting the procedure.[62]

Instead of deciding directly whether or not patients have a liberty interest to decide to terminate their lives, the Court addresses the authority of an agent of the federal government.

In 1997, members of the U.S. Congress critical of the Oregon Death with Dignity Act sought to federally prosecute Oregon physicians who assisted in life-ending decision making. Then Attorney General Janet Reno concluded it was not the position of the federal government to displace the states regarding the regulation of the medical profession, and she declined to prosecute. Legislation was then introduced in Congress to the same effect, but it failed to pass.

John Ashcroft was appointed Attorney General in 2001.When he served in the Senate, he opposed physician-assisted suicide and then as Attorney General, he had another occasion to remedy what he believed to be an immoral law. In 2002, he attempted to suspend the license of a physician under the federal Controlled Substance Act for prescribing listed drugs for the purpose of assisting a dying patient end his life.[63] Ashcroft exercised his powers as Attorney General by issuing an Interpretive Rule which empowered him to criminally charge the physician under the federal Act. The Interpretive Rule was intentionally aimed at undermining the Oregon statute. Ashcroft reasoned that using controlled substances for physician-assisted suicide was not a "legitimate medical purpose," and such conduct could be penalized. As the Court later found, the rule was issued "without consulting Oregon or apparently anyone outside his department"[64] as arguably required by the statute. Two lower federal courts held that the Attorney General lacked the authority to punish physicians under that statute, and the case found its way to the Supreme Court. The issue before the Court was: did the Attorney General have the claimed authority to interfere with state-regulated medical practice under the federal Controlled Substances Act?

Justice Anthony Kennedy, writing for the majority, quoted the Court's earlier *Glucksberg* dictum that physician-assisted suicide was a matter of profound national debate. He then framed the issue before the Court: "The dispute before us is in part a product of this political and moral debate, but its resolution requires an inquiry familiar to Courts: Interpreting a federal statute to determine whether Executive action is authorized by, or otherwise consistent with, the enactment."[65] The permissibility of physician-assisted suicide in Oregon, in other words, would be decided as a matter of procedural law, and the Court would not rule on the constitutionality of such conduct. The Supreme Court found that the Attorney General lacked that authority.

The Controlled Substances Act was passed in 1970 for the purpose of fighting drug abuse and illicit drug trafficking. By law, every prescription for certain controlled substances could only be issued for a, "legitimate medical purpose by an individual practitioner acting in the usual course of his professional practice."[66] The purpose of the statute was to regulate physicians to avoid the diversion of drugs into illicit trafficking and to that end, physicians were required to register with the federal government. The Attorney General, in turn, could deny, suspend, or revoke a physician's registration to curtail the illegal drug trade. The Attorney General could not regulate the medical profession more generally.

The Court found that the statute was clear, and that it was not intended to alter the balance of federal-state power concerning the regulation of the medical profession. The Court decided *Gonzales* again on a procedural rule, statutory interpretation, which honored an institutional value, federalism. Procedural rules, though, cut both ways. The dissent also argued that the case should be decided on another procedural rule—deference to the executive branch.

Justice Scalia, writing in dissent, argued strongly for deference to the Attorney General's interpretation of what constituted a legitimate medical purpose which excluded physician-assisted suicide. The Scalia opinion involves several matters of statutory interpretation, but ultimately his deference to the executive branch is clear. Scalia argued that Ashcroft's interpretation of "legitimate medical purpose" was clearly valid, and that the Attorney General can determine the public interest in matters of public health and safety. Scalia writes: "virtually every source of authoritative meaning confirms that the phrase 'legitimate medical purpose' does not include intentionally assisting suicide."[67] Fair enough, but irrelevant. The Controlled Substances Act is intentionally and narrowly aimed at illicit drug trafficking, and is not intended to be the federal regulation of the medical profession through physician registration.

Scalia criticized the majority for not invalidating physician-assisted suicide as inconsistent with legitimate medical practice: "the only explanation for [its ruling] is that the Court confuses the *normative* inquiry of what the boundaries of medicine *should be*—which it is laudably hesitant to undertake—with the objective under *inquiry* of what the accepted definition of 'medicine' is."[68] Scalia falls victim to his own criticism. His opinion confuses the *normative* inquiry of what the Controlled Substances Act *should* say with the *objective* inquiry of what it *should do*—control the illicit drug trade as intended.

In *Gonzales* and *Glucksberg*, the Court based its decisions on procedural rules. Both cases determine a matter of highly charged moral and political content. Neither, however, addresses the merits of the issue. They do not address the substantive matter of whether or not all United States citizens have a legally protected right to physician-assisted suicide as a matter of constitutional law. This is not all bad.[69] Clearly, the justices know that their choice of procedural rules has a substantive impact. In Oregon, dying patients can end their lives according to the dignity they believe is theirs; in other states this can be, and has been, criminalized. By deferring to the states, then, federalism is honored and so are the wishes of a state's citizens. Procedural rules avoid making decisions on substantive grounds which may be frustrating but procedural rulings may further institutional values.

The Vices, the Virtues, and the Inevitability of Procedural Justice

First we will discuss the vices of procedural justice. The central problem with procedural justice is that even the most perfect and fair procedures can yield unjust results for at least two reasons. First, rules of law, whether procedural or substantive, must be forward-looking and must be generally applied. Consequently, law cannot address and fine tune every controversy and reach every individual case and situation. Rules of law are inherently over- and under-inclusive. Justice is not always done for everyone in every specific instance. Second, decisions must be made so that society can put conflicts in the past and move on even in the most dramatic cases. The argument is, that there exists an institutional value in finality so that even the death penalty and habeas corpus appeals must end sometime.[70] Thus, the most serious vice of procedural justice is that unjust results can occur and even the innocent can be executed because decisions must be made. Procedural justice in such cases is clearly at odds with substantive justice.

Another vice of procedural justice is that it can mask power. We must recognize the role that political power plays in procedural theory. It is not enough to accept institutional determinations simply because its procedures satisfy history and tradition, because the procedures can be revised, or because the pronouncements can be criticized. Substantively unjust results occur, even from the much vaunted Supreme Court, as in the infamous case of poor Joshua, a brain-damaged child left uncompensated for his appalling injuries,[71] and in the case of the brutally battered inmate, also left uncompensated for his injuries.[72] In both Supreme Court cases, procedural reasons and institutional values trumped what many consider the substantively just result. The majority of the Court did not want to allow compensation for the injuries in those horrific cases for fear that government agencies, a child welfare agency and a state prison respectively, would be exposed to too much financial liability. Institutional politics wins out over individual compensation.

Supreme Court opinions are legitimate because they are the Court's opinions. This circular argument was made famous by justice Robert's Jackson quip that the Supreme Court is not final because it is infallible; it is infallible only because it is final.[73] So goes human decision making. Controversies must end sometime, and decisions must be made in the face of uncertainty. Legitimacy, though, is a tricky thing. Legitimacy both brings power under the rule of law and justifies (or mystifies) its exercise to the point that we no longer see power as corrupting.[74] Accepted procedures may legitimate exactly the unjust power that elites wield.[75] Accepted procedures may legitimate the condemnation of Antigone and Socrates or the injuries to children and prisoners all in the name of state protection.

The third vice of procedural justice is its distorting effect. Procedural systems distort the substantive questions posed and the answers given. In other words, people engaged in conflict or controversy want to know, "Who's right?" They want to know what is legally permissible or prohibited. They do not want to prolong the controversy by having it sent to another decision maker, decided on a "technicality," or sent back for reargument.

The distortions then come in three directions, each of which seems unavoidable. The first distortion is that moral questions such as Piergiorgio's are turned into legal questions. The translation entails moving from individual moral claims to collective legal rights. Piergiorgio wishes to end a life of pain after years of suffering, and he has made the individual moral determination to do so. However, by publically asking for assistance from his physician, Piergiorgio brought the state into the equation, and the state then questioned whether or not Piergiorgio had a collective *legal* right to his individual *moral* position because the state was concerned not only with Piergiorgio but with all of its citizens.

The second distortion comes from the process itself. A game of law is not much different in this regard from the game of telephone where one person whispers a statement to another and that person in turn to another and so on down the line. It is inevitable that the statement first uttered is distorted by the end of the game. Similarly, cases that are argued in front of a trial judge will change on intermediate appeal, and they will change by the time they reach the U.S. Supreme Court. At each level in the legal process, the decision maker has institutional concerns and values that must be honored. The trial court, for example, is constrained by the evidence before it and the existing law on the books. The appellate court cannot see the witnesses and must decide the legal matter before it on the basis of a cold record and often on the arguments of counsel. By the time a case makes its way to the Supreme Court, it will be one of about 100 cases the Court decides to hear annually out of the hundreds of thousands of lower court decisions and out of the thousands that petition it for review. The institutional concerns of the Court speaking for the country may dwarf and most likely will distort the concerns of the original litigants.

The third distortion is that procedural rules enable decision makers to resolve conflicts without declaring substantive positions or identifying legal rights. In this way, procedure can be seen to function as a delay or avoidance mechanism. Decision makers might prefer to avoid declaring rights for several reasons. Sufficient data may be unavailable. The social consensus on a particular moral or political matter may be unformed. Multiple reasonable alternatives are competing for attention. Or, a decision maker may chose to buy more time for debate and deliberation by putting off the question for another time or for another forum. A procedural rule can be used to mask the desired substantive outcome. If the substantive decision is politically unpopular or not well-established in law, then the decision maker can rule on a matter of procedure without declaring a substantive position.

We can argue that these distortions, converting moral issues to legal ones, requiring a process for conflict resolution, and masking substantive decisions have a tempering and mediating effect. After all, the chief function of the law is to order future conduct and behavior within a society. It is not the function of law to dispense justice in each individual case. As desirable though that may be, individual justice is impossible to achieve. Instead, society attempts to reduce violence and aspires to justice for the many in the service of the Good.

The issue facing Piergiorgio was whether or not his physician could assist him in ending his life. He wanted to know if his conduct was legally allowed. Neither *Glucksberg* nor *Gonzales* directly answered this question. Instead, both cases issued procedural rulings which left the matter open as an issue of constitutional right. *Glucksberg's* answer to the question of physician-assisted suicide was to let the states decide through democratic processes. Under that ruling, Piergiorgio would have been denied that right. *Gonzales's* response was quite different. The Court denied the U.S. Attorney General the right to interfere with state law, and therefore in Oregon, Piergiorgio would have been permitted to end his life with the dignity he chose.

The theory of procedural justice has counteracting virtues. Chief among them is that cases in complex matters or matters of moral indeterminacy are at least settled temporarily. Settlement may be provisional, but resolutions are achieved while the matter is kept alive for further consideration. A procedural ruling can shift the matter to a more appropriate institution which allows moral and political decisions to be made openly and publicly with the intent of achieving acceptability and legitimacy after further discussion and deliberation. Justice Kennedy's argument was that physician-assisted suicide is a matter open for debate and that the debate should take place in the political arena of state legislatures rather than decided as a matter of constitutional law by the nine on the Bench. In this way, procedural justice can actually further substantive justice through processes which allow moral and political disagreement to be aired and addressed constructively. Through procedural justice, conflict resolving institutions are sustained, and conflicts in society are managed more justly.

Samantha Beeson argues for just such a conception of procedural justice and conflict resolution. In *The Morality of Conflict*,[76] she asserts that there is a politically moral good that comes from democratic disagreement. She recognizes, as do Hampshire and Rawls, that in a pluralistic society that "persistent and wide spread reasonable disagreement . . . about justice and the law" exists.[77] Consequently, while procedural justice can be a primary mode of settling moral conflicts, it is important to understand that procedural rules can be used for conflict elucidation as well as for conflict resolution. Beeson sees indeterminancy as a source of discourse and productive conversation that can yield information about our political societies and about our moral lives in them, and the law can help shape and form the nature of those conversations.[78] She recognizes that law's "ultimate aspiration" may be substantive justice, but that its real function in society is to construct a, "framework of practical reasoning designed to unify public political judgment and coordinate social interaction."[79] While neither *Glucksberg* nor *Gonzales* determined whether there is a constitutional right or liberty interest in physician-assisted suicide, both cases allowed democratic processes to continue to debate the issue.

Beeson's theory of procedural justice amplifies those of Rawls and Hampshire. She labels the "democratic paradox" the notion that legal procedures for resolving political and moral conflicts should appear to be independent of those conflicts but cannot be entirely so.[80] Beeson's analysis gives full vent to the virtues of procedural justice. Procedural justice is possible and desirable because it is necessarily linked with substantive justice. Beeson's conception of substantive justice tracks well with what we have seen before from Rawls and Dworkin. Individuals should be treated with equal dignity and respect, and they should live in circumstances of freedom and equality. This goal of political morality, that humans should flourish, is a goal of substantive justice which can be furthered by a set of reliable procedural rules which are consistent with and safeguard it.

Do the virtues outweigh the vices? Perhaps, but the question may be beside the point. Procedural justice is not unconnected to substantive values even in coin tossing. Procedural justice may also help us think through difficult moral and political questions by helping us frame them more clearly, have more time for deliberation, engage trained professionals and experts in decision making, and give us respite from conflict and controversy during resolution. More important, diversity, uncertainty, indeterminacy, pluralism, and democracy itself all point away from a single and final conception of justice, and all point toward reliance on accepted decision-making institutions and procedures as a second best and maybe desirable alternative. In other words, procedure is inevitable.

Conclusion

Hampshire published *justice Is Conflict* in the summer of 2000. I would have liked to ask him if, after the Supreme Court's decision in *Bush v. Gore,*[81] he would hold the Court in the same high esteem given the charged criticism of that decision as political[82] and the broader claim that the Court is a political body.[83] My guess would be that he would still consider the Court as having satisfied his conditions. He would also support the Court's determination either for or against physician-assisted suicide. But how can it be that the Court's highly political decisions or morally disagreeable opinions can be called just by Hampshire? He answers: "No one is expected to believe that its decisions are infallibly just in matters of substance; but everybody is expected to believe that at least its procedures are just because they conform to the basic principle governing adversary reasoning—that both sides in a conflict should be equally heard."[84]

De Toqueville famously wrote, "there is almost no political question in the United States that is not resolved sooner or later into a judicial question."[85]

In a similar vain, Judge Guido Calabresi has written, "there once was a time when the law and its judges were not called upon to make choices for human beings lying in the twilight between life and death."[86] Legal and political theorists debate whether or not moral decision making is the proper function for courts. They cannot, however, debate either that it often occurs or that it is often divisive. A solid theory of procedural justice, one which incorporates substantive values, provides some support for allowing courts to determine delicate and controversial matters of moral and political disagreement. Man's law may not satisfy the demands of the higher law through procedure, but it can keep the desire for it and the struggle to attain it alive and vibrant.

As we close, we should heed the caution of Grant Gilmore. "In Heaven, there will be no law and the lion will lie down with the lamb . . . in Hell, there will be nothing but law, and due process will be meticulously observed."[87] Procedure brings comfort only to a degree and can, therefore, be no substitute for justice. Our rules of procedure, properly crafted, are necessary for achieving justice, but they do not constitute it. If the settled procedures result in cases of obvious injustice; then those procedures must be changed. Where, however, the obvious justness of an outcome is lacking, because justice is ambiguous or indeterminate, then procedure enables a society to make determinations, resolve conflicts, and move on with its daily business. There may be no law in heaven but on this earth, lawyers keep alive the sense of justice by distinguishing shadows and light through processes committed to principles of fairness.

Conclusion

CREON'S GHOST HAS BEEN INHABITED by a band of outlaws and misfits, mystics and martyrs. Antigone dies by her own hand, Socrates by his at the command of the state, and Martin Luther King Jr. by an assassin's bullet. Machiavelli is exiled for his presumed part in a conspiracy against the Medici, Aquinas allegedly becomes a mystic who brushes away his *magnus opus* as just so much straw, and Holmes's legacy continues to be debated. Each of these sojourners is connected by a central story of the humanities. Each storyteller encounters the ever-present conflict between man's law and the higher law. While each voyager tells a different version of the story, and while some prefer to deny or ignore the higher law, the several stories are connected, nonetheless, because they are the stories of human experience—frustrating, but not extinguishing—the human desire for Justice.

The tension between desire and experience was first presented through the conflict between Antigone and Creon and ended with Hampshire's personal conflict between his desire for social justice amid pluralistic, competing moral claims which, as his experience demonstrated, were resolved—if only provisionally—through legal processes. Instead of staking out a substantive definition of Justice, Hampshire retreated to a process for conflict resolution as a second-best solution. He is not alone either in his skepticism about finding Justice or in his desire for continuing the search even if only procedural substitutes are the best alternatives available.

The humanities exposed this conflict of laws in many guises: a conflict between an individual and the state, a conflict between conscience and power, a conflict between natural law and positive law, a conflict between religious faith and rational thought, and a conflict between private interest and public good. Ultimately, though, we are assessing a conflict between law and Justice. The conflict is a difficult one because we lack permanent, agreed-upon definitions for either law or Justice. Nevertheless, we have been able to converse and disagree about both, and this disagreement is as healthy and positive as the conversation is necessary. Conversation and disagreement can take place because we have a relatively stable and reliable understanding of positive law, man's law. We recognize authoritative orders backed by state power when we see them. Our understanding of Justice or the higher law, however, is more elusive. Defining any ideal escapes us. Still, we rely and act upon our sense of Justice as individuals and as participants in political communities. Since conversation is possible, disagreement is healthy because through disagreement we demonstrate our commitment to Justice and we use Justice to assess and evaluate the good of man's law. Justice is the fitting and proper virtue to seek in a study of law and the humanities because it orients us to the Good and guides us as we design our social and political living arrangements.

It is neither a damning admission to say that we have not found Justice; nor is it a damning admission to say that we continue on our journey precisely because the stories told throughout this book have revealed something about that journey. Over the centuries, the quest has taken us down three not-unrelated paths, and as we have traveled these paths we have learned something about the relationship between man's law and the higher law, between law and Justice, even as we acknowledge that definitions of both are unsettled. In the Introduction, the method and the message of *Creon's Ghost* was described. Now that we have taken our journey of 2500 years, method and message begin to merge, and we find that they complement each other.

The Method

Law has long held a fascination for the humanities. The conflict between man's law and the higher law and the search for Justice has provided a fertile ground for dramatists, novelists, and poets over the centuries. In Aeschylus's *The Eumenides*, the trial of Orestes for the murder of his mother, Clytemnestra, was presided over by the world's first jury in search of Divine Justice. Twenty-five hundred years later, the conflict can also be found in the antithesis of the search for Divine Justice in Cormac McCarthy's *Blood Meridian*. In this novel, the Judge dispenses an evil Justice through the hands of man in total disregard for the higher law. As readers, we are more painfully aware of the absence of Justice in McCarthy's hell that we are of the *contrapasso* Justice in Dante's *Inferno*. Evil disturbs us because without hope for Justice, we are perched on the abyss of despair. Law, even imperfect man's law, has the power to pull us back from the edge of the abyss, to revive hope in Justice, and more than occasionally delivers on that hope as societies are constructed, as lives improve, as art is created, and as science progresses all through law.

Philosophers, too, have been significant contributors to the conversation about the conflict between man's law and the higher law. As the heroic Justice of Homer gave way to the philosophical inquiry of Socrates and then through the ages to Rawls's political theory and his critics' analyses, Justice is a central philosophical investigation. Like the novelists, dramatists, and poets, the philosophers have provided us with multiple stories about and definitions of Justice without concurring on any single one. Whether we define Justice as harmony in the City and the Soul or as various normative spheres which rotate over the ages and among different cultures;[1] or even as a process of political participation or conflict resolution, this philosophical inquiry continues to attract us.

Literature and philosophy have aided our search in other special ways. The words of the poets help us experience the ineffable, those of the dramatists enable us to see Justice revealed or Justice denied, and those of the novelists help us better understand the stories of Justice which run through our lives and our histories. Additionally, the philosophers have given us valuable tools, methods of inquiry from Socrates' use of elenchus and the dialectic, and through Rawls's original position and his veil of ignorance to help us find Justice as a way to understand how to lead the good life as individuals and live in community. The method of *Creon's Ghost,* using the humanities to help us understand jurisprudence, has demonstrated the essential, maybe eternal nature of this quest and its power to engage us.

The stories from the humanities revealed that in searching for Justice, we have traveled three distinct but not completely unrelated paths. There are those among our travelers who sought the marriage between law and Justice while others accepted—favored even—a divorce between them. Others apparently abandoned the search altogether in an effort to simply and practically reduce any conflicts between law and Justice and reduce conflicts among ourselves and over our beliefs.

Let's ask, then: Have we solved the mystery of *Creon's Ghost*? Is there one true path to merging man's law with the higher law? It seems that each of the three paths that we traveled on our journey have not been as sure as we might have hoped to enable us to reach Justice nor have the arguments that sustain them been robust enough to support it. The marriage of law and Justice fails because we cannot successfully connect man's law with the higher law as we continue to experience man's imperfections which become embodied in man's law. The positive man's law of racial slavery, even as a conscious political compromise in the name of Union, does not escape the label unjust. The divorce between them fails because we cannot live in a society with an absence of Justice. A democratic society without women's suffrage and equality cannot be sustained. Nevertheless, we are frustrated because we cannot agree on a single higher law to follow, and conflicts between man's law and the higher law do not disappear. Finally, the third path of second-best solutions leaves us wanting when the outcomes generated such as discriminating against homosexuals, detaining people indefinitely, or prohibiting religious practices are judged unjust. We cannot successfully separate man's law from the higher law by relying on procedure because our desire for Justice compels us to reform or eliminate those laws, institutions, and processes which fall short of our sense of Justice.

Still, we remain uncertain about what constitutes our sense of Justice. The sojourners who desired a marriage between law and Justice throughout this book have offered several higher law alternatives to man's law. Man's law can be overturned and disregarded by Divine or religious law. Man's law can be contradicted by eternal law or unsayable law. And man's law can be invalidated, ignored, or rebutted by natural law. None of these candidates for the higher law have proved to be sturdy enough to win wide acceptance among different peoples over the centuries.

Divine or religious law is defective because we cannot live by monotheism in pluralistic democracies. More to the point, however, is that Divine or religious law is about salvation in the next world; it is not about peace and harmony in this one. Eternal law or the law of the Sun also go wanting because they present insurmountable epistemological problems of knowledge and communication; and while they may guide our conscience, they cannot guide our civil communities because we can neither know nor adequately articulate or specify the eternal or ideal law. We cannot promulgate the eternal law because we can no more know it than we can gaze directly into the Sun. Consequently, our attempts to specify its contents will be either too general to apply to particular controversies or too ad hoc to maintain consistency. Natural law is deficient because it has been shown to be both too broad and too corrupted by political ideology. The first principles of Aquinas, the principle of noncontradiction and the principle that we should do good and shun evil, provide insufficient detail about our social and political lives. While current natural law advocates generate any number of policy positions, they inevitably run into the same problem we encounter with Divine and religious law; contemporary natural law is about individual ethics and moral beliefs—it is not about rational civic interaction.

In short, the three paths revealed to us through literature and philosophy appear to have lead to dead ends. Have they? Or has the path to Justice been illuminated in some other way?

The Message

Something continues to nag us after we have traveled these three paths. None is true; all are incomplete. Yet, we continue to try them one then another; and, together, while they do not reach the Sun, they do reveal its light and its warmth. Each path alone, as well as together, reveals a relationship between law and Justice. While the connection thesis is explicit that there is a necessary relationship between law and Justice, and while the separation thesis and the second-best approaches deny any necessary connection, the latter approaches also betray a magnetic relationship between the two.

Strict positivists like Hart admit that the positive law can incorporate moral principles or the virtue of Justice, thus raising the question: Under what compulsion? Why, for the true positivist, would man's law bother to incorporate the higher law? Hart would also concede that legal systems possess at least some form of procedural justice—laws must be publically promulgated, prospectively applied, and applied fairly. Machiavelli, too, acknowledges that a prince who changes, let alone tramples on the laws of the people, does so at risk to his rule. Justice may be instrumental for Machiavelli, but it is not absent. Thrasymachus also ultimately conceded to Socrates that Justice was preferable to injustice for an individual to lead a worthy life. In short, these most committed separatists acknowledge the attraction of the higher law.

Finally, second-best solutions do not avoid the need to identify and articulate the higher law because majoritarian democratic participation too often disadvantages minority interests and must be tempered by the need for the protection of individual rights and liberties. Mechanisms of procedural justice for conflict resolution cannot wander too far from substantive justice; otherwise the procedures are empty and void. In other words, we can accept procedurally correct outcomes of our most contentious moral and political issues even when we disagree with them because we know that these resolutions are temporary; that other solutions and responses are possible, if not likely; and that times and attitudes as well as cultures and politics change and that other, more desirable, outcomes are available and might be forthcoming. Temporary peaceful resolution of conflict is not only acceptable, it is preferable to continued agitation. More to the point, however, accepting procedural Justice for its instrumental ends does not entail abandoning substantive Justice. We accept the procedural justice of conflict resolution processes because through these processes the possibility of Justice remains alive. Our vision of a just society with a better, fairer distribution of economic wealth and political power serves as a basis to criticize, reform, and change the undesirable outcomes generated by agreed-upon and accepted legal and political devices. In short, procedural Justice, our second-best solution, is dynamic, not static, and it is susceptible to reform based on substantive principles of Justice.

For all the weaknesses that these three paths have exhibited, each, separately and collectively, yields an important idea. The idea is told through 2500 years of law's stories and through 2500 years of stories from the humanities. Human fallibility and variability do not devolve to chaos. Man's law does not wander too far afield from the higher law even as we continue to struggle to find and define it. Law's promise goes beyond serving as a social institution to reduce violence and chaos and resolve conflicts. Law's promise aspires and serves as an institution which not only protects but helps fulfill us as individuals and as communities because for all of its imperfections, man's law is fastened, no matter how loosely, to the higher law—man's law is attached to Justice. Nigel Simmonds calls this idea of man's desire for the higher law and for Justice, "law as a moral idea."[2]

We look to man's law to distribute power and resources, protect the weak, preserve the environment and the creatures in it; and stabilize societies. We look to man's law to promote the creation of wealth and stimulate innovation as well as to create and promote engagement and participation in political and economic marketplaces. And we look to man's law to enable conversation among diverse peoples and cultures, to connect with tradition while enabling progress, and to seek common ground.

If law is a moral idea; if there is a higher law; and if we continue, at least for the next 2500 years to disagree about the moral content of the higher law, then what follows? On the one hand, we can ask: Is the higher law simply and always contentious territory? Or is there no territory here at all? On the other hand, we can ask: If the law has no discernable moral content, then why do we continually seek it? Or more simply, why do we voluntarily obey it? What, then, is the proper (necessary) relationship between law and Justice? Are they connected? Separated? Always distinct? Always in tension? And yet, are they thus somehow always related no matter how mysteriously?

We will not tolerate man's law which privileges procedure and process over substance; embraces immorality or evil; or adopts one comprehensive, political, or moral world view to the exclusion or denigration of other beliefs and commitments. We will not impose a single religious law, moral code, or political ideology on all citizens in the name of Justice. We retain our commitment to Justice amid a jumble of man's imperfect and expedient laws and we can live with Creon's ghost because we are human. We take Plato at his word—the matter of Justice—of the higher law—is a matter of struggle between shadows and light. We will reject the marriage of man's law and the higher law when that higher law is dogmatically oppressive and stagnant. We will reject the divorce between the two when man's law is manifestly unjust. We will correct the imbalance when legal procedures produce unjust outcomes, and we will adjust political processes which do not deliver fairness. This impulse to have the higher law influence and improve man's law—the essence of law as a moral idea—is true for us as individuals and as societies; it is true in City and Soul.

Law and Justice, then, can be seen as twin stars in a celestial *pas de deux*—each star entranced and held onto by the other—both within each other's gravitational orbit. True, neither collapses into the other; but then again, doesn't our experience of law and our desire for Justice prove exactly that point?

Law needs Justice as justification just as Justice needs law to do the necessary practical work of our day-to-day lives even though Justice remains foggy and unclear. Justice is Plato's Sun; it is an ideal never to be fully owned or realized by us human creatures. Law—man's law—man's imperfect law does not exist to do evil for evil's sake. Even Machiavelli, arch instrumentalist, knew that to be true. Law is the tool we use to strive for or emulate and approach the Good. Man's law is a rough, jagged tool which must be honed by our concept of Justice. Law's connection to Justice, "almost sexual in its force," as Ziolkowski tells us,[3] is honed through the stories told through writer's pens and is ground on philosophers' stones.

Law, then, acts in the world; law allows our markets to trade; our politics to function; and our societies and cultures to develop. Law empowers individuals, restrains public and private power, influences City and Soul, and allows us to keep the ideal of the Good alive. Law cannot, and does not, act blindly without purpose. Creon's edict could not withstand many Antigones; it could not withstand only one. American slavery could not forever silence Abolitionist prayers. Law cannot help princes acquire and maintain power unless tempered by some common purpose or public good, whether it is happiness in the principality or the unification of Italy. Democratic participation and political processes cannot be established by law unless they serve some useful purpose such as honoring freedom and dignity of all individuals while reducing moral and political conflicts.

Creon's Ghost is neither curse nor prayer; it is Plato's invitation to struggle for Justice. In our fight to reconcile our deep desire for the Sun with the reality of the shadows of our lives, we use law, man's law, to guide us. Man's law aids the search when we sense Justice, even when we realize that we can know it imperfectly at best. Man's law can be used to order society, avoid or reduce evil, and protect our freedoms. But it cannot do this perfectly. Sometimes our societies are chaotic, sometimes evil is cast into law, and sometimes the innocent suffer or die.

The perennial and constant challenge is to sustain man's law with some argument or justification touching Justice. We sustain man's law by allowing it to change and adapt. The conflict between desire and experience, between Justice and law, allows us to adapt through changing and challenging times and circumstances. The one warning that we must heed is that we must avoid foolish arrogance. We must avoid believing, like Creon, that man's law constitutes Truth or Justice. And we must avoid orthodoxy for is the death of Justice, it is the end of Truth.

The twin stars of man's law and the higher law neither collapse into nor spin away from one another. They maintain their separate dimensions but are attracted, compelled even, to each other. Man's law needs the higher law for its legitimacy and efficacy. The higher law needs man's law to function and operate in the world, to enable the warmth of the Sun to be felt; the unsayable said, and the eternal glimpsed.

We are confident that we know man's law when we see it. Do we know Justice when we see it? Let's return to *Antigone* and the play's final chorus:

Our happiness depends
on wisdom all the way.
The gods must have their due.
Great words by men of pride
bring greater blow upon them.
So wisdom comes to the old.[4]

It is curiously and appropriately ironic that we return to the beginning and conclude with Creon. Creon intended to dishonor his nephew Polyneices for his traitorous attack on Thebes. What Creon never understood and what led, not only to his tragedy but also to Creon's ghost, was his overreaching. Creon wanted man's law to exist independently of the gods, and yet he tread on their sacred territory. Creon wanted man's law to exist independently of legend and fate, yet he tread on the customs, the *nomos*, of the people of Thebes. His edict, if followed, would have left Polyneices' soul wandering forever without rest, between the world of the living and the world of the dead—between man's world and a higher world. Antigone's brave act settled the travails of her brother's unsettled soul but unleashed another unsettled apparition–Creon's ghost. Creon's ghost, the inability of man's law and the higher law to meet in complete harmony and coalescence is Creon's legacy to humanity.

We honor the gods through our desire for the higher law. We honor our humanity and gain wisdom by not abandoning our search for Justice either in frustration or skepticism or in cynicism or pride. We honor the gods and our humanity by embracing the struggle and haggling over the shadows and light of Justice in law courts and elsewhere. These several stories from literature and philosophy confirm the existence of Creon's ghost; validate the value of the struggle; and acknowledge the magnetic, sexual even, attraction between man's law and the higher law; between law and Justice. We know this connection to be true, and we can test this hypothesis with a jurisprudential quiz:

It is 2 AM, you are driving home and reach a stop sign at a deserted intersection. What do you do and why?

Notes

Introduction

1 Pub. L. 109-3 (2005). The bill gave federal courts jurisdiction over the Schiavo case. At the hearing, the federal judge ruled that the feeding tube was not to be reinserted, and Terri Schiavo was allowed to die.

2 Carl Hulse & David D. Kirkpatrick, *Congress Passes and Bush Signs Legislation on Shiavo Case,* N.Y. TIMES A1 (March 21, 2005).

3 W. H. AUDEN, SELECTED POEMS 89–91 (Edward Mendelson ed., 1989).

4 Four fairly common usages of the word law can be identified and should be familiar to the general reader.

(1) We can ask, "What is Law?" meaning what is the nature or *concept* of law?

(2) We can ask, "What is law?" meaning what is a working *conception* of law? Is law nothing other than political power by way of illustration?

(3) The question can be put, "What is a law?" A 25 mph speed limit near schools is an example of "a law" used in this way.

(4) Law can be seen as a social activity or institution. Law in this sense is the practice engaged in by "we" of the legal priesthood, i.e., lawyers, judges, law teachers and students, and citizens qua citizens, when referring to some set of legal institutions or practices or to a legal system or the legal profession.

Another way of paying attention to how we use the word "law" is to understand the context in which it is used. By way of contrast, if we use the word "law" in a synagogue when talking with a rabbi, he will refer us to the Torah, not to the U.S. Constitution. Similarly, if we use the word with a scientist in a chemistry laboratory, she will refer us to Bernouilli and neither to Hart nor Dworkin. When we use the word in a courtroom, the judge will ask to us to cite concrete *examples* and neither *concepts* nor *conceptions* of law in support of an argument even though we should possess both *concepts* and *conceptions* in order to formulate valid *examples.* And when we use the word in a law school, things get sticky because now we are back to trying to define either the *concept* or *conception* of the word "law" and here conversation starts but does not end.

5 I often wonder if the entire enterprise of jurisprudence and legal philosophy does not revolve around the doubt that the word "law" is even susceptible of definition. *See, e.g.*, RONALD DWORKIN, JUSTICE IN ROBES 4 (2006) (Such a "taxonomic" exercise is a "scholastic fiction."); Danny Priel, *The Boundaries of Law and the Scope of Legal Philosophy* (February 11, 2008), available at http://papers.ssrn.com/sol3/papers.cfm?abstract_id=1086389; (Attempting to determine "what counts as law" "may simply be indeterminate."); Jules Coleman & Ori Simchen, "*Law*," 9 LEGAL THEORY 1 (2003); *see also* Timothy Endicott, "Law and Language," in THE STANFORD ENCYCLOPEDIA OF PHILOSOPHY (Winter 2002), available at http://plato.stanford.edu/archives/win2002/entries/law-language/.

6 THOMAS L. PANGLE (trans.), THE LAWS OF PLATO 53 (¶313b) (1980).

7 JOHN AUSTIN, THE PROVENCE OF JURISPRUDENCE DETERMINED, 185 (W.E. Rumble ed., 1995) (1832).

8 *Id.*

9 Regarding concepts and conceptions *see* RONALD DWORKIN, TAKING RIGHTS SERIOUSLY 134–36 (1977); LAW'S EMPIRE ch. 1 and 90–96; JUSTICE IN ROBES ch. 8 (2006); *see also* Timothy A. O. Endicott, *Herbert Hart and the Semantic Sting*; Nicos Stavropoloulos, *Hart's Semantics*; and, Joseph Raz, *Two Views of the Nature of the Theory of Law* in HART'S POSTSCRIPT: ESSAYS ON THE POSTSCRIPT TO THE CONCEPT OF LAW chs. 1, 2, & 3 (Jules Coleman ed., 2005).

10 HAROLD BLOOM, THE BEST POETRY IN THE ENGLISH LANGUAGE 28–29 (2007) (Quoting Owen Barfield, "Strangeness, in fact, arouses wonder when we do not understand: aesthetic imagination when we do.").

11 *See also* THEODORE ZIOLOWSKI, THE MIRROR OF JUSTICE: LITERARY REFLECTIONS OF LEGAL CRISES x (1997).

12 *See, e.g.*, JOSEF PIEPER, THE FOUR CARDINAL VIRTUES 43–113 (1966).

13 The usual formulation is that "law and morality" are either connected or separated. I use "Justice," "morality," and the "higher law" relatively interchangeably and treat Justice as a moral virtue.

14 Oliver Wendell Holmes, *The Path of the Law*, 10 HARV. L. REV. 457, 464 (1897).

Chapter 1 Creon's Ghost

1 CINDY SHEEHAN, NOT ONE MORE MOTHER'S CHILD (2005); W. LEON SMITH & CINDY SHEEHAN, THE VIGIL: 26 DAYS IN CRAWFORD, TEXAS (2005).

2 Seamus Heaney, as a most recent example, said that his new translation of *Antigone* was a letter to President Bush as criticism of the Iraq War. Seamus Heaney, *A Story That Sings Down the Centuries*, LONDON SUNDAY TIMES 41 (March 21, 2004). SEAMUS HEANEY, A BURIAL AT THEBES: A VERSION OF SOPHOCLES ANTIGONE 5 (2004).

3 GEORGE STEINER, ANTIGONES 1 (1984).

4 *See, e.g.*, Gary Wills, *Red Thebes, Blue Thebes,* N.Y. TIMES BOOK REV. December 5, 2004 at 43; *see also* SOPHOCLES, ANTIGONE 3–6 (Reginald Gibbons & Charles Segal trans., 2003).

5 STEINER, *supra* note 3, at 22–42.
6 *See, e.g.*, JUDITH BUTLER, ANTIGONE'S CLAIM: KINSHIP BETWEEN LIFE AND DEATH (2000).
7 *See also* THEODORE ZIOLKOWSKI, THE MIRROR OF JUSTICE: LITERARY REFLECTIONS OF LEGAL CRISES ch. 8 (1997). Ziolkowski, in a masterful study of law and literature, also argues that *Antigone* is about a conflict of laws. He writes that the play is about a conflict between man's written law and the unwritten law of the gods, but is "not a conflict between law and justice," at 154. I agree with Ziolkowski about the conflict between written and unwritten laws but argue that the conflict is exactly about the relationship between law and justice.
8 Albert Camus quoted by Ted Freeman in his Commentary in JEAN ANOUILH, ANTIGONE XIV (Barbara Bragg trans., 2000).
9 *See generally* JOSEPH RAZ, THE AUTHORITY OF LAW: ESSAYS ON LAW AND MORALITY (1979).
10 SOPHOCLES, ANTIGONE 21 (Richard Emil Braun trans., 1973).
11 HEANEY, *supra* note 2, at 5.
12 SOPHOCLES, ANTIGONE (Elizabeth Wyckoff trans.) in SOPHOCLES I 159 (David Grene & Richard Lattimore eds., 1954).
13 HEANEY, *supra* note 2, at 6.
14 STEINER, *supra* note 3, at 35.
15 HEANEY, *supra* note 2, at 10.
16 GRENE, *Introduction*, *supra* note 12, at 3.
17 HEANEY, *supra* note 2, at 20.
18 *Id.* at 21.
19 *Id.* at 23.
20 *Id.* at 26.
21 *Id.* at 29.
22 *Id.*
23 *Id.*
24 STEVEN D. SMITH, LAW'S QUANDARY chs. 1–2 (2004).
25 Various translations capture the essence of Antigone's Law. (1) "God's ordinances, unwritten and secure," DAVID GRENE, SOPHOCLES I 178 (1991); (2) "the unwritten and unfailing ordinances of the gods," HUGH LLOYD-JONES, SOPHOCLES II 43–45 (1994); (3) "unwritten and unfailing" REGINALD GIBBONS & CHARLES SEGAL, SOPHOCLES: ANTIGONE 73 (2003); (4) "Statutes utter and immutable—/Unwritten, original, god-given laws." HEANEY, *supra* note 2, at 29; (5) "the gods' unwritten and unfailing laws," DAVID GRENE (ed.) SOPHOCLES I 174 (Wyckoff trans., 1954); (6) laws that "the gods have not written merely, but made infallible," RICHARD EMIL BRAUN, SOPHOCLES ANTIGONE 39 (1973).
26 Joseph Raz argues that claims of authority in every legal system encompass claims for both *de facto* and legitimate authority. "[E]very legal system which is in force anywhere, has *de facto* authority. That entails that the law either claims that it possesses legitimate authority or is held to posses it, or both." He continues that, "every legal system claims that it possesses legitimate authority" and that "A legal system may lack legitimate authority. It lacks the moral attributes required to

endow it with legitimate authority then it has none." JOSEPH RAZ, ETHICS IN THE PUBLIC DOMAIN: ESSAYS IN THE MORALITY OF LAW AND POLITICS 215 (rev. ed. 2001).

27 PHILLIPE NONET, *Antigone's Law* (2005) available at http://repositories.cdlib.org/cgi/viewcontent.cgi?article=1047&context=csls.

28 *Id.* at 12. *See also* SMITH, *supra* note 24 at ch. 1; law talk as "just words" or "nonsense."

29 NONET, *supra* note 27, at 11.

30 *Id.* at 11; *see also* Tony Burns, *Sophocles'* Antigone *and the History of the Concept of Natural Law,* 50 POLITICAL STUDIES 545 (2002).

31 *Id.* at 25.

32 HEANEY, *supra* note 2, at 30–31.

33 *Id.* at 41.

34 *Id.* at 42–43.

35 *Id.*

36 *Id.* at 44.

37 *Id.* at 46.

38 WYCKOFF, *supra* note 12, at 184–85.

39 HEANEY, *supra* note 2, at 44–45.

40 The myth behind Tiresias' blindness is that while walking in the woods, he saw two snakes copulating and, after hitting them with his stick, he was turned into a woman. Seven years later, he saw the same snakes copulating and was turned back again into a man. When Zeus and Hera were arguing over whether men or women enjoyed sex more, they asked Tiresias for his opinion since he had been both man and woman. Tiresias agreed with Zeus that women enjoyed sex more and Hera struck him blind. Zeus, as compensation, gave Tiresias the gift of prophecy.

41 HEANEY, *supra* note 2, at 57.

42 *Id.* at 58.

43 *Id.* at 59.

44 *Id.* at 61.

45 WYCKOFF, *supra* note 12, at 201.

46 HEANEY, *supra* note 2, at 63.

47 *Id.* at 70.

48 *Id* at 63–64.

49 *Id.* at 73.

50 WYCKOFF, *supra* note 12, at 203.

51 RAZ, *supra* note 26, at 211.

52 *Id.* at 211. A leader such as Creon who claims *de facto* authority either claims "to be legitimate or is believed to be so, and is effective in imposing [his] will on many over whom [he] claims authority, perhaps because [his] claim to legitimacy is recognized by many of [his] subjects."

53 What is never fully determined throughout the *Theban Trilogy* is Creon's rightful claim to the throne. His is not a path of clear ascension. In *Antigone,* Creon succeeds to the throne after Eteocles and Polyneices kill each other by the double blow of the sword, a fate foretold in the Theban legend. In the other two parts of the *Trilogy,* Creon succeeds Oedipus in *Oedipus the King;* and,

in *Oedipus at Colonus*, the sons first defer to Creon's rule before taking over governance themselves. We might say, then, that Creon's ambiguous claim to official authority is the result of the world's first disputed election. *See* SETH BENARDETE, SACRED TRANSGRESSIONS: A READING OF SOPHOCLES' ANTIGONE 23–28 (1999); *see also* AESCHYLUS, SEVEN AGAINST THEBES (1985); WYCKOFF, *supra* note 12, at 159; GRENE, *supra* note 16.

54 *See* ANNE NORTON, LEO STRAUSS AND THE POLITICS OF AMERICAN EMPIRE 39 (2004) ("The enemy presented the threat of death, of annihilation, not merely to a person, but to the nation, and the nation's form of life.").

55 HEANEY, *supra* note 2, at 15. *See also* WYCKOFF, *supra* note 12, at166 ("This revolution, Creon, is your own,/ in the matter of the traitor and the true./ For you can make such rulings as you will/about the living and the dead.").

56 WYCKOFF, *supra* note 12, at 165.

57 HEANEY, *supra* note 2, at 16–18.

58 *Id.* at 42.

59 *Id.* at 21–22.

60 *Id.* at 33.

61 *Id.* at 24.

62 *See e.g.*, HANS KELSEN, THE PURE THEORY OF LAW (1967); BRIAN BIX, JURISPRUDENCE: THEORY AND CONTEXT ch. 3 (2nd ed. 1999); COSTAS DOUZINAS & ADAM GEARY, CRITICAL JURISPRUDENCE: THE POLITICAL PHILOSOPHY OF JUSTICE ch. 5 (2005); ANDREI MARMOR, *Exclusive Positivism* in, THE OXFORD HANDBOOK OF JURISPRUDENCE AND PHILOSOPHY OF LAW 104–124 (Jules Coleman & Scott Shapiro eds., 2002).

63 HERODOTUS, THE HISTORY 600 (¶8.118) (David Grene trans., 1988).

64 H. L. A. HART, THE CONCEPT OF LAW (2nd ed. 1997). THE CONCEPT OF LAW has received a significant amount of critical commentary ever since it was published. *See e.g.*, RUTH GAVISON, ISSUES IN CONTEMPORARY LEGAL PHILOSOPHY: THE INFLUENCE OF H. L. A. HART (1987); P.M.S. HACKER & JOSEPH RAZ, LAW, MORALITY, AND SOCIETY: ESSAYS IN HONOUR OF H. L. A. HART (1977).

Hart's most noted critic, Ronald Dworkin, has addressed Hart throughout his own scholarly career. *See* TAKING RIGHTS SERIOUSLY chs. 1–4 (1977); A MATTER OF PRINCIPLE (1985); and, LAW'S EMPIRE (1986). (LAW'S EMPIRE will be examined more closely in Chapter 2). Regarding the significance of THE CONCEPT OF LAW and Dworkin's criticism, *see* A. W. Brian Simpson, *Herbert Hart Elucidated*, 104 MICH L. REV. 1437, 1452 (2006) ("As is the way with notable books, it has spawned a very considerable secondary literature and the academic career of Ronald Dworkin was launched by his self-presentation as Herbert's major critic.").

In 1994, two years after his death, Hart's reply to his critics, edited by Penelope A. Bulloch and Joseph Raz, was published as a postscript to the second edition of *The Concept of Law*. Hart's postscript itself has generated considerable response. *See* HART'S POSTSCRIPT: ESSAYS ON THE POSTSCRIPT TO THE CONCEPT OF LAW (Jules Coleman ed., 2005 ed.). The continuing significance of THE CONCEPT OF LAW and its postscript is attested to by the fact that Dworkin has recently published an additional response to Hart. *See* RONALD DWORKIN, JUSTICE IN ROBES ch. 6 (2006).

Nicola Lacey's excellent biography of Hart, A LIFE OF H. L. A. HART: THE NIGHTMARE AND THE NOBLE DREAM (2004) discusses the POSTCRIPT and Hart's relationship with Dworkin, *see especially* 347–55.

65 Hart's inside look at law is sometimes called the internal point of view. *See e.g.,* Stephen R. Perry, *Interpretation and Methodology in Legal Theory,* in LAW AND INTERPRETATION (Andrei Marmor ed., 1995). Not unlike many matters of jurisprudence, the internal point of view is not free from controversy as indicated by Symposium, *The Internal View in Law and Ethics*, 75 FORD. L. REV. 1143–1316 (2006).

For brevity's sake, I have equated an "insider" account of law with the 'internal point of view." *But see* Scott J. Shapiro, *What is the Internal Point of View?*, 75 FORD. L. REV. 1157 (2006). By internal, Hart means that a member of a group acknowledges the rules of the group and "accepts and uses them as guides to conduct." HART, *supra* note 73, at 91. This definition does not mean that the group member accepts the moral implications of the rule. It means that they act accordingly.

66 HART, *supra* note 64, at 20–25.

67 *See* LACEY, *supra* note 73; Frederick Schauer, *(Re)Taking Hart,* 119 HARV. L. REV. 852 (2006) (book review of the Lacey biography and good discussion of Hart as philosopher).

68 HART, *supra* note 64, at 51–61.

69 *Id.* at 52.

70 *Id.* at 77.

71 Hart is not completely persuasive here. People "voluntarily" enter contracts, as an example of a power conferring rule, because they can rely on the power of the state to enforce them when breached. Simply, a rule backed by sanctions is moved down a step.

72 HART, *supra* note 64, at 91–94.

73 *Id.* at 94–99.

74 GIBBONS & SEGEL, *supra* note 25, at 69.

75 *Id.* at 69–70.

76 HANS KELSEN, THE PURE THEORY OF LAW 64 (1978 ed.).

77 HEANEY, *supra* note 2, at 74.

78 In addition to the Hart-Dworkin debate noted above, *compare* THE CONCEPT OF LAW with LON L. FULLER, THE MORALITY OF LAW (1964) and *compare* Hart, *Positivism and the Separation of Law and Morals, with* Lon F. Fuller, *Positivism and Fidelity to Law—A Reply to Professor Hart,* 71 HARV. L. REV. 630 (1958).

Also compare MATTHEW H. KRAMER, WHERE LAW AND MORALITY MEET (2004) and MATTHEW H. KRAMER, IN DEFENSE OF LEGAL POSITIVISM (1999) *with* ROBERT ALEXY, THE ARGUMENT FROM INJUSTICE: A REPLY TO LEGAL POSITIVISM (2002) and ROBERT P. GEORGE (ed.), THE AUTONOMY OF LAW (1996).

79 *See* MATTHEW H. KRAMER, IN DEFENSE OF LEGAL POSITIVISM (1999).

80 *See* KENNETH EINAR HIMMA, *Inclusive Legal Positivism* in THE OXFORD HANDBOOK OF JURISPRUDENCE & PHILOSOPHY OF LAW, *supra* note 62, at 125; JULES COLEMAN,

THE PRACTICE OF PRINCIPLE: IN DEFENSE OF A PRAGMATIST APPROACH TO LEGAL THEORY (2001).

81 Religion, law, and politics have intrigued Americans from the founding of our country. Today is no exception. According to which author you read, there is either too much religion in America and in the world or not enough. For the former proposition *see e.g.*, STEPHEN L. CARTER, GOD'S NAME IN VAIN: THE WRONGS AND RIGHTS OF RELIGION IN POLITICS (2000); STEPHEN L. CARTER, THE CULTURE OF DISBELIEF: HOW AMERICAN LAW AND POLITICS TRIVIALIZE RELIGION (1993); MICHAEL J. PERRY, UNDER GOD?: RELIGIOUS FAITH AND LIBERAL DEMOCRACY (2003). For the latter proposition, *see* MARCI A. HAMILTON, GOD VS. THE GAVEL: RELIGION AND THE RULE OF LAW (2005); NOAH FELDMAN, DIVIDED BY GOD: AMERICA'S CHURCH-STATE PROBLEM—AND WHAT WE SHOULD DO ABOUT IT (2005); SAM HARRIS, THE END OF FAITH: RELIGION, TERROR, AND THE FUTURE OF REASON (2004).

82 Another way of conceptualizing these two relationships is contained in the First Amendment's prohibition of establishing religion and its promotion of the free exercise thereof. *See also* RONALD DWORKIN, IS DEMOCRACY POSSIBLE HERE? PRINCIPLES FOR A NEW POLITICAL DEBATE 55–60 (2006).

83 *See also* KEVIN PHILLIPS, AMERICAN THEOCRACY 99–262 (2006).

84 "We citizens of the United States are perennially divided about the proper role of religiously grounded morality in our politics. This is due in substantial part, no doubt, to the fact that we are perennially divided in our judgments about a host of important moral issues—and about a host of connected political issues." PERRY, *supra* note 89, at 21.

85 *See* MARTHA NUSSBAUM, LIBERTY OF CONSCIENCE: IN DEFENSE OF AMERICA'S TRADITION OF RELIGIOUS EQUALITY (2008).

86 *Rosenberger v. Rector and Visitors of the Univ. of Virginia*, 515 U.S. 819, 861 (1995) (Thomas, J. concurring).

87 *Employment Division Dep't of Hum Res. Of Oregon v. Smith*, 494 U.S. 872 (1990).

88 494 U.S. at 911 (Blackmun, J., dissenting).

89 494 U.S. at 878–79.

90 *Minersville School Dist. Bd. Of Ed. v. Gobitis*, 310 U. S. 586, 594–95 (1940).

91 *West Virginia At. Bd. Of Ed. v. Barnette*, 319 U.S. 624 (1943).

92 LORD PATRICK DEVLIN, THE ENFORCEMENT OF MORALS (1965).

93 494 U.S. at 890.

94 494 U.S. at 893.

95 494 U.S. at 902.

96 42 U.S.C. §200bb-1.

97 *Gonzales v. Centro Espirita Beneficente Unaio do Vegetal*, 546 U.S. 418 (2006). In *Gonzales*, members of the Church O Centro Espírita Beneficente Unãio do Vegetal receive communion by drinking *hoasca*, a tea brewed from plants unique to the Amazon rain forest, that contains a hallucinogen. The hallucinogen DMT is a Schedule I drug listed in the federal Controlled Substances Act. United States customs seized a quantity of the drug intended for the church and threatened to prosecute church members. The church sought declaratory and injunctive relief

so that its 130 members could continue the sacramental use of *hoasca*. At a trial court hearing, the government conceded that its confiscation would substantially burden church members. The government argued that it had a compelling state interest to control drug trafficking domestically and internationally. The Supreme Court, in a unanimous opinion, said that the government failed to sustain its burden of proof that *hoasca* needed to be controlled.

98 "[C]ourts must not presume to determine the place of a particular belief in a religion or the plausibility of a religious claim." 494 U.S. at 887.

99 Stanley Fish calls First Amendment jurisprudence "unprincipled" in STANLEY FISH, THE TROUBLE WITH PRINCIPLE CHS. 8–13 (1999). For Fish, "The trouble with principle is, first, that it does not exist, and second, that nowadays many bad things are done in its name," at 2. The "many bad things" means that instead of neutral principles or solid theory, that principle is nothing more than a marker for partisan politics. A neat example of the problem involves tax exemptions for religious institutions. If the government gives a tax exemption to a church, is it impermissibly favoring the "establishment" of religion? If the government denies a tax exemption to a church, then is it interfering with the church's "free exercise" of religion? The choice between the two positions, in this case the granting of tax exemptions for churches as for other nonprofit institutions, is a political, not a principled, choice according to Fish, and I suspect to many others.

100 *See e.g., Zelman v. Simmons-Harris*, 536 U.S. 639 (2002) (allowing public school voucher funds to go to parochial schools); *Agostini v. Felton*, 521 U.S. 203 (1997) (allowing public school teachers to provide remedial education to disadvantaged students in parochial schools); *Rosenberger v. Rector and Visitors of the Univ. of Virginia*, 515 U.S. 819, (1995) (allowing public student fund to pay for the printing of a Christian-oriented newspaper); *Mitchell v. Helms*, 530 U.S. 793 (2000) (allowing federal funds to be used for materials for parochial schools).

101 *Santa Fe Independent School Dist. V. Doe*, 530 U.S. 290 (2000) (student-led school prayer before public school football games disallowed); *School Dist. of Abington Twp. v. Schempp*, 374 U.S. 203 (1963) (bible study in public schools disallowed); *Stone v. Graham*, 449 U.S. 1104 (1980) (display of Ten Commandments in public schools disallowed).

102 *Stone v. Graham*, 449 U.S. 39 (1980).

103 *Van Orden v. Perry*, 545 U.S. 677, 691 (2005).

104 545 U.S. at 707 (Stevens, J., dissenting).

105 *McCreary v. ACLU of Kentucky*, 545 U.S. 844 (2005).

106 *Church of the Lukumi Babalu Aye, Inc. v. City of Hialeah*, 508 U.S. 520 (1993).

107 508 U.S. at 535.

108 At the city council meeting, religious and moral claims were also made in support of the restrictive ordinances:

> Councilman Mejides indicated that he was 'totally against the sacrificing of animals,' and distinguished kosher slaughter because it had a 'real purpose.'

The 'bible says we are allowed to sacrifice an animal for consumption,' he continued, 'but for any other purposes, I don't believe that the Bible allows that.' . . . The chaplain of the Hialeah police Department told the city council that Santeria was a sin, 'foolishness,' 'an abomination to the Lord,' and the worship of 'demons.'

508 U.S. at 542.

109 508 U.S. at 543.

110 508 U.S. at 546.

111 508 U.S. at 548.

112 Justice Souter's concurring opinion nicely states this position. The "Free Exercise Clause bars government action aimed at suppressing religious beliefs or practice." 508 U.S. at 560.

113 *Edwards v. Aguillard*, 482 U.S. 578 (1987).

114 EDWARD J. LARSON, SUMMER FOR THE GODS: THE SCOPES TRIAL AND AMERICA'S CONTINUING DEBATE OVER SCIENCE AND RELIGION (1997).

115 *Stone v. Graham*, 449 U.S. 39 (1980).

116 *Wallace v. Jefferies*, 472 U.S. 38 (1985).

117 *Epperson v. Arkansas*, 393 U.S. 97 (1968).

118 *Lemon v. Kurtzman*, 403 U.S. 602 (1971). The three prongs of the test are (1) the legislature must adopt the law with a secular purpose, (2) the primary effect of the statute should neither inhibit nor advance religion, and (3) the statute must not result in an excessive entanglement of government with religion. The challenged statute must satisfy each of the three prongs.

119 482 U.S. at 578.

120 482 U.S. at 592 (Brennan, J.).

121 482 U.S. at 597.

122 *See e.g.,* S.B. 24, 126th Gen. Assem., Reg. Sess. (Ohio 2004): H.B. 481, 124th Gen. Assem., Reg. Sess. (Ohio 2001); KANSAS STATE DEPARTMENT OF EDUCATION, KANSAS SCIENCE EDUCATION STANDARDS (2007).

123 The plaintiffs were absolutely correct in this claim. One bit of damning evidence revealed the sham. The intelligent design proponents argued that ID had a scientific basis and introduced a text, OF PANDAS AND PEOPLE, to make their point. The plaintiffs, however, introduced an earlier version of that text which used the phrase "creationism" instead of "intelligent design" The authors simply did a search and replaced one term for the other. And, as we learned in our earlier discussion in *Edwards v. Aguillard*, government cannot order that creationism be taught as science in public schools.

124 *Kitzmiller v. Dover Area School Dist.*, 400 F. Supp. 2d 707, 765 (M.D. Pa. 2005).

Chapter 2 Shadows and Light

1 The phrase "the consolation of philosophy" is the title of a book by the fifth-century scholar Boethius. The allusion is apt. Boethius was born in Rome at the end of its Imperial rule. He was educated at the Platonic Academy in Athens in its waning

years and served in the court of the Ostrogoth Theordoric. Boethius was accused of conspiring against Theodoric and thrown in prison. While he was awaiting the death that was to come, he wrote *The Consolation of Philosophy*. Published in 524, the *Consolation* is in the form of a Platonic dialogue between Boethius and the muse of philosophy, thus making the Socratic reference complete. *See also* JOSEF PIEPER, SCHOLASTICISM: PERSONALITIES AND PROBLEMS OF MEDIEVAL PHILOSOPHY 26–36 (1960).

2 ROBERT AUDI (ed.), *Socrates, in* THE CAMBRIDGE DICTIONARY OF PHILOSOPHY 859–60 (2nd ed. 2001); *see also* SARAH KOFMAN, SOCRATES: FICTIONS OF A PHILOSOPHER (Catherine Porter trans., 1998).

3 *See Apology in* PLATO, FIVE DIALOGUES: EUTHYPHRO, APOLOGY, CRITO, MENO, PHAEDO (G. M. A. Grube trans., 1981); *see also* THOMAS C. BRICKHOUSE & NICHOLAS D. SMITH, THE TRIAL AND EXECUTION OF SOCRATES: SOURCES AND CONTROVERSIES (2002); IRVING F. STONE, THE TRIAL OF SOCRATES (1989); JAMES A. COLAIACO, SOCRATES AGAINST ATHENS: PHILOSOPHY ON TRIAL (2000).

4 "The print maker and publisher John Boydell wrote to Sir Joshua Reynolds that it was 'the greatest effort of art since the Sistine Chapel and the stanze of Raphael. . .. This work would have done honor to Athens at the time of Pericles.'" http://www.metmuseum.org/Works_of_Art/viewOne.asp?dep=11&viewmode=1&itgem=31%2E45#a.

5 GARETH B. MATTHEWS, SOCRATIC PERPLEXITY: AND THE NATURE OF PHILOSOPHY (1999).

6 The late philosopher Bernard Williams has written that Plato "invented" philosophy. *See also* BERNARD WILLIAMS, THE SENSE OF THE PAST: ESSAYS IN THE HISTORY OF PHILOSOPHY 148 (2006); ALEXANDER NEHAMAS, VIRTUES OF AUTHENTICITY: ESSAYS ON PLATO AND SOCRATES 317 (1999) ("The *Republic* is therefore not only a work of philosophy. It is in fact the first work of philosophy ever written." Another philosopher, Alfred North Whitehead, has said that all of Western philosophy is merely a series of footnotes to Plato. ALFRED NORTH WHITEHEAD, PROCESS AND REALITY: AN ESSAY IN COSMOLOGY 39 (D. R. Griffin & D. W. Sherburne eds., 1978).

See also Richard Kraut, *Introduction to the Study of Plato, in* RICHARD KRAUT (ed.), THE CAMBRIDGE COMPANION TO PLATO 1 (1992) ("He may in this sense be said to have invented philosophy as a distinct subject, for although all of these topics [e.g., art, metaphysics, epistemology, language, etc.] were, of course, discussed by his intellectual predecessors and contemporaries, he was the first to bring them together by giving them a unitary treatment.").

7 I rely mostly on ALLAN BLOOM (trans.), THE REPUBLIC OF PLATO 6–7 (¶331) (2nd ed. 1991) and will provide page numbers as well as standard paragraph references. In addition to BENJAMIN JOWETT'S classic translation REPUBLIC (3rd rev. ed. 1888), other useful translations include PLATO, REPUBLIC (G. M. A. Grube trans., C. D. C. Reeve ed., rev. 1992); PLATO, THE REPUBLIC (Tom Griffith trans., G. R. F. Ferrari ed., 2001).

8 BLOOM, *supra* note 7, at 7 (¶331e).

9 *Id.* at 8 (¶332d).

10 *Id.* at 12–13 (¶335d).

11 Whether this story is myth or fact continues to be debated. It does serve the purpose of providing a consequentialist example. *See, e.g.,* Anthony D'Amato, *Legal and Moral Dimension of Churchill's Failure to Warn,* 20 CARDOZO L. REV. 561 (1998); Peter J. McIver, *Leading Churchill Myths (3): "Churchill let Coventry Burn to Protect His Secret Intelligence," available at* http://www.winstonchurchill.org/i4a/pages/index.cfm?pageid=107.

12 BLOOM, *supra* note 7, at 13–14 (¶336b-d).

13 *Id.* at 13 (¶336c-d).

14 *See, e.g.*, Gregory Vlastos, *Socratic Irony* in HUGH H. BENSON (ed.), ESSAYS ON THE PHILOSOPHY OF SOCRATES (1992).

15 *Id.* at 15 (¶338c).

16 *Id.* at 16 (¶¶338e–339a).

17 Joseph Raz, Hart's philosophic successor, makes the point of law's connection with authority forcefully in ETHICS IN THE PUBLIC DOMAIN: ESSAYS IN THE MORALITY OF LAW AND POLITICS chs. 9 and 10 (2001); AUTHORITY OF LAW: ESSAYS ON LAW AND MORALITY 3–33 (2002).

18 There is no shortage of recent corporate and political scandals that can be used as examples of profits going to wrongdoers. Some of the scandals that come easily to mind include: Martha Stewart, Kenneth Lay, Jeffrey Skilling, Bernard Ebbers, Richard Scrushy, Jack Abramhoff, Randy "Duke" Cunningham, to name the prominent ones.

19 BLOOM, *supra* note 7, at 28–29 (¶350).

20 Id. at 31 (¶352d) (emphasis added).

21 The idea of justice as a personal or individual virtue may appear a bit odd to us. Today, for the most part, we discuss justice as an attribute of social institutions. *See, e.g.*, JOHN RAWLS, A THEORY OF JUSTICE 3 (1971) ("Justice is the first virtue of social institutions, as truth is of systems of thought."). For Plato and Aristotle, however, justice as personal virtue was central to their systems of ethics or morality. Plato's view is discussed in this chapter. For Aristotle, *see* NICOMACHEAN ETHICS BOOK FIVE AT 116–47 (Terence Irwin trans., 1985); NANCY SHERMAN, THE FABRIC OF CHARACTER: ARISTOTLE'S THEORY OF VIRTUE (1989); RICHARD KRAUT, ARISTOTLE 118–125 (2002). For authors who attempt to reconnect public and private virtue, *see* STUART HAMPSHIRE (ed.), PUBLIC AND PRIVATE MORALITY (1978); ONORA O'NEILL, TOWARDS JUSTICE AND VIRTUE: A CONSTRUCTIVE ACCOUNT OF PRACTICAL REASONING (1998).

22 *See e.g.*, LEO STRAUSS, THE CITY AND MAN ch. II (1964); Bernard Williams, *The Analogy of City and Soul in Plato's Republic* in RICHARD KRAUT (ed.), PLATO'S REPUBLIC: CRITICAL ESSAYS ch. 4 (1997).

23 *See* RICHARD KRAUT, ARISTOTLE 148–50 (2002); ARISTOTLE, NICHOMACHEAN ETHICS 125–28 (Terence Irwin trans., 1985). Irwin translates corrective justice as rectificatory justice.

24 *See* BERNARD GERT, COMMON MORALITY: DECIDING WHAT TO DO 19–53 (2004).

25 Discussing Thrasymachus's definition of Justice, *see* STANLEY ROSEN, PLATO'S REPUBLIC: A STUDY 39 (2005) ("If justice is the interest of the strong, then they

have the right to take away the benefits of the weak. But this is true even among the strong; the strongest have the right to take away the benefits of the less strong. In other words, if might makes right, then life is a perpetual war of each against all, as Hobbes teaches: we are all enemies. If there is such a thing as friendship, it is an allegiance to dominate others; the moment there is a shift in the balance of power, friends become enemies and enemies friends. Today we call this realpolitik.").

26 "[J]ustice has been shown [by Socrates] to be a state that is worth having for itself and not only its consequences." JULIA ANNAS, AN INTRODUCTION TO PLATO'S REPUBLIC 168 (1981). In Chapter 6 of her book, Annas argues that Socrates and his interlocutors do talk past each other. She says that Cephalus, Polemarchus, and Thrasymachus give examples of acts of Justice when Plato is asking for a discussion of how people, as moral agents, behave. ". . . Plato makes the shift from justice as a matter of acts to justice as a state of the agent," at 163.

27 Socrates' claims of ignorance cannot be taken at face value. *See* Gregory Vlastos, *Socrates Disavowal of Knowledge* in GAIL FINE (ed.), PLATO 1: METAPHYSICS AND EPISTEMOLOGY 64 (1999). Vlastos argues that Socrates uses the word "knowing" variably throughout the dialogues, and that close attention must be paid to its precise use.

28 BLOOM, *supra* note 7, at 34 (¶354c).

29 *See e.g.,* EMILY WILSON, THE DEATH OF SOCRATES (2007).

30 While I will discuss the Allegory in connection with law and Justice, the Allegory also connects with previous stories about the Sun and the Line which address education, knowledge, and the search for the Good.

31 *See e.g.,* ANDREW LAWLESS, PLATO'S SUN: AN INTRODUCTION TO PHILOSOPHY (2005).

32 ROSEN, *supra* note 25, at 274.

33 Donald R. Morrison, *The Utopian Character of Plato's Ideal City* in G. R. F. Ferrari (ed.), THE CAMBRIDGE COMPANION TO PLATO'S REPUBLIC 232, 242–43 (2007).

34 R. C. CROSS & A. D. WOOZLEY, PLATO'S *REPUBLIC*: A PHILOSOPHICAL COMMENTARY 219–220 (1964) discuss *eikasia* in terms of the prisoners looking at the images on the cave wall. *Eikasia*, they write, is a state of mind but it "is not one of guessing at originals through their likenesses (conjecture in that sense), but on in which likeness is accepted as reality, without any realisation that it is a likeness, i.e., one concerned solely with likenesses or images; and it would then be parallel to the state of mind of the prisoners in the Cave." *See also,* FRANCIS CONFORD, THE REPUBLIC OF PLATO 223 n. 3 (1966 ed.).

35 Bloom, *supra* note 7, at 194 (¶515c).

36 *Id.* at 195 (¶516b–c).

37 *See, e.g.*, CROSS & WOOZLEY, *supra* note 34, at 196–230; ANNAS, *supra* note 26, at ch. 10; SETH BENARDETTE, SOCRATES' SECOND SAILING: ON PLATO'S REPUBLIC ch. 29 (1989); *see also* IRIS MURDOCH: EXISTENTIALISTS AND MYSTICS: WRITINGS ON PHILOSOPHY AND LITERATURE 386–463 (1997) (This passage contains Murdoch's essay *The Fire and the Sun: Why Plato Banished the Artists.*).

38 Bloom, *supra* note 7, at 196 (¶517b-c). *See also,* J. C. B. GOSLING, PLATO 26 (1983 ed.).

39 Later in the Allegory, Plato tells Glaucon why the philosopher-rulers must go back into the Cave. Plato would say to them because you have been better educated:

> So you must go down, each in his turn, into the common dwelling of the others and get habituated along with them to seeing in the dark things. And, in getting habituated to it, you will see ten thousand times better than the men there, and you'll know what each of the phantoms it, and of what it is a phantom, because you have seen the truth about fair, and just, and good things." Bloom, *supra* note 7, at 199 (¶520c).

40 Bloom, *supra* note 7, at 196 (¶517d).

41 *Id.* at 198 (¶519d).

42 *Id.* at 212–14; *see also,* SEAN SAYERS, PLATO'S REPUBLIC: AN INTRODUCTION 128–30 (1999).

43 *See* Richard Kraut, *Return to the Cave:* Republic 519–21, in GAIL FINE (ed.), PLATO 2: ETHICS, POLITICS, RELIGION, AND THE SOUL 235 (1999). ("By putting oneself into the best position to lead the philosophical life, one develops the intellectual and emotional skills that we look for in a completely just person," at *id.*) Kraut argues that the compulsion is not unjust because of the privilege that rulers have had is seeing the Sun and because of the need to rule. He does not, mistakenly I believe, discuss the compulsion of the law which imposes an obligation to serve the common good. *See also,* Richard Kraut, *The Defense of Justice in Plato's* Republic in RICHARD KRAUT (ed.), PLATO'S *REPUBLIC*: CRITICAL ESSAYS 209 (1997); Richard Kraut, *Reason and Justice in Plato's* Republic, in E. N. LEE ET AL. (eds.), EXEGESIS AND ARGUMENT: STUDIES IN GREEK PHILOSOPHY PRESENTED TO GREGORY VLASTOS 207, 213–14 (1973).

44 Bloom, *supra* note 7, at 198 (¶¶519d–520a).

45 *See* GREGORY VLASTOS, PLATONIC STUDIES 114,115 n. 12 (2nd ed. 1981) in which Vlastos gives the slogan as "does its own." *See also,* ANNAS, *supra* note 26, at 121 ("Doing one's own."); ROSEN, *supra* note 25, at 146 ("Justice, to repeat, is minding one's own business and avoiding *polupragmosun,* busying oneself with many things and so minding someone else's business."); *see also,* Kraut, EXEGESIS AND ARGUMENT, *supra* note 43, at 208 (1973).

46 ANNAS, *supra* note 26, at 119.

47 KRAUT, *supra* note 43, at 324–27.

48 GREGORY VLASTOS, PLATONIC STUDIES 113–15 (2nd ed. 1981).

49 *Id.* at 111–12.

50 "[A]n ideal of justice is none the worse for being non-realizable in practice if its purpose is to inspire the individual person to be as just as he or she can be. . . . Socrates says that it does not matter if the just society is an unattainable ideal, as long as it does serve as an ideal for the just person to realize in his or her life." ANNAS, *supra* note 26, at 185.

51 "[T]he unexamined life for man is not worth living." R. E. ALLEN, EUTHYPHRO, APOLOGY, CRITO, MENO, GORGIAS, MENEXENUS: THE DIALOGUES OF PLATO VOLUME I 100 (¶38a) (1984).

52 BLOOM, *supra* note 7, at 197 (¶518c). *See also,* Iris Murdoch, *The Sovereignty of the Good Over Other Concepts,* in Iris Murdoch, EXISTENTIALISTS AND OTHER MYSTICS

363–85 (1998); Gerasimos Santas *The Form of the Good in Plato's* Republic, in GAIL FINE (ed.), PLATO 1: METAPHYSICS AND EPISTEMOLOGY 247 (1999).

53 ARISTOTLE, NICHOMACHEAN ETHICS 9–12 (Terence Irwin ed., 1985).

54 *See, e.g.*, RONALD DWORKIN, LAW'S EMPIRE 73–74 (1986) ("But we each—some more reflexively than other—form a sense of justice that is an interpretation nonetheless, and some of us even revise our interpretation from time to time.). *See also*, IRIS MURDOCH, THE SOVEREIGNTY OF GOOD 95 (1971). Commenting on the *Republic*, Murdoch writes:

> Good has often been said to be indefinable for reasons connected with freedom. Good is an empty space into which human choice may move. . . . I [offer that] we do really know a certain amount about Good and about the way in which it is connected to our condition. . . . We are not usually in doubt about the direction in which Good lies. Equally we recognize the real existence of evil: cynicism, cruelty, indifference to suffering. However, the concept of Good still remains obscure and mysterious. We see the world in the light of Good, but what is the Good itself?"

55 VIRGIL, THE AENIED 186 (Robert Fagles trans., 2006).

56 JOWETT, *supra* note 7, at cxii:

> The den or cave represents the narrow sphere of politics or law . . . and the light of eternal ideas is supposed to exercise a disturbing influence on the minds of those who return to this lower world. In other words, their principles are too wide for practical application; they are looking for a way into the past and future when their business is with the present. The ideal is not easily reduced to the conditions of actual life, and may often be at variance with them.

57 KRAUT, *supra* note 43, at 205. Reason is "the most worthwhile capacity of our souls because it is only through reason that we can possess the Forms."

58 BLOOM, *supra* note 7, at 211 (¶532b).

59 JOWETT, *supra* note 7, at ccvii.

60 R. E. ALLEN, *supra* note 51, at 170–71 (¶¶85c–86c).

61 For the *Crito*, *see id.* at 117–29. *See also*, A. D. WOOZLEY, LAW AND OBEDIENCE: THE ARGUMENTS OF PLATO'S *CRITO* (1979); GERASIMOS XENOPHON SANTAS, SOCRATES: PHILOSOPHY IN PLATO'S EARLY DIALOGUES 43 (1979).

62 For the *Apology*, *see* ALLEN, *supra* note 51, at 79–104. *See also*, THOMAS C. BRICKHOUSE & NICHOLAS D. SMITH, SOCRATES ON TRIAL (1989); C. D. C. REEVE, SOCRATES IN THE APOLOGY: AN ESSAY ON PLATO'S *APOLOGY OF SOCRATES* (1989).

63 SANTAS, *supra* note 61, at 43 ("[I]n the *Apology* and the *Crito* Socrates' whole life and work is on public trial, and in these works Socrates is making some of the most important decisions of his life.").

64 ALLEN, *supra* note 51, at 122 (¶48c).

65 *Id.* at 123 (¶49b).

66 *Id.* at 125 (¶50b).

67 The distinction between Antigone's and Socrates' is clear. Socrates bases his obedience to the Laws on his contract with the state; a contract that Antigone

did not have with Creon's state. The idea of civil disobedience will be discussed further in Chapter 6.

68 ALLEN, *supra* note 51, at 125 (¶50c).

69 *Id.* at 125–27 (¶¶50e–52b).

70 *Id.* at 129 (¶54c).

71 WOOZLEY, *supra* note 61, at 60–61. "The answer would appear that in the *Crito* it is real laws, or only such actual laws as are real laws, that he has in mind, and consequently that in that discussion the problem what a man should do when and with an unjust law does not get serious consideration." A better interpretation, I think, is that in the *Crito* Plato is addressing an idealized form of law—the Laws.

72 *Id.* at 22–25. *But see,* R. E. Allen, *Law and Justice in Plato's* Crito, 69 J. Phil. 557 (1972); R. E. ALLEN, SOCRATES AND LEGAL OBLIGATION 100–13 (1980) in which the author argues that Socrates obeyed laws which may be just or unjust as all citizens are under an obligation to obey them because they are laws. "The binding claim of law in the Crito is the claim of positive law: positive law as positive, the actually existing law of a given municipal system." I disagree with Allen's positivist analysis for reasons stated by Socrates and recounted in the text above. Again, Socrates is addressing the Laws as idealized form. *See also,* SANTAS, *supra* note 61, at 43–49; WOOZLEY, *supra* note 61, at 25, 40–61.

73 Leo Strauss, *On the Minos, in* THOMAS L. PANGLE (ed.), THE ROOTS OF POLITICAL PHILOSOPHY: TEN FORGOTTEN SOCRATIC DIALOGUES 67 (1987).

74 THE LAWS OF PLATO 3 (¶264a) (Thomas L. Pangle trans.,1980):

> Is it a god or some human being, stranger, who is given the credit for laying down your laws?
>
> A god, stranger, a god—to say what is at any rate the most just thing.

75 *Id.* at 53 (¶313b).

76 *Id.* at 54–55 (¶341c).

77 *Id.* at 55 (¶314d–e).

78 *Id.* at 59 (¶¶316e–317a).

79 STRAUSS, *supra* note 73, at 68. These two views are inseparable:

> While being distinct, the theoretical and the practical questions are inseparable from each other. One cannot know to which law one is subject without having some knowledge however vague and dim, of law as such; one cannot know what law is without possessing at least a directive toward law to which one is subject.

This quotation is a fine summary description of the ongoing Hart/Dworkin debate about the use of the word law. *See also,* Brian Leiter, *Beyond the Hart/Dworkin Debate: The Methodology Problem in Jurisprudence*, 48 AM. J. OF JURIS. 17 (2003).

80 PANGLE, *supra* note 74, at 57–58 (¶316a-b). Leo Straus argues that Plato is articulating a vision of law in quest of itself. "[T]he only definition proposed by Socrates: the law wishes to be finding out what it is." STRAUSS, *supra* note 73, at 69–70.

81 *See e.g.*, RONALD DWORKIN, JUSTICE IN ROBES 168 (2006) discussing the value of legality or the rule of law:

> This picture of political philosophy is not only wildly ambitious—it can only even be imagined in a cooperative way—but it is also, as I conceded, very much against contemporary fashion. It is not in the spirit of modest value pluralism. It aims at a utopian and always unrealized goal—Plato's unity of value.

82 *See, e.g.*, Scott J. Shapiro, *The 'Hart-Dworkin' Debate: A Short Guide for the Perplexed* in THE CAMBRIDGE COMPANION TO DWORKIN (Arthur Ripstein ed., forthcoming).

83 *See* DUNCAN KENNEDY, A CRITIQUE OF ADJUDICATION {FIN DE SIÈCLE} ch. 1 (1997).

84 H. L. A. Hart, *American Jurisprudence Through English Eyes: The Nightmare and the Noble Dream*, 11 GEORGIA L. REV. 969 (1977). *See also*, Michael Bayles, *Hart vs. Dworkin*, 10 LAW & PHILOSOPHY 349 (1991).

85 *Id.* at 972 (Hart quoting Lord Radcliffe). *See also*, RONALD DWORKIN, LAW'S EMPIRE 36 (in which Dworkin criticizes the American Legal Realist skepticism that "[T]here is no such thing as law, or that the law is only a matter of what the judge had for breakfast."

86 *Id.* at 982.

87 *Id.* "The judge, in cases where particular rules—paper rules as they are sometimes deprecatingly called—prove indeterminate, is to 'carve' his decision with the '*grain*' of the system as a whole, that is, in accordance with its broad principles and established values. Faced with the indeterminacies of the positive law the judge is not simply to decide without further attention to the system, as his thinks best."

88 RONALD DWORKIN, TAKING RIGHTS SERIOUSLY 81 (1978).

89 *Id.* at 106–15.

90 *Id.* at 126.

91 Hart, *supra* note 84, at 985; *see also*, A.D. Woozley, *No Right Answer*, 29 PHIL. Q. 25 (1979).

92 RONALD DWORKIN, A MATTER OF PRINCIPLE ch. 5 (1985).

93 DWORKIN, *supra* note 81, at 41.

94 In LAW'S EMPIRE, *supra* note 54, Dworkin distinguishes law from justice, and he distinguishes law from morals while maintaining that law is embedded in the political morality of the community. I do not find Dworkin's disclaimers about distinguishing law from morality and from justice either persuasive or coherent. He says that law is different from each because law's "content may depend on the other." Popular morality is not the political morality of law which may develop over time. As for distinguishing law from justice, Dworkin writes, "Law is also different from justice. Justice is a matter of the correct or best theory of moral and political rights, and anyone's conception of justice is his theory, imposed by his own personal convictions, of what their rights actually are. Law is a matter of which supposed rights supply a justification for using or withholding the collective force of the state because they are included in or implied by actual political decisions of the past" at 96–97.

95 *Id.* at 93. Dworkin is adamantly committed to avoiding the semantic game of defining the word law. He believes the game is a trap he calls the semantic sting that ensnares unwary legal philosophers into a debate about the semantics of the word. Still, we must mean something when we use the word law and when Dworkin uses the word law, he is attempting to justify a state's use of force. *See* LAW'S EMPIRE, *supra* note 54, at 45–46; *see also*, Jules Coleman, *Law*, 9 LEGAL THEORY 1 (2003); Timothy A. O. Endicott, *Law and Language*, *in* THE STANFORD ENCYCLOPEDIA OF PHILOSOPHY (Winter 2002), EDWARD N. ZALTA (ed.), available at http://plato.stanford.edu/archives/win2002/entries/law-language/; Joseph Raz, *Two Views of the Nature of the Theory of Law*, *in* HART'S POSTSCRIPT: ESSAYS ON THE POSTSCRIPT TO THE CONCEPT OF LAW 1 (Jules Coleman ed., 2005); Timothy A. O. Endicott, *Herbert Hart and the Semantic Sting*," *in* HART'S POSTSCRIPT: ESSAYS ON THE POSTSCRIPT TO THE CONCEPT OF LAW 39 (Jules Coleman ed., 2005); Nicos Stavropoulos, *Hart's Semantic's*, *in* HART'S POSTSCRIPT: ESSAYS ON THE POSTSCRIPT TO THE CONCEPT OF LAW 59 (Jules Coleman ed., 2005).

96 DWORKIN, LAW'S EMPIRE, *supra* note 54, at 225.

97 *Gregg v. McClesky*, 428 U.S. 153 (1976).

98 *Atkins v. Virginia*, 536 U.S. 304, 311–12 (2002); *Trop v. Dulles*, 356 U.S. 86, 101 (1958).

99 *Baze v. Rees*, 128 S. Ct 1520 (2008).

100 *See, e.g., Uttecht v. Brown*, 127 S. Ct. 2218 (2007).

101 *McCluskey v. Kemp*, 481 U.S. 279, 366 (1987).

102 *Baze* at 1520 (Stevens, J., concurring); *Furman v. Georgia*, 408 U.S. 238, 312 (White, J., concurring).

103 *Baze* at 1552.

104 *Callins v. Collins*, 510 U.S. 1141, 1145 (1994) (Blackmun, J, dissenting).

105 In the same case, Justice Scalia chides Justice Blackmun for referring to "'intellectual, moral, and personal' preferences, but never to the text and tradition of the Constitution." 510 U.S. at 1141. In fact, Justice Blackmun says explicitly that the death penalty violates the positive law of the Eighth Amendment and he then provides a list of reasons with supporting authority.

106 *Callins v. Collins*, 510 U.S. 1141, 1145 (Blackmun, J., dissenting). This opinion written by Justice Blackmun dissenting from the denial from *certiorari*.

107 *See Furman v. Georgia*, 408 U.S. 238 (1972) (The *Furman* court effectively halted the death penalty because of arbitrariness and discrimination).

108 *Callins* at 1147.

109 WALLACE STEVENS, *Notes Toward a Supreme Fiction*, *in* COLLECTED POEMS 331(1984).

Chapter 3 Rule and Measure

1 For the quotations given in the above paragraph, *see* JAMES A. WEISHEIPL, O.P., FRIAR THOMAS D'AQUINO: HIS LIFE, THOUGHT, AND WORKS 321 (1983). For biographical information about Aquinas, *see* THOMAS F. O'MEARA, O.P., THOMAS

AQUINAS: THEOLOGIAN 1–40; ANTHONY KENNY, AQUINAS 1–31 (1980); F. C. COPELSTON, A QUINAS 9–15 (1955); JOHN FINNIS, AQUINAS: MORAL, POLITICAL, AND LEGAL THEORY 1–19 (1998).

2 *See* ERICH AUERBACH, DANTE: POET OF THE SECULAR WORLD 1–2 (2006 ed.) (1929).

3 R. J. HENLE, S. J. (ed.), ST. THOMAS AQUINAS: THE TREATISE ON LAW 9 (1993).

4 JOSEF PIEPER, SCHOLASTCISM: PERSONALITIES AND PROBLEMS OF MEDIEVAL PHILOSOPHY (Richard & Clara Wilson trans., 1965).

5 ST. THOMAS ACQUINAS, TREATISE ON LAW v (Ralph McInery ed., 1998).

6 *See* John Finnis, Aquinas' Moral, Political, and Legal Philosophy, in EDWARD N. ZALTA (ed.), THE STANFORD ENCYCLOPEDIA OF PHILOSOPHY at http://plato.stanford.edu/archives/spr2006/entries/aquinas-moral-political/.

7 Professor Anthony Lisska dates the revival of the natural law tradition from Elizabeth Anscomb's 1958 paper, *Modern Moral Philosophy*, 33 PHILOSOPHY 124 (1958). *See* ANTHONY J. LISSKA, AQUINAS' THEORY OF NATURAL LAW: AN ANALYTIC RECONSTRUCTION ch. 1 (1996). We might date the modern revival a bit earlier to the Nuremberg Trials. These extra-nation state trials raised an as yet unanswered question about legitimacy. What was basis of law for the Nuremberg Trials? Clearly, the Holocaust constituted unspeakable acts of human violence. But on what legal basis were the Nazi officials tried? No positive law existed. Was natural law available on which to base these judicial proceedings? *See e.g.*, ELLEN FRANKEL PAUL, FRED D. MILLER, JR., & JEFFREY PAUL, NATURAL LAW AND MODERN MORAL PHILOSOPHY vii (2001).

8 LISSKA, *supra* note 7, at 120–21.

9 *See* ROGER COTTRELL, THE POLITICS OF JURISPRUDENCE: A CRITICAL INTRODUCTION TO LEGAL PHILOSOPHY ch. 5 (2nd ed. 2003).

10 *See e.g.*, John Finnis, *Natural Law: the Classical Tradition*, in THE OXFORD HANDBOOK OF JURISPRUDENCE AND PHILOSOPHY OF LAW 1 (Jules Coleman & Scott Shapiro eds., 2002); Brian Bix, *Natural Law: the Modern Tradition*, in THE OXFORD HANDBOOK OF JURISPRUDENCE AND PHILOSOPHY OF LAW at 61; BRIAN TANAMAHA, ON THE RULE OF LAW: HISTORY, POLITICS, THEORY chs. 1 & 2 (2004); JOHN MURPHY, A SHORT HISTORY OF WESTERN LEGAL THEORY (1992).

11 This distinction may be honored more in the breach than in the observance. *See* Finnis, *supra* note 6.

12 LISSKA, *supra* note 7, at 111.

13 In Chapter 1, I argued, following Nonet, that Antigone's law is the unsayable law that even the gods must obey. As such, it serves the role of Plato's Sun as an ideal. Antigone's law, then, is not a form of natural law certainly not in the Thomist tradition. For the contrary reading, *see* Tony Burns, *Sophocles'* Antigone *and the History of the Concept of Natural Law*, 50 POLITICAL STUDIES 545 (2002); Daniel Robinson, *Antigone's Defense: A Critical Study of Natural Law Theory*, 45 REVIEW OF METAPHYSICS 382 (1991). Antigone's law is better seen as an example of Aquinas's description of eternal law and, thus, as an example of the concept of higher law. *See e.g.*, Daniel Robinson, *Antigone's Defense: A Critical Study of Natural Law Theory*, 45 REVIEW OF METAPHYSICS 382 (December 1991).

14 *See* Brian Bix, *Natural Law: the Modern Tradition* in THE OXFORD HANDBOOK OF JURISPRUDENCE, *supra* note 10, 61–62 n. 2 and 70 ("Contrary to a lay person's expectations, natural law theory often has little if anything to do with 'law' as that term is conventionally used.").

15 TREATISE, *supra* note 5, at vi–x.

16 *Id.* at 3.

17 *Id.*

18 *Id.*

19 *Id.* at 10–11 (bracketed numbers added).

20 *Id.* at viii; *see also*, JOHN FINNIS, AQUINAS: MORAL, POLITICAL, AND LEGAL THEORY, 255–56 (1998).

21 *Id.* at 9.

22 LON FULLER, THE MORALITY OF LAW 40, 123 (rev.ed. 1969).

23 Aquinas's structural morality of law has its modern counterpart. The most noted legal philosopher that addresses the morality of law is Lon Fuller whose list of essential elements of law incorporate Aquinas's list and adds the following: law must be mostly non-retroactive, clear, non-contradictory, not impossible to follow, constant, and consistent with official action. This list comprises what Fuller called the inner morality of law and constituted the heart of his procedural theory of natural law. *See* FULLER, *id.* at 46–49.

24 TREATISE, *supra* note 5, at 6.

25 *Id.* at 12.

26 LISSKA, *supra* note 7, at 91–95.

27 TREATISE, *supra* note 5, at 40–42.

28 FINNIS, *supra* note 1, at 307.

29 *Id.* at 308.

30 LISSKA, *supra* note 7, at 112.

31 FINNIS, *supra* note 1, at 266. *See also* John Finnis, *The Truth in Legal Positivism* in THE AUTONOMY OF LAW 195 (Robert P. George ed., 1996).

32 TREATISE, *supra* note 5, at 20–22.

33 *Id.* at 35.

34 *Id.* at 33.

35 JOHN FINNIS, NATURAL LAW AND NATURAL RIGHTS 77–78 (1980).

36 TREATISE, *supra* note 5, at 57.

37 *Id.* at 57.

38 Finnis argues that synderesis is equivalent to Aristotle's (and Aquinas's) use of *intellectus*—we grasp first principles and once grasped they are etched on our minds. Therefore,"nothing whatever turns on that curious medieval word." FINNIS, *supra* note 1, at 89 n. 138.

39 *See* Robert A. Greene, *Synderesis, the Spark of Conscience, in the English Renaissance*, 52 J. HIST. OF IDEAS 195 (1991); Robert A. Greene, *Instinct of Nature: Natural Law, Synderesis, and the Moral Sense*, 58 J. HIST. OF IDEAS 173 (1997; *see also* John Finnis, *Aquinas' Moral, Political, and Legal Philosophy* §3 in EDWARD N. ZALTA (ed.), THE STANFORD ENCYCLOPEDIA OF PHILOSOPHY at 60 available at http://plato.stanford.edu/entries/aquinas-moral-political/. I read

Aquinas differently to say that *synderesis* pertains to matters of conscience as a part of our human nature.

40 TREATISE, *supra* note 5, at 59.

41 *Id.*

42 *Id.* at 59–60.

43 Germain G. Grisez, *The First Principle of Practical Reason: A Commentary on the Summa Theologiae, 1–2, Question 94, Article 2*, 10 NATURAL L. FORUM 168 (1965).

44 TREATISE, *supra* note 5, at 58 and 65.

45 *Id.* at 60.

46 *Id.* at 60–61.

47 *Id.* at 66.

48 *Id.* at 69–72.

49 *Id.* at 71.

50 *Id.* at 70. *See also* HOWARD P. KAINZ, NATURAL LAW: AN INTRODUCTION AND RE-EXAMINATION 89–91 (2004).

51 *Id.* at 81.

52 FINNIS, *supra* note 35, at 363.

53 TREATISE, *supra* note 5, at 81.

54 *Id.* at 96.

55 *Id.* at 44.

56 *Id.* at 74.

57 *Id.* at 76.

58 *Id.* at 81.

59 *Id.* at 85–88; FINNIS, *supra* note 1, at 255–58.

60 TREATISE, *supra* note 5, at 79.

61 *Id.* at 94.

62 *Id.* at 97.

63 FINNIS, *supra* note 1, at 273.

64 TREATISE, *supra* note 5, at 102.

65 *Id.*

66 *Id.* at 109.

67 FINNIS, *supra* note 1, at 354–66.

68 *See e.g.*, Finnis, *Natural Law Theories*, *supra* note 6, at §3.1.1 (regarding the Nuremberg Trials); JACQUES MARITAIN, NATURAL LAW: REFLECTIONS ON THEORY AND PRACTICE (2001) (regarding the UN Declaration of human Rights).

69 *See* COTTRELL, *supra* note 9, at 123–38.

70 *See e.g.*, PIERRE SCHLAG, THE ENCHANTMENT OF REASON (1998); Symposium, *Beyond Right and Reason: Pierre Schlag, The Critique of Normativity, and the Enchantment of Reason*, 57 U. Miami L. Rev. 475 (2003).

71 *See e.g.*, DANIEL A. FARBER & SUZANNA SHERRY, BEYOND ALL REASON: THE RADICAL ASSAULT ON TRUTH IN AMERICAN LAW (1997); THOMAS NAGEL, THE LAST WORD (1997); STEPHEN TOULMIN, RETURN TO REASON (2001).

72 *See* Germain Grisez, *The First Principle of Practical Reason: A Commentary on the Summa theologiae*, 1–2, question 94, Article 2, 10 NATURAL LAW FORUM 168 (1965); Germain Grisez, Joseph Boyle, & John Finnis, *Practical Principles,*

Moral Truth, and Ultimate Ends, 32 AM. J. JURIS. 99 (1987); FINNIS, *supra* note 35; *see also* Jeffrey Goldsworthy, *Fact and Value in the New Natural Law Theory*, 41 AM. J. JURIS. 21 (1996); Robert P. George, *A Defense of the New Natural Law Theory*, 41 AM. J. JURIS. 47 (1996); ROBERT P. GEORGE, IN DEFENSE OF NATURAL LAW (2000); JEAN PORTER, NATURE AS REASON: A THOMISTIC THEORY OF THE NATURAL LAW (2005); DAVID BAYBROOKE, NATURAL LAW MODERNIZED (2001); JOHN GOYETTE, MARK S. LATKOVIC & RICHARD S. MYERS, ST. THOMAS AQUINAS AND THE NATURAL LAW TRADITION: CONTEMPORARY PHILOSOPHICAL AND THEOLOGICAL PERSPECTIVES (2004); Anthony J. Lisska, *On the Revival of Natural Law: Several Boos from the Last Half-Decade*, 81 AM. CATH. PHILO. Q. 617 (2007); HENRY B. VEATCH, SWIMMING AGAINST THE CURRENT IN CONTEMPORARY PHILOSOPHY (1990); ALASDAIR MACINTYRE, AFTER VIRTUE (1981); LLOYD, L. WEINREB, NATURAL LAW AND JUSTICE (1987).

73 GEORGE, IN DEFENSE OF NATURAL LAW, *id.* at 86.

74 Howard Kainz had recently written that the epistemological question actually presents three distinct philosophical problems. *See* KAINZ, *supra* note 50, at 69–79; *see also* LISSKA, *supra* note 7, at ch. 3; PORTER, *supra* note 72, at 123–39; LAWRENCE B. SOLUM, *Natural Justice*, 52 AM. J. JURISPRUDENCE 65, 66–69 (2006). First, the new natural lawyers must address Hume's is-ought distinction. At its most rudimentary, Hume says that a moral norm, as a matter of logic, cannot be derived from a matter of fact. No *ought* can be derived from an *is*. The fact that slavery has existed throughout history does not mean that human slavery is a moral good which *ought* to exist. First principles of natural law, then, must come from elsewhere.

The second and related problem is known as the fact-value distinction addressed by Descartes and Kant among others. Kainz writes that this problem is often used as a "litmus test" for the validity of ethical theories such as the theory of natural law. KAINZ at 75; FINNIS, *supra* note 35, at 33–48; *see also* John Finnis, *The Natural Law Tradition in Ethics* at http://plato.stanford.edu/natural-law-ethics/(2002). This problem is broader than the is-ought prohibition because values can be, among other things, aesthetic and political values as well as moral ones. It is also a deeper problem because while is-ought is a logical argument, the fact-value problem is a metaphysical assertion that we should not confuse the realm of objective facts with the subjective realm of moral values. For an argument to the contrary, *see* PHILLIPA FOOT, VIRTUES AND VICES AND OTHER ESSAYS IN MORAL PHILOSOPHY 96–131 (2002). Facts in the world, such as a general disapproval of same-sex marriage, does not of itself generate a moral value of approval or disapproval.

The third, and again related, problem is G. E. Moore's naturalistic fallacy. According to Moore, once we identify some *x* as "good," we cannot escape asking the question, "But is *x* good?" To maintain that saying "'*x* is good'" is the same as saying 'good is good' is to fall into the naturalistic fallacy." KAINZ, at 77. At the heart of natural law theory is the injunction to "pursue good," therefore, on the face of it, Moore's naturalistic fallacy would seem to apply as he challenges us to define 'good" in intelligible and non-tautological terms.

75 ARISTOPHANES, *THREE COMEDIES*: *THE CLOUDS* 21 (William Arrowsmith trans. & ed., 2003).

76 Grisez, *supra* note 43, at 175; *see also* Finnis, *The Natural Law Tradition in Ethics*, *supra* note 74, at §2.1.

77 *Id.* at 178.

78 *See* GEORGE, IN DEFENSE OF NATURAL LAW, *supra* note 72, at 85 ("[The basic reasons for human action] are known in non-inferential acts of understanding in which we grasp possible ends or purposes as worthwhile for their own sakes. The most basic reasons for action are those reasons whose intelligibility does not depend on deeper or still more fundamental reasons. As *basic* reasons, they cannot be derived; for there is nothing more fundamental that could serve as a premise for logical derivation. Therefore, they must be self-evident.").

79 FINNIS, AQUINAS, *supra* note 1, at 87–89. *See also* GEORGE, *supra* note 72, at 143 ("Intrinsic value cannot, strictly speaking, be demonstrated. . . . Such acts [of understanding] require imaginative reflection on data provided by inclination and experience, as well as knowledge of empirical patterns, which underlie possibilities of action and achievement.").

80 David F. Forte, *The Natural Law Moment*, in NATURAL LAW AND CONTEMPORARY PUBLIC POLICY 7 (David F. Forte ed., 1998).

81 GEORGE, *supra* note 72, at 1.

82 Grisez, Boyle & Finnis, *supra* note 72, at 107.

83 *Id.* at 131.

84 GERMAIN R. GRISEZ, THE WAY OF THE LORD JESUS, VOL. 1: CHRISTIAN MORAL PRINCIPLES, 121–22 (1983).

85 FINNIS, *supra* note 35, at 86–90.

86 John Finnis, *Is Natural Law Theory Compatible with Limited Government*, in NATURAL LAW, LIBERALISM, AND MORALITY 5 (Robert P. George ed., 1996).

87 *Id.* at 3.

88 FORTE, *supra* note 80.

89 *See e.g.*, George Weigel, *Just War and Iraq Wars* in FIRST THINGS: A JOURNAL OF RELIGION, CULTURE, AND PUBLIC LIFE (April 2007) available at http://www.firstthings.com/article.php3?id_article=5465.

90 *See e.g.*, JEAN PORTER, NATURE AS REASON: A THOMISTIC THEORY OF THE NATURAL LAW 33–44 (2005), Natural law is not *necessarily* Catholic. Still, the key journal in the field, *The American Journal of Jurisprudence* (formerly *The Natural Law Journal*), is published at the University of Notre Dame and many of the chief expositors of natural law are Catholic—some, like Robert George and John Finnis, explicitly ground their theories of natural law in their religious tradition.

91 Grisez, *supra* note 43, at 184.

92 *See e.g.*, BENJAMIN FLETCHER WRIGHT, JR., AMERICAN INTERPRETATIONS OF NATURAL LAW: A STUDY IN THE HISTORY OF POLITICAL THOUGHT (1962). Natural law in American law is also addressed in Chapter 5.

93 *See e.g.*, PAULINE MAIER, AMERICAN SCRIPTURE: MAKING HE DECLARATION OF INDEPENDENCE (1997).

94 *See* GEORGE, *supra* note 72, at ch. 18.

95 For some demographics, see the American National Health Interview, D. Dawson & A. M. Hardy, National Center for Health Statistics, Center for Disease Control, Advance Date 204 (1990–92) (2–3 percent male homosexuality); *National Health and Social Life Survey*, http://cloud9.norc.uchicago.edu/faqs.sex.htm (4.1 percent female, 4.9 percent male homosexual experience since 18 years old); Alan Guttmacher Institute, John O. G. Billy et al., *The Sexual Behavior of Men in the United States, Family Planning Perspectives*, The Alan Guttmacher Institute vol. 25, no. 2 (March/April 1993) at http://www.gutmacher.org (2.3 percent male, 20–39 years old in last 10 years and 111 percent exclusively).

96 *See, e.g.*, Nicholas Wade, *Pas de Deux of Sexuality Is Written In the Genes*, N. Y. TIMES D1 (April 10, 2007) (Desire between the sexes is not a matter of choice. Straight men, it seems, have neural circuits that prompt them to seek out women; gay men have those prompting them to seek other men. Women's brains may be organized to select men who seem likely to provide for them and their children. The deal is sealed with other neural programs that induce a burst of romantic love, followed by long-term attachment.").

97 As soon as the California Supreme Court ruled that same-sex couples were constitutionally entitled to be called "married" and receive all of the legal benefits of marriage, referenda were drafted to declare, as a matter of state constitutional law, that marriage was the union of one man and one woman. *See e.g., In re Marriage Cases*, Dkt. No. 147999 (Sup. Ct. Cal. May 15, 2009), available at http://www.courtinfo.ca.gov/opinions/documents/S147999.PDF.

98 TREATISE, *supra* note 5, at 63.

99 FINNIS, *supra* note 10, at 28.

100 *See* GEORGE, *supra* note 72, at 147–51.

101 FINNIS, *supra* note 10, at 44; *see also* FINNIS, "AQUINAS' MORAL, POLITICAL AND LEGAL PHILOSOPHY," *supra* note 39 at § 6.1.

102 FINNIS, AQUINAS, *supra* note 1, at 97–98.

103 GEORGE, *supra* note 72, at 141. *See also* Robert P. George & Gerard Bradley, *Marriage and the Liberal Imagination*, 84 GEO. L. J. 301 (1995). *But see* Stephen Macedo, *Homosexuality and the Conservative Mind*, 84 GEO. L. J. 261 (1995).

104 *See* ROBERT P. GEORGE, THE CLASH OF ORTHODOXIES: LAW, RELIGION, AND MORALITY IN CRISIS 269 (2001), reprinted in GEORGE, *supra* note 72, at ch. 8.

105 GEORGE, *supra* note 72, at 143.

106 ANDREW SULLIVAN, VIRTUALLY NORMAL (1995); Jean Porter, *Human Nature and the Purposes of Marriage* (March 6, 2006).

107 *Id.* at 14–15. Sullivan's book is critically reviewed in GEORGE, THE CLASH OF ORTHODOXIES, *supra* note 104, at ch. 13.

108 *Id.* at 17.

109 *Id.* at 6.

110 See Porter, *supra* note 106.

111 GEORGE, *supra* note 72, at 143.

112 *Id.* at 144.

113 Porter, *supr*a note 106, at 19 ("The reproductive purpose of sex sets a paradigm for understanding sexuality and giving it institutional expression, but that does not necessarily mean that this purpose must be expressed, or even retained as a possibility, in each and every sex act.").

114 GEORGE, *supra* note 72, at 140–47.

115 Kent Greenawalt, *Questions About the Place of Natural Law* in FORTE, *supra* note 80, at 370; *see also* Porter, *supra* note 106, at 18.

116 GEORGE, *supra* note 72, at 145. (George quoting Grisez, "'Even if the mated pair is sterile, intercourse, provided it is the reproductive behavior characteristic of the species, makes the copulating male and female one organism.'")

117 KAINZ, *supra* note 50, at 122.

118 478 U.S. 186 (1986).

119 Any claim that a right to engage in such conduct is "deeply rooted in this Nation's history and tradition" or implicit in the concept of ordered liberty" is, at best, facetious, at 194.

120 *Id.* at 196 (Burger, C.J., concurring).

121 *Id.* at 194.

122 *Id.* at 196.

123 Chief Justice Burger's concurring opinion argued that "decisions of individuals relating to homosexual conduct have been subject to state intervention throughout the history of western civilization. Condemnation of these practices is firmly rooted in Judaeo-Christian moral and ethical standards," at 196.

124 478 U. S. at 199 (citations omitted).

125 WILLIAM N. ESKRIDGE JR., GAYLAW: CHALLENGING THE APARTHEID OF THE CLOSET 150 (1999).

126 *Id.*

127 539 U.S. 558 (2003).

128 539 U.S. at 578.

129 539 U.S. at 562.

130 539 U.S. at 567.

131 *See also* ESKRIDGE, *supra* note 125, at ch. 4.

132 539 U.S. at 568.

133 Note, however, that Justice Scalia had no hesitancy in overruling a precedent that only was 11 years old in another case. *See Hudson* v. *Michigan*, 547 U.S. 1096 (2006).

134 478 U.S. at 216.

135 539 U.S. at 599.

136 539 U.S. at 602.

137 539 U. S. at 603 (Scalia, J., dissenting).

138 478 U.S. at 216 (Stevens, J., dissenting). Justice Stevens that cites *Loving v. Virginia*, 388 U.S. 1 (1967) in support. *Loving* held that miscegenation was once treated as a crime and was no longer constitutional.

Chapter 4 The Ancient Courts of Ancient Men

1 Letter from Niccolò Machiavelli to Francesco Vettori (December 10, 1513), quoted in NICCOLÒ MACHIAVELLI, THE PRINCE 109 (Harvey C. Mansfield trans., 2nd ed. 1998).

2 MAURIZIO VIROLI, NICCOLÒ'S SMILE: A BIOGRAPHY OF MACHIAVELLI ch. 21 (2000).

3 *See* Anthony Grafton, *Introduction* in NICCOLÒ MACHIAVELLI, THE PRINCE xv–xxix (George Bull trans., 1999) in which he discuses the parallels between Machiavelli and Savonarola.

4 Carnes Lord, *Machiavelli's Realism*, in NICCOLO MACHIAVELLI, THE PRINCE 114 (Angelo M. Codevilla trans. and ed., 1997) (hereinafter Codevilla trans.), quoting Frederick the Great, "I have always considered Machiavelli's *Prince* as one of the most dangerous works ever to be disseminated in the world.").

5 *See, e.g.*, LEO STRAUSS, THOUGHTS ON MACHIAVELLI 9 (1958) ("We shall not shock anyone, we shall merely expose ourselves to good-natured or at any rate harmless ridicule, if we profess ourselves inclined to the old-fashioned and simple opinion according to which Machiavelli was a teacher of evil.").

6 STRAUSS, *supra* note 5, at 10.

7 CODEVILLA, *supra* note 4, at vii.

8 MANSFIELD, *supra* note 1, at vii–viii; STRAUSS, *supra* note 5, at 54–55 ("The *Prince* is a scientific book because it conveys a general teaching that is based on reasoning from experience and that sets forth that reasoning. That teaching is partly theoretical (knowledge of the nature of princes) and partly practical (knowledge of the rules with which the prince must comply.").

9 MANSFIELD, *supra* note 1, at 3.

10 *See* HARVEY C. MANSFIELD, MACHIAVELLI'S VIRTUE 8–11(1998 ed.); *see also* JACOB BURCKHARDT, THE CIVILIZATION OF THE RENAISSANCE IN ITALY 59 (Modern Library ed. 1995) ("But of all who thought it possible to construct such a State, the greatest beyond all comparison was Machiavelli. He treats existing force as living and active, takes a large and accurate view of alternative possibilities, and seeks to mislead neither himself or others.").

11 *Compare* Robert Black, *Machiavelli, servant of the Florentine republic*, with John M. Najemy, *The controversy surrounding Machiavelli's service to the republic*, both in GISELA BOCK, QUENTIN SKINNER & MAURIZIO VIROLI (eds.), MACHIAVELLI AND REPUBLICANISM, at respectively 71–99 and 101–117 (1990); *see also* QUENTIN SKINNER, MACHIAVELLI chs. 1 & 2 (1981).

12 In addition to *The Prince*, Machiavelli's historical studies include FLORENTINE HISTORIES (Laura F. Banfield & Harvey C. Mansfield trans., 1990); ART OF WAR (Chirstopher Lynch trans., 2005); DISCOURSES ON LIVY (Harvey C. Mansfield & Nathan Tarcov trans., 1996);THE MANDRAGOLA (Mera J. Flaumenhaft trans., 1981 ed.).

13 MANSFIELD, *supra* note 1, at 61.

14 MANSFIELD, *supra* note 1, at 14.

15 CICERO, THE REPUBLIC THE LAWS (Niall Rudd trans.,1998).

16 ARISTOTLE, NICHOMACHEAN ETHICS (Terence Irwin trans., 1985).

17 W.B. Allen, *Machiavelli and Modernity,* in CODEVILLA, *supra* note 4, at 101.

18 "The name of Machiavelli has become almost the symbol of pure politics. . . . Machiavelli discovers the necessity and autonomy of politics, of politics which is beyond or, rather, below moral good and evil, which has its own laws against which it is useless to rebel, politics that cannot be exorcized and driven from the world with holy water." BENEDETTO CROCE, POLITICS AND MORALS 58–59 (1945).

19 *Contrast* BALDESAAR CASTIGLIONE, THE BOOK OF THE COURTIER (George Bull trans., 1976).

20 MANSFIELD, *supra* note 1, at 3.

21 *Id.* at 4.

22 *Id.*

23 STRAUSS, *supra* note 5, at 56.

24 *Id.* at ch. I and ch. IV.

25 MANSFIELD, *supra* note 1, at 14–15; STRAUSS, *supra* note 5, at 54.

26 STRAUSS, *supra* note 5, at 61–62 ("It is characteristic of the *Prince* to partake of two pairs of opposites: it is both a treatise and a tract for the times, and it has both a traditional exterior and a revolutionary interior.").

27 MANSFIELD, *supra* note 1, at 8.

28 *Id.* at 9.

29 *Id.* at 23.

30 *Id.* at 23 (emphasis added).

31 *Id.* at 24.

32 *Id.* at 27.

33 *Id.* at 32.

34 *Id.* at 30.

35 *Id.* at 32–33.

36 *Id.* at 35.

37 *Id.* at 37–38.

38 *Id.* at 45.

39 *Id.* at 46.

40 *Id.* at 47.

41 *Id.* at 47 n.7.

42 *Id.* at 47.

43 *See* LOUIS ALTHUSSER, MACHIAVELLI AND US (1999 ed.).

44 MANSFIELD, *supra* note 1, at 48.

45 H. L. A. HART, THE CONCEPT OF LAW 6 (1997 ed.).

46 MANSFIELD, *supra* note 1, at 57.

47 *Id.* at 58.

48 *Id.* at 43.

49 MANSFIELD, *supra* note 10, at ch. 1.

50 MANSFIELD, *supra* 1, at xix.

51 SKINNER, *supra* note 11, at 35.

52 MANSFIELD, *supra* note 1, at 61.

53 Id. at 61(emphasis added).

54 CODEVILLA, *supra* note 4 at 57.

55 MANSFIELD, *supra* note 1, at 70.
56 *Id.* at 62.
57 ISAIAH BERLIN, AGAINST THE CURRENT: ESSAYS IN THE HISTORY OF IDEAS 25–79 (1980).
58 MANSFIELD, *supra* note 1, at 61–62.
59 *Id.* at 64
60 *Id.* at 66.
61 *Id.* at 71.
62 *See e.g.,* ANDREW LAWLESS, PLATO'S SUN: AN INTRODUCTION TO PHILOSOPHY 172–76 (2005).
63 "We must not say that divine inspiration is being lowered to the level of *realpolitik* without adding that *realpolitik* is being raised to the level of divine inspiration." J. G. A. POCOCK, THE MACHIAVELLIAN MOMENT: FLORENTINE POLITICAL THOUGHT AND THE ATLANTIC REPUBLICAN TRADITION 171 (1973).
64 *Id.* at 101.
65 *Id.* at 96.
66 *Id.* at 102.
67 *Id.* at 105.
68 The Medici were exiled from Florence from 1494 until 1512. *See, e.g.,* CHRISTOPHER HIBBERT, THE HOUSE OF MEDICI: ITS RISE AND FALL (1974).
69 LAURO MARTINES, FIRE IN THE CITY: SAVONAROLA AND THE STRUGGLE FOR RENAISSANCE FLORENCE 94–95 (2006). *See also* POCOCK, *supra* note 63, at 104 (1973) ("These often lucid and intellectual addresses reveal to the eschatological coexisting with the other modes of expounding the affairs of particular political systems, which our model disposes us to expect as crucial in early modern republican thought."), at 106 ("He came to believe that the church was to be reformed through a spiritual renewal beginning at Florence—apocalyptic thought identifying spiritual history with the secular community—and more important still, he came to equate this renewal with a restoration of republican citizenship.").
70 As one biographer puts it, "The story of Savonarola in Florence is the story of what happened when, as the result of an agreement with one political faction, an apocalyptic preacher became the de facto ruler of the republic—when, in short, religion and politics were allowed to mix." RACHEL ERLANGER, THE UNARMED PROPHET: SAVONAROLA IN FLORENCE 3 (1988).
71 MANSFIELD, *supra* note 1, at 35.
72 *Id.* at 70.
73 MAURIZIO VIROLI, NICCOLÒ'S SMILE: A BIOGRAPHY OF MACHIAVELLI 168 (2000).
74 SEBASTIAN DE GRAZIA, MACHIAVELLI IN HELL 341 (1989).
75 *See e.g.,* Justin Pope (AP), *Backers of Harvard President Cite Politics,* http://www.abcnews.go.com/us/wirestory?id=1664619; Alan Finder, Patrick D. Healy & Kate Zernike, *President of Harvard Resigns Ending Stormy 5-Year Tenure,* N.Y.TIMES A1 (February 22, 2006).
76 John Deutch, *Time to Pull Out. And, Not Just Iraq,* N. Y. TIMES A21 (July 15, 2005).

77 A majority of Americans, for example, were polled as favoring the appointment of a U.S. Supreme Court justice who favors, "allowing displays of the Ten Commandments on government property." *See* Sarah Vowell, *Moses' Top Ten*, N.Y. TIMES A27 (July 16, 2005).

78 "It is a Hobbesian world in which men pursue their own ends without regard to any structures of law . . ." POCOCK, *supra* note 63, at 165 (1975).

79 H. L. A. HART, THE CONCEPT OF LAW 52–53 (2nd ed. 1994).

80 J. L. AUSTIN, THE PROVINCE OF JURISPRUDENCE DETERMINED 13–15 (1832) (1954 ed.).

81 STRAUSS, *supra* note 5, at 62.

82 NICCOLÒ MACHIAVELLI, DISCOURSES ON LIVY (Harvey C. Mansfield & Nathan Tarcov trans., 1996).

83 SKINNER, *supra* note 11, at 64–67.

84 "[M]en conform to the legal norm not because they make it or choose it, but for fear of sanctions if they violate it." DE GRAZIA, *supra* note 74, at 109. *See also* DISCOURSES, *supra* note 82 at 48–52 at which Machiavelli discuses the corruptions of the people and ruler of Rome. In face of corruption, even "well-ordered laws do not help unless indeed they have been put in motion by one individual who with an extreme force ensures their observance so that the matter becomes good," at 48. Machiavelli then notes that he does not know if this has ever happened or if it is even possible.

85 DISCOURSES, *supra* note 82, at 110; SKINNER, *supra* note 11, at 67–73.

86 DISCOURSES, *supra* note 82, at 16, 32.

87 DE GRAZIA, *supra* note 74, at 107. *See also* DISCOURSES, *supra* note 82, at 15 ("Where a thing works well on its own without the law, the law is not necessary; but when some good custom is lacking, at once the law is necessary.").

88 MANSFIELD, *supra* note 1, at 9.

89 *Id.* at 20.

90 *Id.* at 23–25.

91 *Id.* at 48.

92 *Id.* at 50.

93 *Id.* at 73.

94 *Id.* at 69.

95 *Id.* at 69.

96 *See, e.g.,* the opening paragraph of the American Bar Association report, *Task Force on Presidential Signing Statements and the Separation of Powers Doctrine* (July 2006):

> RESOLVED, That the American Bar Association opposes, as contrary to the rule of law and our constitutional system of separation of powers, the issuance of presidential signing statements that claim the authority or state the intention to disregard or decline to enforce all of part of a law the President has signed, or to interpret such a law in a manner inconsistent with the clear intent of Congress.

97 SKINNER, *supra* note 11, at 64–67; VIROLI, *supra* note 2, at ch. 2; *see also* A. J. Parel, *Machiavelli's Notions of Justice*, 10 POLITICAL THEORY 528 (1990).

98 MANSFIELD, *supra* note 1, at 90.

99 *Id.* at 101–05.

100 SKINNER, *supra* note 11, at 65.

101 DISCOURSES, *supra* note 82, at 10–14, 30, 46.

102 VIROLI, *supra* note 2, at ch. 2; BURCKHARDT, *supra* note10, at Part One.

103 IRIS MURDOCH, THE SOVEREIGNTY OF GOOD ch. 2 (2002 ed.).

104 MANSFIELD, *supra* note 1, at 67.

105 "What has pleased the prince has the force of law," quoted in BRIAN TAMANAHA, ON THE RULE OF LAW 13 (2004).

106 *See* ROGER COTTERRELL, THE POLITICS OF JURISPRUDENCE: A CRITICAL INTRODUCTION TO LEGAL PHILOSOPHY ch. 7 (2nd ed. 2003).

107 MANSFIELD, *supra* note 1, at 58–60.

108 Karl Llewellyn, *Some Realism About Realism—a Response to Dean Pound*, 44 HARV. L. REV. 1222 (1931).

109 *But see*DAVID KENNEDY & WILLIAM W. FISHER III (eds.), THE CANON OF AMERICAN LEGAL THOUGHT Part I (2006).

110 *Southern Pacific Co. v. Jensen*, 244 U.S. 205, 222 (Holmes, J., dissenting).

111 Felix S. Cohen, *Transcendental Nonsense and the Functional Approach*, 35 COLUM. L. REV. 809 (1935).

112 JEROME FRANK, LAW AND THE MODERN MIND 6 (1963 ed.).

113 OLIVER WENDELL HOLMES, THE COMMON LAW 5 (1963 ed.).

114 *Id.* at 1.

115 *See, e.g.*, BRIAN BIX, JURISPRUDENCE: THEORY AND CONTEXT 166 (2nd ed. 1999); *see also* Brien Leiter, *American Legal Realism*, in MARTIN GOLDING & WILLIAM EDMUNDSON (eds.), THE BLACKWELL GUIDE TO THE PHILOSOPHY OF LAW AND LEGAL THEORY (2003).

116 KARL LLEWELLYN, THE COMMON LAW TRADITION: DECIDING APPEALS 121–57 (1960).

117 BENJAMIN N. CARDOZO, THE NATURE OF THE JUDICIAL PROCESS 103–04 (1949 ed.).

118 *Roscoe Pound, Mechanical* Jurisprudence, 8 COLUM. L. REV. 605 (1908).

119 *See Rapanos v. United States*, 547 U. S.715 (2006) in which the Court split 5–4 on exactly this issue.

120 Compare the majority and dissenting opinions in *Hernandez v. Robles*, 7 N.Y. 3d 338 (2006).

121 *See* COTTRRELL, *supra* note 106, at 178.

122 LLEWELLYN, *supra* note 116, at 509–10.

123 *Id.* at 23.

124 RONALD DWORKIN, *Justice in Robes* 244 (2006).

125 *See* GLENN M. ANDRES, JOHN M. HUNISAK & A. RICHARD TURNER II, THE ART OF FLORENCE (1994) ("probably the single most famous sculpture ever created") (965) ("Michelangelo's *David* crystallizes a conception of young manhood idealized and raised to godlike status in the manner of ancient statues.") (966) ("The triumphant David, standing at the entrance to the seat of government became an emblem of the Florentine republic.") (967). *See also* GEORGIO VASARI, THE LIVES OF THE ARTISTS 427 (Julia Conaway Bondanella & Peter Bondanell

trans., 1998 ed.) ("Thus, Michelangelo did a wax model depicting a young David with a sling in hand, as the symbol of the palace, for just as David had defended his people and governed them with justice, so, too, those governed this city should courageously defend it and govern it with justice. . . .").

126 ISAIAH BERLIN, AGAINST THE CURRENT: ESSAYS IN THE HISTORY OF IDEAS 44 (1980).

127 HANS KELSEN, THE PURE THEORY OF LAW 64 (1978 ed.).

128 BERLIN, *supra* note 126, at 43.

Chapter 5 Law Breaking

1 "In truth, the numbers of runaway slaves who were not returned to their masters within 12 months appeared to have numbered several hundred annually, perhaps as many as a thousand, by the early 1850's. . . ." This number contrasts with estimations of over 60,000 escaped slaves between 1810 and 1850. SEAN WILENTZ, THE RISE OF AMERICAN DEMOCRACY: JEFFERSON TO LINCOLN 648 (2005).

2 *See, e.g.,* DAVID W. BLIGHT, A SLAVE NO MORE: TWO MEN WHO ESCAPED TO FREEDOM, INCLUDING THEIR OWN NARRATIVES OF EMANCIPATION, (2007); *see also* ANN HAGEDORN, BEYOND THE RIVER: THE UNTOLD STORY OF THE HEROES OF THE UNDERGROUND RAILROAD (2002).

3 HARRIET BEECHER STOWE, UNCLE TOM'S CABIN, VOL. I, Chs. ix–xii (pp. 67–115) (Norton Critical Edition, 1994).

4 JOAN D. HEDRICK, HARRIET BEECHER STOWE: A LIFE vi (1994).

5 JAMES MCPHERSON, BATTLE CRY OF FREEDOM: THE CIVIL WAR ERA 88 (1988).

6 The Massachusetts Anti-Slavery Society charter, written by abolitionist William Lloyd Garrison, read: "Resolved, that the compact which exists between the North and the South is a covenant with death and an agreement with hell—involving both parties in atrocious criminality—and should be immediately annulled." Available at http://www.fff.org/freedom/fd0307f.asp.

7 *See* DON FEHRENBACHER, THE SLAVE HOLDING REPUBLIC: AN ACCOUNT OF THE UNITED STATES GOVERNMENT'S RELATIONS TO SLAVERY (Ward M. McAfee ed., 2001).

8 *See generally* PETER KOLCHIN, AMERICAN SLAVERY 1619–1877 (1993).

9 PAULINE MAIER, AMERICAN SCRIPTURE: MAKING THE DECLARATION OF INDEPENDENCE 120 (1997).

10 *Id.* at 146.

11 WILLIAM M. WEICEK, THE SOURCES OF ANTI-SLAVERY CONSTITUTIONALISM IN AMERICAN, 1760–1848, 62–63 (1977).

12 U.S. CONST., Art. I, Sec. 1, Cl. 3.

13 U.S. CONST., Art. I, Sec 9, Cl. 1.

14 U.S. CONST., Art. IV, Sec. 1, Cl. 3; *see also* AKHIL REED AMAR, AMERICA'S CONSTITUTION: A BIOGRAPHY 256–64 (2005).

15 WIECEK, *supra* note 11, at 98.

16 *Prigg v. Pennsylvania,* 16 Pet. (41 U.S.) 539 (1842).

17 *See, e.g.,* Christopher L. M. Eisgruber, *Justice Story, Slavery, and the Natural law Foundations of American Constitutionalism,* 55 UNIV. OF CHI. L. REV. 273, 297 n. 21 (1988).
18 *Prigg, supra* note 16, at 611.
19 *Id.* at 612.
20 *Id.* at 611.
21 *Somerset's Case,* quoted in ROBERT M. COVER, JUSTICE ACCUSED: ANTISLAVERY AND THE JUDICIAL PROCESS 17 (1975).Available at http://medicolegal.tripod.com/somersetvstewart.htm.
22 WILENTZ, *supra* note 1, at 648.
23 Parallels between Fugitive Slave Acts of 1793 and 1850 and today's treatment of enemy combatants at Guantanamo Bay are multiple. Fugitive slaves and enemy combatants were denied any or all of the following rights: right to a jury trial; right to counsel; right to habeas corpus; right to know the charges against them; right to confront evidence; right to contest one's status as a fugitive slave or an enemy combatant; and, the right not to be held for unlimited detention without charges. *See* the discussion of *Boumediene v. Bush,* 476 F. 3d 981 (D.C. Cir. 2007), in Chapter 6, *infra.*
24 MCPHERSON, *supra* note 5, at 78–79.
25 *Id.* at 80.
26 HEDRICK, *supra* note 4, at 206–07.
27 Harriet Beecher Stowe, *The Free Man's Dream: A Parable,* NATIONAL ERA, August 1, 1850.
28 HARRIET BEECHER STOWE, THE KEY TO UNCLE TOM'S CABIN VI (reprint ed. 1987) (1854). In response to critics of *Uncle Tom's Cabin,* Harriet Beecher Stowe planned on writing a brief statement about her sources. The result, however, was a 500-page detailed list of her research for the book. The subtitle of THE KEY is revealing, "presenting the original facts and documents upon which the story is founded, together with corroborative statements verifying the truth of the work."
29 The quotations in this section appear in STOWE, *supra* note 3, at 67–80.
30 Ferenc M. Szasz, *Antebellum Appeals to the "Higher Law," 1830–60,* ESSEX INSTITUTE HISTORICAL COLLECTION 33, 47 (1974).
31 *See, e.g.,* HARRIET BEECHER STOWE, THE ANNOTATED UNCLE TOM'S CABIN (Henry Louis Gates, Jr. & Hollis Robbins eds., 2007). See Introduction at xi–xxx.
32 STOWE, KEY, *supra* note 28, at 381–404.
33 *Id.* at 34–36; HAGEDORN, *supra* note 2, at 138–39 (2002). Hagedorn tells the story of John Rankin, a conductor on the Underground Railroad in Ripley, Ohio.
34 STOWE, KEY, *supra* note 28, at 381.
35 For an intellectual history of the Great Separation *see* MARK LILLA, STILLBORN GOD: RELIGION, POLITICS, AND THE MODERN WEST (2007).
36 STOWE, KEY, *supra* note 28, at 384.
37 *Id.*
38 *Id.* at 385.
39 ALBERT J. RABOTEAU, SLAVE RELIGION: THE "INVISIBLE INSTITUTION" IN THE ANTEBELLUM SOUTH 152 (1978).

40 *Id.* at 390.
41 *Id.* at 391.
42 STOWE, KEY, *supra* note 28, at 466.
43 *Id.* at 493.
44 *Id.* at 497.
45 The quotations in this section appear in STOWE, UNCLE TOM'S CABIN, *supra* note 3, at 81–89.
46 The quotations in this section appear in STOWE, UNCLE TOM'S CABIN, *supra* note 3, at 100–115.
47 WILENTZ, *supra* note 1, at 656–57.
48 RABOTEAU, *supra* note 39, argues that the religious practices of the slaves gave them sustenance and community and were not only an instrument of repression.
49 ERNST J. GAINES, A LESSON BEFORE DYING (1997).
50 HEDRICK, *supra* note 4, at 102–03.
51 STOWE, UNCLE TOM'S CABIN, *supra* note 3, at 89–100.
52 *See* ROBERT M. COVER, JUSTICE ACCUSED: ANTI-SLAVERY AND THE JUDICIAL PROCESS 62 & 125 (1975).
53 PLATO, FIVE DIALOGUES: EUTHYPHRO, APOLOGY, CRITO, MENO, PHAEDO (G. M. A. Grube trans., 1981).
54 *See* EDWIN S. CORWIN, THE "HIGHER LAW" BACKGROUND OF AMERICAN CONSTITUTIONAL LAW (1955 ed.); *see also* Eisgruber, *supra* note 17, (discussing Justice Joseph Story's natural law basis for his opinion in *Prigg v. Pennsylvania* and Dworkin's criticism of Story); Ronald Dworkin, *Law of Slave-catchers*, TIMES LITERARY SUPPLEMENT 1437 (December 5, 1975); RONALD DWORKIN, LAW'S EMPIRE (1986) (on political morality and constitutional interpretation generally).
55 *Dred Scott v. Sandford*, 60 U.S. 393 (1857). *See also* DON FEHRENBACHER, THE DRED SCOTT CASE: ITS SIGNIFICANCE IN AMERICAN LAW AND POLITICS (1978).
56 *Id.* at 407.
57 *Id.* at 451.
58 *See* MARK GRABER, DRED SCOTT AND THE PROBLEM OF CONSTITUTIONAL EVIL (2006).
59 Paul Finkelman, Scott v. Sandford, *The Courts' Most Dreadful Case and How It Changed History*, 82 CHI-KENT L. REV. 3 (2007).
60 *Thomas Sims's Case*, 61 Mass. 285 (1851).
61 COVER, JUSTICE ACCUSED, *supra* note 52, at 6.
62 *Id.* at 2–6.
63 Leonard W. Levy, *Sims's Case: The Fugitive Slave Law in Boston in 1851*, 35 J. NEGRO HISTORY 39, 40 (1950).
64 *Id.* at 43.
65 *Id.* at 46.
66 *Id.* at 47.
67 *Id.*
68 One avenue open to antebellum anti-slavery judges was the avenue offered by the anti-slavery lawyers—read and apply the fugitive slave laws narrowly or ascribe procedural safeguards to the hearings. As examples, a warrant may be defective, the court may lack jurisdiction, the fugitive may have a right to be

heard, etc. Cover demonstrates that judges did not take this route. Regarding such tactics he writes: "Such side tracks could be avoided only by asserting an alternative formal (legal) principle that either maintained the identity of moral and legal imperative through requiring the law to conform to some "natural law," or presumed the identity of law and morality subject only to explicit defeasance by express legislative action." COVER, *supra* note 52, at 199. Cover's judges found the alternative moral principle not in the natural law of individual equality, but in the positive law of the Constitution's compromise with evil. They believed that they could not do otherwise. After all, slaves were not citizens; that was what the whole fight was about.

Cover's "side-tracks," he argues, could be interpreted not as naked evasions of the law but as consonant with the political morality of the Constitution and the Founding. Dworkin's argument, *see supra* note 54, may have let the judges sleep only a little better at night but he (and they) must then respond to the argument about the noncitizen status of slaves. The Constitution explicitly denied them citizenship; to now argue that they have citizenship rights of habeas corpus or due process or the like undercuts the fundamental deal cut in Philadelphia in 1787.

69 Previously in *Commonwealth v. Aves*, 18 Pick. 193, Shaw held that a slave who voluntarily came into a free state such as Massachusetts with his master was not subject to Article IV of the U.S. Constitution because they were not fugitive and did not escape from slavery.

70 *See Boumediene v. Bush*, 476 F. 3d 981 (D.C. Cir. 2007). The denial of habeas corpus relief was overturned by the Supreme Court in *Boumediene v. Bush*, 553 U.S. _____ (2008).

71 SZASZ, *supra* note 30, at 33.

72 *See* DAVID BRION DAVIS, THE PROBLEM OF SLAVERY IN THE AGE OF REVOLUTION 1770–1823. 11 (1975).

73 COVER, JUSTICE ACCUSED, *supra* note 52, at 62 & 125.

74 *See* BRUCE ACKERMAN, WE THE PEOPLE: FOUNDATIONS (1991); BRUCE ACKERMAN, WE THE PEOPLE: TRANSFORMATIONS (1998); *See also* Bruce Ackerman, *Higher Law Making*, in SANFORD LEVINSON (ed.), RESPONDING TO IMPERFECTION: THE THEORY AND PRACTICE OF CONSTITUTIONAL AMENDMENT, ch. 4 (1995); CORWIN, *supra* note 54.

75 Robert M. Cover, *Forward:* Nomos *and Narrative*, 97 HARV. L. REV. 4 (1983) (footnotes omitted).

76 *Id.* at 5 (footnote omitted).

77 *Id.* at 9.

78 Cover labels this creation of legal meaning "jurisgenesis." *See id.* at 11–19. Cover draws inspiration from this creation of meaning from scholars writing both about the Old Testament and the New Testament.

79 *Id.* at 19.

80 Robert M. Cover, *Violence and the Word*, 95 YALE L. J. 1601 (1986). Cover's critics point out that as ugly as violence is, it can, and has, operated in the service of justice and we can point to the Civil War as well as the civil rights movement as

examples. *See* Martha Minow, *Interpreting Rights: An Essay for Robert Cover*, 96 YALE L. J. 1960 (1987); Austin Sarat (ed.), LAW, VIOLENCE, AND THE POSSIBILITY OF JUSTICE (2001). *See also* DAVID KENNEDY & WILLIAM W. FISHER III, "ROBERT COVER, IN DAVID KENNEDY & WILLIAM W. FISHER (eds.) THE CANNON OF AMERICAN LEGAL THOUGHT, 735–51 (2006).

81 Cover, *id.* at 1607.

82 Cover, *Nomos,* and Narrative, *supra* note 75, at 35.

83 *See* BENJAMIN FLETCHER WRIGHT JR., AMERICAN INTERPRETATIONS OF NATURAL LAW: A STUDY IN THE HISTORY OF POLITICAL THOUGHT (1962); CORWIN, *supra* note 54.

84 STEPHEN L. CARTER, GOD'S NAME IN VAIN: THE WRONGS AND RIGHTS OF RELIGION AND POLITICS, 83 (2000).

85 WIECEK, *supra* note 11, at ch. 11.

86 Cover, *Nomos and Narrative, supra* note 75, at 39.

87 COVER, JUSTICE ACCUSED, *supra* note 52, at 250.

88 JOHN LOCKE, THE SECOND TREATISE ON CIVIL GOVERNMENT ¶¶ 220–21 (Prometheus Books ed., 1986).

89 Ackerman argues that the country has experienced three constitutional transformations—the Founding, Reconstruction, and the New Deal. *See* BRUCE ACKERMAN, WE THE PEOPLE: FOUNDATIONS (1991); BRUCE ACKERMAN, WE THE PEOPLE: TRANSFORMATIONS (1998); *See also* Bruce Ackerman, *Higher Law Making*, in SANFORD LEVINSON (ed.), RESPONDING TO IMPERFECTION: THE THEORY AND PRACTICE OF CONSTITUTIONAL AMENDMENT ch. 4 (1995).

90 BRUCE ACKERMAN, WE THE PEOPLE: TRANSFORMATIONS, *id.* at 115.

91 BRUCE ACKERMAN, WE THE PEOPLE: FOUNDATIONS, *supra* note 90, at 266.

92 *See also* MARTHA NUSSBAUM, THE LIBERTY OF CONSCIENCE (2007).

93 *See, e.g.*, MICHAEL PERRY, UNDER GOD? RELIGIOUS FAITH AND LIBERAL DEMOCRACY (2003) MICHAEL J. PERRY, RELIGION IN POLITICS (1997); CARTER, *supra* note 84; STEPHEN L. CARTER, THE CULTURE OF DISBELIEF: HOW AMERICAN LAW AND POLITICS TRIVIALIZE RELIGIOUS DEVOTION (1994).

94 Transcript of Sen. Obama's March 18, 2008 speech at the National Constitution Center in Philadelphia, Pennsylvania. Available at http://www.cnn.com/2008/POLITICS/03/18/obama.transcript/index.html?iref=newssearch.

Chapter 6 Law's Practical Theory

1 The enduring significance of this remarkable essay is confirmed by the several symposia held on its centenary. *See, e.g.*, Symposium, *The Path of the Law 100 Years Later: Holmes's Influence on Modern Jurisprudence*, 63 BROOK. L. REV. 1 (1997); Symposium, *The Path of the Law Today*, 78 B.U. L. REV. 691 (1998); Symposium, *The Path of the Law After One Hundred Years*, 110 HARV. L. REV. 989 (1997); *see also THE PATH OF THE LAW* AND ITS INFLUENCE: THE LEGACY OF OLIVER WENDELL HOLMES, JR. (Steven J. Burton ed., 2000). For a description of the occasion, *see* David J. Seipp, *Holmes's Path*, 77 B.U. L. REV. 515 (1997).

2 Letter from Oliver Wendell Holmes to Clare Fitzpatrick, Lady Castleton (Jan. 11, 1897) quoted in Symposium, *The Path of the Law After 100 Years: Introduction*, 110 HARV. L. REV. 989 (1997).

3 Mark DeWolfe Howe, *The Positivism of Mr. Justice Holmes*, 64 HARV. L. REV. 529 (1951) (positivist); JEROME FRANK, LAW AND THE MODERN MIND 253–60, (1930) (realist); John Dewey, *Justice Holmes and the Liberal Mind*, in MR. JUSTICE HOLMES (Felix Frankfurter ed., 1921) (liberal); ALBERT W. ALSCHULER, LAW WITHOUT VALUES: THE LIFE, WORK AND LEGACY OF JUSTICE HOLMES (2000) (cynic).

4 *See* CATHERINE DRINKER BOWEN, YANKEE FROM OLYMPUS (1944).

5 SHELDON M. NOVICK, HONORABLE JUSTICE: THE LIFE OF OLIVER WENDELL HOLMES (1989); G. EDWARD WHITE, JUSTICE OLIVER WENDELL HOLMES: LAW AND THE INNER SELF (1993); LIVA BAKER, THE JUSTICE FROM BEACON HILL: THE LIFE AND TIMES OF OLIVER WENDELL HOLMES (1991).

6 Holmes's contribution to classical pragmatism and his active membership in the Metaphysical Club have been questioned. Nevertheless, Holmes's legal pragmatism greatly informed his theory of the law. *See, e.g.,* LOUIS MENAND, THE METAPHYSICAL CLUB (2001); Thomas C. Grey, *Holmes and Legal Positivism*, 41 STAN. L. REV. 787, 864–70 (1989) (Appendix, *Holmes and the Pragmatists*).

7 Seipp, *supra* note 1, at 534–35.

8 Thomas C. Grey, *Holmes and Legal Pragmatism*, 41 STAN. L. REV. 787 (1989); Thomas C. Grey, *Plotting The Path of the Law*, 63 BROOK. L. REV. 19 (1997); Thomas C. Grey, *Molecular Motions: The Holmesian Judge in Theory and Practice*, 37 WM. & MARY L. REV. 19 (1995). *See also* Thomas C. Grey, *Freestanding Legal Positivism*, THE REVIVAL OF PRAGMATISM: NEW ESSAYS ON SOCIAL THOUGHT, LAW AND CULTURE 255 (Morris Dickstein ed., 1998).

9 Grey, *Plotting*, *supra* note 8, at 27–29.

10 Pragmatism is a word of many meanings. Susan Haack lists 20 definitions of pragmatism in her paper, Susan Haack, *On Legal Pragmatism: Where Does "The Path of the Law" Lead Us?*, 50 AM. J. JURIS. 71 (2005); to that we can add the three schools of philosophical pragmatism as the classical school of Pierce, Dewey, and James, the neo-pragmatists such as Rorty, and the radical pragmatism of Roberto Unger. A useful compendium of classical and neo-classical pragmatism can be found in PRAGMATISM: A READER (Louis Menand ed., 1997); for radical pragmatism *see* ROBERTO UNGER, THE SELF AWAKENED: PRAGMATISM UNBOUND (2007).

Legal pragmatism shares some of the general attributes of philosophical pragmatism but does not involve itself with more abstract philosophical issues such as issues of language and reality, free will and determinism, and the like. *See, e.g.,* Thomas C. Grey, *Freestanding Legal Pragmatism*, *supra* note 8, at 254, 259. Instead, legal pragmatism is intended to serve less as theory of how the world does or ought to function and more as an accurate description of how law is best practiced and then as a useful guide for practicing it. *See also* THE INTERNET ENCYCLOPEDIA OF PHILOSOPHY, *Legal Pragmatism* at http://www.iep.utm.edu/l/leglprag.htm; Brian E. Butler, *Legal Pragmatism: Banal or Beneficial as*

A Jurisprudential Position?, in ESSAYS IN PHILOSOPHY, at http://www.humboldt.edu/~essays/butler.html.

11 I distinguish the term "inside" from how H. L. A. Hart uses "internal" to convey his particular positivist view of law. *See* H. L. A. HART, THE CONCEPT OF THE LAW, 89–91 (2ND ed. 1997). I use inside or internal to mean law as viewed from a participant (lawyer or judge, student or citizen). Such an "inside" view is largely, but not exclusively, descriptive. The external or outsider view of law is the view of an observer who wishes to make evaluative comments about law. *See* ROBERT ALEXY, THE ARGUMENT FROM INJUSTICE: A REPLY TO LEGAL POSITIVISM, 25 (2002) (*internal* as a participant's perspective; *external* as an observer's).

This usage differs significantly from Hart's and I want to avoid confusion. The necessary component of Hart's internal point of view is a normative idea that a person inside a legal rules system "accepts and uses them as guides to conduct," or as "a standard of behavior and an obligation," and is "the way in which the group regards its own behavior." *See* THE CONCEPT OF THE LAW at 89–91. *See also* Scott J. Schapiro, *What is the Internal Point of View?*, 75 FORDHAM L. REV. 1157 (2006). *See generally* Symposium, *The Internal Point of View in Law and Ethics*, 75 FORDHAM L. REV. 1143 (2006); *compare* Stephen R. Perry, *Holmes v. Hart: The Bad Man in Legal Theory in Burton*, in THE PATH OF THE LAW AND ITS INFLUENCE, *supra* note 1, at 158; *with* Scott J. Shapiro, *The Bad Man in the Internal Point of View*," in THE PATH OF THE LAW AND ITS INFLUENCE, *supra* note 1, at 197.

12 Grey, *Holmes and Legal Pragmatism*, *supra* note 8, at 830–44.

13 Oliver Wendell Holmes, *The Path of the Law*, 110 Harv. L. Rev. 991 (1997) (hereinafter *The Path*) at 1006.

14 *The Path*, *id.* at 991.

15 *See* Grey, *Holmes and Legal Pragmatism*, *supra* note 8, at 82.

16 *See e.g.*, Susan Haack, *On Legal Pragmatism: Where Does "The Path of the Law" Lead Us?* 50 AM. J. JURIS. 71, 81 (2005) (". . . Holmes's briskly practical opening and his visionary closing are seamlessly integrated.").

17 *The Path*, *supra* note 13, at 992.

18 *See* David Luban, *The Bad Man and the Good Lawyer*, in THE PATH OF THE LAW AND ITS INFLUENCE, *supra* note 1, at 33, 43–44 (2000) (criticizing the bad man as a heuristic device for law study).

19 *See also* OLIVER WENDELL HOLMES, THE COMMON LAW (Mark DeWolfe Howe ed., 1963).

20 *The Path*, *supra* note 13, at 995.

21 *But see* CHARLES FRIED, CONTRACT AS PROMISE; A THEORY OF CONTRACTUAL OBLIGATION (1981).

22 *The Path*, *supra* note 13, at 994.

23 Perry, *supra* note 11, at 159 and *passim*.

24 *The Path*, *supra* note 13, at 992.

25 *See, e.g.*, MICHAEL HOFFHEIMER, JUSTICE HOLMES AND THE NATURAL LAW (1992).

26 On Holmes and logic, *compare* Scott Brewer, *Traversing Holmes's Path Toward a Jurisprudence of Logical Form*, *in* THE PATH OF THE LAW AND ITS INFLUENCE,

supra note 1, at 94 with Thomas C. Grey, *Holmes on the Logic of the Law,* in THE PATH OF THE LAW AND ITS INFLUENCE, *supra* note 1, at 133.

27 HOLMES, *supra* note 19, at 5.

28 *The Path, supra* note 13, at 997.

29 HOLMES-POLLOCK LETTERS 17 (Mark DeWolfe Howe ed., 1941) (Letter of April 10, 1881). (Holmes's criticism of Langdell).

30 *The Path, supra* note 13, at 998.

31 EDWARD H. LEVI, AN INTRODUCTION TO LEGAL REASONING (1948).

32 *The Path, supra* note 13, at 998.

33 *Id.*

34 *Id.*

35 *Id.* at 999.

36 *Id.*

37 *Id.* at 1000.

38 *The Path, supra* note 13, at 1001.

39 *Id.*

40 *Id.*

41 *Id* at 1005.

42 Grey, *Plotting, supra* note 8, at 43.

43 *The Path, supra* note 13, at 1007.

44 *Id.* at 1009.

45 JOHN DONNE, SELECTED POEMS (2006).

46 *See* G. EDWARD WHITE, JUSTICE OLIVER WENDELL HOLMES: LAW AND THE INNER SELF (no full theory of the law); Thomas C. Grey, *Molecular Motions, supra* note 8 (no full theory of judging).

47 Jurisprudents and philosophers of law who engage grand or unified theories of law do so from the outside and their external perceptions of law may be become so embedded in philosophical categories so as to miss the practical dimension of law. *See e.g.,* Jules Coleman, *Against Jurisprudence: Preliminary Reflections* (November 22, 2006), at http://www.law.upenn.edu/academics/institutes/ilp/2006papers/Coleman-AgainstJurisprudence.pdf.

48 Grey, *Plotting, supra* note 8, at 19–20.

49 Learned Hand, *Mr. Justice Holmes,* 43 HARV. L. REV. 857 (1930).

50 *See also* Thomas C. Grey, *Holmes on the Logic of the Law, supra* note 26, at 136–38.

51 Again, we encounter a classic Holmes aphorism:

> The felt necessities of the time, the prevalent moral and political theories, institutions of public policy, avowed or unconscious, even the prejudices which judges share with their fellow-men, have had a good deal more to do than the syllogism in determining how men should be governed.

HOLMES, *supra* note 19, at 5; *See also* Grey, *Plotting, supra* note 8, at 52.

52 Grey, *Holmes and Legal Pragmatism, supra* note 8, at 800.

53 Grey, *Molecular Motions, supra* note 8, at 27.

54 *Id.* at 22, 36, 45.

55 *Id.* at 805.

56 RICHARD A. POSNER, THE PROBLEMATICS OF MORAL AND LEGAL THEORY 241 (1999). Posner calls such a judge a "rule pragmatist."

57 *See, e.g.*, Law "is better, though not fully, described as an activity of the licensed professionals we call judges." RICHARD A. POSNER, THE PROBLEMS OF JURISPRUDENCE 456–57 (1990).

58 *See* POSNER, PROBLEMATICS, *supra* note 56, at chs. 3 & 4.

59 *Id.* at 207.

60 POSNER, PROBLEMATICS, *supra* note 56, at 227.

61 RICHARD A. POSNER, LAW, PRAGMATISM, AND DEMOCRACY 59–85 (2003).

62 RICHARD A. POSNER, HOW JUDGES THINK ch. 9 (2008).

63 *See, e.g.*, "The ingredients of reasonableness include, but are not exhausted in, conventional legal materials such as precedence and the principles for using precedence. Often the judge will have no choice but to reason to the outcome by non-legal methods from non-legal materials, and sometimes he will have to set inarticulate intuition against legal arguments." POSNER, PROBLEMS OF JURISPRUDENCE, *supra* note 57, at 456.

64 *Id.* at 457.

65 POSNER, LAW, PRAGMATISM, AND DEMOCRACY, *supra* note 61, at 64.

66 Thomas C. Grey, *The New Legal Formalism* available at http://ssrn.com/abstract=200732.

67 *See* Richard A. Posner, *The Problematics of Moral and Legal Theory*, 111 HARV. L. REV. 1638 (1998) and *compare* Martha Nussbaum, *Still Worthy of Praise*, 111 HARV. L. REV. 1776 (1998). *See generally* POSNER, PROBLEMATICS, *supra* note 56.

68 POSNER, PROBLEMATICS, *supra* note 56, at 242.

69 RICHARD A. POSNER, OVERCOMING LAW 400–01 (1996).

70 POSNER, LAW, PRAGMATISM, AND DEMOCRACY, *supra* note 61, at 49–56.

71 *See also id. at* 84–85 for a summary of Posnerian pragmatism.

72 *See* Andrew J. Morriss, *Some Challenges for Legal Pragmatism: A Closer Look at Legal Reasoning* (March 1, 2007). Available at SSRN: http://ssrn.com/abstract=967440.

73 Regarding criticism of legal pragmatism, *see* RONALD DWORKIN, JUSTICE IN ROBES 60–65 and ch. 3 (2006); John F. Manning, *Statutory Pragmatism and Constitutional Structure*, 120 HARV. L. REV. 1161 (2007); *see also* POSNER, LAW, DEMOCRACY AND PRAGMATISM, *supra* note 61, at 93–96; POSNER, PROBLEMATICS, *supra* note 56, at 255–56.

74 *See, e.g.*, "This account should help us see why internal 'truth' is a problematic concept for a pragmatist . . . The pragmatists real interest is not in truth at all but in belief justified by social need." POSNER, PROBLEMS OF JURISPRUDENCE, *supra* note 57, at 464; *see also* William James, *Pragmatism's Conception of Truth* in PRAGMATISM (1907).

75 *The Path, supra* note 13, at 991.

76 Among the judges Posner names as pragmatists include Holmes, Brandeis, Cardozo, Frankfurter, Jackson, Douglas, Brennan, Powell, Stevens, White, and Breyer. *See* POSNER, PROBLEMATICS, *supra* note 56, at 240. Among the scholars Posner lists as pragmatists are Cass Sunstein, Richard Rorty, Cornel West,

William Eskridge, Thomas Grey, Martha Minnow, Daniel Farber, among others. *See* POSNER, OVERCOMING LAW, *supra* note 69, at 389; regarding Dworkin, *see also* POSNER, PROBLEMATICS, *supra* note 56, at 252–55.

77 POSNER, PROBLEMATICS, *supra* note 56, at 242.

78 *See Boumediene v. Bush*, 476 F.3d 981 (2007). For denial of the writ of certiorari, *see Boumediene v. Bush*, 549 U.S. __ (2007) (Stevens, J. and Kennedy J., statement respecting the denial of certiorari) and *Boumediene v. Bush*, 549 U.S. __ (2007) (Breyer, J., dissenting).

I drafted these moot court opinions before the Supreme Court issued its decision in *Boumediene v. Bush*, 553 U.S. ___ (slip op. June 12, 2008). The Court decided in favor of the detainees in a 5–4 decision with the Court's opinion written by Justice Kennedy who adopts the Holmesian analysis with a dissent by Roberts and Scalia which parallels the Posnerian analysis.

79 RICHARD A. POSNER, NOT A SUICIDE PACT: THE CONSTITUTION IN A TIME OF NATIONAL EMERGENCY 1 (2006).

80 U.S. CONST, art. I sec. 9, cl. 2.

81 *See, e.g., Rasul v. Bush*, 542 U.S. 466 (2004).

82 *Id.*

83 POSNER, NOT A SUICIDE PACT, *supra* note 79, at 60–62.

84 *Id.* at 54.

85 *See* Adrian Vermeule, *Posner on Security and Liberty: Alliance to End Repression v. City of Chicago*, 120 HARV. L. REV. 1251 (2007).

86 *See* RICHARD A. POSNER, UNCERTAIN SHIELD; THE U.S. INTELLIGENT SYSTEM IN THE THROWS OF REFORM (2006); RICHARD A. POSNER, REINVENTING SURPRISE ATTACKS: INTELLIGENCE REFORM IN THE WAKE OF 9/11 (2005); RICHARD A. POSNER, REMAKING DOMESTIC INTELLIGENCE (2005); *See also* RICHARD A. POSNER, CATASTROPHE: RISK AND RESPONSE (2004).

87 POSNER, NOT A SUICIDE PACT, *supra* note 79, at ch.1.

88 *Id.* at ch. 2.

89 The facts recited here are found in petition for a Writ of Certiorari, *Boumediene v. Bush*, U.S. Sup. Ct. Dkt. No. 06—____(2007).

90 *See* Haack, *supra* note 10, at 54–57.

91 Grey, *Molecular Motions*, *supra* note 8, at 27.

92 *See* JACK GOLDSMITH, THE TERROR PRESIDENCY: LAW AND JUDGMENT INSIDE THE BUSH ADMINISTRATION (2007).

93 *See* William Glaberson, *Court Asked to Limit Lawyers at Guantanamo*, N.Y. TIMES, Apr. 26, 2007.

94 *See, e.g.*, Mark DeWolfe Howe, *The Positivism of Mr. Justice Holmes*, 64 HARV. L. REV. 529, 530 (1951) (Quoting Westbrook Pegler's remark of Holmes as a "cynical and senile brutalitarian."); *see also* ALBERT W. ALSCHULER, LIFE WITHOUT VALUES: THE LIFE, WORK, AND LEGACY OF JUSTICE HOLMES (2000).

95 *The Path*, *supra* note 13, at 1009.

96 *Oliver Wendell Holmes, The Profession of the Law in* THE COLLECTED LEGAL PAPERS 29–32 (1921).

Chapter 7 Timeliness and Justice

1 *See* TAYLOR BRANCH, PARTING THE WATERS: AMERICA IN THE KING YEARS, 1954–63, 725–40 (1988); MARTIN LUTHER KING, JR., WHY WE CAN'T WAIT (2000). *See also* Lee W. Bains, *Birmingham 1963: Confrontation Over Civil Rights* in DAVID J. GARROW (ed.), MARTIN LUTHER KING, JR. AND THE CIVIL RIGHTS MOVEMENT (1989).

2 *Brown* v. *Board of Education*, 347 U.S. 483 (1954).

3 *Brown* v. *Board of Education*, 349 U.S. 294, 301 (1955).

4 *See* John Hart Ely, *The Supreme Court 1977 Term: Foreword: On Discovering Fundamental Values*, 92 HARV. L. REV. 5 (1978).

5 BRANCH, *supra* note 1, at chs. 4 & 5. Rosa Parks consented to becoming a plaintiff in a civil rights lawsuit which successfully ended with the U.S. Supreme Court declaring that segregated buses were unconstitutional. *Owen* v. *Browder*, 352 U.S. 903 (1956).

6 The wording of the injunction can be found in *Walker v. City of Birmingham*, 388 U.S. 307 (1967) (Brennan, J., dissenting).

7 BRANCH, *supra* note 1, at 731.

8 KING, *supra* note 1, at 57. King adds "[w]e did not take this radical step without prolonged and prayerful consideration."

9 David Luban writes that the letter conforms closely in style to that of St. Paul's Epistles as he provides a description of the religious references in the letter in addition to a political reading. *See* David Luban, *Difference Made Legal: The Court and Dr. King*, 87 MICH. L. REV. 2152, 2193–95 (1989). For another interpretation of the history of the *Letter*, *see* S. JONATHAN BASS, BLESSED ARE THE PEACEMAKERS: MARTIN LUTHER KING, JR., EIGHT WHITE RELIGIOUS LEADERS, AND THE "LETTER FOR A BIRMINGHAM JAIL" ch. 6 (2001).

10 *See* http://www.hoboes.com/html/FireBlade/Politics/niemoller.shtml.

11 Pub. L. No. 88–352, 78 Stat. 241 (1964).

12 *See generally* TAYLOR BRANCH, PILLAR OF FIRE: AMERICA IN THE KING YEARS, 1963–65 (1998).

13 42 U.S.C. § 1973aa-6.

14 *Reynolds v. Sims*, 377 U.S. 533 (1964).

15 *Bush v. Gore*, 531 U.S. 98 (2000).

16 *See, e.g., The League of United Latin American Citizens v. Perry*, 548 U.S. 399 (2006).

17 *See, e.g., Crawford* v. *Marion County Election Board*, 553 U.S. ____ (2008) (Petitioners argue that Indiana's voter identification laws adversely affect racial minorities.). *But see* Jimmy Carter & James A. Baker, III, *A Clearer Picture on Voter ID*, N.Y. TIMES, Feb. 3, 2008, available at http://www.nytimes.com/2008/02/03/opinion/03carter.html (Carter and Baker chaired a bipartisan commission on federal election reform and argued that states should provide free voter photo identification cards for eligible citizens).

See also, Andrew Hacker, *Obama: The Price of Being Black*, N.Y. REV. BOOKS 12 (September 25, 2008) (arguing that voter registration rules and recent US Supreme Court cases may disadvantage black voters in the 2008 election).

18 JOHN HART ELY, DEMOCRACY AND DISTRUST: A THEORY OF JUDICIAL REVIEW (1980). The central focus of Ely's book is judicial review, the process through which a court can overturn a legislative act. Judicial review has been criticized as anti-democratic because it is anti-majoritarian. How can unelected judges overturn an act of a democratically elected legislature? Hart's book answers that question and along the way provides us with another path to the higher law.

19 ELY, *supra* note 4, at 7 (footnote omitted).

20 *Id.*

21 *See* Federalist Paper No. 10 (James Madison) in STEVEN M. CAHN, CLASSICS OF MODERN POLITICAL THEORY: MACHIAVELLI TO MILL 626–31 (1997).

22 *United States v. Carolene Prods. Co.*, 304 U.S. 144, 152 n. 4 (1938).

23 *Id.*

24 Indeed, DEMOCRACY AND DISTRUST has been called perhaps the "single most perceptive justificatory account of . . . modern constitutional law . . ." Michael C. Dorf, *The Coherentism of* Democracy and Distrust, 114 YALE L. J. 1237, 1238 (2005).

Ely has been influenced by the discussion of democratic theory in the mid-twentieth century and by skepticism about finding values and cites the work of Robert Dahl and others. *See, e.g.*, ROBERT DAHL, A PREFACE TO DEMOCRATIC THEORY (1956); *ROBERT DAHL, DEMOCRACY IN THE UNITED STATES* (3d ed. 1976). *See also* CAROLE PATEMAN, PARTICIPATION IN DEMOCRATIC THEORY, ch. 1 (1970).

25 Herbert Wechsler, *Toward Neutral Principles of Constitutional Law*, 73 HARV. L. REV. 1 (1959).

26 *See also* HENRY M. HART, JR. & ALBERT M. SACKS, THE LEGAL PROCESS: BASIC PROBLEMS IN THE MAKING AND APPLICATION OF LAW (William N. Eskridge Jr. & Philip P. Frickey eds., 1994).

27 Weschler, *supra* note 30, at 12.

28 *Id.* at 19.

29 *Id.* at 31.

30 *Id.* at 34.

31 *Id.* at 33.

32 Ely points out, "neutral principles" have often served as a code for judicial conservatism. *See* ELY, *supra* note 18, at 55.

33 *See, e.g.*, Lon F. Fuller, *The Forms and Limits of Adjudication*, 92 HARV. L. REV. 353 (1978).

34 FRIEDRICH NIETZSCHE, BEYOND GOOD AND EVIL 36–37 (Penguin Classics 1990).

35 ELY, *supra* note 18, at 74.

36 *Id.*

37 *Id.* at 77.

38 *See* CHARLES BLACK, STRUCTURE AND RELATIONSHIP IN CONSTITUTIONAL LAW (1969).

39 ELY, *supra* note 18, at 87 (footnote omitted).

40 The criticism of Ely, of course, is that he is making value judgments himself. *See, e.g.*, Laurence H. Tribe, *The Puzzling Persistence of Process-Based Constitutional*

Theories, 89 YALE L. J. 1063 (1980); RONALD DWORKIN, FREEDOM'S LAW: THE MORAL READING OF THE AMERICAN CONSTITUTION (1996).

41 ELY, *supra* note 18, at 102.

42 ELY, *supra* note 18, at 103 (footnote omitted).

43 *Romer v. Evans*, 517 U.S. 620 (1996).

44 STEPHEN BREYER, ACTIVE LIBERTY: INTERPRETING OUR DEMOCRATIC CONSTITUTION (2005).

45 *Id.* at 3.

46 Breyer's analysis recalls Isaiah Berlin's two conceptions of liberty. Berlin believed that individuals have a positive liberty to be our own masters and a negative liberty to be free from coercion by the state. *See* ISAIAH BERLIN, FOUR ESSAYS ON LIBERTY ch. 3 (1969).

47 "[W]e can define deliberative democracy as a form of government in which free and equal citizens (and their representatives), justify decisions in a process in which they give one another reasons that are mutually acceptable and generally accessible, with the aim of reaching conclusions that are binding in the present on all citizens but open to challenge in the future." AMY GUTMANN & DENNIS THOMPSON, WHY DELIBERATIVE DEMOCRACY? 7 (2004) (footnote omitted). *See also* JAMES S. FISHKIN, DEMOCRACY AND DELIBERATION: NEW DIRECTIONS FOR DEMOCRATIC REFORM (1991); AMY GUTMANN & DENNIS THOMPSON, DEMOCRACY AND DISAGREEMENT (1996); JOHN ELSTER, DELIBERATIVE DEMOCRACY (1998); STEPHEN MACEDO (ed.), DELIBERATIVE POLITICS: ESSAYS ON DEMOCRACY AND DISAGREEMENT (1999); JOHN DRYZEK, DELIBERATIVE DEMOCRACY AND BEYOND: LIBERALS, CRITICS, CONTESTATIONS (2000).

48 ELY, *supra* note 18, at 136.

49 President Lyndon B. Johnson, Commencement Address at Howard University: "To Fulfill These Rights," (June 4, 1965) available at http://www.lbjlib.utexas.edu/johnson/archives.hom/speeches.hom/650604.asp.

50 *See, e.g.,* GUNNAR MYRDAL, AN AMERICAN DILEMMA (1964); ANDREW HACKER, TWO NATIONS: BLACK, AND WHITE, SEPARATE, HOSTILE, UNEQUAL (1992).

51 ELY, *supra* note 18, at 170.

52 ELY, *supra* note 18, at 170. *See also* John Hart Ely, *Constitutionality of Reverse Racial Discrimination*, 41 U. CHI. L. REV. 723 (1974).

53 BREYER, *supra* note 44, at 82—83 ("they find some form of affirmative action necessary to maintain a well-functioning participatory democracy" at 82).

54 *See* JOHN DEWEY, DEMOCRACY AND EDUCATION ch. 1 (1966 ed.).

55 *See* HARRIET BEECHER STOWE, UNCLE TOM'S CABIN 223–37 (Norton Critical ed. 1994). In Stowe's story about Topsy, who was taught to read the Bible, and Henrique, a youth who learned to mistreat his slaves, the role of education, and it suppression, is central. ("We [Alfred a slaveowner says] must set our face against all this educating, elevating talk, that is getting about now; the lower class must not be educated," at 233).

56 See *also* AMY GUTMANN, DEMOCRATIC EDUCATION (1987).

57 *See* JULIA B. ISSACS, ISABEL V. SAWHILL & RON HASKINS, GETTING AHEAD OR LOSING GROUND: ECONOMIC MOBILITY IN AMERICA (2008) (education is necessary for

economic mobility, and education is unequally available to racial minorities). Report available at http://www.economicmobility.org/assets/pdfs/Economic_Mobility_in_America_Full.pdf.

58 *Brown* v. *Board of Education*, 347 U.S. 483, 493 (1954).

59 *Id.*

60 *Id.*

61 *Regents of the Univ. of Cal.* v. *Bakke*, 438 U.S. 265 (1978).

62 The most notorious legislation was Proposition 209 in California outlawing racial preferences in higher education. The text that amended the California state constitution is available at http://cla.calpoly.edu/~hhellenb/diversity/Prop_209/209text.html. Similar measures have been adopted in Michigan and Texas. For a discussion of the Texas legislation, *see Hopwood v. Texas*, 78 F.3d 932 (5th Cir. 1996). The Michigan legislation is the subject of *Grutter* v. *Bollinger*, 539 U.S. 306 (2003).

63 *Gratz* v. *Bollinger*, 539 U.S. 244 (2003) (undergraduate program); *Grutter* v. *Bollinger*, 539 U.S. 306 (2003) (law school).

64 Ely, *supra* note 52.

65 *See* RONALD DWORKIN, SOVEREIGN VIRTUE: THE THEORY IN PRACTICE OF EQUALITY 412 (2000) (quoting Gerald Gunther in footnote 9).

66 *Brown* v. *Board of Education, supra* note 58, at 494 n.11.

67 *Sweatt v. Painter*, 339 U.S. 629 (1950).

68 *Gutter* at 332 (citation omitted).

69 *Id.*

70 *Id.* at 343.

71 *Id.* at 346–47 (Scalia, J., dissenting).

72 *See Grutter* at 378 (Thomas, J., dissenting) (quoting *Plessy v. Ferguson*, 163 U.S. 537, 559 (1896) (Harlan, J., dissenting)).

73 *Grutter* at 347 (Scalia, J., dissenting).

74 *See* Joseph P. Tomain, *Introduction to Law, Ethics, and Affirmative Action in America*, 72 U. CIN. L. REV. 873 (2004).

75 *See* MARTHA C. NUSSBAUM, CULTIVATING HUMANITY: A CLASSICAL DEFENSE OF REFORM IN LIBERAL EDUCATION ch. 5 (1997).

76 Lani Guinier, *Admissions Rituals as Political Acts: Guardians at the Gates of Our Democratic Ideals*, 117 HARV. L. REV. 113 (2003).

77 *Parents Involved in Community Schools* v. *Seattle School District 1*, 551 U.S. ___ ; 127 S. Ct 2738 (2007).

78 *Parents*, at 127 S. Ct 2754.

79 *Id.* at 2767.

80 *Id.* at 2768. (Thomas, J. concurring Slip Opinion at 1).

81 *Id.*

82 Linda Greenhouse, *Justices Limit the Use of Race in School Plans for Integration*, N.Y. TIMES (June 29, 2007).

83 *See also* JEFFERY TOOBIN, THE NINE (2007).

84 *Parents, supra* note 76, at 2833 (Breyer, J., dissenting) This argument is contested by Justice Thomas at 2778–81.

85 *See Swann v. Charlotte-Mecklenberg Bd. of Ed.*, 402 U.S. 1, 16 (1971).
86 *Parents*, supra note 76 (Breyer, J., dissenting).
87 *Id.* at 2823 (Breyer, J., dissenting), Slip Opinion at 42–43.
88 *Id.* at 2834.
89 Martin Luther King, *I Have a Dream* (August 28, 1963). Available at http://www.usconstitution.net/dream.html.
90 *Parents, supra* note 76, at 2837 (Breyer, J., dissenting).
91 Ely, *supra* note 52, at 727.

Chapter 8 A Poet Dies

1 Ian Fisher, *A Poet Crusades for the Right to Die His Way*, N.Y. Times A4 (Dec. 20, 2006); at A4; *Italian Poet Dies with Help from Doctor*, N.Y. Times (Dec. 22, 2006).
2 Stuart Hampshire, Justice is Conflict (2000).
3 *See, e.g.*, Lawrence Solum, *Procedural Justice*, 78 S. Cal. L. Rev. 181 (2004).
4 John Rawls, A Theory of Justice 85 (1971). *See also* John Rawls, Political Liberalism 72–75 (1993); Cristina Lafont, *Procedural Justice?: Implications of the Rawls-Habermas Debate of Discourse Ethics,* 29 Philosophy & Social Criticism 163 (2003). For the "debate," *see* Jurgen Habermas, *Reconciliation through the Public Use of Reason: Remarks on J. Rawls's Political Liberalism,* 92 J. of Philo. 109 (1995) *and* John Rawls, *A Reply to Habermas*, 92 J. Phil. 132 (1995).
5 *Id.* at 85.
6 *Id.* at 86.
7 Truth always being stranger than fiction, the Anchorage Daily News reports that given high votes, candidates for the democratic nomination to run for a U.S. House seat would be determined by the toss of a coin, Available at http://www.adn.com/news/politics/elections/story/8220761p-8118676c.html.
8 John H. Wigmore, A Kaleidoscope of Justice, 5–17 (1941).
9 *See, e.g.*, Henry M. Hart, Jr. & Albert M. Sacks, The Legal Process: Basic Problems in the Making and Application of Law (William N. Eskeridge Jr. & Philip P. Frickey eds., 1994). The introduction to this classic text by the editors is an excellent analysis of the legal process school that has played a significant role in modern jurisprudence.
10 *See, e.g.*, James E. Fleming, Securing Constitutional Democracy: The Case of Autonomy (2006).
11 Stuart Hampshire, Innocence and Experience 8 (1989).
12 *Id.* at 67.
13 Jane O'Grady, *Sir Stuart Hampshire: Philosopher Whose Moral Awareness Was Heightened by the Practical Demands of Wartime Work as an Interrogator*, The Guardian (June 16, 2004), Available at http://www.guardan.co.uk/obituaries/story/0,3604,1239568,00. This incident certainly seems to have stayed with him. "Men and women generally recognize that there may be some exceptional circumstances in which they will hold that considerations of procedural justice and of rationality ought to be over-ridden in order that some other essential value,

which is dominant in their morality, may be protected, such as the avoidance of widespread misery of the preservation of life." JUSTICE IS CONFLICT, *supra* note 2, at 36.

14 Mark Lilla, *Philosophy for a Messy World*, N.Y. REV. BOOKS 48 (July 11, 2000). *See also* CHARLES H. HAHN, THE ART AND THOUGHT OF HERACLITUS: AN EDITION OF THE FRAGMENTS WITH TRANSLATION AND COMMENTARY 67, 205–07 (2004 ed.).

15 Hampshire, *supra* note 2, at ix.

16 STUART, MORALITY AND CONFLICT chs. 5 & 7 (1983).

17 HAMPSHIRE, *supra* note 11, at 14 & 72.

18 *See* HAMPSHIRE, *supra* note 11, at 13; STUART HAMPSHIRE, MORALITY AND CONFLICT 140–42 (1983).

19 *Id.* at xi. *See also* HAMPSHIRE, *supra* note 11, at 12.

20 *Id.* at xiii.

21 *Id.* at 13.

22 *Id.* at 16.

23 *See* HAMPSHIRE, *supra* note 18, at 160 ("[W]e ought not to plan for a final reconciliation of conflicting moralities in a perfect social order; we ought not even expect that conflicts between moralities, which prescribe different priorities, will gradually disappear, as rational methods in the law and sciences are diffused.").

24 HAMPSHIRE, *supra* note 2, at 4.

25 *Id.* at xi.

26 *Id.* at 94.

27 Oliver Wendell Holmes, *The Path of The Law,* 10 HARV. L. REV. 457, 466 (1897).

28 HAMPSHIRE, *supra* note 2, at 51.

29 *See, e.g.,* FRANCIS FUKUYAMA, THE END OF HISTORY AND THE LAST MAN (1992); SAMUEL P. HUNTINGTON, THE CLASH OF CIVILIZATIONS AND THE REMAKING OF WORLD ORDER (1996).

30 HAMPSHIRE, *supra* note 11, at 72.

31 *Id.* at 68–69.

32 HAMPSHIRE, *supra* note 2, at xii.

33 *Id.* at 47.

34 *Id.* at 53.

35 *Id.* at 54.

36 *Id.* at 55–56.

37 RONALD DWORKIN, LAW'S EMPIRE 247–48 and *passim* (1986).

38 *See also* JOHN RAWLS, POLITICAL LIBERALISM (1993).

39 *Id.* at 35–40.

40 *Id.* at 35.

41 *Id.* at 212–54; JOHN RAWLS, JUSTICE AS FAIRNESS at 26–29 and *passim* (2001);*see also* John Finnis, *Public Reason,* Available at http://papers.ssrn.com/sol3/papers.cfm?abstract_id=955815; Lawrence B. Solum, *Public Legal Reason,* 92 VA. L. REV. 1449 (2006).

42 RAWLS, *supra* note 38, at 32–38.

43 RAWLS, *supra* note 38 at 212–20. *See also* RAWLS, *supra* note 41, at xvi; John Rawls, *Justice as Fairness: Political Not Metaphysical,* 14 PHILO. & PUB. AFFAIRS, 223 (1985).

44 RAWLS, *supra* note 38, at 220–22.
45 RAWLS, *supra* note 41, at 2.
46 *Id* at 24.
47 *Id.* at 19.
48 RAWLS, *supra* note 38, at 44.
49 RAWLS, *supra* note 41, at Part II; JOHN RAWLS, A THEORY OF JUSTICE ch. II (1971).
50 RAWLS, *supra* note 46, at 58.
51 Indeed, Rawls says as much when he writes, "Justice as fairness is not procedurally neutral. Clearly, its principles of justice are substantive and express far more than procedural values, as do its political conceptions of society and person . . ." RAWLS, *supra* note 41, at 153 n.27; *see also* RAWLS, *supra* note 38, at 191–92.
52 RAWLS, *supra* note 46, at 59.
53 *Id.* at 35–243.
54 HAMPSHIRE, *supra* note 2, at 95.
55 RAWLS, *supra* note 38, at 231–40.
56 *Id.*
57 SPIRO KOSTOF, A HISTORY OF ARCHITECTURE 21 (1985).
58 *Washington v. Glucksberg*, 521 U.S. 702 (1997).
59 From the transcript of the oral argument in *Glucksberg*. The transcript can be found at http://www.oyez.org.
60 521 U.S. at 735.
61 Ore. Rev. Stat §127–800 *et seq.*, (2003).
62 *Gonzales v. Oregon*, 546 U.S. 248, 249(2006).
63 21 U.S.C. §801 *et seq.*
64 546 U.S. 253 (2006).
65 546 U.S. 249 (2006).
66 21 C.F.R. §1306.04 (a) (2005).
67 546 U.S. at 285 (2006) (footnote omitted).
68 546 U.S. at 286.
69 *See e.g.,* CASS R. SUNSTEIN, ONE CASE AT A TIME: JUDICIAL MINIMALISM ON THE SUPREME COURT (2001).
70 *But see* http://docket.medill.northwestern.edu/archives/004184.php.
71 *DeShaney v. Winnebago County Dept. of Social Services,* 489 U.S. 189 (1989).
72 *Hudson McMillian,* 503 U.S. 1 (1992).
73 *Brown v. Allen,* 344 U.S. 443 (1953).
74 Jack Balkin, *Critical Legal Theory Today* in FRANCIS J. MONTZ (ed.), ON PHILOSOPHY AND AMERICA LAW (2008).
75 Duncan Kennedy, the progenitor of the Critical Legal Studies, writes that most judicial decisions mask political choices and are either acts of denial, avoidance, duplicity, or insincerity. DUNCAN KENNEDY, A CRITIQUE OF ADJUDICATION {FIN DE SIÈCLE} 4 (1997).
76 SAMANTHA BEESON, THE MORALITY OF CONFLICT: REASONABLE DISAGREEMENT AND THE LAW (2005).
77 *Id.* at 1.
78 *Id.* at 5–6.

79 *Id.* at 123.

80 *Id.* at 213–14. Beeson's procedural justice, then, is an amalgam of deliberative democracy as channeled through a robust idea of Dworkin's notion of law as integrity at 375–86. For Dworkin, the ideal of law as integrity is embodied in the notion that law should cohere in a set of political principles and values such that there are correct solutions to legal problems. Beeson takes a step further and argues that not only should legal decisions be "made to cohere as much as possible within themselves, but also with past decisions, as if they convey the single view of justice," at 416.

81 *Bush v. Gore,* 531 U.S. 98 (2000).

82 *See, e.g.,* ALAN M. DERSHOWITZ, SUPREME INJUSTICE: HOW THE HIGH COURT HIJACKED THE ELECTION (2000); RICHARD A. POSNER, BREAKING THE DEADLOCK: THE 2000 ELECTION, THE CONSTITUTION, AND THE COURTS (2001); CASS R. SUNSTEIN & RICHARD A. EPSTEIN, THE VOTE: BUSH, GORE, AND THE SUPREME COURT (2001).

83 *See* RICHARD A. POSNER, HOW JUDGES THINK ch. 10 (2008).

84 HAMPSHIRE, *supra* note 2, at 95.

85 ALEX DE TOQUEVILLE, DEMOCRACY IN AMERICA, 257 (Harvey C. Mansfield & Delba Wynthrop eds., 2000).

86 *Quill v. Vacco,* 80 F.3d 716 (2nd Cir. 1996).

87 GRANT GILMORE, THE AGES OF AMERICAN LAW 110–11 (1977).

Conclusion

1 *See* MICHAEL WALZER, SPHERES OF JUSTICE: A DEFENSE OF PLURALISM AND EQUALITY (1983); ALASDAIR C. MACINTRYE, WHOSE JUSTICE? WHICH RATIONALITY? (1988).

2 NIGEL SIMMONDS, LAW AS A MORAL IDEA (2007).

3 THEODORE ZIOLKOWSKI, THE MIRROR OF JUSTICE: LITERARY REFLECTIONS OF LEGAL CRISES 17 (1997).

4 SOPHOCLES, ANTIGONE (Elizabeth Wyckoff trans.) in SOPHOCLES I 204 (David Grene & Richard Lattimore eds., 1954).

Index